HOFMANNSTHAL'S
FESTIVAL DRAMAS

HOFMANNSTHAL'S
FESTIVAL
DRAMAS

JEDERMANN

DAS SALZBURGER GROSSE WELTTHEATER

DER TURM

BY

BRIAN COGHLAN

Professor of German Language and Literature
University of Adelaide

CAMBRIDGE UNIVERSITY PRESS

MELBOURNE UNIVERSITY PRESS

1964

PUBLISHED BY
THE SYNDICS OF THE CAMBRIDGE UNIVERSITY PRESS

Bentley House, 200 Euston Road, London, N.W. 1
American Branch: 32 East 57th Street, New York 22, N.Y.
West African Office: P.O. Box 33, Ibadan, Nigeria

AND

MELBOURNE UNIVERSITY PRESS
Parkville N. 2, Victoria, Australia

Printed in Great Britain at the University Printing House, Cambridge
(Brooke Crutchley, University Printer)

Again and again a great nation may bring forth poets and thinkers who represent her intellectual being. Most of them, however, are objects of this intellectual life; extremely few are subjects of it. Buch der Freunde

Spiritual and intellectual forces are seldom lacking in Austria. But more frequently the will to make use of them is absent. Grillparzers Politisches Vermächtnis

CONTENTS

PREFACE

I T is perhaps, in traditional manner, easier to indicate the purpose of this study by noting certain things which it does not include, by naming qualities which it would not pretend to possess.

In the first place, it is neither a personal nor an intellectual biography of Hugo von Hofmannsthal. In the second place, it does not and—by definition of its title—cannot devote equal attention to all aspects of Hofmannsthal's genius mentioned in its pages. The earlier works, for example, are mentioned for one of two reasons: either to demonstrate a line of continuity—concealed or modified, as it may be—or to point a contrast, to stress the particular outlook, even impasse, from which Hofmannsthal progressed towards the achievement of his artistic and ethical objectives. I have tried as far as was possible to assemble these comments and references in the introduction, and thus leave myself free to concentrate on the three festival dramas (*Festspiele*) which are the subject of this study.

I believe and have tried to show that Hofmannsthal's development of the festival drama is a highly significant aspect of his work, and that the works themselves demonstrate a certain continuity and progress in technique and thought. I have thus tried to deal with these *Festspiele* both from the dramatic and ethical point of view. In using the latter term I deliberately include in it Hofmannsthal's function as a *Kulturpolitiker*, an important part of which is seen in the three dramas discussed.

From this statement it follows that the temptation to include other works of the later period was often great. When speaking of Hofmannsthal's 'Austrianism', for example, there was a temptation to devote a whole section, at least, to *Der Schwierige* which is by fairly general agreement one of Hofmannsthal's two or three most important works. When writing of Hofmannsthal's growing tendency in the dramas discussed to express himself in terms of 'mythical' figures, the temptation to expatiate at length on, for example, *Die Frau ohne Schatten* and Hofmannsthal's use of the fairy-tale (*Märchen*) tradition was likewise considerable. Not least among these temptations was the enigma presented by such fragments as *Xenodoxus* and the various stages of a projected *Semiramis*. These two dramas might well have become 'festival dramas' in their own right. *Xenodoxus* indeed was planned for the Salzburg Festival. But they remain fragments and despite their fascination and importance (recently demonstrated, incidentally, by Edgar Hederer in his *Hugo von Hofmannsthal*) I thought it wise—if I were to retain at least some trace of form and clarity—to take a leaf from Ronald Peacock's *Goethe's Major Plays* and limit myself to those festival dramas which 'fulfil two conditions. First, they should be complete, and secondly, they should have had a life on the stage, even if a chequered one, and not only in the study.' One of my main purposes in this book is, after all, to consider Hofmannsthal as a writer for the living stage.

It proved, indeed, impossible to discuss *in vacuo* Hofmannsthal's developing ideas in the *Festspiele*, impossible, that is to say, without all manner of necessarily vague or sweeping references to works, like those mentioned above, which fall outside the confines of the study. I have therefore compromised and have selected for fairly detailed treatment six essays which were written during the period 1914–18. This choice seems to be justifiable for several reasons. The essays themselves all fall in their date of origin between *Jedermann* and *Das Salzburger Große Welttheater* and, in their medial position in the study, may serve a useful purpose in helping to link the pre-war and post-war Hofmannsthal. The essays chosen, quite apart from Hofmannsthal's own statement to this effect, obviously belong together as evidence of his attempted creation of an Austrian 'myth'. It was thus relatively easy to consider them in relation to each other as also to the subject of the study as a whole.

These essays are in addition evidence of Hofmannsthal's

characteristic technique, demonstrated in the *Festspiele*, of using the forms and figures, the achievements and spirit of the past in order to invigorate the present, and to join the present to what is thus realized to be a live and inspiring past. One recalls Hofmannsthal's own words about 'the cumulative force of forebears who are shrouded in mystery . . . layer upon layer of supra-personal memory towering up into the present'.

In these essays the *kulturpolitische* side of Hofmannsthal is very apparent, and possibly more so than in any comparable group of his essays. They seem thus to serve my present purpose. I am aware, however, that this choice is not the only one. One might with equal justice include in such a group the *Raimund* essay, *Wert und Ehre deutscher Sprache*, *Das Schrifttum als geistiger Raum der Nation*, the *Beethoven* addresses, the *Grillparzer* speech of 1922, the *Lessing* essay—to name several examples.

Some economy of choice and space was clearly necessary in view of the detail and length involved in the treatment of the festival dramas. I shall, moreover, deal with at least some of these works in a later study, which will be devoted primarily to *Der Schwierige* and various other of Hofmannsthal's *Lustspiele*.

My choice of essays therefore represents but one of several possibilities. I hope that the sections devoted to them may indicate at least some logic and clarity of purpose.

Regarding the *Festspiele* themselves, I have tried to analyse them in such a way as to demonstrate Hofmannsthal's methods, his sources and possible influences. At the same time, however, I have tried constantly to keep the larger ethical or cultural-political picture in view. *Jedermann* has been analysed in considerable detail. Being the first of these festival dramas it has, quite apart from its own merits, much to tell us in advance, as it were, about Hofmannsthal's characteristic interests and ideals, some of which are developed in the two later *Festspiele*.

Hofmannsthal himself admitted that the success of *Jedermann* led him to create the *Große Welttheater*, and the connection between the two works—the kind of stage for which they were written, the folk-theatre background, etc.—allowed me, justifiably I hope, to dispense with such a detailed textual study and consideration of the background of *Große Welttheater*. I realize, of course, that the 'models' for the two plays, the English morality and the Spanish *auto*, are indeed widely different. As I hope to have shown, however, this difference in background is not, perhaps, of decisive significance; and Hofmannsthal has converted both *Stoffe* into something individual and Austrian, and the two pieces reveal certain basic similarities together with certain vital differences. These latter, however, have little to do with the origin of the themes of Everyman and of the Great World Theatre. In any case, my object has not been to compare the original works with what Hofmannsthal 'made' of them.

If *Große Welttheater* has been treated at rather shorter length and in rather more general terms, the treatment of *Der Turm* has been very detailed—linguistically (producing, I believe, some quite interesting and original results), dramatically and ethically. This has been done for several reasons. *Der Turm* is to my mind a very difficult work and one whose content is not at all obvious at first sight: the history of the work in the theatre seems to bear out this assertion. Secondly, Hofmannsthal himself regarded this work as his artistic last will and testament, and intended it to be the coping-stone of his life's achievement. Finally, there is, as far as I am aware, no really detailed textual study of *Der Turm**
—in the sense of those that exist, for example, of *Faust* I and II, of Wagner's *Parsifal*, and other 'occasional' dramas which fall into the category both of would-be comprehensive *Alterswerk* and last will and testament.

Such treatment has meant that the section on *Der Turm* is very long in comparison with the rest of the study. I must also add apologetically that for the above reasons the notes become rather profuse as the book progresses. I can only hope that these do not hinder the reader, and that the additional information in them may perhaps be illuminating and on occasion interesting!

* See Bibliography for works consulted.

The section on *Der Turm* proved very difficult to divide into logical divisions or chapters—logical, that is to say, if the analysis were not to degenerate into an anatomical, physiological, genetical —and thus quite soulless—treatise. Accordingly I have devoted a relatively short chapter to outlining the plot and to indicating such background and influences as may be helpful in setting the play in its right context. This is followed by a very long chapter in which the play itself (first version, 1925) is discussed in detail. In pursuit of greater clarity this chapter is divided into sections: Act I, Act II, and so on. This is followed by another completely separate and comparatively short chapter in which the revised (1927) version of *Der Turm* is examined in the light of what has gone before. Some conclusions, in respect both of *Der Turm* and of Hofmannsthal in general, are put forward in the final chapter of the book.

It can probably be maintained of most academic works that they are provisional in character, and I should not wish to claim Hofmannsthal as a special case. On the other hand, it is probably true to say that there is at present very considerable activity in the field of Hofmannsthal studies—in a way, moreover, which rather complicates the critic's task. This remarkable increase over the last few years has kept pace with the appearance during the period 1945–59 of the first complete edition of Hofmannsthal's works. With the publication of *Aufzeichnungen* the full edition is now complete. However, I understand from Dr Herbert Steiner, editor of the Fischer *Gesamtausgabe*, that some seven or eight volumes of letters, fragments, etc., will also appear in due course.

Much as one appreciates the complete edition one must envy the Hofmannsthalian of ten years hence, whose task will not be complicated by the periodic arrival of basic texts and the anticipation of others. The appearance a few years ago of the Hofmannsthal–Burckhardt correspondence was a good instance of this kind of thing. This work, not actually part of the Fischer *Gesamtausgabe*, is a vital contribution to our knowledge of Hofmannsthal, and has forced one to change or modify several opinions.

A further and probably more typical instance is the case of *Der Turm*. The bibliographical history of this play is almost wilfully complicated and for many years one had to pick one's way through its erratic course. The appearance of *Dramen IV* has somewhat simplified one's task but not wholly. An account of these particular problems is given in the Bibliographical Note at the end of chapter 8.

Concerning the supplementary volumes which have yet to appear: thanks to the courtesy of Dr Steiner and the Houghton Library, I was able, during a visit to Harvard, to see sufficient of the unpublished papers there to convince myself that a good deal therein will prove relevant to the later period in Hofmannsthal's career, which is the particular concern of this book. I might mention by way of illustration a draft for a *Salzburgische Große Welttheater* of 1919. The sub-title for this draft is *Christianus der Wirtssohn* and the work was to be a 'a play in the manner of the seventeenth century'. Many of the figures are quite different from those in the play familiar to us, and the setting is clearly that of the Salzburg district. But critical treatment of such papers as these must necessarily await their publication. It will be several years before this is complete.

To some extent, therefore, this book is provisional. If, however, it in any way clears the ground for a comprehensive study of Hofmannsthal at a later time, or if any of its allegedly original findings prove to be of value in Hofmannsthalian scholarship, I shall be more than satisfied.

It would be difficult to name all those whose help and interest have had some part in this book. But I should wish to express my particular gratitude to various colleagues and writers associated with Hofmannsthal and his work, whose contributions have been quite indispensable.

My warm appreciation goes to Herbert Steiner for his unfailing kindness and patience in answering numerous queries and volunteering all manner of information. I owe much to Derek van Abbé who, in years of stimulating daily discussion, has helped me greatly. In comparable manner I am grateful to Richard Samuel and Ralph Farrell for their unfailing interest and encouragement, and to Heinz Wiemann for views on many a tricky point. I am also very pleased to acknowledge Henry Basten's constant encouragement and unobtrusive advice over a period of many years.

My former teachers Roy Pascal and Hinton Thomas have aided me vitally from the very beginning of my interest in Hofmannsthal, and I should add a particular word of thanks to Professor Pascal for his criticism and general encouragement over a number of years. A discussion with Erich Heller was a vital factor in the composition of the final chapter, while I am very grateful to Adolf Klarmann for hours of stimulating discussion on *Der Turm*. I have ventured to use some of his verbal and epistolary arguments in chapter 8, and wish to express my thanks for the way in which these have modified—even if they have not entirely transformed—my earlier views on the controversial ending to *Der Turm I*.

I wish particularly to thank William Rey for most stimulating conversations on our joint *Steckenpferd* in two continents and correspondence in three. Detlev Schumann's interest and advice, gained during a short visit to Philadelphia, were invaluable, and I am greatly indebted to Robert Kann for much discussion and detailed advice. Many German and Austrian colleagues have been ready with interest and good counsel: I wish particularly to mention Wilhelm Emrich, Wilhelm Grenzmann, Fritz Martini, Josef Nadler, and Paul Requadt.

My debt to Carl Burckhardt for discussion, reminiscence and advice is very great. In this context I also wish to pay tribute to the kindness and consideration of Felix Braun, Bernt von Heiseler, Max Mell, and the late Rudolf Alexander Schröder.

Helmut Fiechtner of *Die Furche* was very helpful to me during my visit to Vienna a few years ago, and I also wish to thank Walter Ritzer, Librarian at the Technische Hochschule there, for indispensable bibliographical assistance.

It goes without saying, however, that I alone can be held responsible for the shape and form taken in my book by all this generous help.

To the publishers thanks are due for literary and critical guidance, much technical aid, and—last but not least—patience unlimited.

In conclusion I wish to thank my university for its generous help in many ways: for handsome financial assistance in the publication of this book, for granting study leave, for the constant and courteous co-operation of the Barr Smith Library, and for providing the particularly invigorating atmosphere (especially amongst the staff and students of the Department of German) which is indispensable to work of this kind, especially when undertaken so far from the sources. I must also thank the Australian Humanities Research Council and the University of New England at Armidale, New South Wales, for their generous financial support in the publication of the book. A good deal of the later work was done while I was at New England. I received every help and encouragement there, notably from the Vice-Chancellor, the Dixson Library and the members of my own department. All these demand and receive my sincere thanks.

In dedicating the book to my wife I wish to express in some measure my appreciation of her help at every stage and especially her supervision of the several hundred pieces of translation scattered throughout the following pages. She must take credit for any felicities therein: for exuberance and licence I alone am to blame.

BRIAN COGHLAN

ADELAIDE
February 1963

ACKNOWLEDGMENTS

THE author's grateful thanks are also due to the following:

S. Fischer Verlag for permission to translate and quote extracts from the works of Hofmannsthal, from volumes of correspondence (e.g. Hofmannsthal–Burckhardt), from various articles in *Die Neue Rundschau*, and from an essay by Thomas Mann.

Emeritus Professor L. A. Willoughby and the Modern Humanities Research Association (England) for permission to quote from *On Some Problems in the Study of Goethe's Imagery*.

Professor E. M. Wilkinson and the English Goethe Society for permission to use material (in chapters 3 and 4) from my essay 'The Cultural-Political Development of Hugo von Hofmannsthal during the First World War'. This appeared in *Publications of the English Goethe Society*, vol. XXVII (1958), pp. 1–32.

Dr Willy Haas for permission to translate and quote an extract from an article in *Die Literarische Welt*.

Professor Allardyce Nicoll for permission to quote translations of *El gran teatro del mundo*.

George Allen and Unwin Ltd for permission to use a personal translation of an extract from Albert Schweitzer, *Aus meinem Leben und Denken*. Messrs Allen and Unwin are the publishers of the English version of this work, *My Life and Thought*.

August Bagel Verlag for permission to translate and quote extracts from William H. Rey, '*Der Turm*' (in *Das Deutsche Drama*, vol. 2) and Benno von Wiese, *Die Deutsche Novelle*.

Etablissements Benziger et Cie S.A. for permission to translate and quote extracts from Theodor Rall, *Katholisches Schrifttum Gestern und Heute*.

A. and C. Black Ltd for permission to use personal translations of extracts from Albert Schweitzer, *Verfall und Wiederaufbau der Kultur*. A. and C. Black own the English rights of this work which was published by them in 1923 under the title *The Decay and Restoration of Civilization*.

Basil Blackwell for permission to quote from Mary Gilbert's Introduction to *Selected Essays of Hugo von Hofmannsthal* and Felix Braun, 'Encounters with Hofmannsthal', which appeared in *German Life and Letters*.

Hermann Böhlaus Nachf. for permission to translate and quote extracts from Rudolf Kiszling, *Erzherzog Franz Ferdinand von Österreich-Este. Leben, Pläne und Wirken am Schicksalsweg der Donaumonarchie* (Graz and Cologne, 1953) and Fritz Fellner (ed.), *Schicksalsjahre Österreichs 1908–1919. Das Politische Tagebuch Josef Redlichs*, 2 vols. (Graz and Cologne, 1953–4).

Wilhelm Braumüller, Universitätsbuchhandlung, for permission to quote a translated extract from Ignaz Seipel, *Nation und Staat*.

Carnegie Endowment for International Peace for permission to quote from Josef Redlich, *Austrian War Government*.

Wm. Collins Sons and Co. Ltd for permission to quote from Neville Cardus, *Autobiography*, and to use personal translations of extracts from the correspondence between Hofmannsthal and Strauss prepared before the appearance in autumn 1961 of *The Correspondence between Richard Strauss and Hugo von Hofmannsthal*, translated by Hanns Hammelmann and Ewald Osers, with an introduction by Edward Sackville-West. The publisher of the German original, *Richard Strauss–Hugo von Hofmannsthal. Briefwechsel: Gesamtausgabe* (1952) is Atlantis Verlag, Zürich.

Columbia University Press for permission to quote from Robert Kann, *The Multi-National Empire*.

Constable and Co. Ltd for permission to quote from Ernst Kantorowicz, *Frederick the Second, 1194–1250* (trans. E. O. Lorimer).

Eugen Diedrichs Verlag for permission to translate and quote extracts from *Briefe der Freundschaft: Hugo von Hofmannsthal–Eberhard von Bodenhausen*.

The Editor, *DU* (Zürich), for permission to translate and quote extracts from Rudolf Kassner, *Erinnerungen an Hofmannsthal*.

Frau Lisa Farga for permission to translate and quote extracts from Franz Farga, *Die Wiener Oper von ihren Anfängen bis 1938*.

Francke Verlag for permission to translate and quote extracts from Ernst Robert Curtius, *Kritische Essays zur europäischen Literatur* and Richard Alewyn, 'Geist des Barocktheaters' (in *Weltliteratur: Festgabe für Fritz Strich*).

Freies Deutsches Hochstift for permission to translate and quote extracts from Walther Brecht, 'Hugo von Hofmannsthals "Ad me ipsum" und seine Bedeutung' which appeared in the *Jahrbuch* of the F.D.H.

The General Editor of the *Germanic Review* (Professor W. T. H. Jackson) for permission to quote from Arnold Bergstraesser, 'The

Holy Beggar, Religion and Society in Hofmannsthal's Great World Theatre' and Wolfgang Michael, 'A Swiss Resurrection Play of the Sixteenth Century' (review).

Walter de Gruyter and Co. for permission to translate and quote extracts from Friedrich Naumann, *Mitteleuropa*.

Carl Hanser Verlag for permission to translate and quote extracts from Curt Hohoff, 'Hofmannsthals Lustspiele' which appeared in *Akzente*.

George G. Harrap and Co. Ltd for permission to quote from Allardyce Nicoll, *World Drama*.

Professor Robert A. Kann and Thames and Hudson for permission to quote from Robert A. Kann, *A Study in Austrian Intellectual History from Late Baroque to Romanticism*.

Ernst Klett Verlag for permission to translate and quote an extract from Rudolf Borchardt, 'Hofmannsthals Wirkung'.

Vittorio Klostermann for permission to translate and quote extracts from Max Kommerell, *Beiträge zu einem deutschen Calderón*.

Alfred Kröner Verlag and Professor Fritz Martini for permission to translate and quote extracts from Fritz Martini, *Deutsche Literaturgeschichte von den Anfängen bis zur Gegenwart*.

Verlag Helmut Küpper vormals Georg Bondi for permission to quote from Stefan George, *Dem Andenken des Grafen Bernhard Uxkull*.

Dr Jakob Laubach for permission to translate and quote extracts from *Hugo von Hofmannsthals Turm-Dichtungen — Entstehung, Form und Bedeutungsschichten*.

The Listener for permission to quote from Thomas Mann, 'Germany and the Germans'.

Manchester University Press for permission to quote from Ronald Peacock, *Goethe's Major Plays*.

Manesse Verlag for permission to translate and quote extracts from Carl J. Burckhardt, *Gestalten und Mächte*, and Max Rychner, *Zur europäischen Literatur*.

Methuens Ltd for permission to quote from Jethro Bithell, *Modern German Literature*, and from Hugo F. Garten, *Modern German Drama*.

J. B. Metzlersche Verlagsbuchhandlung for permission to translate and quote from various articles in the *Deutsche Vierteljahrsschrift*.

Siegbert Mohn Verlag for permission to translate and quote extracts from Bernt von Heiseler, *Ahnung und Aussage*.

Otto Müller Verlag for permission to translate and quote extracts from Josef Nadler, *Literaturgeschichte Österreichs*.

The Nonesuch Press Ltd for leave to quote from its edition of North's translation of Plutarch's *Lives*.

Österreichische Verlagsanstalt for permission to translate and quote extracts from Erika Brecht, *Erinnerungen an Hofmannsthal*.

Verlag der Österreichischen Staatsdruckerei for permission to translate and quote extracts from Ernst Marboe (ed.), *Das Österreichbuch*.

Oxford University Press for permission to quote from James Fitz-maurice-Kelly, *A New History of Spanish Literature*.

Penguin Books Ltd for permission to quote from Nikolaus Pevsner, *Outline of European Architecture*.

Verlag Hermann Rinn for permission to translate and quote extracts from Carl J. Burckhardt, *Erinnerungen an Hofmannsthal und Briefe des Dichters*.

Wolfgang Rothe Verlag for permission to translate and quote extracts from *Deutsche Literatur im XX. Jahrhundert*.

Routledge and Kegan Paul for permission to quote from Hermann Broch, Introduction to *Selected Prose of Hugo von Hofmannsthal* and I. A. Richards, *Principles of Literary Criticism*.

Direktion der Salzburger Festspiele for permission to translate and quote an extract from the *Festspielführer 1947*.

Verlag der Bücherstube Fritz Seifert for permission to translate and quote extracts from Grete Schaeder, *Hugo von Hofmannsthal und Goethe*.

University of North Carolina Press for permission to quote from *University of North Carolina Studies in Language and Literature*, no. 26, *The Works of Stefan George*, translated by Olga Marx and Ernst Morwitz.

Verlag Vandenhoeck und Ruprecht for permission to translate and quote extracts from Richard Alewyn, *Hofmannsthals Wandlung* (in *Über Hugo von Hofmannsthal*).

Wissenschaftliche Verlagsgesellschaft for permission to quote an extract from Claude Hill, 'Hugo von Hofmannsthal—A Classic of German Poetry in the Twentieth Century' which appeared in *Universitas* (English language ed.).

Rainer Wunderlich Verlag Hermann Leins for permission to translate and quote extracts from Theodor Heuss, *Hugo von Hofmannsthal: Eine Rede*.

NOTE ON TRANSLATIONS

THE many quotations from Hofmannsthal's works and others presented a problem. I was undecided whether to quote original texts or to risk the inevitable second-best of translation. I was, however, happy to take the publishers' advice on this point. In the hope, therefore, that the book may as a result interest a larger circle in the works of Hofmannsthal, I have translated virtually all prose quotations. In general verse quotations are printed in the original. In special circumstances—to demonstrate a stylistic point, for example—both German and English versions are given. Where a particularly felicitous translation of verse was available and the context demanded it, the translation has been given. In general, however, I thought it wise to leave well alone.

The particularly evocative prose of *Der Turm*, together with its unusual range of idiom and type of expression, placed me in a dilemma. Translation cannot hope to give much idea of the manifold overtones and multi-coloured images of this kind of language. And there is as a rule no precise English equivalent. Something, however, had to be sacrificed and I have tried to translate all quotations from this work too. Those who do not know the play may perhaps be encouraged to make its acquaintance. Those who do will appreciate the problem here.

In all cases page references indicate the source of the German original, unless otherwise stated.

INTRODUCTION

As the closing epoch of the Habsburg empire recedes in time, we are, although still involved in the after-effects of its collapse and dismemberment, able to see in some perspective the salient features of its last decades and to assess their importance, not only for developments of that time, but—what is of much greater significance—to trace with some clarity their cause, influence and effect, which reach out along the intervening years into contemporary times.

The collapse of 1918 was utter and complete, and at the outset it is as well to recall just how complete it was. Imperial Austria had a population of some fifty-two million people, a major port on the Adriatic and a sea-going fleet. She had a smoothly functioning internal economy: heavy industry in Bohemia, grain in Hungary, dairy products in the alpine provinces were but three leading features. Her land frontiers were *inter alia* with Italy, Germany and Russia. The whole great complex centred on Vienna which was in both cultural and economic senses the heart of the empire.

This political and polyglot colossus blocked effectively any expansionist drive from the north to the Mediterranean Sea. It had prided itself for a thousand years on being the frontier province of western civilization, a barrier against the east and at the same time a permanent thrust into it.

This self-conscious bearer of the Roman imperial mission was shattered virtually overnight and a vestigial fragment remained, to a great extent mountainous and with approximately one eighth of its pre-war population. This splinter state was in no way self-supporting and was scarcely capable of maintaining its political independence save by the charity or whim of powerful, modern, national states on its northern and southern frontiers. From the start it was clear that Germany to the north must always be tempted by the existence of several million German-speaking Austrians and by several provinces which, if not of rich productive potential, were at all events a useful little annex to an overcrowded *Reich*—a *Reich*, moreover, in which in some quarters nationalist feeling was as unrepentant as it was humiliated. The new and easy accessibility of the Mediterranean Sea and of southern Europe— a rather fateful motive in German history—was bound to be a constant attraction as Germany regained her power. Nor must feeling in Austria itself be ignored. Pan-Germanism in Austria was not new and Austria's seemingly hopeless situation after 1918 stimulated a good deal of agitation for an *Anschluß*, expressly forbidden by the peace treaty which had brought the new Austria into being.

The new Austria was not alone in its isolation, for other fragments of the Habsburg empire had been resolved into small states whose prospects of political, economic and strategic safety were equally doubtful. The existence of the *Nachfolgestaaten* or 'succession states' was codified and ratified by various post-war treaties, notably that of St Germain.

The history of the nationalist movements which were to a considerable extent responsible for their creation is both long and in many ways distinguished. For present purposes it must suffice if, as a good example, the work and tactics of such groups as the Masaryk (Czech) organization be recalled. This was a prototype of the Free French or Polish *émigré* type of political body characteristic of World War II. The allies adopted towards such agitation a policy which put the defeat of the central powers as the main or even the only objective. By encouraging such movements and their practical expression the allies hastened the disintegration of the Habsburg empire with unpredictable consequences. It is not readily clear to what extent this was the inevitable concomitant of allied short-sightedness, opportunism on the 'win at any price' basis, or a genuine desire to assert and support the national rights of Central European minorities—an idealistic notion certainly. Lloyd George is on record as having said that the dismemberment of the Habsburg empire was not one of the allied war-aims but that events got out of hand and the allies were faced with a new *status quo* and the necessity for regularizing it.

However, had the *Nachfolgestaaten* themselves been organic national unities there would certainly have been some hopeful future for Central Europe after 1918. But from the start, by reason of their amorphous structure, both geographically and ethnically, jealousy and open enmity were ever present. Tensions within the states themselves were also of calamitous potential. Two instances will illustrate this. Czechoslovakia was made up of at least five linguistic and racial groups. These were the large (three million) Sudeten German minority in the west, the fiercely nationalistic Czechs of Bohemia, the intensely Catholic and separatist Slovakia in the south-east and east, a considerable Hungarian-speaking minority in the south, and the Ruthenian minority in the north-east. Each group, with its own background of tradition, culture, interest and aspiration, was inherently hostile to the other four, as events later proved. This unhappy state of affairs came to pass despite the enlightened and far-sighted efforts of Thomas Masaryk himself—efforts which won for him among his Czech countrymen the reputation of being the friend of the Sudeten Germans. The ultimate failure of Masaryk's efforts and the sad and changing fortunes of his country are a significant commentary on the difficulties which sprang into being as the Habsburg empire fell apart.

In the case of another new state, Yugoslavia, conditions of similar explosive intensity were created, notably by the fusion of Orthodox Serbia and Catholic Croatia, with their differing traditions and allegiances. The whole, originally termed the Kingdom of Serbs, Croats and Slovenes, was subject to a Serbian monarchy of somewhat dubious record.

Hungary, formerly an equal partner with Austria within the empire, was forcibly split off from her. After abortive attempts to gain control on the part of Communists (Béla Kun) and

Habsburg monarchists the country settled down to an uncomfortable twilight existence as a permanent regency. The regent, Admiral Horthy of the Imperial Austro-Hungarian Navy, whose uniform he insisted on wearing throughout his many years of office, ruled on behalf of a vacated throne to which no legal heir was permitted.

This brief outline may suffice here to indicate the magnitude of the change and the political perils latent within the new order. It should not be thought, however, that the forcible break-up of the empire was solely due to the revolutionary activities of nationalist groups. Signs of internal decomposition had been disturbingly apparent for a long time. Austria never really regained full prestige after the Napoleonic *débâcle* and with the passage of time became steadily more unfitted to carry out the task laid on her in 1815, that of being at once the arbiter and balancing force of central and south-east Europe.

Grave weaknesses were apparent in the system of government, which in any case varied from district to district. Within the boundaries of German-speaking Austria the method of despotic rule was quite out of tune with the spirit of the age and was seemingly blind to new political realities. Law-making, taxation and state spending were subject to no parliamentary control. The strictest of censorships—of a particularly mean and craven kind—was enforced by the notorious Metternich police system which in consequence maintained a rigid grip on the press, all publishing activity, education and the theatre: witness the experience of Austria's accepted national poet, Franz Grillparzer. The large and cumbersome bureaucracy was directed in the main by Viennese officials, noted neither for their efficiency nor for their incorruptibility, who were—in the accepted tradition—grossly underpaid and overworked.

Elsewhere in the Habsburg empire strong feudal systems of government and administration still prevailed. The local prince, count or petty aristocrat ruled more or less according to whim. After the *Ausgleich* of 1867 Hungary was constitutionally a separate kingdom enjoying only a Habsburg monarch in common with Austria. Government of a kind was dispensed largely by the Magyar nobility which fiercely asserted a great degree of independence. There was, it is true, a diet which assembled periodically in Pressburg but this was a rather quaint survival of the medieval estates and had minimal power. What might conceivably have been a rallying point of the empire, or at least a sounding board for grievances and a means of achieving some degree of equalization amongst the constituent elements, was all too often an opportunity for general indiscipline and even separatist sentiment.

Clearly, therefore, it was virtually impossible to effect unanimous agreement or joint action in any cause whatsoever. Much less was it possible to mobilize the full potential of the Habsburg empire in any emergency. Given such a proliferation of regional systems any change at all was deemed dangerous and threatening to the whole. Thus the policy of imperial statesmen was in the main that of preserving the *status quo*. Metternich himself, who was from 1815 until the risings of 1848 the *spiritus rector* of the empire, was known to say that he had to dedicate himself to propping up a mouldering edifice.

The Habsburg monarchy did indeed, as in former times, provide some bond of union between the various factions, and the traditional loyalty to the royal house cannot be dismissed lightly. It was, however, rather less of a unifying force than its sentimental apologists often maintain. Nowhere was this more evident, for example, than amongst the Czech population where the *Schwarz-Gelben* were becoming increasingly unpopular.

The accession after the risings of 1848 of the youthful and active Francis Joseph seemed at first to presage positive developments in imperial affairs. After order had been forcibly restored in Vienna, Prague, Budapest and northern Italy a new constitution was certainly introduced, but it provided for the complete centralization of government in Vienna.

Metternich's successor, Prince Schwarzenberg, was a man of

iron will who was also an inflexible anti-liberal. He determined to suppress all forms of provincial independence and perpetuate a system of complete absolutism. This was in effect the beginning of the end. Rising nationalism in the constituent states was not something ephemeral or spontaneous. It was an expression of the conviction that peoples of differing language, culture and historical tradition have the right to some degree of self-government.

It was the tragedy of the Habsburg empire that neither Francis Joseph nor his advisers recognized this early enough, if at all. The consequence was that what could well have been encouraged, fostered and ultimately given scope within the empire's framework was instead suspected, branded as criminal and, from the start, put down with savage non-comprehension.

Austria's history in those last seven decades of the empire's existence was indeed a series of 'ifs'. It is not merely idle speculation which makes one ponder the destiny of the empire had the Crown Prince Rudolf not shot himself (1889). Rudolf was something of an exception amongst latter-day Habsburgs. Broad-minded and unusually far-seeing where the future of the empire was concerned, he was also decidedly liberal in his political outlook and was pronouncedly anglophile. He suffered deeply under the obscurantism of his father and the ageing advisers who surrounded him. He resented bitterly the fact that he was little more than a cipher at the imperial court and he longed for the opportunity to direct the affairs of state while time remained to re-form the empire on lines in accord with the spirit of the age.

When one recalls the massive power which was vested in the emperor and the considerable and widespread regard for Rudolf the conclusion can only be that his despairing suicide was as much a tragedy for Austria as was the unprecedentedly long reign of Francis Joseph, who lingered on until 1916 as little more than a memorial of a bygone age.

Such was the political background of the society into which Hugo von Hofmannsthal was born. He was fifteen when Rudolf shot himself—and at eighteen Hofmannsthal was a mature

6

genius. He was forty-four when the Habsburg empire crumbled into dissolution. He died at the age of fifty-five, four years before the advent of National Socialism in Germany and nine years before the *Anschluß* with Austria.

It is important to stress this background at the outset because Hofmannsthal was to an unusual degree formed by his environment. He was in many ways the expression of his age—at first, perhaps, involuntarily, but later with increasing self-awareness. He tried, moreover, to face up to the problems and the dilemma of his age. Some appreciation of his immediate environment may therefore be helpful before considering his actual work.

But in the fabric of existence there are strands without number and each one has a strong and deep colour and in their play with one another they can sometimes gleam forth like a piece of strong old brocade shot through with gold.

The above passage is taken from what on the surface is a routine essay, *Österreichische Bibliothek*,[1] written in 1915 to introduce a new series about to be published by the Insel-Verlag. As is often the case, however, Hofmannsthal's words are an unconscious projection of himself, of his own intellectual constitution. He was, as perhaps few other men of letters of his time, a gathering up and embodiment of the many strands—racial, spiritual and moral—which combined to make up the cultural fabric of his time. He does, moreover, stand out amongst his contemporaries in his awareness of his position at the end of a great cycle. An aristocrat of several strains—Italian, Jewish and native Austrian at least—he was also a Viennese by birth and by conviction, deeply conscious too of the folk element, of the land about him, its instinctive culture and traditional way of life.

Simultaneously, however, he was Viennese in quite a different sense. He had much of that cosmopolitanism of outlook, both political and cultural, which has for long been a distinguishing feature of Vienna, standing from Roman times at a crossroads in

Europe, the gateway to the Balkans, to the Slavonic East and the Near East, to the Germanic North and to the Mediterranean South.

Sensitive to currents flowing into Vienna from all directions, Hofmannsthal presents a finely balanced dualism, for this supranational side of his intellectual character appears with equal strength alongside his abiding love for simple rural custom, folk language and traditions, which are depicted in his work with marked sympathy. This dualism, which becomes apparent only in his middle creative years (from 1910 approximately), was with time to become a dominating characteristic.

Such considerations are, however, chronologically out of place in this introduction. The young Hofmannsthal was to all appearances a vastly different man. He was one of those phenomena which an old civilization brings forth without effort from time to time. Hofmannsthal, even more perhaps than Mozart or Richard Strauss, sprang fully armed at all points into the intellectual world. To say this is not, of course, to attempt any evaluation of respective genius. It is merely to record that at the age of seventeen, while still a schoolboy, Hofmannsthal was using the German language with an ease, a coruscating magic and wealth of overtone and suggestion whose like had not been experienced since the death of Goethe. In making this bold assertion one recalls Richard Alewyn's assessment of this early phase in Hofmannsthal's career:

Verses which will live as long as our language, verse which is of seemingly dream-like inspiration, apparently without body or weight, but at the same time of a sweetness and maturity of which one would previously not have thought German capable.[1]

Allied with this facility was a brooding, even resigned cynicism of outlook which would have aroused comment in a mature artist three times his age. In the well-known prologue to Schnitzler's *Anatol* Hofmannsthal wrote:

> Early ripened, sorrowful, tender,
> The comedy of our own soul.

Stefan Zweig has told of his own sensations when attending a lecture by the mysterious new genius and expecting to find a man of ripe years speaking from the height of vast experience. Instead a youth mounted the platform, a youth to whom fore-knowledge and fore-experience seemed to have been given and who was yet forced to publish his early work under a pseudonym. The rules of the *Gymnasium* forbade the publication of independent signed work.[1]

The phenomenon is probably inexplicable and is in itself of little significance. What is more important is the fact that the young Hofmannsthal, born at the sunset of the Habsburg empire, as it were, seemed to have within him the accumulated cultural achievement, experience, wisdom and final resignation of the centuries which preceded him. At the outset of his career he was deeply affected by the spiritual malaise of his time, which existed beneath the outward splendour of the empire. The consciousness of the glorious and legendary past, which was later to be such an inspiration to him, was at this stage a crushing burden.

This aspect of Hofmannsthal's talent is of course familiar enough. The artist-philosopher of *Gestern*, for example, of *Der Tod des Tizian*, of the *Terzinen* or of the *Ballade des äußeren Lebens*, tended formerly to distract attention from the work of Hofmannsthal's later years. There was in consequence a tendency to see him as a Keats-like figure who had the misfortune not to die as soon as his best work was done: this is in fact a paraphrase of a much-quoted remark by Hermann Bahr, made jocularly no doubt, but expressing what was a widespread idea. The work of such critics as Alewyn, Walther Brecht, Broch, E. R. Curtius, Requadt and Rey (to name several of the most significant) has exploded this notion.

This widespread sentimental view of Hofmannsthal, however, is not the only obstacle to a true assessment of his work. It is equally misleading to consider his career as one of distinct phases in the course of which the later Hofmannsthal, the 'socially responsible' artist, is regarded as having made a complete break with his brilliant but rather unhealthy youth. Certain marked turning-points in his work are indeed quite obvious. *Der Kaiser und die Hexe* (1897) and *Ein Brief* (1902: this is the *Chandos Letter*) are clear examples of this.

The value of the *Chandos Letter*, the most noted of Hofmannsthal's 'crisis' works, has been argued eloquently—if at times turgidly—by Hermann Broch.[1] Of interest in this connection is Kluckhohn's 'Die Wende vom neunzehnten zum zwanzigsten Jahrhundert in der deutschen Dichtung'.[2] Kluckhohn develops an interesting theory of 'crisis' in Hofmannsthal and several of his major contemporaries.

It may be useful for the present purpose—that of establishing the place of certain of the later works in Hofmannsthal's development—if a few characteristic traits or portents in the early work are noted here, to indicate a certain continuity in Hofmannsthal's ideas.

The most obvious such trait arises from Hofmannsthal's sense of the past, a leading feature of his work which is in its diverse phases much discussed throughout the present study. Rudolf Borchardt summed up this dominating feature in Hofmannsthal—with which are associated his cosmopolitan cultural sympathies—in the following comprehensive manner:

He had personal dealings with three millennia, with every language of cultured peoples, with all literatures which have developed form, with their leading spirits and with their essential spirit...he was the son of an ancient and glorious imperium also in the fact that in his spiritual realms the sun never set.[3]

It is a commonplace of criticism to recall the constancy of that technique, fundamental to Hofmannsthal's artistic being, which searched the achievement of bygone ages for inspiration. The milieux of *Gestern* (1892), of *Der Tod des Tizian* (1893), of the prologue to *Anatol* (1892), are noted cases in point. A study of the lyrical dramas reveals in fact a wide range of period in the setting of the plays and a marked disinclination to set them in the present day. This preoccupation with the past is of particular interest from another point of view. Hofmannsthal chose not only the historical event or epoch as inspiration and often as providing an artistic analogy with his own times; he also sought out and adopted or adapted the actual forms of the past in which to express himself. This characteristic likewise runs through his entire poetic and dramatic output. It is, as shown later, a feature which by constant modification he brought to considerable re-finement in the works of his closing period.

A further feature of this use of the past, in effect an extension of it, is found in such works as *Das Bergwerk zu Falun* (1899), *Das Kleine Welttheater* (1897) or *Der Kaiser und die Hexe* (1897). Here the setting is of no particular period or style. There are echoes—of Calderón perhaps, as in *Das Kleine Welttheater*—and there are vague indications as to the dress of the characters: in *Das Kleine Welttheater* it is 'in the style of the twenties of last century'. In *Der Kaiser und die Hexe* there are faint suggestions that this play is set in mid-Byzantine times—notably the name (Porphyrogenitus) of the emperor, presumably a reminiscence of Constantine VII, Porphyrogenitus (912–59).

In all these works, however, Hofmannsthal's main purpose and effect seem to be to create a kind of timeless and almost mythical atmosphere. This technique was likewise developed in the work of the later period, notably, as demonstrated in some detail later, in the Poland of *Der Turm* which is 'more that of saga than of history'.

Alongside this feeling for the past in its various modifications may be set another feature of Hofmannsthal's early work. It is neither constant nor quite so obvious. There are, especially in certain early prose writings, signs of the social and moral interest which later became such a prominent characteristic of his work. In *Hofmannsthals Wandlung*, cited on p. 8, Alewyn showed how even in this early period, when 'the literary world regarded Hofmannsthal as the reincarnated myth', the young poet was aware of the danger of his situation, that of the 'aesthetic man'. Alewyn places this awareness very early in Hofmannsthal's career and proves his assertion in an interpretation of *Das Märchen der 672. Nacht* which was written in 1894 and was therefore contemporary with those works which brought the 'Loris' legend into being. Alewyn considered the *Märchen* in some detail and showed how it was part of a constant development which ultimately led Hofmannsthal away from his own myth and out into life:

The young Hofmannsthal had every reason to feel that he was one of the elect. He was blessed with hours when he...seemed to be transmuted into the heart of things...the young Hofmannsthal certainly did not cease to treasure the preciousness of this blessed state. But he was not tardy in warning against its ambiguousness....In his poetic work—in many disguises—he revealed the deeply questionable nature of this 'completeness'.[1]

Alewyn then pointed to various of the young poet's creations who substantiate this assertion:

There are the rich men whose possessions shut them off from their fellow-men, there are the beautiful ones to whom love is not granted, there are the proud ones who pine away in powerless isolation... there are the adventurers on whom life showers all its gifts abundantly and who let everything run through their hands.

It cannot be maintained, however, that Hofmannsthal's attitude at this stage in his career was particularly constructive. To be aware of a danger, to point to shortcomings in oneself or in one's environment is only one step in the right direction. Benno von Wiese has demonstrated the existence in *Reitergeschichte* (1898) of a new ethical awareness and concern.[2] He did not, however, attempt to place this *Novelle* within the framework of Hofmannsthal's development.

Such awareness and concern certainly represent a clearing of ground and are positive in that limited sense, but only the use made by the artist of his awareness and new insight can be of decisive value. In other words he clears the ground and thus metaphorically rejects old error. What does he build on his newly gained vantage-point? The *Chandos Letter* relates how the final clearing and rejecting was done and why it was done. It is, however, to *Der Dichter und diese Zeit* (*The Artist in the Present Age*), a significantly titled essay-speech written a few years later (1906–7), that one turns to get an authoritative statement as to the positive course which Hofmannsthal was to adopt as he approached middle age and the composition of those three dramas which are the main object of this study.

It is fortunate that one of Hofmannsthal's most distinguished *ex cathedra* statements was delivered during the period immediately preceding the appearance of *Jedermann* (1911) which, as shown in chapters 1 and 2, sprang from a new conception of his purpose as a dramatist. The essay-lecture *Der Dichter und diese Zeit* was written at the end of the year (1906) which had seen the final break with Stefan George and it was delivered publicly in Munich, Frankfurt, Göttingen and Berlin.[1] These two facts are in themselves of some significance. An essay by Paul Requadt demonstrates this. In summing up the polarity of the two men Requadt also assessed Hofmannsthal's attitude to his own work:

External factors are again relevant to Hofmannsthal himself. How did he publish his work? To what sort of reader did he address himself? The relationship between the poet and his times is the actual question.

George's attitude is quite unambiguous...the poet withdraws from the vulgar mob, at first in aesthetic isolation and later as judge and prophet....Hofmannsthal's attitude is not so clearly defined. On the one hand he gives George poems for publication in *Blätter für die Kunst* and also allows George to bring out a small edition of his poems. At the same time, however, he writes for the daily press. It would be wrong to conclude without further ado that Hofmannsthal was anxious for popularity. Often, like Oscar Wilde, he merely wants to shake up the public by the force of his paradoxes, and he knows the temptations in this *feuilleton* writing....On the whole Hofmannsthal increasingly gave up his tendency to address himself only to those who were aesthetically initiated....In the Shakespeare address he is speaking to the...learned, in *Das Schrifttum als Geistiger Raum der Nation* to the academic youth of the country, in the *Deutsches Lesebuch* to the people. In the same way his plays free themselves from the exclusiveness of the 'little theatre' until, at the Salzburg Festival, he reaches and moves the masses....He thought about the 'reader' a good deal and with good reason. Later on, however, this reader is pushed aside by the sensuously receptive spectator.

In turning his back on aesthetic realms Hofmannsthal becomes contemporary in a very actual sense, especially because he realizes at an early stage that his personal problem is that of his century.[1]

In *Der Dichter und diese Zeit* Hofmannsthal achieved balance between the world of internal, personal experience and critical observation of the world in which he lived. With this balance went an attempt to reconcile feeling and reason. For all the magic of language, the familiar technique of word-pictures perceived fleetingly, there is in this essay a clarity and precision of thought not felt in Hofmannsthal's earlier work, where one is often more impressed by brilliant intuition.

Hofmannsthal revealed in this essay an exalted view of the artist's mission. At the same time, however, he confined himself to the situation as it is in a confused and contradictory age, rejecting the temptation to set up a grand ideal of the artist as the preacher, teacher, seer and prophet of old—and of the fairly recent past. This meant a decisive break with what might be called the Romantic tradition. Probably, however, Hofmannsthal was also thinking of Stefan George:

They are perturbed to see how little the poets of today seem to realize the dignity of their office; how with pride mingled with something like contempt they leave to others...the task of playing the part of ...spokesman for our time. It is as if there were an abyss between their attitude and the attitude of Schiller who was so very much the eloquent and conscious herald of his epoch, between their attitude and that of Hebbel who with sleepless eyes, standing in the darkness, constantly felt the scale of values moving up and down in his hands.[2]

It seems that Hofmannsthal was here close to the real point of a question much asked of the creative writer in the present age: should he grapple with actual problems of his times—social, political, cultural problems? Hofmannsthal has sometimes been attacked because he is assumed not to have dealt with specific problems of his day, because he did not advance positive solutions. Solutions to such problems, however, tend unfortunately to be ideological and ephemeral. The artist is not there to answer all questions which may arise in his lifetime. He is neither a statesman nor a political scientist. By being true to himself, however, by creating *aus sich heraus* he can stir the imagination and perceptive faculty of his contemporaries—of those contemporaries, at least, who have the ears to hear and the patience to go with him without preconceived notions and demands as to what should be revealed to them. To make men alive to possibilities, to reveal the interconnection of past and present, to make his readers vitally aware of what is in them and the world about them—that was Hofmannsthal's view of the artist's mission, and it seems to be a valid one.

Hofmannsthal seems in fact to claim for the literary artist a quality of inevitability. The artist is for him a seismograph of his times:

The artist is there and it is nobody's concern to bother about his presence. He is there and he changes his position without a sound and he is nothing but eye and ear and he takes his colour from the colour of those things upon which he rests. He is the spectator—no—the concealed companion, the silent brother of all things, and the changing of his colour means intense torment for him: for he suffers in and with all things, and yet as he suffers he enjoys them. This suffering enjoyment is the whole content of his life. He suffers because he feels things so deeply. And he suffers in and with the individual as much as with the mass of people; he suffers their isolation and their relation to each other; the exalted and the worthless, the sublime and the mean; he suffers their conditions and their thoughts; he suffers the mere objects of thought, those phantoms and insubstantial children of the age. For to him men and things, thoughts and dreams are one; he only knows phenomena. ...He can omit nothing.... It is as if his eyes were lidless. He may not shun any single thought which presses in upon him.... For everything must fit into his order of things. All things must and will come together in him. He it is who joins together the disparate elements of the age. The present is to be found nowhere if not in him.[1]

At this stage in Hofmannsthal's career, and in this essay in particular, a further and fairly consistent pattern becomes apparent. The theory of his personal development was often fully discussed—even argued—and his changing outlook clarified and defined in a prose essay which preceded the expression of at least some of these ideas in a drama.[1] It was, however, the tragedy of his career that the spiritual weariness, so early apparent, haunted him throughout. Constantly one has the impression that what was revealed in the dramas was only a fragment of what had been postulated in the prose works. These, in their turn, were often brilliant sketches or vignettes, studies for works of great scale and scope which were never completely carried out. The fragmentary nature of much of Hofmannsthal's work is scarcely to be denied. His correspondence, with Richard Strauss and Eberhart von Bodenhausen for example, shows just what efforts were necessary for him to drive on with his work.

Some expression of the ideas put forward in *Der Dichter und diese Zeit* is found, however, in *Jedermann* (1911).

CHAPTER I

'JEDERMANN': BACKGROUND AND PURPOSE

'JEDERMANN' was the first drama of Hugo von Hofmannsthal which, while written with deep personal conviction, was at the same time quite consciously written for and addressed to the outside world. It can be regarded as the decisive work of his middle years. It would be unjust, however, to regard it as primarily a stepping-stone, a distinguished introduction to something great and complete. As shown in chapters 5 and 6 *Jedermann*, *Das Salzburger Große Welttheater* (1922) and *Der Turm* (1925–7) may be considered together as aspects of an integrated vision of God and of human society. *Jedermann* was nevertheless complete in itself.

In *Jedermann* style, form and content were united in such a way as to make the work as satisfying to the most sensitive stylist as it is accessible to the anonymous masses to whom the play is primarily directed. This latter idea made here its initial appearance in Hofmannsthal's work. For the first time he aimed at the widest possible circle of readers or, ideally and more accurately, spectators—a far cry from the aristocratic seclusion of his early lyrics, yet in two ways a consistent line may be traced.

In *Jedermann* Hofmannsthal was still deeply aware of the forces of decline which had weighed so heavily on him as a young man. But he had won his way to a positive standpoint. This was expressed in a traditional form (the medieval mystery play) and embodied a wholly traditional code of morality. It can make a direct and deep impression on a modern audience, however, because of its stark, straightforward approach and certain modifications in and additions to the old English play on which it is based. These factors are discussed in some detail in chapter 2.

The second consistent line was of course the flight to the past for inspiration. Now, however, Hofmannsthal returned from his flight vigorous and ready to adapt what he had gained in order to deal with what he regarded as the great evil of his time.

There is little doubt that Hofmannsthal was greatly concerned by the growing materialism of the early twentieth century. Attention has already been drawn to his prescience in spiritual-cultural values (see pp. 7–8 and 11–12) and to the fact that he was aware of impending doom, of standing at the end of a great progress on the edge of the pit of dissolution. He saw the corporeal, flatly materialistic projection of this in the complacent *laissez-faire* prosperity inseparable from the terms Edwardian, Wilhelminian and Dual Monarchy. Earlier than the majority of men he understood the legacy of the nineteenth century. The conviction of inevitable progress based on the new science, the cheerful overthrow of old beliefs and their systems of personal and public morality did not, he realized, lead automatically into the promised land.

This anti-materialistic attitude can be said to be part of a movement in German letters which began with Nietzsche. In Hofmannsthal's own time its most obvious exponents were to be found in Stefan George and the circle round him. A highly characteristic statement of these anti-materialistic convictions is for example the opening paragraph of Gundolf's work on George himself:

Language and poetry are for us here simply the most tangible signs of a situation which in its totality ranges from everyday affairs to religion. They are at the same time the basis of the means by which the individual human being is most likely to be able to redeem the world when all around him the state, economy, society...have fallen into materialism and the attitudes of the herd.[1]

It is significant that the protest of George's group led in the drama to those *Kultspiele* which in rejecting society turn away from it. Such works are in effect aestheticism's counterpoise to Hofmannsthal's revival of the ancient morality form with a practical social end in view, namely the regeneration of society through individual reform.

Thus we find Hofmannsthal moving in the opposite direction from his former associates. His attitude can be summed up in the words of Albert Schweitzer, not usually regarded as in any way a contemporary of Hofmannsthal. Not only, however, is Schweitzer of the same generation (he was born in 1875), but he like Hofmannsthal foresaw disillusionment in ideas which were widely accepted at the turn of this century.

It is of considerable significance, however much at first sight surprising, that we can associate Hofmannsthal's views with those of a man who has always stood in the midst of life accepting its burdens, a man who has always been a practical visionary. Discussing the social climate round about the turn of the century Schweitzer wrote:

Right from my early university years I had begun to view with concern the idea that mankind was engaged in sure and steady progress. My feeling was that the fires of idealism were burning low and that nobody ...was worried about it. In so many cases I could not help noticing how public opinion, far from indignantly rejecting publicly proclaimed inhumane sentiments, accepted them and approved inhumane actions of states and peoples as being opportune. But it also seemed that there was only a very lukewarm zeal left where justice and the appropriate were concerned. So many symptoms forced me to conclude that our proud and industrious race was intellectually and spiritually tired. It seemed to me that people were persuading themselves that previous hopes for the future of mankind had been too exalted and that we should have to limit ourselves to striving for what was within reach. The watchword *Realpolitik*—applied to all topics—really meant that a shortsighted nationalism was approved and a pact was made with forces and tendencies which had previously been fought because they were the enemies of progress.... Towards the end of the century people reviewed the past and tried to evaluate its achievements in all spheres of activity. They did this with an optimism which I found quite incomprehensible. Everywhere people seemed to assume that we had not only advanced in knowledge and inventiveness but that in a spiritual and ethical sense we had likewise reached a standard never reached before and never to be lost in the future. It seemed to me, however, that in our spiritual and intellectual life we had not only failed to surpass bygone generations but that in many respects a good deal of their achievement was running away between our fingers.[1]

Hofmannsthal's appraisal of the same period was metaphysical and highly abstract where Schweitzer was blunt and almost commonplace in expression—a characteristic which (in Schweitzer's original German) gives his written thought a hard and tempered force. A passage from *Der Dichter und diese Zeit* is relevant here. Hofmannsthal's words seem to run in sombre counterpoint to those of Schweitzer and each strand of thought complements the other:

Our time is full of things which seem to be alive but which are in reality dead. It is full of things which are supposed to be dead but which are in fact very much alive. Considering its various phenomena it seems to me that in almost every case those things which according to popular assumption are in the game are in fact out of it, whilst those whose importance is denied are of very actual significance and effectiveness. Our time is—to a diseased extent—full of unrealized possibilities. At the same time it is stuffed with things which seem to exist only because of their living content and which do not really have life within them. The essential nature of our time is expressed in the fact that nothing which really has power over men expresses itself in any visible metaphor. On the contrary everything is carried inwardly. But that period which we call the Middle Ages—that period whose ruins and phantoms tower right into the present—gathered together all its essential facets and shaped them into an enormous cathedral of metaphor which was raised up right out in the open.[2]

In the sense of this passage *Jedermann* is an 'enormous cathedral of metaphor'. Its foundations are in the Middle Ages and it bears within itself the associations and overtones accumulated over half a millennium. The impact of this metaphor is, however, of today. This claim is investigated in the following sections of this chapter.

The English *Everyman* play is probably the most famous of all medieval mysteries and moralities. It is notable for its vigour, direct wit of an obvious kind, and for its simple moral pressed home with realistic effect to a naïve audience of believers. It recounts simply the mission of Death to summon Everyman before God to give an account of his stewardship on earth; how Everyman, a figure who symbolizes all humanity, despairs and tries to find someone or something to accompany him on his last journey; how he fails and all his fair-weather friends desert him; how he is brought to timely repentance and dedication of himself by his religion and his own few good works; how, shriven and solaced, he sets out on his pilgrimage into eternity. The moral is that of the rich man for whom it is as easy to get into heaven as it is for a camel to pass through the eye of a needle.

Hofmannsthal was evidently impressed by the strength of this mystery play[1] and by its sense of unchanging values:

It made a great and pure impression on me....Its actual essence revealed itself more and more as being absolutely valid for all humanity, belonging to no particular age and not even bound up indissolubly with Christian dogma. What is expressed here in allegorical-dramatic form is simply this: that an unconditional striving for higher things— for the most high—must come to man's aid decisively when all earthly relationships—of loyalty and possession—have shown themselves to be illusory. Is there anything that could be more relevant to us?[2]

Accordingly, Hofmannsthal set out to bring *Everyman* into the living possession of the German people, rescuing it from a fate where the many versions, in his own academically icono-clastic phrase, 'wash around in the dead waters of scholarly ownership'! His aim was clear. He was determined that in evoking the spirit of the Catholic Middle Ages he would protest against and offer a timeless solution for the abject materialism which, he felt, was the source of the decay existing on all sides. He expressed himself on this point, which is the spiritual core of *Jedermann*, with unusual vehemence:

For we are in the darkness and in sore straits; in a different way from that of medieval man but to no less a degree. We survey and penetrate many things and yet our actual spiritual power of sight is weak. We have power over many things but we are not rulers. What we ought to possess possesses us; and what has become the remedy above all remedies—money—is now, by devilish perversity, a goal to be set above every other. The modern age looks on Mammon in a different, more free and benevolent way than did the old pious ages.[1]

Thus what is felt as implicit in the medieval English play is brought to the surface and treated as the central theme of Hofmannsthal's *Erneuerung*,[2] from which all character and motive spring:

The relationship to this demon [i.e., money] has become dark and involved. This relationship permeates and suffuses every other relationship in human existence. The extent to which it determines them all is quite terrifying.[3]

An allegory based on this kind of idea might well present a bleak prospect for a drama. It might indeed have formed the basis for one of those essays in cultural-political philosophy which were characteristic of the older Hofmannsthal. However, he was able to deal with this objection as soon as it arose. Such an allegory, he insisted, is not cold and lifeless. On the contrary, an essential part of the idea which should imbue drama is 'to condense the nebulous essence of the world into tangible antitheses in this [allegorical] way'.[4]

This justification for the use of allegory is followed by one of those strange, seer-like sayings, latter-day Goethean *Sprüche*, which were characteristic of Hofmannsthal in his middle and later years: 'It is the danger and the glory of our time, on whose threshold the aged Ibsen stands, that we have again arrived at a point where we are forced to prove ourselves in allegorical terms.'

Hofmannsthal's growing tendency to use timeless or mythical symbols is further explained by two aphorisms in the *Buch der Freunde*, which also demonstrate his distaste for naturalistic techniques and their limitations:

Allegory is a great vehicle which should not be despised. What two friends really mean to each other can be better shown by the exchange of magic rings and horns than by psychology.

Naturalism is a long way from nature because in order to reproduce the surface of things it has to neglect the inner wealth of relationships and connections, the actual mystery of nature.[1]

Hofmannsthal wrote *Jedermann* with a marked feeling for double values: while the voice of his social and religious conviction spoke to the immediate present of present problems, an inner voice was speaking *sub specie aeternitatis* in the prophetic knowledge that some things not understood or only darkly felt in his own times would be revealed to succeeding generations. An obvious illustration of this might be seen in the history of *Jedermann* since its completion. It was an irony of fate that *Jedermann* was established at Salzburg only after the collapse of the Habsburg empire and in the midst of the old Europe whose coming dissolution Hofmannsthal had so clearly perceived.

If the impact of *Jedermann* was correspondingly greater in the years of bitterness following World War I, such was immeasurably more the case when it was revived at Salzburg immediately after the National Socialist collapse in 1945. In those years, after the deluge had receded and a shattered society set out to build anew, the spectacle of Jedermann at his banquet, insouciant, willingly ignorant of the plight of others, made an impression which was frighteningly intense. Here it could be felt how the rise of devilish power in civilized countries can become possible. Frivolity, superficiality, material egotism, a cynically personal *Realpolitik*, allow a Moloch to arise unchecked until it affects personal interests, and then it is usually too late. To see Jedermann rejoicing in the pleasures of the day, wilfully unaware of death circling over him, was to understand something of Hofmannsthal's prophetic vision. As an artist he was of course *untragbar* in National Socialist Germany and in post-*Anschluß* Austria. It is tolerably certain that the Jewish strain in his genetical constitution was not wholly to blame for this.

In *Jedermann* Hofmannsthal is continually widening the implications of the old play. He treats the ancient Christian concepts of tolerance, generosity and love of neighbour, and points to the fatal consequences of a refusal to countenance these values. A new austerity of conscience is strongly felt as Hofmannsthal shows the uselessness of mere lip-service to religion. Jedermann is a 'good Christian' who, in his own words, goes to church and puts something on the plate. Hofmannsthal points, however, not only to the mere negative uselessness of this. He demonstrates in addition the inevitable slackening of all personal morality which must occur when principles and beliefs openly professed are ignored when convenient. Religious belief does not bring with it a source of comfortable consolation on tap whenever the need be felt. Religion is not something external. Hofmannsthal shows it as a series of truths and commands which must be lived to the last in face of all difficulties.

Hofmannsthal's actual message in *Jedermann* was of course not new. What, however, has in many mouths become a tiresome pulpit platitude, bearing little relation to the realities of earthly and eternal life, is here given uncompromising expression. For Hofmannsthal in *Jedermann* a belief is alive and active or it is nothing. That Hofmannsthal achieves this uncompromising tone despite the lavish baroque-style staging of the play is demonstrated during the analysis of the play itself (chapter 2) and in the conclusion to the present chapter.

The unequivocal message of the play comes to reader and audience in an idiom more than tinged with dialect (Bavaro-Austrian) and showing a pronounced archaic bias. This idiom is deceptively simple, for its simplicity in *Jedermann* is as polished and sophisticated as any of the earlier bejewelled and empurpled dramatic poems such as *Der Tod des Tizian* or *Gestern*. The words of *Werke* (Good Works) in addressing Jedermann provide an ideal illustration:

> Ich war ein Kelch der vor dir stand,
> Gefüllt von Himmel bis an den Rand,
> Von Irdischem war darin kein Ding.
> Drum schien ich deinen Augen gering.

The language here is simple and direct. There is no word which would be in any way unfamiliar to the average hearer. 'Chalice', 'heaven', 'earth', 'eyes': around these four picture-words the artist builds his idea of good works as a chalice filled to the brim with grace, the gift of heaven, God-given to Jedermann as to all. With the aid and benison of this grace Jedermann could have wrought those things which would have brought him well-being and satisfaction on earth, eased the lot of others and ensured his own salvation.

Also associated with the chalice is the symbol of the central reality of the Catholic faith: the living presence of God in Holy Communion, fortifying all who are free from mortal sin.[1] This double symbol is strengthened by the second line: 'Gefüllt von Himmel bis an den Rand.' Two ideas are suggested: the chalice filled with the heavenly grace of God; the chalice filled by heaven itself and coming down to this world, having nothing earthly about it—'von Irdischem war darin kein Ding'—and, like the Grail's descent to Montsalvat, bearing with it the aura of heaven. This second idea exalts an already exalted image. From this image to *von Irdischem* is a stark contrast and *irdisch* in its turn has diverse overtones of worldliness, sensuality and the merely human.

The style of *Jedermann* is simple and unadorned yet there is no trace of *naïveté* of thought. In fact it is by the combination of high seriousness with homely idiom that *Jedermann* achieves its aim. This simplicity of diction—the presentation of Christian idealism in language essentially of peasant and soil—was designed to make a deep effect on Hofmannsthal's primarily south German audience. It may be appropriate here to recall that *Jedermann* was written principally for outdoor performance. It has gained its world-wide reputation as a result of the annual performances at the Salzburg Festival where, on the enclosed cathedral square with the façade of the baroque cathedral as evocative background, it has become a firm tradition.

But the brilliance of the Reinhardt production should not be allowed to divert attention from certain facets of the play which cannot be completely demonstrated at a festival performance. Such a performance, however *volkstümlich*, must have something of the 'occasional' atmosphere about it. Moreover, the particular achievement of the Salzburg performance in realizing Hofmannsthal's ideal is discussed later in this chapter.

Relevant here is an average performance in the suburbs of a town or in a village community, the sort of performance which is encountered any summer anywhere in Austria. What do the people in the audience hear and see? They hear a familiar language similar to that in which, like their ancestors, they conduct their everyday affairs. The dialogue, its familiarity heightened in this dramatic way, is spoken perhaps before their own parish church or on their market square, places in and around which their lives run their course. And so the force of the play can make a deep and direct impact.

This is a vital consideration for there, where the history of the community is ever-present—where victory and defeat, general joy and personal sorrow, baptism and requiem, and also all the little countless, nameless, unremembered acts of everyday life— where all these have been celebrated, mourned, discussed, lived in youth and age, the audience now sees the eternal play of its own earthly progress on its own familiar and well-loved ground.

Although *Bodenständigkeit*, the sense of identity with folk, soil and immediate homeland, is the essential for the kind of realization which has just been described, it should be remembered that this type of feeling, together with the sense of unchanging values and oneness with ancestors and with the past, is most strongly marked in peasant communities. As Hofmannsthal remarked:

If you go amongst the peasants you flee from the world of today. The peasant and the world of today are engaged in a healthy and eternal struggle, and above nature and the stars there hovers a realm of time which never fades and which knows nothing of the insipid present.[1]

In a short essay written in 1919, *Festspiele in Salzburg*,[1] Hof-mannsthal discussed the fundamental and natural aptitude for the theatre to be found amongst the Bavaro-Austrian people. What, he asked, was the purpose of musical-theatrical festivals in Salzburg? In his answer one sees the linking of past and present in a new guise:

It means: to give new life to what has been alive for centuries, it means to do again on an ancient site, chosen for its appropriateness, what was done there throughout the ages; it means allowing full play to the basic urge of the Bavaro-Austrian peoples and thereby helping these peoples, amongst whom 'the gift of song, of the drama, of painting and musical composition is very widely distributed', to find their way back into their real spiritual element.[2]

Hofmannsthal pointed to the Bavaro-Austrian's love of action, by which external, visible action is meant, combined with a dis-taste for solely abstract thought. Hofmannsthal proves this in the variety and extent of theatrical art in the regions under discussion. After attributing the creation of the German folk-play to the people of this area and noting the Oberammergau Passion Play as the most celebrated instance of this, Hofmannsthal gives in a brief suggestive passage a picture both of the range and serious-ness of approach natural to these districts:

And the villages and little towns, the abbey and monastery schools along the Inn and the Etsch, on the Danube and on the Mur, gave birth to the same kind of thing. In the Tyrol alone we can, in the half century between 1750 and 1800, count up eight hundred performances of folk dramas in a hundred and sixty different places. In these fifty years the Tyrolean peasant saw just about everything that had been put on in German theatres since 1600—and a good deal of what had been staged in other European theatres. We find state tragedies in the grand manner, passion plays, plays on the theme of the 'world theatre' and last judgment, German and Italian operetta; there are legends, there are comedies and tragedies from the repertories of all German court theatres of that generation; old Shrove-tide plays.

At this point it may be interesting to note that all quotations used by Hofmannsthal in this essay were taken from Josef Nadler's *Literaturgeschichte der deutschen Stämme und Landschaften*. The aim and method of Nadler's work are sufficiently well known to make superfluous any attempt at a summary. Hofmannsthal had a great though not altogether uncritical admiration for the controversial literary historian and amongst his posthumous notes was a sketch of a projected large-scale essay: *Zu Josef Nadlers Literaturgeschichte*.[1] This sketch dates from the years 1924–8 and according to Herbert Steiner the work had held Hofmannsthal's attention since 1917.[2] This is substantiated in Hofmannsthal's correspondence with Bodenhausen. Hofmannsthal's interest in Nadler's work is relevant not only because of the later political controversy around Nadler himself, but mainly because Hofmannsthal's sketch contains several very characteristic leading motives in his own cultural-political thought. Here are some fragments from the sketch, relevant to the present study:

He describes a past which works on into our own day. Landscape and tradition take hold of the individual soul...he puts forward the idea that great stems of poetically endowed men have shaped the intellectual face of the nation.

Proof of the homogeneous folk culture of the Bavarians throughout their history.

...no landscape, no town from Murten to Danzig, from Flensburg to Graz, no part of the nation more than the Bavarians. Open the book anywhere...turn up anything you like—landscape and atmosphere stick to it—Viennese theatre in the eighteenth century.

The whole is like a power-charged atmosphere. Nothing is ever finished with, nothing ever concluded....Each individual carries within him his inheritance and what destiny has seen fit to lay upon him—it breaks forth from him, here in the form of a poetic work, there as a political essay....The dramatic element within the nation.

It can be seen how these large concepts in note form accord with Hofmannsthal's thought at the time when, with *Jedermann* written and ready for its first Salzburg performance (not, admittedly, its first performance, which took place under Reinhardt's direction in Berlin, 1912), he was envisaging Salzburg and *Jedermann's* place there in terms of a revival of an ancient

28

form of folk theatre, a revival designed to exert a powerful influence on the nation.

It is odd, however, that in *Festspiele in Salzburg* Hofmannsthal concentrated exclusively on the dramatic achievement of the seventeenth and eighteenth centuries. There could be several reasons for this. Hofmannsthal, as Viennese and Austrian, was imbued with the living baroque tradition and the achievement of the Counter-Reformation. This essay was written primarily to publicize and explain the idea underlying the newly instituted Salzburg Festival. Salzburg is of course the baroque city *par excellence*, both in style and in its more recent and predominating traditions. It was thus perhaps natural that Hofmannsthal should emphasize the later age.

The traditions of the folk theatre in Austria are indeed much older than *Festspiele in Salzburg* might seem to indicate. The very numerous medieval mysteries and moralities in towns and villages from Tyrol to Styria are of course clear proof of this.[1] Hofmannsthal himself was well aware of these early beginnings of the theatre. This is clear not only from his own commentaries on and explanations of *Das Salzburger Große Welttheater* (discussed at some length in chapter 5). It is also clear from a very short essay written in the same year as *Festspiele in Salzburg*. This bears the confusing title *Deutsche Festspiele in Salzburg*![2] Here Hofmannsthal wrote:

The foundation of a festival theatre on the frontier between Bavaria and Austria is the symbolic expression of some very deep tendencies which go back five hundred years....South German life can be seen here in its entirety. The mighty foundation is medieval...in Mozart you find the real peak and centre at once: drama and music are one—high drama and opera, separate from each other only in a conceptual sense but in fact inseparable and actually already united in the baroque[3] theatre of the seventeenth century....What in Goethe was the real stuff of theatre...is a great piling-up of every theatrical form which has sprung from south German soil: from the mystery and the morality to the puppet plays and the Jesuit school drama, and from there to the court opera with its choirs, machines and a great parade of pomp.

Hofmannsthal trusted in this instinctive receptivity to and practice of the living theatre. The interpenetration of sophisticated and intuitive elements can be constantly noted in his account. In the present case this means the mutually complementing influence of the baroque spirit (usually sacred Baroque) and of peasant folk art. In Bavaria and Austria, probably more than anywhere else in the German-speaking lands, the age-old connection between church and people is still firm and apparent. This has little to do with external fervour, still less with exacting religious observance. One cannot imagine Melk or Ettal, St Florian or Wilten existing either in monastic seclusion or as admired museum-pieces, which is often the case elsewhere:

That is how things are in town after town, village after village. The great abbeys, on their beautiful hills, look out far into the countryside. Every one of them has its own theatre for high drama and spectacular opera....Every single one is a focal point from which this popular folk art flows forth in all directions. Wherever the sledge-hammers thunder in a forest-valley the smiths and journeymen have their own theatre. They put on knightly dramas, fairy-tales and sagas.[1]

Hofmannsthal recalls these theatres—at Kieferach, at Lauffen an der Salzach—and notes how, for example, in the Saltmen's Guild at Lauffen a man's fame as an actor counted for more than his skill as a salt-shipper: 'It is indeed an elemental yearning which expresses itself there; and when times are dark and a hard and cruel reality presses down on men, this urge becomes stronger, not weaker.'[2] The famous oath of the Oberammergauer peasants is an obvious instance, but no less striking were the events of 1683 and the years following the siege and relief of Vienna:

In 1683 when the Turks besieged Vienna...there was theatrical activity of scarcely precedented intensity in those parts of the alpine provinces which had been spared. Seven years later Kara Mustapha was a stock figure on twenty stages. There is something in this activity, this unconquerable urge towards visual depiction—in which tableau and sound, feeling gesture and dance rhythm come together—which reminds one of Attica.[3]

This analogy with Greece led Hofmannsthal to the notion of the power of the landscape itself—the mountain land.[1] For this passion for the theatre follows the mountain ranges of South Germany and Austria; north as far as Lower Bavaria; eastward to the Hungarian plain; westward almost to the shores of Lake Geneva; in the south throughout the Dolomites.

A further analogy, some recent performances of Aeschylus' plays in the antique theatre at Syracuse in Sicily, brought Hofmannsthal to the direct purpose of *Jedermann* in Salzburg. In Syracuse ancient drama of great exaltation, played under the bright, clear Sicilian sun (as visualized by Aeschylus himself), was able to impress the spectator with its directness, its veritable folk-quality. It seemed, Hofmannsthal continues, as natural and as much 'of the people' as the procession of Our Lady in Ghent.

Because of these considerations, this accumulated wealth of traditional practice, Hofmannsthal felt that he could with confidence stage *Jedermann* on the cathedral square in Salzburg.

In view, however, of Hofmannsthal's work as co-founder of the Salzburg Festival[2] and of the vital part which Salzburg was to play in his further progress as a dramatist—not only where *Jedermann* is concerned—it may be interesting to look a little more closely at the factors which drew him to the actual city of Salzburg when he arrived at the last stage of his creative career.

Hofmannsthal, as already noted in connection with the tradition of the folk-theatre, felt as few men the living power of Austrian–South German Baroque with its manifold overtones: of the Counter-Reformation, of the Jesuit and Benedictine sacred drama, of the secular court spectacle, of the wave of rejoicing and enterprise which followed the long and painful struggle against the Turks.

The inherent antitheses of the Baroque were Hofmannsthal's familiars: the sacred and the profane, sensuous joy in living and a brooding sense of death in the midst of all things, a fervently pious spirituality and a solidly tangible way of expressing it.

This antithesis is probably best expressed in terms of sacred baroque architecture. A church such as the former Benedictine abbey church of St Michael in Bamberg is a case in point. One is simultaneously impressed by the solid, massive and sombre brilliance of the interior and by the fervent spirituality which it expresses—and which it can induce in the congregation or individual. Vierzehnheiligen (near Bamberg), St John Nepomuk (Munich) or St Florian (near Linz) are perhaps even more pointed examples. They seem almost as solid, yet the illusion of heavenly splendour is more intense.

Nikolaus Pevsner summed up this aspect in a manner which is quite relevant to the present discussion. Writing of Vierzehnheiligen he observed

a decidely theatrical effect. This is one of the chief objections against such churches.... Besides, why did architects and artists so fervently strive to deceive and create such intense illusion of reality? What reality was the Church concerned with? Surely that of the Divine Presence. It is the zeal of an age in which Roman Catholic dogmas, mysteries, and miracles were no longer, as they had been in the Middle Ages, accepted as truth by all. There were heretics, and there were sceptics. To restore the first to the fold, to convince the others, religious architecture had both to inflame and to mesmerize. But it is brought forward as another argument against Baroque churches that they seem worldly as compared with the churches of the Middle Ages. Now it is true that the character of Baroque decoration in a church or palace is identical. But is not the same true of the Middle Ages? The idea behind the identity is perfectly sane. By the splendour of the arts we honour a king; is not supreme splendour due to the King of Kings? In our churches today and in those churches of the Middle Ages which the nineteenth century restored, there is nothing of this. They are halls of worship with an atmosphere to concentrate the thoughts of a congregation on worship and prayer. A church of the Baroque was literally the house of the Lord.

Still there is no denying the fact that we, observers or believers, never feel quite sure where in a church such as Vierzehnheiligen the spiritual ends and the worldly begins.[1]

The Baroque, however, 'with all its power of living and dying',[2] was one of several factors destined to make Salzburg and *Jeder-*

mann inseparable. To this sensuous architectural quality a perfect complement was added in the natural setting and historical-geographical significance of the city itself. The city is layer upon layer of living history, tangible and obvious to the eye. Hofmannsthal already felt this as a youth of seventeen:

In Salzburg Baroque and Rococo still hold sway over the poor styles of modern times. And the sovereign lords of Salzburg, in their ecclesiastical-secular elegance, always did understand the art of representation. If you look at the characterless bourgeois town of today it is easy to trace out the old city of the princely tyrants. An aura of genuine individuality hovers over the patricianly houses with their stairways, over the mannered groups in sandstone and the over-ornate summer-houses.[1]

Thus when *Jedermann* was performed in Salzburg a number of factors of widely different categories combined with a result which was 'folkish, natural and direct'.[2] As has been shown, Hofmannsthal was very aware of the ruling passion for theatre amongst the Bavaro-Austrian mountain folk. He went on to assert that Salzburg is the heart of this area at a point where the lines of cultural influence and counter-influence cross: Munich–Vienna, Tyrol–Bohemia, Nürnberg (that is, Lower Bavaria)–Styria and Carinthia. He cites Nadler again when he notes how from the middle of the seventeenth century Salzburg was 'the undisputed spiritual and intellectual leader of all the free land between Munich, Vienna and Innsbruck. Humanism, Renaissance and Baroque had an historical content here which was unrivalled by that of any other landscape.'[3] What particularly appealed to Hofmannsthal in this was the idea of the concentrated heritage of the past, with every aspect simultaneously visible:

Nowhere else do the centuries flow into each other as they do here [Salzburg]; the Baroque of the Middle Ages—the Franciscan epoch struggling to find its characteristic expression[4]—and the Baroque of the [seventeenth][5] century. The peasant element, constant and close to nature, joins these two together. The cathedral square, enclosed by palaces and pillared arches, is Italian and almost timeless. The mountains of a German landscape, crowned by a German castle, gaze down on all this. The Franciscan Church towers up nearby—pure Middle Ages. The statues in front of the cathedral are early baroque.[1]

This passage illustrates something essential to the understanding of Hofmannsthal's peculiar genius. The lines cited are apparently wholly 'external' in character and coolly objective. And yet, rather in the manner of August von Platen seeing, consciously or unconsciously, the symbol of himself and his declined aristocratic line in the wondrous, hollow façade of Venice, Hofmannsthal found in Salzburg the symbol of his own personal and artistic constitution. For Hofmannsthal was Italian-German in ancestry and in his culture. He had the medieval sense of universality and of mysticism. He had the humanist's classic poise, dignity, and pride in the achievement of man. The latter includes those three features so characteristic of the traditional man of the Renaissance: the sense of one all-embracing European culture, a super-refined feeling for beauty, and a certain speculative trait. Finally, there was in Hofmannsthal a fervent piety, a sense of the bitter transience of earthly things, and a markedly plastic-sensuous gift of expression. These things were all derived from his baroque heritage. It is perhaps not an exaggeration to say that Salzburg was in T. S. Eliot's sense Hofmannsthal's own personal 'objective correlative'!

The firm enduring fundament, however, was his *Volkstümlichkeit*, by which one means an awareness of belonging, of instinctive sympathy with and (a rarer attribute) understanding for one's countrymen. This means a warmly spontaneous and deep appreciation of custom, manner and speech. This quality in Hofmannsthal, which sustained his far-ranging, more brilliant qualities, usually prevented him from soaring into the realm of the ideal and abstract. It was the peasant-folk element in Salzburg —amidst, surrounding, softening the aristocratic and ecclesiastical splendours of a millennium—which completed for him the identification of *Jedermann* with Salzburg:

The great...marble statues, between which the actors entered and left the stage, had the effect of something self-evident and appropriate; likewise the cries of 'Jedermann' from the towers of the nearby church, from the castle, from St Peter's Cemetery; likewise the pealing of the great bells at the end of the play, the six angels moving into the dusky portals of the cathedral, the Franciscan monks looking on from their tower, the clerics at a hundred windows in St Peter's Convent; likewise the symbolic elements, the tragic and joyful elements, and the music. All this seemed right and proper to the peasants who streamed in, at first from the edge of the town, then from villages nearby, and then from further and further afield. They said 'There's a play on again. And that's as it should be.'[1]

To bring about this response the theatre presented had to measure up to the immanence of its setting. Referring to Mozart's *Don Giovanni* and to *Jedermann* Hofmannsthal put forward an ideal:

For they are both true theatre, born not of rhetoric and psychology, but of that elemental desire 'which wants to see superhuman things in tangible shape before its eyes and which has a deep aversion to any formless abstraction'.[2]

Salzburg thus presented Hofmannsthal with the opportunity of realizing an ideal. Earlier in this chapter it was averred that certain qualities in *Jedermann* cannot be fully realized at a festival performance, by which one would usually mean the Salzburg Festival. The Salzburg *Jedermann*, however, played before a very mixed and cosmopolitan audience, can attempt, by *demonstrating* its implicit *Volkstümlichkeit*, by concentrating into the span of a performance the disparate factors discussed in this chapter, to show the way to what is for a space a supra-national community. It can summon those present to interpret and apply its significance to their own traditions and customs.

The extent to which this can be achieved depends of course on individual sensibility. But the effort, at any rate, was made. It is, incidentally, scarcely a coincidence that the post-1945 period has seen a very considerable increase in several countries of emulations of the *Jedermann*-Salzburg tradition. These have taken several forms. The rejuvenation of medieval miracles and moralities (as at Chester, Coventry, York, etc.) is one instance. The highly successful revival at the Edinburgh Festival of Sir David Lindsay's *Satyre of the Thrie Estaitis* (1540) is a further development of the Salzburg tradition. Even more significant of this development are, however, the new works specially written for the new-old style of setting and the particular occasion. Mr Eliot's *Murder in the Cathedral* (1935) was in this respect an important forerunner.

The subject of the influence exerted by *Jedermann* at Salzburg is, however, very large and has many ramifications. These hints at its significance for others must suffice here, where the main purpose has been to clear the way for some study of *Jedermann* itself.

CHAPTER 2

'JEDERMANN': STRUCTURE AND MEANING

In the previous chapter the ethical and artistic motivation of *Jedermann* was discussed. Something was also said of its effect, ideal and actual, and of its place in a tradition which developed organically over a long period. An examination of the play itself may now be of greater relevance.

At the same time, however, a detailed examination such as that which follows may seem to negate Hofmannsthal's aim: *Jedermann* is a 'simple' play, as it has to be to fulfil one of Hofmannsthal's purposes, that of making a direct effect on an unsophisticated peasant audience. *Jedermann*, one might say, tells its familiar story of sin, repentance, and redemption by faith in terms still well known in every Christianized country. To follow the action step by step might seem to aim at an altogether too elementary level. Moreover, if so much has to be explained one might assume that the play could not make the direct effect which its author planned.

Against this, however, it should be emphasized that Hofmannsthal's mind was complex in its very nature. In *Jedermann* he was trying to write in a way simple enough to be understood by the peasant and subtle enough to satisfy more sophisticated audiences and more complex demands. Even in the 'simplicity' of the drama there was nothing naïve or spontaneous. If, indeed, the contrived nature of this simplicity does not on the whole show through this can be regarded as a tribute to Hofmannsthal's artistic skill. It is not suggested that the subtleties detailed in the following pages are always immediately obvious in performance. They may be on occasion. On the other hand it is probably a truism to say that what often makes a great and direct impact in the theatre—seemingly spontaneous and intuitively perceived—is revealed on subsequent scrutiny to have been a feat of skilful and conscious construction.

Perhaps the detailed examination which follows will at least give some idea of Hofmannsthal's characteristic method at this period in his career. Perhaps, too, it may be able to give some sense of that lucid and radiant quality in the play which one also encounters in Claudel (for example, *L'Annonce faite à Marie*)—what might perhaps be called its essentially 'Catholic' quality.

Structurally *Jedermann* is certainly very simple. It can be considered in two ways, each related to the other. In the first place it is a series of variations on the one central character who—save for a few moments during his repentance—is on the stage throughout. Thus the sequence of characters and incidents, one succeeding the other and rarely overlapping, takes on a pronouncedly musical quality as the various facets of Jedermann's character are revealed in turn. The resulting continual changes of mood give the whole a liveliness which holds the interest throughout, and Hofmannsthal is at pains not to allow the changes of mood to be either too sudden or crass. In consequence, when a sudden, sharp change of mood is called for, as in the sound of the voices calling Jedermann and at the appearance of Death, these impressions are all the stronger because of the sparing use of such virtuosity both beforehand and afterwards.

In the second place the play, although on the surface an extended one-acter, falls naturally into three acts with two prologues, one of secular type, the other—an integral part of the action—of sacred character. The first act runs from Jedermann's admonitions to his servants to the end of the scene with his mother. Here the straightforward worldly character of Jedermann is revealed. The second act, dramatically the climax of the play, takes in the assembly for the banquet, the banquet itself, the appearance of Death, and terminates with the end of the Mammon scene. The final act shows Jedermann in despair, deserted by all and helped finally to redemption by *Werke* (Good Works) and

Glaube (Faith) who ward off the Devil and lead Jedermann to his grave.

It will be appreciated that if the dramatic centre of gravity lies in the second act, the moral climax comes towards the end of the play and is made the more impressive by the austerity of its presentation in contrast to and following the flamboyance of the banquet scene. This staggering of effect illustrates I. A. Richards's comment on dramatic technique: 'Even a good dramatist's work will tend to be coarser than that of a novelist of equal ability. He has to make his effects more quickly and in a more obvious way.'[1] Hofmannsthal evidently realized this and completely separated the two major impacts in order to ensure his effect. In a novel, no doubt, the conflicting elements would have been subtly intertwined.

The action, then, is straightforward, uncomplicated by sub-plot and subsidiary interest. All character-drawing—the broad comedy of the two cousins, the bitter-sweet visionary poetry of Jedermann's mother, the remote grandeur of Faith—are of no interest in themselves but solely in so far as they relate to Jedermann and his destiny.

The secular prologue, spoken formally by a herald, is important in two ways. First, he tells in outline the purpose and action of the play:

> Wie unsre Tag und Werk auf Erden
> Vergänglich sind und hinfällig gar...

This is quite in tradition and in itself merits no special comment. The lines which follow, however, establish the essential mood of the play and point to the final universal moral: the audience is drawn into the action, cautioned against taking lightly the simple action of the play, summoned to brood well upon it and profit accordingly:

> Der Hergang ist recht schön und klar,
> Der Stoff ist kostbar von dem Spiel,
> Dahinter aber liegt noch viel,
> Das müßt ihr zu Gemüt führen
> Und aus dem Inhalt die Lehr ausspüren.

The participation of the audience in and its self-identification with the developing progress of the play are fundamental to Hofmannsthal's aim.[1]

The figure of God is not usually seen in productions of *Jedermann* despite Hofmannsthal's stage direction ('God the Father becomes visible on his throne and speaks'). Max Reinhardt's solution, which has become established tradition, is the most satisfactory way of dealing with a difficult problem. The voice of God is *heard*, coming from no definable direction. This move, which appears to have had Hofmannsthal's approval,[2] means that to the onlooker the divine voice of authority comes from nowhere and everywhere, from the air around and above, from within the conscience itself.

God's words are direct and stark in effect. The cross is the 'wood' on which he gave his blood. The crown of thorns becomes a symbol for the ills, cares and sins of mankind. These 'thorns of life' he has drawn from man's feet (the picture of life as a pilgrim's way is thus introduced), and in taking the woes of man upon himself and atoning for them he has set the crown of thorns on his own head. Thus at the outset we have the mental image of God as King of Sorrows, angry and sad at once: the vigour of

> In Sünd ersoffen, das ist was sie sind,

is balanced by the mournful tone of

> Soviel ich vermocht habe ich vollbracht,
> Und nun wird meiner schlecht geacht.

With the appearance of Death in response to the divine summons the drama moves forward. Jedermann must undertake a pilgrimage and the pilgrimage is to lead from his earthly life to God's throne. In this way the essential unity of life (earthly and eternal) and, moreover, the dramatic unity of the play are established by the use of one of the oldest of archetypal symbols: the journey, quest, or pilgrimage. This symbol and variants of it have been used to portray the career of *Bildungshelden* and picaresque heroes from Parzival to Felix Krull.

A realistic touch is given by God's insistence: 'Und heiß ihn mitbringen sein Rechenbuch'—Jedermann's book of accounts with the credit and debit of his life totalled and the accounts drawn up. This variation on the symbol of the recording angel is bold and strangely moving in its earthy directness.

Death's reply is coldly grim and contemptuous. There are biblical overtones in his reply[1] which extends his vision of man and the world to almost apocalyptic proportions:

> Herr, ich will die ganze Welt abrennen
> Und sie heimsuchen, Groß und Klein,
> Die Gotts Gesetze nit erkennen
> Und unter das Vieh gefallen sein.

In this way the universal quality of the allegory is established. Death's icy rage hovers over all, and the thrust of his threat gives an almost physical shock:

> Den will ich mit einem Streich treffen,
> Daß seine Augen brechen
> Und er nit findt die Himmelspforten.

This is a cunning extension of the idea introduced in God's words:

> Des geistlichen Auges sind sie erblindt,
> In Sünd ersoffen, das ist was sie sind.

Spiritually blinded by his own evil, man shall now suffer the final eternal blindness, that of death and deprivation of the sight of God, for in his double blindness (that is, sin and death) he will not find the gates of heaven, originally destined to be the goal of his pilgrimage.

Hofmannsthal, however, tempers the stern aspect of Death as he concedes that although man, left to himself, is irredeemable, the crowning grace of divine mercy can befriend and aid him. This, it should be emphasized, is the ethical core of the play:

> Es sei denn, daß Almosen und Mildtätigkeit
> Befreundt ihm wären und hilfsbereit.

With the knowledge of divine anger and sorrow in the audience's mind, with the dark sense of Death in the air winging his way earthward, the play begins. It is important to realize that all which follows is, as it were, framed within this mood of gathering doom. Hence the crassly domineering cavortings of Jedermann and the sensuous exuberance of the banquet gain by contrast, unconscious for the players but very real for the audience. The resulting tension is considerable and a high degree of dramatic irony is sustained. This latter is analysed in some detail later in this chapter.

Jedermann enters, obviously at the height of his powers and authority. His creed is material, luxurious, living for the day with no heed for the future:

> Einen schönen Schatz von gutem Geld
> Und vor den Toren manch Stück Feld, . . .
> Daß ich mir wahrlich machen mag
> So heut wie morgen fröhliche Tag.

Immediately two aspects of Jedermann's power and its influence are introduced. Power and property corrupt and harden the personality of their master, as is seen in Jedermann's carelessly brutal treatment of his servants, but this characteristic is fairly obvious and too well known to need further discussion. The second and more subtle aspect is the corruption which great wealth and power bring about in others. The obsequiously flattering *Guter Gesell* (Good Companion) is the expression of this. Fawning, pliable, apparently without a will of his own, the Good Companion is in a little, mean way as bad as Jedermann himself. He is the classic example of the petty power-worshipper. Without talent or originality himself, he is the amoral cheer-leader for these qualities in others—with the sole object of drawing in return as much profit from his idol as possible.

Throughout the two succeeding episodes the comments of the Good Companion, oily and ingratiating, are in complementary accord with those of his master-friend. His treatment of the Poor Neighbour who begs alms from Jedermann, his erstwhile equal, is more brutal than that of Jedermann himself:

> Selbig ist besessen alls!
> Hättst tausend Bettler auf dem Hals,
> Was tausend, hunderttausend gleich!

This is mild compared with his scandalously cynical comment on the Debtor who is led past on the way to the debtors' prison:

> Mich dünkt, das geht an ein Schuldturmwerfen,
> Hätt sich auch mehr in acht nehmen derfen,
> Jetzt muß ers bei Wasser und Brot bedenken
> Oder sich an einen Nagel henken.
> Ja, Mann, du hast halt ein Reimspiel trieben
> Und Schulden auf Gulden, die reimen gar gut.

The coarseness and sarcasm of his language—*Schuldturmwerfen*, *an einen Nagel henken*—together with the superior *besser wissen wollen* of *Schulden auf Gulden* make a sickeningly realistic impression. The emphasis given to the Good Companion in these two episodes is important for it demonstrates that Jedermann's sin is not confined to himself. Nothing less than the corruption and consequent decadence of his society is involved.

The two scenes, however, are equally notable for Jedermann's shameless statement of his creed. His distorted apologia for power and wealth abounds in false premises:

> Mein Geld muß für mich werken und laufen,
> Mit Tod und Teufel hart sich raufen,
> Weit reisen und auf Zins ausliegen,
> Damit ich soll, was mir zusteht, kriegen,
> Auch kosten mich meine Häuser gar viel,...

The picture of the rich man with his manifold responsibilities and cares is tellingly drawn: Jedermann even feels justified in self-pity.

His apologia is a good instance of the magnate blinding his victims with financial science. He reaches the incontrovertible conclusion that if all his money were divided amongst those who needed help, the Poor Neighbour would certainly get no more than the shilling which Jedermann carelessly tosses to him.[1] But of course Jedermann does not divide even a part of his wealth, and so his perfect argument falls to the ground.

In the *rencontre* with the Debtor, Hofmannsthal demonstrates the debasing effect of material values on all concerned. Jedermann is right, although he is the last person who should claim to be, when he reproaches the Debtor:

> Gibst vor, du achtest das Geld gering
> Und war dir schier ein göttlich Ding!
> Nun möchtest ihm sein Ansehn rauben,
> Bist wie der Fuchs mit sauern Trauben.

It is notably at this point in these early sequences of the drama that Hofmannsthal's essentially modern interpretation of the medieval allegory-drama is seen. Although in the English play— and in Hans Sachs's *Comedi* to which Hofmannsthal also acknowledged a debt[1]—due emphasis is laid on Everyman's materialism and worldliness, there is neither the vehement detail nor the bitter urgency which one senses in Hofmannsthal's version. Jedermann responds to the Debtor's reproaches with a cynically realistic defence of money which he sets up as a god. Although in these lines there is no anachronism in idea and theme, it is fairly clear that Jedermann's words may be applied to the times in which Hofmannsthal was living:

> Dadurch ist unser ganze Welt
> In ein höher Ansehn gestellt
> Und jeder Mensch in seinem Bereich
> Schier einer kleinen Gottheit gleich,...

It would be inaccurate to represent Hofmannsthal as being a polemical anti-capitalist in any rigid or doctrinaire sense. This speech is nonetheless a commentary on the degradation brought about by nineteenth-century economic liberalism of the unrestricted *laissez-faire* type, which under the guise of protecting the sacred rights of every individual conceded a power into the hands of small groups of men.[2] This power, although neither so obvious nor so spectacular as that of absolutist monarchs in less 'enlightened' times, was total in that it enslaved body and spirit.

Hofmannsthal expresses the insidiously indirect nature of the system in stark terms:

> Und ohn viel Aufsehn und Geschrei
> Beherrscht er abertausend Händ.[1]

The very fact that Jedermann does not know the Debtor personally is doubly significant in this context. For Hofmannsthal it is not so much a matter of ideologies as of individual human decency between men on the one hand, and on the other the personal, individually responsible relationship between man and God which should inspire and sustain the moral conscience. Hofmannsthal allows Jedermann to reach blasphemous heights:

> Du kaufst das Land mitsamt dem Knecht,
> Ja, von des Kaisers verbrieftem Recht,
> Das alle Zeit unschätzbar ist
> Und eingesetzt von Jesu Christ,
> Davon ist ein gerechtsam Teil
> Für Geld halt allerwegen feil, . . .

At this point Hofmannsthal's dramatic instinct impels him to a little masterpiece of character-drawing. Thus far Jedermann has been revealed as arrogant, self-sufficient and heartless. The author realizes, however, that a wholly one-sided character cannot attain the universal validity and human reality which are vital if his significance is to be appreciated fully by the audience. He must be depicted so that onlookers may perceive in him qualities of the average human being, even facets of character which are reflected in their own souls. Thus at a moment when Jedermann is about to assume the moral proportions of an inhuman and untypical monster another side of his character is revealed. This aspect of Jedermann was tersely summed up by the programme note on the Salzburg production which described him as 'a rich man who is not exactly bad'.[2] Not exactly bad in the conventional sense—this phrase certainly describes Jedermann, whose outlook is a curious mixture of cynicism, thoughtlessness, grossness, naïveté and sentiment. The plight of the Debtor's wife stirs his conscience: not deeply, but what today is called the 'human interest' of the situation calls forth his sympathy without impelling him to probe the deeper causes of such a situation:

> Tu mir's zulieb, geh da hint nach
> Und sieh im stillen zu der Sach.
> Der Mann kommt in Turm, da mag nichts frommen,
> Dem Weib gewähr ich ein Unterkommen
> Und was sie nötig hat zum Leben
> Zusamt den Kindern, das will ich ihr geben.

It follows from this that for Jedermann money, impersonal material help, can achieve all and also salve the hardest conscience. The moral problem is not really involved:

> Doch will ich Plärrens ledig gehn,
> Ihre Not nicht wissen, noch Gejammer.

The remainder of this speech is in the form of a rather obvious apologia. This is psychologically accurate: Jedermann's wordiness and aggrieved tone show him to be at least dimly conscious of his own shortcomings. *Qui s'excuse, s'accuse*—especially when it is done at this length. Towards the end of his diatribe, however, there comes one of those apparently innocuous lines, quite logical and factual in their context, but laden with association and dramatic irony, in this instance of an ominous kind:

> Jetzt aber, daß ich es ehrlich sag,
> Steht mir der Sinn nit mehr darnach,
> Daß ich einen Lustgarten anschau,
> Auch wird es duster schon und grau.

This is the first indication as to the time of day and it is dramatically and imaginatively appropriate that Jedermann's last hours, which the audience knows have been determined by God, should pass in the progression from afternoon to twilight, evening and night. Thus *duster und grau* have here a second meaning: the audience knows that Death is already on his way and this line falls like a deathly shadow across the scene which is now 'dark and grey' in both natural and supernatural senses.[1]

46

The succeeding episode, which forms a bridge to the scene with Jedermann's mother, shows a familiar side of Hofmannsthal in a new function. So far the lyrical impulse has been strictly under control. The action has thus been able to move forward easily and rapidly. However, before the tense and sad scene with Jedermann's mother Hofmannsthal evidently felt that his audience needed some slackening in tension, some relief in mood. We are therefore given a colourful description of the garden of pleasure which Jedermann is about to build for his mistress. The richness of this section, after the sharp discussion and bitter mood of the preceding episode, is balm to ear and imagination alike. It should be noted, however, that the description is not a static purple passage but a rapidly ranging, impressionistic sound panorama which, because the audience knows it is destined to remain a dream, is heavy with dramatic irony:

> Und dann ich die Anlag also führ,
> Daß unter dem Morgen- und Abendwind
> Ein Ruch von Blumen mancher Art
> Daher streich allezeit gelind
> Von Lilien, Rosen und Nelken zart.

It is obvious, from this alone, that the magic of Hofmannsthal's early lyric poetry has been toned down and is now subordinate to the dramatic exigencies of the whole piece.

The introduction of Jedermann's mother and the importance given to her are significant. That she embodies the voice of morality, of conscience and also of experience is clear. That she represents authority to some extent is likewise obvious. Hitherto Jedermann has been seen only with inferiors or dependants. Now he is seen in relation to a higher law and timeless principle:

> Und wird die Frag dich recht beschweren,
> Wenn ich dich mahn, ob deine Seel
> Zu Gott gekehrt ist, ihrem Herrn?

Jedermann's responses show the fundamental weakness of his kind. Shifty, prevaricating, begging the question, he demonstrates that his life and conduct are based on no firm principle whatever. Cliché succeeds cliché as he avoids discussing what he knows to be the only point at issue:

> Doch weiß ich, die Pfaffen drohen halt gern.
> Das ist nun einmal ihr Sach in der Welt,
> Ist abgesehen auf unser Geld, . . .

He then works himself into a quite irrelevant rage and tries to sidestep the problem:

> Doch kränkts mich, wie sie Alten und Kranken
> In Kopf nichts bringen als finstre Gedanken.

Throughout the scene the replies of Jedermann's mother are marked by their directness and sense of Christian reality:

> Wer recht in seinem Leben tut,
> Den überkommt ein starker Mut
> Und ihn erfreut des Todes Stund,
> Darin ihm Seligkeit wird kund.

Jedermann almost caricatures himself with his feeble, verbose excuses:

> Wir sind gute Christen und hören Predig,
> Geben Almosen und sind ledig.

Here Hofmannsthal is pillorying what he evidently regarded as a characteristic Christian phenomenon of the twentieth century: the man who has not the faith nor the courage to live his Christianity, and has neither the nerve nor the moral strength to deny it publicly.

The vagueness of Jedermann's comments is emphasized by the aphoristic phrasing of his mother's statements. These, couched in a homely idiom, have the ring and strength of well-tried proverbs:

> Mein Sohn, es ist ein arg Ding zu sterben,
> Doch ärger noch auf ewig verderben.

Her words, moreover, have the effect of heightening the dramatic tension and atmosphere of expectancy which have hovered over the play from the outset. Her warnings are a compound of urgency, rising from her love for her son, and of clairvoyant sense of prophecy, which under the circumstances can only be divinely inspired:

> Willst du den Kopf in den Sand stecken
> Und siehst den Tod nit, Jedermann,
> Der mag allstund dich treten an?

This is followed by another 'sand simile':

> Das Leben flieht wie Sand dahin,
> Doch schwer umkehret sich der Sinn.

These repeated allusions to sand recall the hour-glass and the traditional figure of Death bearing it, with the sands of time (life) forever running through. Thus without direct reference or blood-curdling symbol Hofmannsthal indicates the inexorable approach of Death, so that from this point onward, throughout the tumult of the banquet, Jedermann's actions and speech take on a feverish and hectic quality as Death is sensed circling above. This rising urgency is conveyed by the brusque dialogue towards the end of this scene in which, sharply and abruptly with thrust and parry, tempers rise and Jedermann is forced to placate his mother with vague promises:

> *Jedermann.* Ist halt noch allweil die Zeit nit da.
> *Mother.* Und doch der Tod schon gar so nah.
> *Jedermann.* Ich sag nit ja, sag auch nit nein.
> *Mother.* So muß ich allweg in Ängsten sein.
> *Jedermann.* Auch morgen ist halt noch ein Tag.
> *Mother.* Wer weiß, wer den noch sehen mag.

Jedermann's mother, characteristically, clutches at the merest straw of hope which her son holds out to her and blesses him for his promise to marry, settle down and lead a Christian life. It is with warm-heartedly human touches such as this that Hofmannsthal is able to use her as the mouthpiece of morality and order, and yet at the same time to present her to the audience as a sympathetic and living figure.

The scene closes with Jedermann wishing his mother a peaceful night's slumber and with her foreboding of imminent death. Ironically she sees it as destined for her. With this in mind Jedermann's last words to his mother are noteworthy and, in a quiet way, moving:

Viel gute Nacht, Frau Mutter nun,
Ich wünsch, du mögest sänftlich ruhn.

These are his last words to her on earth. The idea of *sanfte Ruhe* is of course associated in the mind of a German-speaking audience with death, particularly with the gravestone inscriptions—*Ruhe sanft in dem Herrn*, *Er ruht sanft*, etc. Hence one realizes the implication of these words here and recalls them with added poignancy later in the drama. Both he and she will *sänftlich ruhn*: he will have peace of soul on his pilgrimage through the valley of shadows to the gate of heaven, she will rest in peace in the knowledge of his soul redeemed and on its way to God. At her appointed time she will die peacefully and with joy.

The banquet scene which now erupts on to the stage makes a fascinating study both in its dramatic and lyric content and in its form. The abrupt change from the elegiac tone of Jedermann's *rencontre* with his mother to the brash tumult of the banquet is a contrast of the 'façade and reality' (*Schein und Wirklichkeit*) type which was a typical feature of Hofmannsthal's baroque heritage.

But the banquet scene is actually a theatrical depiction of the medieval symbol of the Dance of Death (*Totentanz*). It might seem odd to find such a markedly medieval scene in this exuberantly baroque setting, but the Dance of Death and the idea embodied in it were in characteristically modified form also a prominent feature of the baroque interpretation of life.[1] Hofmannsthal's fusion of medieval and baroque elements was therefore quite logical.

The scene itself opens on a note of ominous merriment. Against a background of gathering gloom on the stage and of metaphysical gloom in the audience's mind, the revellers arrive, as Jedermann's mother departs, led by Jedermann's mistress *Buhlschaft*. She, like Jedermann himself, is an allegorical personification. She stands for earthly, sensual passion, its undeniable charms and its fatal stultifying of the soul. Age against youth, saintly virtue set against flamboyant and careless passion: this characteristic baroque antithesis sets the mood of the whole episode.

The mood is heightened by the sense of eternal darkness drawing ever closer as the hectically reeling banqueteers sing, drink and sport in a blaze of light while the night draws on. Death's approach is indicated in a subtle manner. Following the opening affectionate exchanges between Jedermann and Buhlschaft, Jedermann is troubled by thoughts of approaching age and loss of his powers of attraction. The flattering consolations of Buhlschaft cannot completely dispel his reverie. Suddenly the thought of death takes shape in his mind—the result, one feels, of his mother's warning, the dawning awareness in him of God's messenger on the way, and his melancholy realization that he is standing on the threshold of middle age. This sense, at times of great earthly happiness, of the approach of age and physical dissolution is yet another (although not exclusively) baroque theme.

Jedermann's words are interesting, however, in an additional respect:

> Wenn eins gemahnt wär an den Tod
> Und hätt Melancholie und Not
> Und säh auf deine Lieblichkeit,
> Dem tät sein trübes Denken leid.

It is characteristic of Hofmannsthal that the dawning of an idea as yet unclear—a dim presentiment in the mind of the speaker— is introduced in a series of conditionals and subjunctives: *gemahnt wär, hätt Melancholie, säh auf, dem tät*. To these sentiments Buhlschaft makes the unconsciously prophetic reply:

> Das Wort allein macht mir schon bang,
> Der Tod ist wie die böse Schlang,
> Die unter Blumen liegt verdeckt,
> Darf niemals werden aufgeweckt.

This reply is notable for two reasons. In the first place it demonstrates that craven attitude towards death which tries to ignore it and conceal its existence under a welter of diversions. In ignoring the simple morality of life this attitude blinds itself to reality and to consequences. In the second place Buhlschaft, with the same premonition apparent in Jedermann, unwittingly sums up the actual situation where Death is in effect the unseen guest at the banquet; and the banquet itself is the feast of life. It is interesting to note, moreover, that for Buhlschaft the symbol of death is the snake. This is of course an archetypal symbol of Satanic evil, an evil for which Jedermann must shortly account.

With this episode and the frivolous distortion of the snake symbol into an elaborate conceit, in which cares are buried under forgetfulness and lovers' snake-like arms entwine and hold each other fast, the banquet scene moves to its next phase with the arrival of the guests and the emergence of the festive table from the ground. Hofmannsthal's stage direction has a marked pictorial-formal quality which demands comment:

Some of the boys run up and strew flowers and fragrant herbs. A table, bearing candles and richly laden, rises up out of the ground. Jedermann and Buhlschaft step one to each side of a stairway which leads to the upper stage.[1] The guests, ten young men and ten maidens, enter from both sides singing and dancing.

The formal musical-balletic quality together with the quite unrealistic and unexplained appearance of the table are features derived from the tradition of the baroque spectacle play, which was a marked feature of courtly entertainment in the seventeenth century and whose tradition still survives.[2]

The song *Ein Freund hat uns beschieden* bursts in with its superficial sentiment and cheerfulness. It contrasts with Jedermann's thoughts of death and it heightens the festive mood with song and dance. A singular feature of the banquet scene is the way in which the abandoned mood is built up to its climax in a series of definite stages until the sudden appearance of Death at the height of the tumult, after a series of increasingly ominous forebodings on the part of Jedermann. These forebodings seem at first to be entirely personal, a dark stirring in his mind, but in marked dramatic contrast to the careless mirth around him:

> Seid allesamt willkommen sehr,
> Erweist mir heut die letzte Ehr.

Each time, however, Jedermann recovers control of himself and after a moment of puzzled silence the festivity begins again. However, the dual nature of mood is established and hence the scene moves onwards with the constant awareness in the audience of a dark deposit of menace and gloom. This duality is underlined when to Jedermann, gazing at the banquet table, the guests seem to be sitting in their shrouds. Thus the *Totentanz* idea and the contrast of *Schein und Wirklichkeit* are introduced again.

Psychologically the development is convincingly contrived as Jedermann, with the prophetic insight of one near to death ('Methinks I am a prophet new inspired...'), castigates his guests and at the same time gives them an opportunity to reveal themselves in their true light with their true opinions of him:

> Ist recht eines reichen Mannes Red,
> Gar überfrech und aufgebläht.

The climax of this section of the scene is reached with Jedermann's plea to Buhlschaft. In attempting to wring from her a pledge of eternal loyalty—into death and beyond—Jedermann falls into the image and metaphor not only of death but also of pilgrimage and even of crucifixion. Thus his words link with those of God in the prologue:

> Tät dir das Blut in Adern stocken,
> Wär mir gedoppelt Marterqual
> Und Gall und Essig allzumal,...

God's words in the prologue were:

> Auf daß sie sollten das Leben erlangen,
> Bin ich am Marterholz gehangen.

Jedermann, moreover, speaks of *Gall und Essig*, a reminiscence of the vinegar mingled with gall which was poured on to a sponge and thrust to Jesus' lips when he cried out in thirst.

In the ensuing section the guests, led by Buhlschaft, try to console Jedermann. With mingled solicitude and frivolity they propose all manner of charms, remedies and popular cures in an impressive array of medieval superstition.

The levity, the *Wichtigtuerei*, the popular scientific superstitions paraded with a show of knowledge and superiority reveal Hofmannsthal in a sharply satirical mood rare enough in his work to warrant special note. The depiction of the guests is sharp to the point of caricature. It recalls certain characteristic features of the expressionist attitude to the hollowness of social life, the 'lie of society'. It is interesting to recall that *Jedermann* (1911) was almost contemporary with *Der Bettler* (R. J. Sorge; published 1912). Sorge's pungent satire on the sensation-hungry 'newspaper readers' is an obvious parallel. Hofmannsthal was certainly not an Expressionist. But there are connections. Fritz Martini summed up the situation as follows:

Hauptmann, Thomas Mann, Hofmannsthal, George,...the great names of the time, remained true to the laws of their own development and stayed outside this movement. Even though one notes various related themes they were at most only peripherally affected. It is certainly true that in those years they also were concerned with a rejuvenation of man in an age which had become extremely problematic. But they brought to their work a rich historical inheritance and—this applies above all to George, Hofmannsthal...—associated the process of renewal with a vigorous activation of this inheritance.... Here also one notes various gradations: in the lyric and in the drama paths lead from George and Hofmannsthal towards Expressionism.[1]

Hofmannsthal's satirical depiction of contemporary society as flighty and materialistic is the more striking when one recalls that there is nothing comparable in the English *Everyman*.

Jedermann, with unconscious irony, now speaks his panegyric on love and friendship, little realizing that this shallow conviviality will be dissipated the moment any strain is put upon it. His sentiment is characteristically sickly and almost maudlin:

> Nun hab ich doppelt Lebenslust.
> Bin froh, daß wir beisammen sein,...
> Ja, Lieb und Freundschaft, die zwei sind viel wert,
> Wer die hat, des Herz nit mehr begehrt.

From this point to the entrance of Death a *coup de théâtre* is sustained in a remarkable manner. As the scene reaches its lowest point morally with the ridiculous song of the Thin Cousin and as the wine-flushed excitement mounts, Jedermann, alone amongst the banqueteers, hears the death-bell. The contrast between Jedermann, alone with his terror and foreboding, and the dull-witted, facetious guests who hear and fear nothing, is striking. So too is the contrast in terms of sheer physical sound as Jedermann peremptorily silences the raucously bawling guests and bids them listen—to nothing save a fearsome silence. The pert comments of the guests, projected into what the onlooker feels to be the vast and inscrutable silence of death, make a bitter antithesis of baroque intensity and imagination.

The riotous mirth and song begin again feverishly as Buhlschaft tries hysterically to whip a rowdy sing-song into life once more. The famous *Floret silva undique* from the *Carmina Burana* collection of vagabond songs serves Hofmannsthal's satirical purpose admirably. Its essentially frivolous tone of light-hearted disloyalty is quite apparent:

Floret silva nobilis,	Floret silva undique,
floribus et foliis.	nah mime gesellen ist mir we.
ubi est antiquus	grünet der walt allenthalben:
meus amicus?	wa ist min geselle alselange?
Hinc equitavit,	Der ist geriten hinnen,
eia, quis me amabit?	owi, wer sol mich minnen?

Equally striking, however, are the associations borne by this song of the worldly cynicism and bold profanity which are characteristic of the *Carmina Burana* as a whole.[1]

As the song dies down and as Jedermann's Good Companion takes his place at the table the penultimate climax of the scene is reached. Voices are heard calling on Jedermann. The action now reels onward again. The sense of doom is strengthened by the realization that Death is now at hand. In most productions of the play the example of Reinhardt's *coup de théâtre* at Salzburg is followed: the voices are heard from all points of the compass, from near and far, impersonal and summoning; Death is literally in the atmosphere.

At this point Hofmannsthal's language is bare and stark, devoid of simile and image. Jedermann's words as he tries to recapture the sound of the voices show how terror of soul is suggested in familiar phrases of otherwise quite pedestrian association:

> Nein, nein! in fürchterlicher Weis
> Und laut und mächtiglich, nit leis...
> Gar fremd und doch bekannt zugleich.
> Aus welchem höllischen Bereich
> Hats müssen also nach mir schreien.

Even now, however, on the brink of death, Jedermann still talks of postponement and delay, thus echoing the conversation with his mother—'there's always tomorrow':

> Ich mein, es könnt ein solches Schrein
> Kein zweites Mal sich hier anheben...
> Will morgen zu gelegner Zeit
> Mit einem Arzten Beratung pflegen,
> Daß solche Zufäll allerwegen
> Er wohlbedacht mir hält hintan.[1]

The age-old superstitions surrounding light and dark are used to presage the actual entrance of Death. Like a child whose candle scares away imagined spirits, reminiscent too of the early ecclesiastical significance of bell, book and candle, Jedermann finds solace in the lights on the banquet table: 'Tut mir recht wohl der Lichterschein'. And then, as he feels Death striding towards him, it seems to him that the lights burn low. The candle is now seen in another symbolic sense, that of time and life, the brief candle guttering and going out:[1]

> Nun aber sag um Gott, mein Lieb,
> Was brennen die Lichter also trüb?
> Und wer kommt hinter mir heran?
> Auf Erden schreitet so kein Mann.

The implacable nature of Death, his remote, aloof will and eternal majesty are conveyed in the rhythms of his speech and in his calm elemental words:

> Von deines Schöpfers Majestät
> Bin ich nach dir ausgesandt,...

The banquet scene closes summarily with this long-sensed appearance of Death, the last phase in the progressively intensified *coup de théâtre* which forces the scene to its inevitable climax.

What follows is in effect a long *entr'acte* which prepares Jedermann's repentance, amendment and final humility before God. Death himself sets the note of despair with his dark and bare phrases, stripping off the façade of illusion in which Jedermann has lived and still lingers:

> Nun ist Geselligkeit am End.
> Ring nit vergebner Weis die Händ,
> Schleun dich, jetzt gehts vor Gottes Thron.
> Dort empfängst deinen Lohn.

But Jedermann must learn the hard way what the ultimate realities are. He is granted a space of time to settle his conscience and to seek someone or something so that he need not walk alone into the presence of God.

The succeeding scenes are miserable and quietly bitter as Jedermann turns one by one to his illusions, his friends, his relatives. Their reactions to his present state vary from the smooth consolations and slippery sophistry of his good-time friend, his Good Companion, to the mean facetiousness of his cousins. Their attitude is, however, the same, summed up in Jedermann's bitter comment:

War mein Gesell, solang ich fröhlich war.
Nun trägt er wenig Leid um mich ganz unverstellt.
Hab immer und eh was reden hören,
Das ging mir aber gar nit nah
Bis heute, da mir das geschah.

These words are the heart of the matter. Comment is probably superfluous but some reflections of Albert Schweitzer may help to place Hofmannsthal's idea in a wider social context:

A certain mentality has developed in society which leads people away from the essential spirit of humanity. The politeness which rises from natural feeling is disappearing. In its place appears...behaviour of absolute indifference. This personal remoteness from and lack of sympathy towards strangers, which is emphasized in every possible way, is no longer regarded as springing from innate rudeness, but rather as being the appropriate behaviour for a 'man of the world'. Our society has ceased to acknowledge human dignity and value in all human beings. Various sections of humanity have become mere human material....If for decades we have found it possible to talk with growing insouciance of war and conquest—as if it were a matter of a move on a chess-board—this has come about because a mass attitude had been created which no longer tried to imagine the fate of individual people, but only regarded them as numbers and objects. When the war came, this inhumanity in us had a free hand.[1]

With this in mind the desertion of Jedermann—and also Jedermann's treatment of his neighbour, the debtor and his mother, together with his sudden repentance and abasement when disaster comes—can be seen as an allegory of the morality, the rise and the fall of people and systems in the modern age.

Considered retrospectively these scenes of Jedermann's disillusionment run in ironic counterpoint to those preceding the banquet, and especially the meeting with his mother where the reality of his state, now *visible* to the audience, was first *felt* in her appeals and prophecies.

The following episode with *Mammon* is in a special category. It marks the transition from the human sphere to the supernatural and fantastic. Hitherto, although Death has played a large part and Jedermann has heard supernatural voices, the stage action has been human: for most of the time it has been all too human. The characters, although types, have for the greater part been seen as having certain personal and humanly credible characteristics. Now, however, the action moves wholly into the realm of the general and allegorical.

The Mammon scene, together with the banquet, is the biggest innovation in the play as compared with the English *Everyman* and is of corresponding importance. The scene is of constant tension and is cruelly bitter in tone. Hofmannsthal clearly meant to make a striking effect and to emphasize an important point. Further evidence of this is found in the now traditional manner in which the part of Mammon is played. The sudden appearance from the chest of the bald, semi-naked figure, shining in gold and dripping with coins, gives a theatrical shock which is scarcely diminished by familiarity. This mode of production, established by Reinhardt, was approved by Hofmannsthal:

a figure which is dwarf-like and yet gigantic, half naked but with golden rings on its arms and strings of pearls around its neck. On its fingers, which drip with gold,[1] it has horrible, long claws. This creature has a fearsome voice—one moment it is falsetto like a woman or a eunuch, the next instant it roars savagely, more wildly than a man in battle who yells in order to terrify the foe.[2]

Jedermann, then, turns desperately to what seems the only tangible thing in his disillusioned life: Mammon, his money, which means power. This, his servant in all things, must go with him. But now, in a rapid exchange, cutting and sarcastic on Mammon's part, bewildered and angry and finally downcast on Jedermann's side, the truth is revealed. The technique (noted on p. 49) of rapid, short lines in moments of tension, a dialogue of assertion and counter-assertion, statement and mocking contradiction, raises the scene to an intense climax:

> *Jedermann.* Warst mein leibeigner Knecht und Sklav.
> *Mammon.* Nein, du mein Hampelmann recht brav.
> *Jedermann.* Hab dich allein gedurft anrühren.

This sequence bursts into Mammon's terrible *credo* which, as Jedermann realizes, is at once his own *credo* and his funeral dirge. The position and function of this speech are characteristic of Hofmannsthal's method. It has been seen how at turning-points in the action he brings the physical action to a standstill and allows the intellectual-spiritual action to range far and wide in a set speech, a kind of statement of policy, a summary of the forces at work. Jedermann's sophistical sermon to his poor neighbour, his panegyric on money and interest for the instruction of the debtor, the initial warning of his mother (*Um meine Gesundheit kein Sorg nit hab*), Jedermann's prophetic questioning of Buhlschaft—all are in this category. It might be called an operatic technique. Verdi's *Credo in un dio cruel* (*Otello*) and Mozart's *In diesen heiligen Hallen* (*Die Zauberflöte*) are comparable examples, in which visually static action and declamatory style contribute to make a dramatically intense effect.

In the present instance Hofmannsthal achieves a sad, grim irony as Mammon's domineering talk and humiliation of Jedermann run in a kind of retroactive counterpoint to Jedermann's speech to the Debtor:

> Da ist kein Ding zu hoch noch fest,
> Das sich um Geld nicht kaufen läßt.

Passing reference has just been made to the importance which Hofmannsthal attached to this scene. At this point it is perhaps appropriate to note how the scene figured in the development of his cultural-political ideas as found in some of the essays and speeches written during the war. Some of these are considered more fully in chapters 3 and 4. Here, however, it is worth noting that when in *Aufzeichnungen zu Reden in Skandinavien* (1916) Hofmannsthal discussed the ethical pattern of the twentieth century, he drew certain vital conclusions from the Mammon episode:

Jedermann: type—'money at his side'—Balzac: money as a driving force; all are capable of acting against their own convictions. Money as a demon. The shadowy projection of this idol;—that is the Mammon scene in *Jedermann* . . . the hypocrisy, the mockery of the rich man, . . .

the rattling of a chain on which, as he thinks, he holds the world . . .
the shareholder who sits back while the miners and glassworkers
work themselves to death: I? What is it to do with me? . . . Jedermann's
devilish answers . . . Mammon scene: what is left of you if I leave you?
I was your strength, your boast, your rank in society—I was all that.
Collapse of Jedermann. What sort of an age was it in which this
question had to be asked so anxiously:—the question about ultimate
values, . . . the moral basis of reality? . . . [1]

With this extract in mind Mammon's final castigation of Jedermann
is felt the more urgently:

> Was ich in dich hab eingelegt,
> Darnach hast du dich halt geregt . . .
> Und was ihn itzt noch aufrechthält,
> Daß er nit platt an Boden fällt . . .
> Das ist allein sein Geld und Gut.
> Dahier springt all dein Lebensmut.

The force of Mammon's lines is strengthened by the appropriateness of the language and style. Reference was made on
pp. 24–5 to Hofmannsthal's linguistic virtuosity and to the
deceptive simplicity of the idiom used in *Jedermann*. In the present
instance the unwonted coarseness of the language makes a stark
impression:

> Du Laff, du ungebrannter Narr, . . .
> Und alle Viere von sich reckt, . . .

This coarseness is used with restraint and could scarcely offend.
But the realistic atmosphere thereby created—the everyday
crudity of the personal attack—does ensure that Jedermann's
situation and the memories of his past life which have brought it
about are not obscured in a haze of sentimentality.

Mammon's last words prepare for what is in effect the last
act of the play. They also depict Jedermann's true plight:

> Geh nit, bleib hier, laß dich allein
> Ganz bloß und nackt in Not und Pein . . .
> Fährst in die Grube nackt und bloß,
> So wie du kamst aus Mutter Schoß.

This too is his spiritual state in the eyes of God: 'naked, bare' and dependent on divine mercy.

From these considerations of the Mammon episode it can be seen that expressionist overtones are again present. Fritz Martini gives an acute summary of this connection:

Lyrical elements penetrated deep into the drama. But here also, as for example in Werfel's *Die Mittagsgöttin*, a path was followed which had already been taken by Hofmannsthal, who anticipated certain essential tendencies in form and expression found in Expressionism's ecstatic soul-dramas, mystery plays, and in various operatic features of its style. . . . Expressionist drama brought about a complete change. It searched for the. . .allegorical, for the absolute in both ethical and tragic senses. It wanted to make pantomimic and choral effects; it looked for cultic-mythical and symbolic techniques. Thus it tried to win back a high style in which it could judge values. Expressionist drama also revived and renewed the old religious form of the mystery in its emphasis on such things as the marionette-like nature. . .of horror mingled with the grotesque.[1]

The relevance of this to *Jedermann* and to the Mammon scene in particular, especially 'horror mingled with the grotesque', is obvious. The relevance of Martini's summary becomes very clear as he continues:

Expressionism's advance into the sphere of the supernatural, the visionary and spook-like, goes hand in hand with the activation of the theatre in order to bring about some directly provocative, world-reforming, ethical or political effect.

With the end of the Mammon scene the 'grotesque' element goes out of the play but the 'visionary' element increases. The following scene, dramatically speaking a link between Jedermann's despair and repentance, is noteworthy from the point of view of psychological realism. It might have been expected, with the realization brought about by Mammon so fresh upon him, that Jedermann would plunge immediately into an hysterical self-condemnation and a spectacular repentance. Such short cuts, while for the moment, perhaps, theatrically satisfying, were no solution or conclusion to the situation. Otherwise Bithell's jibe about the 'comic idiocy of redemption by repentance' might have some relevance.[1]

Jedermann, however, absorbed in his own ego, is still too much his old self even to heed the approach of *Werke*, the crippled representative of his own few and feeble good works. And yet, as was seen in his treatment of the Debtor's wife, Jedermann is not all bad. His sins have often been as much of omission as of commission. Hence, though broodingly absorbed in himself, he hopes that the voice he hears is not that of his mother and he calls instinctively on God to spare her the sight of him in his present state.

In the same breath, however, his worldly ego reasserts itself as the voice calls again:

> Seis wer da will, hab itzt nit Muß
> Für irdisch Händel und Verdruß.

This mixture of kindly feeling and hostile reaction within his stricken spirit is quite true to life. The effect is enhanced when the rather portentous note of self-pity is heard:

> Brauch nit ein fremd Gebrest dahier,
> Liegt Angst und Marter gnug auf mir.

The words of Jedermann's 'Good Works' now make their initial impression as she speaks of the 'way' or 'road' which lies ahead. This has been a fatal-sounding *leitmotif* throughout the play:

> Mich brauchst, der Weg ist schreckbar weit,
> Bist annoch ohne ein Geleit.

And then his pride breaks down, his self-pity is pushed to the background and he turns to his Good Works for help and advice: 'Ist mir gar sehr um guten Rat.' This development takes place quietly but its psychological accuracy should not be overlooked, the more so as in Good Works Hofmannsthal is using a character who is entirely a type-figure, an abstract. She has, moreover, few of the dramatic possibilities of Mammon, the only other wholly abstract and non-human figure hitherto introduced into the action (excluding, of course, the sacred prologue). By establishing something of a human association between Jedermann and Good Works—human, at any rate, in tone—Hofmannsthal gives Good Works a warmth and fullness which could scarcely be achieved otherwise.

At the same time, however, he is careful not to let this character upset his general scheme, namely that the figures must speak *sub specie aeternitatis*, both to and for the generality. Hofmannsthal merely ensures that a character may arouse sufficient interest to hold the audience's attention. He does not take the device beyond this point. This formal-general type of character is of great importance in a study of Hofmannsthal's three festival dramas, the more so as it is part of a widespread tendency in modern and contemporary German literature. His development of such characters is discussed in chapters 5 and 7 while some general conclusions are drawn in chapter 9.

The dramatic effectiveness of Good Works thus assured, the action moves forward again. The next stage in Jedermann's repentance is the familiar sensation of joy and pain, the same complex emotion which can cause tears of joy:

> Mir ist, je mehr ich dich anseh,
> So mehr wird mir im Herzen weh,
> Und sänftlich auch, vermischter Weis,
> Daß ich mich nit zu nehmen weiß.

But this joy in new-found insight is still mingled with despair—springing from little faith—that it is too late for forgiveness. Good Works knows that wholesale and emotional repentance is not sufficient, that as in the sacrament of confession a firm purpose of amendment must go hand in hand with repentance for sin and the request for absolution. She senses the danger of his luxuriating in mental flagellation and tries to bring him to a clear-headed realization of his errors. She ignores the heights and depths and concentrates on the simple realities of Christian life.

This episode is particularly Catholic in spirit and it could be asserted that some direct experience of confession is necessary in order to appreciate it fully: Good Works' attitude and words are those of the priest dealing with a self-consciously spectacular sinner whose ego and sense of unusualness must be quietly but firmly humbled. In other words, the emotional experience of 'pouring it all out' with theatrical self-abasement must be replaced by rational realization of the necessity for repentance and hatred of sin.

Good Works' words are interesting from another point of view:

> Wärest bei mir verblieben viel
> Und fern der Welt und bösem Spiel!
> Komm näher, meine Stimm ist leis—:
> Bei Armen wärest eingegangen
> Recht als ihr Bruder, heiliger Weis,
> Und göttlich Leid und irdischen Schmerz,
> Die hättest zu lieben angefangen. . . .

The interpolation in the third line is not incidental. It enhances the necessary human quality already noted in Good Works; it is an indirect reference to the weakness and paucity of Jedermann's good works, and the cry 'come closer' suggests a growing warmth between Jedermann and Good Works—a *rapprochement*, as it were, with the good self which was thought to be dead.

From this point in the action the verse changes subtly in texture. In the scenes of Jedermann's disillusionment and desperation the language has a grey, direct quality: the absence of symbol and image is striking. Now Good Works depicts what might have been—and, as Jedermann will shortly see, what can still be—and the language takes on a heightened, image-charged quality. The 'chalice' image in the lines beginning 'Ich war ein Kelch' was discussed in chapter 1 as a characteristic example of Hofmannsthal's poetic technique in this play. When one considers the entire episode, however, one sees how the chalice image is extended through the dialogue which follows. This is particularly appropriate in a scene which has as its dramatic and spiritual climax the absolution of Jedermann and the administering to him of Holy Communion. Good Works says that instead of drinking from the chalice of grace Jedermann has drunk deeply of the world—a kind of distorted parody of Holy Communion. His thirst will therefore be eternal:

> O weh, nun müssen die Lippen dein
> Auf ewig ungetränket sein!
> Hast wollen dich tränken an der Welt,
> Da ward der Kelch dir weggestellt!

From this to Jedermann's admission of his thirst for divine grace is a short step:

> Des fühl ich ein wütendes Dürsten schon
> Durch alle meine Adern rinnen....

This is the first real step towards God, the burning within him of the necessary longing for repentance and awareness of the tribulation which he has avoided in life. The next step, that of amendment with the aid of faith, has still to come. Thus Jedermann despairs again—the familiar lapse of the penitent into the sin of despair—and in a violent passage portrays the state of mind of man seeing that the end is in sight, the just reward at hand, and crying 'If only I had realized...':

> Zurück! und kann nit! Noch einmal!
> Und kommt nit wieder!...
> Hie wird kein zweites Mal gelebt!

Jedermann thus appeals to Good Works to aid him in giving account for his life before God. At the word *Rechenschaft* (reckoning) the opening scene between God and Death comes to mind and Jedermann's own language takes on the lofty tone of the opening, spanning the universe and all time past and future:

> Vor dem, der ist Herr über Tod und Leben
> Und König in der Ewigkeit,
> Sonst bin ich verloren für alle Zeit!

And so the stern figure of *Glaube* (Faith) is introduced. She is the necessary complement to Good Works, austere, unsentimental, her eyes fixed on God. For her only those things which witness to faith in him are important. Her words to Jedermann are curt and to the point. They sum up what his life has been, what he has become and what, all emotion apart, he is trying to do as Death rises up before him. Throughout his life he has laughed at her and now, at the last moment, he is trying to scramble back to safety:

> Hast mich dein Leben lang verlacht
> Und Gottes Wort für nichts geacht,
> Geht nun in deiner Todesstund
> Ein ander Red aus deinem Mund?

Jedermann's insufficiency and woefully confused soul are demonstrated by his pathetic answer. He calls on his schoolboy catechism for support, thus admitting that his faith has atrophied since those days:

> Ich glaub die zwölf Artikel mit Fleiß,
> Die ich von Kindschulzeiten weiß:
> Was sie vorstellen ganz und gar,
> Nehm ich für heilig hin und wahr.

'What they represent'—Jedermann is not quite sure exactly what they do represent but thinks that all twelve articles should cover him. Faith, not surprisingly, is contemptuous of the easy way out and catechizes him further. Finally, impatient with his stumbling, fragmentary answers, and angry at his heretical despair, she forces him to the point with a clear summary of the Christian faith:

> Glaubst du an Jesu Christ
> Der von dem Vater kommen ist,
> Ein Mensch und unsersgleichen worden,
> Von einem irdischen Weibe geboren,
> Und hat in Marterqual sein Leben
> Um deinetwillen hingegeben
> Und ist erstanden von dem Tod,
> Daß du versöhnet seist mit Gott?

This is one long sentence and in its even flow, its succession of *und* and *um*, the wholeness, continuity and inevitability of Christianity are conveyed. Hofmannsthal reverts here in heightened manner to one of the most marked stylistic habits of his early years: Mary Gilbert called this the 'loose flowing "und" of which Hofmannsthal was so fond in his early poetry'.[1]

In stressing the universal aspect Faith at the same time emphasizes the personal element. Her statement, she says, applies with
equal force to every living creature: Jesus died not for mankind,
an abstract unlimited, but:

> Hat in Marterqual sein Leben
> Um *deinetwillen* hingegeben, . . . [1]

This passage emphasizes Jedermann's role as a living individual
and not merely as a type-figure. Faith, moreover, associates
herself with Jedermann as a human being: 'He became a man
and one of *us*.' But faith is of necessity a human quality and in
any case Hofmannsthal was in this scene faced with the difficulty
—already noted in the case of Good Works—of preserving a
living human quality in a scene which has primarily to do with
spiritual qualities. The pointed personification of Faith as a
human figure helps to bring this about.

The succeeding dialogue portrays two interpretations of God
and serves Hofmannsthal's dramatic-religious purpose. Jedermann sees God as the angry and even vengeful God of the Jews
who is more apparent in the Old Testament. His attitude to this
God is characteristically mercantile:

> Durch gute Werk und Frommheit eben
> Erkauft er sich ein ewig Leben.

But, he thinks, because of the mountain of sin on his shoulders
there can be no forgiving grace for him. Thus he sees God as the
terrible bringer of retribution. Here Hofmannsthal forces to one
point the two vitally differing interpretations of the deity:

> *Jedermann.* Gott straft erschrecklich!
> *Faith.*   Gott verzeiht!
> Ohn Maßen!

Faith's view—Hofmannsthal's own Catholic view—is set up
against that of quasi-Christian fear of God as a kind of puritanical
overseer:

> *Jedermann.* Schlug den Pharao,
> Schlug Sodom und Gomora, schlug,
> Schlug!
> *Faith.* Nein, gab hin den eignen Sohn
> In Erdenqual vom Strahlenthron.

From this Faith progresses to a most moving sequence as she speaks of the mystery of faith, of the ever and all comprehending mercy of God, of his special love and care for sinners. The simple peasant-like idiom, with its overtones of the New Testament, the words charged with centuries of association, can make a decisive impression on the hearer:

> Und keiner ginge mehr verloren,
> Nit einer, nit der letzte, nein,
> Er finde denn das ewige Leben.
> 'Um der Sünder willen bin ich kommen,
> Der Gsund bedarf keines Arztes dann',
> Die Red ist aus dem Munde kommen,
> Der keine Lügen reden kann.
> Glaubst du daran in diesem Leben,
> So ist dir deine Sünd vergeben
> Und ist gestillet Gottes Zorn.

This speech constitutes one of the major moments in the play and merits especially close attention from the stylistic point of view. The simple idiom conceals a subtle use of rhythm and accentuation. The *Knittelvers* metre carries with it the automatic association of simplicity and Hofmannsthal retains this advantage —which gives the words of Faith the sense of long-proven validity already noted. Within this framework he enhances the effect by changes of pace, breaks in the line, the highlighting of one important word by rhythmical device. The first line, for instance, flows calmly in the assurance of its eternal message. The second line, however, is twice broken and this, together with the repetition of *nit* and the *einer-nein* sound, adds a sharp tone of emphasis to the message of the first line. This device eliminates the danger present in the use of *Knittelvers*, namely that the jogging rhythm can so easily run on effortlessly and that the content can get lost in the process. It will be noticed how the natural stresses fall: in the fourth line on the key-word *Sünder*; in the following line on *Gsund*—strikingly similar in sound and its complete antithesis in meaning—and, because of the placing of the extra syllable, on *keines*. In the closing two lines an authoritative *ex cathedra* effect is produced by the repetition of *ist* at the same point in each line. The natural stress falls on the four key-words, *Sünd*, ver*geben*, ge*stillet*, *Zorn*.

From these instances it can be seen how Hofmannsthal, while maintaining the advantages of the naïve folk-verse, is also able to emphasize his message in a sophisticated manner without obtruding his method.

Brought thus to insight and faith, and firm in his purpose of amendment, Jedermann is now ready for confession and absolution. He asks for

> solcher heiliger Quell,
> Daß ich zu ihm mich hintrüg schnell?

Quell as a symbol of purity and of purification is age-old. In the present instance the baptism of Jesus in the Jordan comes to mind as Jedermann attempts at this late hour to restore himself to the image and likeness of God. The word *Quell* has the dual meaning of *spring* and *source*. The Church is here the source of eternal life and the spring which keeps it pure. The monk who now appears to hear Jedermann's confession, to absolve him and give him Holy Communion, is the visible symbol of this Church and its power.

To close the scene of Jedermann's repentance Hofmannsthal again draws the physical action to a standstill and, as it were, sums up the situation. Jedermann, in an appeal to the Saviour, calls with a wealth of image on God; he begs Jesus the Redeemer to intercede for him with God the Father and Creator when Death has him in stranglehold and Satan presses in upon him. Thus in a few lines the realms of heaven, earth and hell are traversed and the speech closes with the vision of God in his glory and of the crucified Christ who has redeemed man.

To achieve the necessary intensity for this vision of eternity Hofmannsthal alters his style abruptly. The rhyming couplet is abandoned and Jedermann speaks a rhythm which is reminiscent of the opening lines of the *Te Deum*, the lines being broken in the middle. A comparison of the respective verses demonstrates this:

O ewiger Gott! O göttliches Gesicht! / Te deum laudamus: te Dominum confitemur.

O rechter Weg! O himmlisches Licht! / Te æternum Patrem: omnis terra veneratur.

The rhythm is that of the Church's greatest song of praise and triumph. The imagery recalls that of the litanies. The *Litany of the Blessed Virgin Mary* provides a characteristic example:

Virgo clemens,	Virgin most merciful,
Virgo fidelis,	Virgin most faithful,
Speculum justitiae,	Mirror of Justice,
Sedes sapientiae,...	Seat of Wisdom,...[1]

Laden with the solemnity with which these reminiscences of the liturgical prayers endue his words, Jedermann's supplication can pierce an audience to its soul;[2] and especially an audience for which these prayers themselves have, consciously or unconsciously, manifold associations.

As Jedermann lies prostrate praying and as the gathering darkness deepens, the scene remains unchanged but the attention of the audience is abruptly distracted. It was a bold and even risky move to bring Jedermann's mother back to the stage at this point. The risk was twofold. In the first place she could tend to recall the mood of the earlier part of the play without notably helping the action along.[3] Secondly, and this is a more delicate point, the action has been moving into ever more spiritual regions. The abrupt reintroduction of the earthly element could have meant bathos—the more so as the lachrymose sentimental possibilities in the reappearance of Jedermann's mother at this juncture are truly alarming. Hofmannsthal, however, attempted a union in the minds of his audience of spiritual things and of earthly goodness as their tangible expression. He was trying to bring before the inward eye a vision of earthly striving, spiritual torment and heavenly peace—all as part of one progress.

Thus Jedermann's mother comes across the stage on a lower level in the gloom, while above and beyond her the praying figure of Jedermann is seen the more clearly. Above him in turn, towering over him, is the majestic entrance to the church, the way to the altar, to God in heaven.[1] The mother feels instinctively that something decisive is happening. Intuitively she feels for it:

> Sind wir denn so verspät't alsdann
> Und hebt sich schon die Frühmett an?
> Ich hör ein also herrlich Klingen,
> Als täten alle Engel singen!

The rough kindness of her servant makes in contrast a strangely moving effect. Puzzled, impatient and at once solicitous, he stands by waiting:

> Wollt Ihr leicht heim in Euer Bett
> Statt nächtlings zu der Morgenmett?

> Verspätet sind wir keinerweis,
> Auch hör ich nichts, nit laut noch leis.

The mother scarcely knows whether it is late at night or very early in the morning, whether the 'grey' of which her attendant later speaks is an allusion to the oncoming night or the grey twilight of dawn. The situation is perhaps best explained by the following words of Hofmannsthal to Carl Burckhardt:

It is important in this play that one should always have something tangible, something in the visible foreground, as it were—an action... of quite concrete nature. Simultaneously and behind this action something more exalted, something of the mind and spirit, something *generally* valid, difficult to put into words, must likewise reveal itself, step by step and keeping pace with the action....[2]

Here the 'more exalted' element, the 'something of the mind and spirit', lie in the fact, sensed by the mother and the audience, that Jedermann is going into the night of death, the Church's 'valley of shadows'—and at the same time towards the dawn of a new day, his new life in the eternal light of God. Hence the *Morgenmett*, the *Frühmett*, is the early morning Mass at which his mother prays for his soul, but it is also an act of thanksgiving for his redemption.

There follows a reminiscence of her previous appearance when, solaced by Jedermann's words, she seemed to hear heavenly sounds:

> als ob ein Ton
> Gar schön wie Flöten und Schalmein
> In deine Worte tön herein.

At that earlier moment she took these sounds as a sign of her approaching death. Now she hears the 'heavenly shawms' and knows that this 'wonderful sound' tells of her son. In the prayer which follows Hofmannsthal achieves a simple intensity. There is no word which could not be in the everyday speech of a mountain-valley peasant, yet in the smooth-flowing, seemingly naïve couplets is expressed the omnipotence of divine love, and all-sacrificing motherly love as an earthly reflection of it:

> Ich spür, zu dieser nächtigen Stund
> Ist seine Seele worden gesund.
> Er ist versöhnet Gott dem Herrn,
> Des sterb ich freudiglich und gern.
> Erhört ist meine große Bitt,
> Und weiß, daß ich einmal hintritt
> Vor Gottes meines Schöpfers Thron
> Und find dort meinen lieben Sohn.

To Jedermann's mother it is obvious and natural that she should appear before God's throne—as natural as her regular walk to early Mass. Her prayer ends appropriately; with an unconscious echo of the final sequence of the *Dies Irae*:

> *Jedermann's mother.* Bald lässest deine Dienerin
> In deinen Frieden fahren hin.
> Amen.

Dies Irae. Pie Jesu, Domine,	In thy mercy, Jesu blest,
Dona eis requiem.	Grant thy servants endless rest.
Amen.	Amen.[1]

Jedermann is now ready to receive absolution to strengthen him on his pilgrim's way. He has striven towards and gained repentance, his Good Works are thus 'freed of their burden'. His faith sustains him, his mother's prayers have interceded for him—a further markedly Catholic touch. Thus he will be able to set out calmly and can say at last:

> Dann ich nit Zögerung noch Aufschub such.

As he thus joyfully takes back his plea for delay he recalls the actual words of God at the outset:

> Und heiß ihn mitbringen sein Rechenbuch
> Und daß er nicht Aufschub noch Zögerung such.

The scene with the Devil now literally breaks loose. It is long. It is overlong when the overall length of the drama is considered and, more particularly, the point which the action has reached. From the dramatic point of view the scene has the effect of holding up the climax and spinning out the duration in a way reminiscent of the tedious Mephistopheles sequences after the death of Faust (*Faust* II). Hofmannsthal's dramatic instinct and sense of tact seem to have deserted him for a space. In his wish to have his drama grow out of the native peasant drama tradition of the southern German lands Hofmannsthal has created a figure who has all the trappings of the medieval devil. He is, true to tradition, a folk character, part serious, mostly comic, who must be defeated ignominiously and swept from the stage to the huge delight of the audience.

But this devil does not ring true. He is so intent on providing rather slapstick light relief that it is impossible to take him at all seriously as a claimant to Jedermann's soul. Like the great *Beckmesser* joke in *Die Meistersinger von Nürnberg* he goes on for rather too long.

It is odd that Hofmannsthal, having recreated *Everyman* for a twentieth-century audience and its spiritual-ethical situation, did not take a leaf from Goethe's book and create a devil to match.[1] Elsewhere in the drama he succeeded in combining medieval form and appearance with essentially modern content and dialectic. As it is, the answers and comments of Faith are simple but crushing:

Vor dem Gericht, vor das er tritt,
Bestehen deine Rechte nit,
Die sind auf Schein und Trug gestellt,
Auf Hie und Nun und diese Welt,
Die ist gefangen in der Zeit
Und bleibt in solchen Schranken stocken,
Wo aber tönet diese Glocken...
Hat angehoben Ewigkeit.

Hofmannsthal expresses the baroque idea of 'façade and reality' quite explicitly here. 'Appearance and deception' are equated with the 'here and now' of the world. These in turn are opposed to the eternal 'reality' symbolized in the death knell. One feels that the remote dignity of Faith—exemplified in her phrase *gefangen in der Zeit*, the elliptical brevity of which is so eloquent[1]—is worth a more dangerous foe than this tail-lashing devil. In any case the power of Satan in Jedermann has been felt strongly throughout, and the audience has had opportunity to suffer Jedermann's visible conquest of the devil with him. Thus save for serving to motivate these remarks by Faith the introduction of this figure is superfluous.

At the same time, however, it may be worth noting that this is probably a specifically Anglo-Saxon view. As far as the present writer is aware this attitude is not shared by German and Austrian audiences and critics. No doubt the stage devil is rooted so securely in tradition that he is taken for granted and does not disturb. Hofmannsthal himself evidently had no doubts and even compared his Devil's cunning with that of Jedermann himself: 'The diabolically clever answers of Jedermann (as cunning as the Devil himself later on [in the play]).'[2]

The disturbing atmosphere of this verbose interlude is, however, quickly dissipated as in a silent scene of great solemnity Jedermann reappears. The stage direction, with its association of the pallor of death and the white light of heavenly transfiguration, re-establishes the essential mood:

Jedermann enters on the upper level. He is dressed in a long white gown and has a pilgrim's staff in his hand. His face is deathly pale but is transfigured.

Good Works now feels at last the strength for the last journey and Jedermann is ready. The ancient ceremony of laying the hand on sword or spear and swearing honour and loyalty is recalled in his words and in the brief but eloquent reply of Good Works:

> *Jedermann.* Leg jeder die Hand an diesen Stab
> Und folge mir zu meinem Grab.
> *Good Works.* Ich heb vom Stab nit meine Händ,
> Zuvor die Reis kam an ihr End.

Now, with Death moving in behind them, what was foreseen in the divine prologue has come to pass. The Dance of Death is over, the sands have run out and the pilgrim's way is about to begin: the way which leads through the dark night of the grave to the light of God. Hofmannsthal created few lines which are simultaneously so unadorned and yet so telling:

> *Faith.* Ich steh dir nah und seh dich an.
> *Good Works.* Und ich geh mit, mein Jedermann.

One notes the immovable, timeless quality obtained by the long vowels on which the natural rhythmic stress falls: *steh, nah, seh* (the repetition of the long *eh* sound enhances this). This contrasts with the almost brisk consonantal movement of *ich/geh/mit* which invites equal stress for each word.

The sturdily possessive tone of Good Works is the last solace. As Jedermann descends with her, Faith, the austere figure of everlasting belief in God, moves down towards the audience, to the world assembled in symbol. She draws each soul into this climax and resolution of the drama. For this, she says, is the lot of man who must appear one day, bereft of all worldly things, before his judge.

As she speaks, warning and comforting at once, she hears the angels sing as Jedermann enters heaven. The steady tread of the verse conveys the inevitability and finality of the human cycle:

Nun hat er vollendet das Menschenlos,
Tritt vor den Richter nackt und bloß, . . .

The death bells ring out; the attendant angels sing as they withdraw from the stage and enter the church. At Salzburg the dying
sun gleams on the crosses at the pinnacles of the twin towers and this
latter-day baroque drama of 'appearance and reality' is at an end.

At the beginning of this chapter reasons were given for the
length and detail of the analysis which has just been concluded.
It is to be hoped that this fairly close analysis has also shown how
in *Jedermann* Hofmannsthal is preoccupied with personal human
destiny and salvation. In this play's insistence on individual,
personal reform ('Das müßt ihr zu Gemüt führen / Und aus dem
Inhalt die Lehr ausspüren.') and personal responsibility there lies
the seed from which grows the cultural-political thought of
Hofmannsthal's later years. This is the principal foundation of
Das Salzburger Große Welttheater, *Der Turm*, and of the prose
essays which are considered in the following two chapters.

There will probably be little disagreement about the existence
of this connection. It is in any case one of the purposes of this
study to justify the claim. But did Hofmannsthal achieve his
object in *Jedermann* itself? Does the play convince morally?
It might well be argued that the dramatic effectiveness of the play,
its luxurious spectacle and *coups de théâtre* militate against what
should be the austerity of its uncompromising message. It may
also be argued that there is no true climax to the play, that
Jedermann does not in fact have to make any great moral decision,
that divine intervention redeems him unassisted by Jedermann
himself. It can of course be argued that Jedermann is saved 'by
faith alone' in the Lutheran sense.[1]

To the reader brought up in the Catholic tradition the dénouement of the drama is at first sight disturbing. It seems to imply
that a man may live a life of evil, ignore every commandment at
convenience, 'repent' when he is too old or ill to be wicked, use
and make a mockery of the sacraments, especially that of penance

(that is, confession, sorrow for sin, carrying out of penance laid upon one, and purpose of amendment). This last is probably the most serious charge, for the abuse of confession has caused not only one of the oldest and most persistent criticisms of the Church but is stigmatized by the Church itself as one of the gravest of sins.

How then can Jedermann's facile repentance and absolution be explained? Surely it is in the fact that Death allows him an hour in which to make his dispositions. This is a dramatic device which allows the playwright to parade before the audience in succession those forces which have brought about the downfall of the central character. Then those forces are shown which alone can save him—if obeyed in life. Any Catholic knows the folly of postponing repentance and amendment. He also knows that Death does *not* give time in which to make one's dispositions. God's mercy may be unending—as it is for Jedermann—but the sin of presumption is a mortal sin. Thus Hofmannsthal's message to his audience is that the ways of God are as mysterious as his mercy is generous. To presume or to postpone is to risk eternal perdition. Each moment must be lived as if it were one's last. A true death-bed repentance will find favour with God. To rely on it ('Ist halt noch allweil die Zeit nit da') invites damnation.

Hofmannsthal himself laid emphasis on the element of personal effort and responsibility when he wrote of *Jedermann*:

an unconditional striving for higher things—for the most high—must come to man's aid decisively when all earthly relationships—of loyalty and possession—have shown themselves to be illusory. Is there anything that could be more relevant to us?[1]

Is *Jedermann*, then, only for Catholic audiences? Hofmannsthal maintained that the message of the play was not necessarily tied to Christianity, let alone to Catholicism. Its content, if the foregoing analysis be accepted together with the theological apologia, will probably find fairly general favour on ethical-moral if not on religious grounds.

Reasons for its possible rejection are paradoxically to be sought in those characteristics which have always ensured its theatrical success, namely in the richness and pageantry of its presentation. These are not mere externals but are clearly part of Hofmannsthal's avowed intention—witnessed, for example, by his enthusiastic acceptance of Reinhardt's production with Moissi's flamboyant performance in the title-role, and by his deliberate association of *Jedermann* and the Salzburg Festival with the traditions of folk and baroque drama.

The richness and pageantry are in the nature of the play: by this is meant that the play is, as has been indicated, baroque. 'Baroque' is the key-word for anyone attempting to interpret or produce *Jedermann*. To audiences for whom the baroque tradition is a living thing, *Jedermann* will present few obstacles. Where, as in Great Britain and the United States, such traditions are limited or non-existent, *Jedermann* may appear to be a gorgeously overloaded canvas not always in the best of taste. If we remember, however, that the aim of the baroque theatre as of the baroque altar was to assail the sight and the senses and to overwhelm them by sheer impression, then *Jedermann* may become more acceptable —to the head if not to the heart. Alewyn's words on the baroque theatre itself help to explain this:

The baroque illusion is...always quite conscious and deliberate. It never tries to seduce the soul or deceive the intellect, but always— and only—the senses....For this precise reason it never delves into the depths of the 'appearance' but always stays on its surface; always ready to leap across the dividing line [between 'appearance' and 'reality'] and dissolve the 'appearance', but at the same time just as ready to redouble its effect.[1]

It would, for instance, be easy to interpret the banquet scene in terms of the 'surface of the appearance' and to demonstrate Hofmannsthal's readiness to 'dissolve the appearance' in the continual sense of God and of Death present throughout the action.

It would be wrong to judge *Jedermann* from the standpoint of English theatrical tradition and primarily Protestant instinct.

We become justifiably irritated when a Voltaire sees Shakespeare in terms of French Classicism or when the stalwarts of the Comédie Française find the Irving or Olivier style difficult to take. The problem with *Jedermann* is comparable in that recognition of local and national tradition, of social and religious history, has to be accorded and due allowance made.

Perhaps an injustice is done to Hofmannsthal if one attempts to find for *Jedermann* a place amongst those dramas which know no frontiers and can be adapted by widely differing styles and traditions in succeeding generations. Hofmannsthal seemed at any rate to suggest this and in spite of himself to stress its dependence on the Christian faith when he replied to Bodenhausen's critique. The exchange between the two friends is particularly interesting because Bodenhausen's comments call forth Hofmannsthal's definition, and because Bodenhausen's critique itself is most reasoned and balanced. It represents in a few words a sincere and non-dogmatic approach to the drama— what might perhaps be called the *Gesund-Normale*!—

The performance of *Jedermann* did not give me what I had expected from it.... The banquet scene was tremendous.... For the decision one way or the other was bound to come from the entrance of Good Works onwards. When I read it the whole final section makes a purely allegorical impression, quite unconvincing and without any impact on my feelings. I have never told you this because I hoped and expected that an actual performance would transform it into a symbol. But this did not happen at all...it was entirely unexpected and I was most surprised and disappointed. Perhaps Dietrich with her sentimental, tearful voice is partly to blame. Instead of being a real experience... it became something wholly unpleasant and untrue—so much so that I greeted the appearance of the devil with genuine relief, and with a certain feeling of hostility to all this I went over on to his side! To my mind your *Jedermann* lacks ultimate decisiveness and I do not think that I should hesitate to tell you so. At the same time I am well aware that it must be some deficiency in me and not in you, since *Jedermann* has become such a great experience and a complete symbol for a man like Schröder.[1]

Hofmannsthal replied:

the old play does not go beyond the allegorical sphere and I have really done nothing apart from restoring the old play with a not unskilled hand. It seems to me that the essence of this art form—the morality play—is that it is two-dimensional. It gets its third dimension by means of its relationship to something outside itself—the truths of faith. What you are looking for in this play seems, however, to be that three-dimensional quality—you call it a symbolical quality—such as one finds in ancient Greek drama and also—to name one of various religious dramas related to it—in *Faust*.

In attempting to draw a final conclusion from the analysis of *Jedermann* a critic can, if he is to remain free of personal prejudice arising from his own convictions, do little more than put forward the views on the play which seem reasonable and can be justified. What for some is obscure or remote or other-worldly in *Jedermann* may be instinctively obvious to others. This may be said perhaps of many plays. Where, however, a play is rooted so deeply in a religious tradition of a particular kind—as is here the case—this assertion may be tenable.

To conclude this consideration of the problem one might well consider the comments of Richard Alewyn on the customary type of criticism of the (sacred) baroque drama from which, as has been shown, *Jedermann* is descended:

The fact that we are concerned here with theology and not with aesthetics has been overlooked. All aesthetic objections to the sacred drama and its descendants right down to our own day are really not of an artistic kind but more a matter of the critics' own attitude to life. The 'passivity' of the hero, the lack of action, the absence of 'tension', the type figures, the use of allegory, supernatural interference—all this is criticized as being 'undramatic'. This is justified if one has developed one's ideas from the secularized world of the Protestant theatre; that is to say, if in order to be 'dramatic' the action of a work has to be entirely a matter of relationships between friend and foe, an action in which strong individuals struggle against each other with a good deal of force—or at least noise—and in which birth and death mark out the area which encompasses all fortune and misfortune. The unpredictable outcome of this action gives rise to a tension which pulls the audience along with it in the flood of time.

This elevation of the 'dramatic' element to such an absolute pitch can be done only by a view of life which puts active values above contemplative ones and earthly values above eternal. On the other hand, wherever worldly things are regarded as valueless or as possessing only symbolic value, a different kind of theatre will arise. This theatre does not need to be any more lacking in tension than the other, but its axes run vertically, not horizontally. It is not concerned with the tension between friend and foe but with the tension between this world and the next. Therefore there are no individual people here but only human beings. This theatre is not concerned with victory but with redemption. Reality is not conquered but truth is revealed. And for this reason the outcome is never in doubt but has been pre-determined in eternity.

This is not always 'dramatic' but it may be 'theatrical' in a most audacious sense.[1]

The relevance of this summary becomes the more marked when one notes that Alewyn, himself a most distinguished critic of Hofmannsthal,[2] alludes not only to the baroque drama itself but also to 'its descendants right down to our own day'. It is surely unthinkable that *Jedermann* is not amongst the works he has in mind.

Whatever one's personal view of *Jedermann* may be, it can scarcely be disputed that it meant a considerable step forward in Hofmannsthal's career; a step, that is to say, towards the pre-occupation with problems of his country and of his age. This preoccupation made him the *Kulturpolitiker* and *Praeceptor Austriae* of the war years. From *Jedermann* to the essays of those years, a selection of which is considered in the two chapters which follow, is as will be seen a short and logical progression.

CHAPTER 3

THREE HISTORICAL STUDIES

The poet's later work is the expression of his strenuous effort to find new order in the chaos around him and to rescue human values. FRITZ MARTINI[1]

Even if our age is to be one of decline, how much still remains, unspent and as pure as it was in the beginning . . . even Rome in decline still bore within it many such seeds of life. . . . With these thoughts in mind we can rise above anything. HUGO VON HOFMANNSTHAL[2]

'JEDERMANN' revealed Hofmannsthal at the height of his powers. Its technical and dramatic accomplishment was matched by the maturity of outlook towards which he had been struggling during the first decade of the century. Chronologically *Jedermann* was in the middle of his career. Dramatically and in its content it was in a sense for Hofmannsthal a parting of the ways. The few years which followed its completion made Hofmannsthal very much aware of 'a destiny which bears in on us from outside'.[3] What had been presaged in such works as *Der Dichter und diese Zeit* and *Jedermann* was realized during the war. His activity as a dramatist, both in his own right and in collaboration with Richard Strauss, continued. But this activity was paralleled and at times—really until *Der Schwierige* (1918, published 1920)— even overshadowed by his work as a *Kulturpolitiker*. This was not a sudden development. It is fairly clear that the outbreak of the war brought into the immediate foreground many problems which had actually occupied Hofmannsthal's mind for some years. The years of European conflict are in consequence notable in his career for a series of prose works in which he strove to postulate an 'Austrian ideal', an intellectual and political *raison*

83

d'être for the Austrian empire, and to show a positive way out of evil and war in the encouragement of a new European ideal.

In the light of these labours *Jedermann* can be seen retrospectively as a 'parting of the ways' in a rather particular way: it was in effect a moral clearing of ground for a campaign to which the war gave but greater urgency. These wartime works in their turn can be seen as a kind of preparation, a working out of certain ideas which found dramatic expression in *Das Salzburger Große Welttheater* and in the (at least partially) political or state drama *Der Turm*.

There is fortunately a good deal of direct evidence as to the way in which the war influenced Hofmannsthal. The distinguished Austrian historian and politician Josef Redlich was a good friend of Hofmannsthal and each man had a high regard for the other.[1] Redlich noted on 23 November 1915:

I spent the whole of today with Hugo von Hofmannsthal...in Rodaun...Hofmannsthal told me a good deal about Germany and Belgium; he talked about politics and plans for peace. The war has influenced Hofmannsthal in a remarkable way. He has become a realist and a politician. He wants to take part in public affairs and bring about tangible results. I am really moved by the practical way in which he expresses his deeply innate Austrianism.[2]

Hofmannsthal seems to have seen the implications of the war quite clearly. The following extract from a letter written early (1915) in the struggle demonstrates this:

For even if other uniformly national states[3] believe that they are entitled to reject the concept of a united Europe and stand alone in hardened self-sufficiency, this is out of the question for my country...Austria needs Europe more than any other country does, for what is Austria but Europe on a smaller scale? For us, therefore, even more than for the others, this war also has a spiritual significance,...[4]

Hofmannsthal was unable to view the war in narrowly national terms. The rise of nationalism—often with selfishly economic motivation—disturbed him even more than the possibility of the defeat of the central powers. He regarded the war as the product of an exclusively materialistic civilization. His ideas on this subject were directly expressed in, for example, *Die Idee Europa* (1916), a speech delivered in Stockholm, Oslo and Berne—all neutral capitals.[1] The full text of this speech does not seem to have been printed but Hofmannsthal's notes have survived. In them one sees those Christian-social ideas already felt in *Jedermann* and particularly in the Mammon scene: 'Without any trace of shame this world worshipped the three idols—health, security, and a long life; the cult of security and comfort. Comfort without beauty.'[2] This is quite evidently an attack on the bourgeois philistinism of the *laissez-faire* era and in particular on the decline in taste and spiritual standards which results from a cult of material prosperity. He continues with a note which is curiously reminiscent of Thomas Mann: 'Nature as an *enemy*,[3] with its refuge in disease.' One recalls in passing the symbolism of disease in Mann's work and especially in the comfortable bourgeois world of *Der Zauberberg* (1924). It is interesting to note that Mann began *Der Zauberberg* in 1912. Thus Hofmannsthal's development of this particular idea is in a sense parallel to a comparable development in Thomas Mann.

The memory of the Mammon scene becomes very distinct as Hofmannsthal develops his point about the diabolically comprehensive influence of money in the world: 'Anyone who faced up to the problem of money had to ask himself this: has not money the power to replace God himself?...A trust in its omnipotence comes into being—in its power to grant us at any moment any individual and base desire.'[4]

Hofmannsthal did not see the war solely from this negative and critical standpoint, however. He was also aware of it as an opportunity, not to restore what was old and effete, but to create a new Europe:

We sense that certain tendencies in the material civilization which we inherited from the nineteenth century will break up like surging waves which crash on the shore. This material civilization will doubtless continue to develop, but—we may surely hope—to a certain extent under a different star and with the possibility of conquering itseif [5]

Although he characterized the war as a 'catastrophe' Hofmannsthal saw in it a chance for Austria to realize her own latent possibilities as a united Europe on a modest scale: he saw in effect a chance for Austria to throw off the weariness and cynical fatalism which seemed to have dogged her progress since 1867 (the *Ausgleich* with Hungary).[1] He realized only too clearly just how perilous Austria's state was; and he saw how wide a gap existed between ideal and reality. In this respect his correspondence with Bodenhausen is especially revealing as regards Hofmannsthal's practical reaction to contemporary affairs.[2] Two letters, both dating from before 1914, demonstrate this. On 30 April 1912 Hofmannsthal wrote:

Then I was back here at home. Things look bad here, Eberhard, bad for old Austria. I often ask myself anxiously—into what sort of a world are my two boys growing up? Our foreign situation...is not the worst part of it. If we were a state like others we could negotiate and act—or we could decide to postpone action until later. As things are here, however, it is really all the same whether one acts or whether the ability to act is for the moment taken away. Everything...points to disaster. The most fearsome problem is the internal one. The southern Slavs within the monarchy...in semi-revolt (arrests which nobody talks about), the Czechs maliciously lying in wait with bared teeth, Galicia...rotten with sedition, Italy just as willing to be our enemy as our ally, Russia...simply yearning to pick a quarrel with us. And at home—half indolence, half sheer incapacity, the problems too complicated...honesty and good intentions here and there... but even these without real conviction...we are going into a dark time...we could easily lose everything between one step and the next—and, this is the worst part of it, even when we win anything we really gain nothing—except more embarrassments.[3]

Hofmannsthal's letter of 21 January 1913 is quietly moving in tone. It demonstrates not only his fears for the future of both Germany and Austria; there is also apparent a compound and complex feeling characteristic of him in maturity: his personal, human warmth on the one hand, on the other a sense of suprapersonal events which determine the course of his life:

This letter of yours—after I came home this evening, one of those now rare times when I can read to the children. These lines in your hand, your words, your feelings...coming across the whole of that great, uneasy and darkly threatened Germany...this touch of your hand—your face which suddenly appears in the circle of my lamp,...I have had strange feelings these last few days, in this confused and rather anxious Austria, this stepchild of history—strange, lonely and anxious feelings. How alone we are, and yet how wonderful that we have each other. I want to beg of you: don't die and leave me....For me all these destinies always seem to flow into each other. But that is my lot in life....[1]

With the outbreak of war and the end of an epoch which had ground itself into ruin Hofmannsthal felt that his course was clear. With the above considerations in mind it is not surprising that his 'patriotic' wartime essays present a twofold aspect. In them he manifests a fervent love of the Austrian empire together with praise for its past achievements. But a warning note is also present, a plea to his motherland to live up to and to perfect the potentialities within her. In this the likeness to Grillparzer is seen. Grillparzer's patriotism was the greater for its clear-eyed appraisal and criticism of his country. Perhaps the most obvious example of this is seen in his characterization of Rudolf of Habsburg in *König Ottokars Glück und Ende*. Through this one figure Grillparzer proclaimed his love for the dynasty, recalled its past glories, and urged both the royal house and his fellow-countrymen to reach those heights again:

> Die Welt is da, damit wir alle leben,
> Und groß ist nur der ein allein'ge Gott!
> Der Jugendtraum der Erde ist geträumt,
> Und mit den Riesen, mit den Drachen ist
> Der Helden, der Gewalt'gen Zeit dahin.
> Nicht Völker stürzen sich wie Berglawinen
> Auf Völker mehr, die Gärung scheidet sich
> Und nach den Zeichen sollt' es fast mich dünken,
> Wir stehn am Eingang einer neuen Zeit...
> Ihr habt der Euren Vorteil stets gewollt;
> Gönnt ihnen Ruh, Ihr könnt nichts besseres geben.[2]

It is a telling fact that in Hofmannsthal's mature years he often found inspiration in Grillparzer's example,[1] and again and again he tried to make it live in the minds of his own generation. One of his several essays wholly or partially devoted to Grillparzer is specially relevant to the present study. *Grillparzers Politisches Vermächtnis* was written in 1915 and is the first of the three historical studies which form the principal matter of this chapter.

In *Grillparzers Politisches Vermächtnis* Hofmannsthal tried to do three things: to see Grillparzer in his age and environment; to demonstrate political sense; and to point to a patriotic ideal. He develops his polemical method in a logical manner. First of all he establishes his premises:

His great and constant themes were as follows: ruling, being ruled, and justice. In order to depict the various forms of these things he created a whole line of great political figures: Bancban and his king, Ottokar and Rudolf of Habsburg, Rudolf II. It has become customary to overlook this side of him because of the magic of his women characters. But in a creative nature all manner of things have their place, and anyone who looks at greatness in a one-sided way is the poorer for it.[2]

There follows an aphoristic definition of politics which is of a kind notably characteristic of Hofmannsthal at this stage in his career. The definition itself seems to be a sudden break with the content of the above paragraph. But in this way Hofmannsthal sets the larger political stage:

Politics is knowledge of men, the art of getting on with people but on a higher plane. An irrational element is involved here just as in one's contact with individuals: the hidden powers obey those who know how to address them. In this way a great politician is revealed. For the poet it is enough if he senses these powers and points to them with unerring instinct.[3]

This passage puts forward Hofmannsthal's general theme. Then, quite naturally it seems, he places inside this framework his particular topic: Austria's historical situation and Grillparzer's position in it:

In Austria's case two of them [that is, 'the powers' referred to in the preceding passage] are relevant and these are merely touched by the political ideas of the age,...the ruler and his people. Grillparzer's spirit and imagination were in constant contact with these two main forces, which were not always clearly recognized as such by the politicians of the day. Some deep sense made him transform himself alternately into both: his nature was of the people but in imagination he saw himself as a ruler. He interwove into both the peculiar, strong, enduring elements of his own Austrian nature.

Perhaps one may here place two of his characters side by side. Somewhat surprisingly they are Rudolf II and the woman of the people in *Der arme Spielmann*, the grocer's daughter. Together they symbolize Grillparzer's Austria. Each has a deep and strong character, patient, wise, God-fearing, unaffected and tenacious. Both are shy and inhibited; both need love in order not to be misjudged by others. But they are at one with God and nature.[1]

This essay is highly concentrated and abounds in implicit instruction—to statesmen and artists with their responsibilities and limitations. But through it all one feels the cultural ideal and essentially 'different' aspect of Austria's being and mission—different, that is to say, as compared with the German *Reich*. Hofmannsthal's sense of the continuity of past and present is specially noteworthy; constantly he makes the reader see the past towering into the present as precept and living inspiration. All these themes, *Gewebe des Daseins* as Hofmannsthal might have called them, acting one on the other, are exposed and discussed in a few short paragraphs. It was this ability to carry along so many seemingly disparate 'threads of existence'—to sense them constantly present in and about him and to bind them together in clear definition—that distinguished Hofmannsthal's prose work at this period:

One often talks about a certain attitude to art in which 'art for art's sake' is the slogan. This idea is vigorously rejected but we are not always clear about its exact meaning. Yet we should not forget that a similar attitude is to be found in all spheres of life, and it is everywhere equally objectionable: wit, business, factiousness, declamation—each for its own sake. There is a certain 'art for art's sake' in politics and it is to blame for a good deal of trouble. The poet who wants to assert himself politically runs a serious risk of falling into rhetoric for the sake of rhetoric. Grillparzer was much too solid a character not to reject this temptation very firmly.... For a man of his character there was only one possible way of entering practical politics; through a personal relationship—as assistant and adviser—to a creative statesman, namely Stadion.[1] For whenever that particular brilliant yet friendly trait of character appears in a professional politician—when he is a man of the world and a philosopher at the same time, like Prince Eugene and Frederick the Great, like Kaunitz and de Maistre—then it is quite possible that he may touch off productive forces other than those which are purely political. For it is in this way that culture comes into being: as a growing awareness of beauty in functional things, as an influence coming from the intellect and transfiguring things which have been built up by power relationships. Goethe's definition was as follows: 'Could culture be anything other than the spiritualization of political and military matters?'[2]

At the end of the above paragraph Hofmannsthal incorporates a Goethian aphorism into his own definition. It is a salutary fact that his own lapidary style and definition are comparable in tone and effect with those of Goethe.[3]

At this stage in Hofmannsthal's career a further quality which he had in common with Goethe becomes apparent. This is perhaps best summed up in two sentences written in another context by Bernt von Heiseler:

The thing which first strikes one on reading his work is a certain... exactness and freshness of observation, his closeness to the thing observed. He combined with this an inexorable and often uncanny incisiveness of thought, a determination to think his ideas through to the end. This combination seldom occurs in Germany.[4]

Hofmannsthal developed this quality most strikingly at a time when his thoughts were turning more and more to cultural-political affairs; to a sphere, that is to say, where it could best be used. In the present instance Hofmannsthal was able to suggest the larger field of history in the light of his own definitions and then to place against that background the figure of Grillparzer himself. As he did so he laid his hand on the historical and fatal weakness of Austria:

But here the stars did not favour Grillparzer: when Stadion first noticed him he was still too immature. Later, when the serious crisis of 1848 made him for a moment a politician in the purest sense of the word and raised him up as an ephemeral intellectual-political force, he was past his best. He had not been called upon in the decades which lay between. Spiritual and intellectual forces are seldom lacking in Austria. But more frequently the will to make use of them is absent.[1]

This last sentence stands at the head of this study. Its relevance to Hofmannsthal himself becomes fully clear only in the light of his last works and utterances. It is significant, however, that he turned to Grillparzer during this middle period of his career. The fact itself is less important than the way in which he interpreted his predecessor.

Hofmannsthal saw Grillparzer as a connecting spiritual link between the Austria of the decades before the French Revolution and the new Austria whose last generation Hofmannsthal himself was attempting to represent in the most positive manner possible. Of Grillparzer's essential representativeness he wrote: 'he stands midway between Maria Theresia's times and our own. His character fits in there as easily as it does here and now, and in both cases as a living element. It is the embodiment of an Austrian character which is indestructible.'[2]

One recalls here Theodor Heuss's assessment of Hofmannsthal, which might equally be applied to Grillparzer:

the intellectual sublimation of the old Austria...to put it crudely Hofmannsthal owed to it [Austria] the atmosphere which was vital for his growth...while owing much to the richness of this social-cultural and intellectual world he also contributed much to it.[3]

In his mature years Hofmannsthal attempted again and again to define what was specifically Austrian in the make-up of the German-Austrian. More significantly, however, he frequently tried to do this by means of a German (that is *Reich* German)–Austrian polarity. In so doing he had much of penetrating wisdom and hard truth to say about Germany, hard truths which were all the more sincere because they were expressed with the insight that grows from love. In the Grillparzer essay he expressed this polarity in a temperate way:

The Austrian spirit gains the palm not through its dark profundity but through its clarity, by the fact that it is of the present. The German has a complicated, inhibited feeling about his own times. Whether it is a whole epoch or simply an instant he does not find it easy to live in the here and now. He is here—and not here; he is above and outside time, not in it. For this reason few people talk about time as much as the Germans. They struggle to find the inner meaning of the present. But we have been granted it. This lucidity, this sense for the here and now, is realized most impressively in the Austrian people; in the upper classes it is most marked in the women. It is the secret source of that feeling of sheer happiness which streams forth from the music of Haydn, Mozart, Schubert and Strauss.[1]

This approach to German-Austrian distinctions should not be confused with chauvinism or nationalism—Hofmannsthal was almost strenuously insistent on his own German heritage[2]—nor was it a digression from his main object in this essay. It was introduced to demonstrate the more clearly the essential quality of Austrianism, of Austrianism as it was in Grillparzer's works, as it could and should exist in Hofmannsthal's own day:

He despised fine phrases and was inexorable in his rejection of new and fashionable words and slogans. Exaggeration in words was for him the true symbol of a spreading weakness and slovenliness. Finally I would mention his Austrian sense for what is appropriate, this wonderful inheritance from our...medieval period which in spite of everything still makes it possible today for us to live together with all manner of peoples in one common homeland; this tolerant vitality which carries us through difficult times and which we must save for the future.[3]

Moderation, sincerity, action and vitality tempered by mutual tolerance: these qualities are the mainsprings of the essay's climax as seen in this passage. It is perhaps not irrelevant to recall in this context a characteristic opinion of Hofmannsthal on a very

characteristic failing of his as of the present time. Carl Burckhardt
has told how Hofmannsthal saw post-war society:

Those artificial characters within the nation, conditioned by literary
fashion, were deeply repugnant to Hofmannsthal—those effect-
merchants, speculators of the intellect who, like dealers in gloom,
prophesy society towards the abyss: the diseased mania of the time for
cheap remedies in order to make an impression, the false masters, the
false peasants, the false saints and the false sinners. When the great
immorality set in after the war—with its 'destinies', a profound term
for just letting oneself go—Hofmannsthal said once in a bored way:
'It's all nothing else than the petty bourgeois in reverse.'[1]

In the light of this later reaction Hofmannsthal's warning in the
Grillparzer essay is seen to have the greater point and accuracy.
The closing paragraph of the essay is in fact simultaneously a
panegyric, a warning, and a summons:

He complained and he criticized, but he loved and he was creative.
His Austria is so great, so rich, so natural; and on his lips 'Austria
erit' sounds completely natural and convincing. He was a mirror of
the older...Austria. When the new Austria looks into this mirror it
can see whether we have not perhaps become poorer, whether we have
lost some of our vital content and warmth of soul. Whether, if his
criticism still applies to us,[2] his praise also is justified—and for whom?
His pride, his confidence—have they any foundation now?—And
where is it?[3]

It may seem dogmatic to claim that the above could equally
well be applied to Hofmannsthal and his own Austrianism.
Writing barely three years before the disappearance of the oldest
empire in the world, Hofmannsthal sensed the shadows gathering
even as he wrote (see pp. 86–7), and the application to himself
of his own words on Grillparzer may be better appreciated in the
light of a consideration of some of those other wartime essays in
which he 'complained and criticized,...loved and was creative'.

In Bemerkungen, written a few years after the war, Hofmannsthal
outlined his purpose in the essays which are discussed in the
following pages:

My own attempt to define this particular kind of spirit—the actual mixture of self-reliance and modesty, sure instinct and occasional *naïveté*, natural balance and poor dialectical capacity—my attempt to depict all these things which make up the essential character of the Austrian is clearly seen...in more sharply defined form in numerous essays and speeches such as *Maria Theresia, Prinz Eugen, Österreich im Spiegel seiner Dichtung*, and in the lectures which I gave during the war in Stockholm, Oslo, Warsaw and Berne. All these were ultimately concerned with one thing only: to remind the nations of Europe that the present German *Reich* does not reveal the whole face of Germanism in Europe, and that this face cannot be recognized unless one also acknowledges those features of an older and higher form of Germanism which have been preserved in Austria.[1]

These assertions should be borne in mind as Hofmannsthal's claims to have been to some extent a preceptor for his countrymen are tested in the remaining part of this chapter and in the one which follows.

Hofmannsthal celebrated Grillparzer as a creative artist who left a political heritage. In his attempt to encourage, to warn, to strengthen his age morally, Hofmannsthal turned also to men and women of the past, some of whose deeds appear at first to have been concerned rather less with the spirit and intellect. At the head of a short essay written in December 1914 to commemorate Prince Eugene,[2] Hofmannsthal set some words taken from Johannes von Müller's (1752–1809) panegyric on Frederick the Great. These, in their present context especially, reveal something of Hofmannsthal's intentions:

When we celebrate the memory of great men we do it in order to become familiar with great thoughts, to banish what weighs heavily upon us....Loss of property can be made good. Other losses are healed by time. Only one evil is incurable: when man gives up hope.

Hofmannsthal was impressed and saddened by the fact that the oldest empire in the world, the inheritor of the empire of Charlemagne and of the Roman imperium, had no national mythology in the sense of those which are the possession of

England, France, or Prussia. For the Englishman Plymouth Hoe
and the little ships are forever present: past time and present
inspiration are one. Henry V at Harfleur has become inextricably
mixed with Shakespeare's evocation of him. Phrases of Shakespeare, Nelson's self-conscious heroism, a saying of Disraeli or of
Pitt—all are particles in a limitless, timeless constellation which
makes up the English myth; to be used, even on occasion
much abused, but incontestably a source of confidence and
strength.

The realization of Austria's disadvantage compared with England
was not an altogether sudden wartime insight on Hofmannsthal's
part. In *Der Dichter und diese Zeit* (1906–7) there is a clear indication of it:

How vitally and impressively the Englishman of today uses his
expression 'man of genius'—and he has been doing this for six
generations. He does not reserve it only for his poets; and yet there
is something poetic about all those to whom he applies this term—
about them or their destinies. . . . But it must be a figure from whom
something extraordinary flashes forth, something incomparable in the
way of boldness, fortune, intellectual strength, or dedication. There is
something tremendous about a concept which is permitted by the
genius of the English language to include Milton and Nelson, Lord
Clive and Samuel Johnson, Byron and Warren Hastings, Pitt the
Younger and Cecil Rhodes.[1]

This realization now assumed larger proportions in Hofmannsthal's mind. He commented ruefully on the great efforts of the
Prussians to preserve and enhance their historical inspiration, and
he drew the inevitable conclusion:

I am not speaking only about Frederick the Great who is celebrated
in book after book, whose least saying. . .keeps a healthy respect alive
for him; but also about their Blücher and Moltke, for others as well,
whose deeds are not so legendary, whose memory is perhaps less
clearly printed on the soul of later generations—Yorck, Stein, Gnei-
senau, Boyen, whose names they keep alive nevertheless, and not only
their names but their whole mental image. Here, however, where
would you even find a really popular account of Maria Theresia?[2]

It is of course clear that there are ever-present dangers in the characteristic and traditional national myth. The likelihood of cheap, propagandist exploitation by press and politicians is obvious. The second danger is not so apparent: the myth can be partly evil in itself if it lays undue emphasis on any one aspect of a nation's achievement. This is especially true of the military aspect and of national glory won at the expense of other equally proud but less coherently vocal nations. Hofmannsthal's preceptors, the constituent elements in his Austrian myth, are examples in the art of avoiding just this danger. Grillparzer is clearly above suspicion in any case. But what of Prince Eugene, Maria Theresia, or Stadion? Eugene was one of the great captains of European history. Maria Theresia ruled for forty years in an age of absolutism. Stadion was a statesman in a time of national humiliation and following insurrection. All three, however, had something fundamental in common. This was the imagination and executive power of the visionary and builder. This may be less apparent in Eugene than in the others. Yet while praising and recreating his military valour Hofmannsthal urged more and more into the foreground what he called 'the secret of all secrets: a creative nature'.[1] The creative nature and achievement of Eugene throughout the thirty-nine years of his campaigns: this was for Hofmannsthal the stout and never-breaking thread running through his life.

In the measured rhetoric of the opening paragraph of the essay on Prince Eugene, Hofmannsthal instilled a new vitality into his old practice of plunging to the past for solace:

When fearsome events bear down on us...and what was won at great sacrifice is for the moment lost[2]...we do not know where to turn. Our spirit ranges anxiously abroad, seeking the meaning of things: we can come to terms with the hardest fate if we can see the necessity for it. But such violence is too much for us to grasp: we have to stand by helplessly and see how individual people are slaughtered in their thousands. And then we ourselves—individuals too—feel humiliated. ...And when we are in this state of mind the deepest features of our nature assert themselves; a great word can raise us up for a few moments; the recounting of heroic deeds will set all our own forces in motion. Never are we more worthy of turning our thoughts to a great man than when we are in this frame of mind.[1]

Boldly but logically, thought and fact following each other, the mind of the reader, anxious and perplexed by present confusion and fear, was led by contemplation of the homeland's plight to think of its architect, Prince Eugene. Thus far in the essay Hofmannsthal had not mentioned him directly, except as 'a great man'. But he then proceeded to fuse past and present and thus Eugene and his lasting significance were brought quite naturally to the forefront of the reader's mind:

Now the forces which he had to combat stand before us;...and now he himself appears before us. The past appears not as a finished... picture but we recognize in its constant and terrifying movement the image of our own time, and the lives of peoples stand revealed as a constant stress and strain one against the other. The only thing which changes is the combination of foes and allies. We see a great epoch which determined the course of history for a quarter of a millennium; Europe in flames,...from Lille to Belgrade, just as it is today. And our Austria is born out of these battles. We do not see how it could happen, only that it did; nowhere can we see the way ahead marked out, but only that everything was constantly uncertain,...threatening; and that one man created the possibility where to eyes less keen no possibility had previously appeared;...we can recognize a man's greatness and it makes us revere him. This is how the Prussians of today think of their Frederick; this is how we Austrians regard the greatest Austrian of all: Eugene of Savoy.[2]

It was not easy to make the many-sided achievement of Eugene a living picture for the reader, the more so because his achievement contained seemingly great contradictions. These contradictions— bloodshed and destruction set against Eugene's works of progress and peace—were demonstrated and resolved by Hofmannsthal in terms of the living contradiction which was the Austrian empire itself. The empire was in Hofmannsthal's view one of peace, peace within its multi-lingual, multi-cultural borders. And yet its task was to assert itself continually in war against the expanding power of France in the west; and in the east first against the sultan and then against the Mediterranean-minded czar. The man to bring this Austria into existence and to ensure her permanence was Eugene. In Hofmannsthal's summary of the situation a warning to the distressed, dissent-ridden Austria of 1914–18 is obviously implicit, together with a clear admonition to the leadership as well as to the people. It is noteworthy that Hofmannsthal expresses himself here in a style which is comparatively terse and military in tone. It abounds, moreover, in antitheses. Thus the actual form and style of the essay at this point prepare the way and establish the mood for one of the greatest human antitheses, Eugene himself:

Austria is the realm of peace but it was born of conflict. Its destiny is to reconcile opposites, and it constantly has to assert and renew itself in battle. The man who was destined to summon this state out of chaos into the world of form had to be a great military captain who at the same time was capable of high statecraft. And such a one was Eugene.[1]

Following this, however, Hofmannsthal's language takes on a heightened and somewhat rhetorical rhythm as he strives to depict the gigantic, tumultuous century which bore Eugene and a new Austria, and to make his readers feel the superhuman strength of that age surging down the centuries:

a mighty century gave birth to him. His shape rises up amongst the gigantic sons of that age: Richelieu, Wallenstein, the Great Elector, William of Orange—he yields to none of them in the unshakeable pursuit of his decisions and in the power to carry them out. And he ranks with them in the greatness of his achievement which has lasted for centuries. In the purity and honesty of his intellect throughout his mighty career he is...closer to our hearts than any of the others.[2]

Hofmannsthal now changes his style abruptly. He seems to have sensed the danger of falling into rodomontade and vague concepts. He realized too his own power of expression, the power which since the turn of the century he had bent to his will and artistic conscience. Hence he avoids the temptation to fall into mere patriotic propaganda (however effective this might be for the moment)[1] and in the vital depiction of Eugene himself the style, while still rhetorical, becomes comparatively curt again, rich in antithesis and the unexpected turn of phrase. The reader must think and follow, for the rhetoric is now more in the antithesis than in any compelling rhythm or imaginative picture:

His destiny called him here from a foreign land. In the same way France's destiny summoned Napoleon from his island a century later. He was a prince's son and he had, moreover, a princely soul; to him it was right and natural that he could only serve a master who embodied for him the very highest qualities. And so he came here and served the Emperor and the *Reich*. He came from a foreign land, he never really learned to speak German properly,[2] and he became a German national hero.... Vienna was the seat of the Roman Emperor, so Eugene came to Austria in order to seek his destiny. And he created our destiny. The decisive qualities were already inborn; fortune offered him the means and the opportunities. A detachment of cavalry and a great epoch—this was all that was given to him.[3]

Stage by stage Hofmannsthal built up the composite figure of a great field captain. Ingeniously he likened Austria's position in 1914—threatened with dismemberment and disgrace—with her plight when the grandiose dreams of Louis XIV of a French imperium in Europe and the Middle East were perilously close to realization. The military genius of Eugene thus assumes huge dimensions in the reader's mind.

Then comes the decisive stroke: psychologically it is a master-stroke. History down to the most recent times is littered with the names of successful generals in the narrow military sphere—generals, however, who were either completely non-political or aggressively political. It is difficult to say which is the greater menace. Ample evidence might be assembled to prove that either was the case. The qualities in Prince Eugene which Hofmannsthal reserved for the climax of his panegyric were those of the political visionary and colonial pioneer. Alongside these great gifts, which are essentially positive and practical, the military feats lose none of their brilliance, but they fall into perspective as a necessary evil; a component and not the ultimate object itself:

War is the work of destruction. But the greatest masters of war rise above their works. Over and above the fact that they were great soldiers, Alexander, Hannibal, Caesar, Gustavus Adolphus, Frederick the Great, and Eugene were also creative statesmen.[1]

Eugene's particular genius was characterized by Hofmannsthal in an effective antithesis: 'Eugene, the mighty master of war, was a most moderate and effective peace-maker.'[2]

The warning note addressed to contemporary Austria was never far away as Hofmannsthal traced the course of Eugene's activity: 'The confused present he handled in a most lucid way; the future—and this was a most rare gift, above all in Austria—with extreme foresight!'[3] Eugene's care for the conquered or reconquered provinces was held up as an example for contemporary Austria: 'He conquered, and wherever he conquered he made secure.... And unexpectedly, everywhere his armies had fought, works of peace bloomed under his creative hands. The plough follows behind his army and the axe of the colonist sounds in the forest. He brings new populations....'[4]

It is a measure of the suggestive properties of Hofmannsthal's prose that he was able at this point to use a symbol of rare poetic quality in order to make vital and idealistic, even miraculous, the sober, practical deeds of reconstruction and development which followed the paths of the armies. The symbol is that ancient one of the rod of Aaron and Moses (Book of Numbers, xvii. 6–11). Here the symbol was boldly modified without losing its near-divine association:

His marshal's baton, symbol of the destructive warlord, fertilizes the provinces and reawakens the life within them which had perished. He subjugates and reconciles, he unites and leads.... Wherever he goes he lays new foundations and what he founds lives on. Trieste is his creation. He builds, he adorns, he ennobles.[5]

Some grounds for a possible comparison between Grillparzer and Hofmannsthal were noted earlier. Hofmannsthal concluded this essay on Prince Eugene with references and sentiments which inevitably recall Grillparzer's fate some eighty years previously. Grillparzer was a devotedly loyal monarchist and an unswerving supporter of the ruling dynasty. This did not prevent him from seeing grave shortcomings in the state of things and from giving expression to these sentiments. For this his career as a creative artist was stultified by the censor and the creative urge ultimately died within him. Hofmannsthal's was in this respect a happier lot. But in these closing sequences of the essay he felt impelled to warn the dynasty and leaders of state in terms which were scarcely oblique. Recalling Eugene's incredible physical and moral fortitude in the field over a span of thirty-nine years he came thus to an account of

the...constant conflict with forces behind him at home, against disfavour, envy, foolishness, dishonesty. The never-ending necessity to assert himself, the struggle against seniority, that parent of jealousy, against obstinacy and intrigue; the unceasing struggle against bureaucratic obscurantism,...stupid slander, cunning and resourceful baseness. A host of enemies in front of him, but what a world behind him— and all sprung from one root, the hereditary Austrian disease— sprouting a thousand shoots but always the same root: laziness of spirit, dull unimaginativeness, a minimal sense of duty, the flight from anything unpleasant into a welter of distraction; not real badness for the greater part, but an evil which is really worse and more hateful, an evil which springs from a heavy, dull slothfulness.[1]

In all Eugene's labours Hofmannsthal felt his self-sacrificing love of Austria and evoked this love in two sentences of simple felicity:

His love for this Austria is unconquerable and in this love is the source of the strength with which he changed our world; because of this love he refused the crown of Poland and the duchy of Mantua. His was a princely spirit which had sought...someone whom it might serve, and then served right through to the end.[2]

The conclusion of the essay is an intricate mixture of idealized history, political realism and hope for the future. Modern Austria, said Hofmannsthal, was essentially the work of Prince Eugene and her situation had not changed fundamentally in the two centuries which had passed. Here Hofmannsthal touched on the present situation of the Austrian empire. Despite the disasters which punctuated the reign of Emperor Francis Joseph, despite the official policy of 'too late and too little', despite the upsurging nationalism within her boundaries and pressure from beyond her borders, Austria still had—in Hofmannsthal's view—the re-surgent, rejuvenating strength to make Eugene's mid-European ideal a new reality.[1] For Hofmannsthal Austria was not an imperialistic power complex. It was a 'structure of the spirit' which had been called into being to meet a necessity.[2] It was his hope, vain as it was, that the times would again bring forth the man of destiny:

The peoples whom he linked together with the golden chain of his deeds are still young, pure and unspoiled. Our spirit was for a long time tormented by faint-heartedness and dull hesitancy,...now it is numbed by the enormity of events. But this one figure Eugene radiates an inexhaustible hope to us all. This Austria is a structure of the spirit, and envious forces are always trying to pull it back into chaos. But one man can achieve incredible things: again and again...providence summons the man from whom mighty things are demanded and who is equal to the task.[3]

In this evocation of idealism and strength combined in one man the reader's mind inevitably leaps forward a decade to *Der Turm* (1925). At the climax of the action, after the overthrow of both the forces of reaction and of chaos, the eldest of the surviving nobles addresses the victorious warrior-idealist Sigismund:

The threat of our times was fearsome without bounds, but still more fearsome was the discord which tore our hearts asunder. Force and the law, these twain pillars of the world, in monstrous conflict before our very eyes! Son against father, ruler against ruler, violence against violence like fire against water—but there came yet a third, as when on the day of judgment the earth opens up and engulfs fire and water: along with the fools and evil-doers, the heretics and fanatics,...Asia itself broke in across our frontiers and tried to be overlord in our house as in the terrible days of our fathers. And then, terrible above the chaos, the standard of the sundered chains was raised by one mighty hand—and to us with heads bowed low in defeat it sounded like the scourge of God. How could we recognize in this hand the hand of our anointed king?

And Sigismund replies:

It was he. It is he. Here am I—your king given to you by strength and necessity.[1]

A similarity between this episode and the conclusion of the essay on Prince Eugene is fairly clear. In both there is in the prose itself a compelling rhythmic quality designedly broken here and there to emphasize an important idea or a name: 'Asia', 'tried to be overlord', 'the hand of our sanctified king', 'this one figure Eugene', 'one man can....'.[2] A parallelism of situation is likewise apparent. It would of course be absurd to equate the figure of Eugene in its 'mythical' proportions with the poetic vision of idealism which is Sigismund. This character is in any case discussed in detail in chapters 7 and 8. It is very probable, however, that when creating Sigismund, the embodiment of so much of his own aspiration and idealism, Hofmannsthal recalled the figure of Eugene. Eugene was for the artist who summoned up both his spirit and his form the perfect preceptor. Deeds and vision, a practical and skilled hand moving at the behest of an idealistic mind: this was Eugene.

But his was not the only face of Austria. It was natural that in his quest to define Austria and her mission Hofmannsthal should turn to one who was also a creator and a practical visionary, but who was at the same time in a very particular sense the mother of her people.

In 1917, on the two hundredth anniversary of her birth, Hofmannsthal published an essay on the Empress Maria Theresia.

The term *Landesvater* has many connotations.[3] In the German-speaking lands it has a long history. The tradition of regional particularism and patriotism lingered more strongly in Germany than elsewhere in Europe. It is probably for this reason that its associations are more varied there than in any other country. The concept of a *Landesvater* seems to appeal more in lands where a parliamentary tradition of representative government is absent than in a country where self-government in one form or another has been long established. It is significant, for example, that there is no single English expression which conveys truly the sense of *Landesvater*. Fully developed political consciousness and paternalism are mutually inimical. Generalizations here may be dangerous but it is probably true to say that the Napoleonic cult of 'mon empereur' owed a good deal to the traditions of a people bred in the atmosphere of absolute monarchy. The esteem enjoyed by Frederick the Great or Bismarck amongst the common people is unthinkable without reference to the structure of Prussia.

These considerations may help to clear the ground for the last of Hofmannsthal's three Austrian preceptors and to allay any instinctive hostility which might be felt towards the lauding and idealization of a great ruler, in this case, as claimed above, the mother of her people, the Empress Maria Theresia.[1] An Austrian was in any case (until 1918) born into a larger atmosphere than a German. His empire, in extent, variety, and in seemingly automatic permanence, could give him a self-assurance which his less secure, less established neighbour in the new, even *parvenu*, German empire could not attain. For an Austrian the kind of *Landesvater* pilloried by Heine[2] was much less a possibility than for the subjects of, for example, Schiller's duke or any of the thirty-six monarchs in whose care Germany 'slept so peacefully' prior to 1871.

Austrian paternalism, at any rate in the German-speaking territories and in Bohemia, was thus by tradition on a large, literally imperial scale. In this sole respect the appeal of Maria Theresia may be compared to that of Elizabeth of England. Maria Theresia differed, however, from most great queens and empresses in that her gentle, womanly qualities were one with her qualities as a ruler. Hofmannsthal emphasizes this in drawing a sharp distinction between her on the one hand and Elizabeth of England and Catherine the Great on the other.[1]

Hofmannsthal chose the two-hundredth anniversary of Maria Theresia's birth to recall a great age in Austrian history and thus to give inspiration to compatriots in the thick of war. Beyond this, however, he exposed those human qualities in a ruler, those qualities of naturalness, kindliness, understanding, without which the pomp and imperial dignity are hollow. As he did so he put forward an ideal of kingly conduct. This was in 1917. In his words on the achievement and character of Maria Theresia the voice of the conservative revolutionary can be heard, rejecting and condemning without fear, but conserving and modifying; developing towards an ideal, but refusing to cut the roots from which Austria has grown. In this respect a remark of Carl Burckhardt is interesting:

But he was very familiar with the political sense of the English, their spacious way of seeing things, their trust in their own sure instinct, their natural, untheoretical way of thinking, untrammelled by any logical method, . . . the tremendous force exerted by the basic Norman strain in the nation.[2]

Hofmannsthal wrote of Maria Theresia that she

possessed that truly Janus-like countenance common to all great and good princes who with their one pair of eyes hold the past firm while with the other they seem to look into the future. She may take the credit for having softened as far as possible—by constant and untiring application of her regal power—the discrepancies between politics and justice, between given circumstances and necessary changes. Her maxim seems simple enough: she took pains to ensure that everything remained fluid and could be solved by a simple, peaceful and just solution. But one must be familiar with the difficulties of political affairs in general and with the particular nature of the lands under her rule in order to realize what it means really to carry out such a maxim throughout a reign of forty years—and, moreover, in the midst of continual war and with the personal burden of numerous pregnancies. . . .

If one considers the sum total of her various measures and laws, by means of which she reformed her states from top to bottom—and in a quiet, unspectacular way—then her achievement is seen to be enormous.[3]

It is interesting to note here how Hofmannsthal again modifies his earlier habit of reinterpreting or seeking solace in the past. In this present case he uses this technique in order to stress the conserving and yet reforming character of the empress—keenly aware of the past, its virtues as well as its shortcomings, but intent on reform and progress as need arises. The Janus image, symbol of the new year with its hopes and also its memories, is of course of Roman origin and was perhaps particularly appropriate for Hofmannsthal's depiction of the Holy Roman Empress at the outset of her reign.

Two phrases in the closing sentence of the above extract are also very characteristic of the mature Hofmannsthal. These are 'from top to bottom' and 'in a quiet unostentatious way'. It is worth noting that in the middle of a life-and-death struggle, where on all sides nationalism knew no bounds and where violent schemes of wholesale revolution and plans for the destruction of states were becoming increasingly clear, a writer of national renown could point to reform and change 'in a quiet unostentatious way'. He emphasized too how Maria Theresia's reforms were designed to affect all classes. In describing the scarcely credible variety of Maria Theresia's reforming activity, Hofmannsthal stressed her unity with the people, her sense of reason and naturalness, how 'in the very smallest measure one sees the same spirit of reason and...complete naturalness, which are on a vast scale the essential foundations of her system'.[1]

There was in fact a certain symbolic aspect to Hofmannsthal's choice of Maria Theresia as a preceptor and living inspiration. Along with her personal qualities she was also the last of the Habsburg line in Austria which was founded by Rudolf I on his election as German king in 1274. With Maria Theresia the great line of kings and emperors died—and was reborn: from her union with Francis I, who was duke of Lorraine, there sprang the modern line of Habsburg rulers, the house of Habsburg-Lorraine (Lothringen). There was therefore in the figure of the empress the double and hopeful symbolism of death and rebirth, such as that which Hofmannsthal so longed for in the Austria of his own day.

This is reflected in an unusual way in the essay: Maria Theresia was the mother of sixteen children. This fact was brought into close connection with her character as ruler. The idea was subtle. The execution offered horrifying possibilities of sentimentality or tastelessness. Hofmannsthal's method was bold and straightforward with the minimum of peripheral comment. He contrived to bring motherhood and imperium together in one life-giving idea. At the beginning of his attempt to convey this particular notion Hofmannsthal cited some words of Jakob Burckhardt which are in themselves a pointer towards the theme of a conservative revolution: 'Great individuals come about when progressiveness and a certain quality of obstinacy coincide in the same person.'[1] This antithesis was the fundament of Maria Theresia's life:

At the beginning of her reign there was a great and dangerous crisis.... At the same time she was about to become a mother. The coinciding of these two situations,...to have to assert herself as a representative figure and, as a woman, to give life to a child—this intermingling is Maria Theresia's signature. She had to deal with crises again and again and she defied them simply by getting through a tremendous amount of constructive work. The calmer moments, which a weaker spirit would have waited for, never came or if they did they were only very short. And she gave birth to sixteen children....Both duties she accepted willingly....She prayed that God would open her eyes for political affairs. But she was praying only for the development of what to an incomparable degree was already born in her. With this prayer on her lips she set about making her German and Bohemian lands into a living unity....She carried over into those territories entrusted to her...her ability to breathe life into a body....There is indeed a complete analogy between her relationship to her children and to her lands. Her letters as ruler and as mother are scarcely distinguishable in tone: there is in both the same measure of untiring solicitude, in both there is the same particular mixture of authority and delicacy of feeling. She had respect for living things.[2]...This respect is part of her wonderful, all-pervading piety.[3]

This depiction, especially in the two final sentences, shows clearly the fusion in Hofmannsthal of intellectual perception and warm human feelings. This personal warmth—the sense that his subject mattered personally, even deeply, to him—together with his reflective, objective intellect made up the characteristic tone of his work in these later years.

From the characterization of Maria Theresia as woman and as ruler Hofmannsthal went on to a description of her actual achievements, but he phrased it in such a way that it was also a rough draft for the urgently needed conservative revolution of his own times:

There have never been reforms like these anywhere else; never carried out with this combination of strength and great perception on the one hand, allied with delicacy of feeling and forbearance on the other. Political administration, the civil and criminal code, . . . the relationship between church and state—all these had to be newly thought out from the beginning.[1]

From these hints of detail Hofmannsthal proceeded to the key phrase, the watchword of the liberal-conservative and apostle of *Ausgleich*:

All that was rigid, individualistic, limited, out of date, had to be raised on to a new and higher plane of existence . . . Maria Theresia's historical greatness is to be found here. The great ideas of the time, the ideas of nature and order, were both embodied in her.[2]

To stress his point Hofmannsthal made an implicit comparison between Maria Theresia and her son, the unhappy Freemason Joseph II. Joseph was a revolutionary, a man of fine intellect and great vision. But he was a theorist who tended to leave the personal element out of his considerations. His was a thoroughness which could cripple or stultify. It may well be that Maria Theresia, in her union of 'nature and order', was more constructive, more revolutionary in the literal sense:

That signified more than if she—like her son—had grasped these ideas only with her intellect. She had the character of a great ruler. That is something more than—and quite different from—a great will, no matter how pure, and a great intellect, no matter how high it may soar.[3]

Hofmannsthal described and interpreted the death of Maria Theresia with moving reticence. It is an essentially matter-of-fact account. Hofmannsthal had in his youth been fascinated by the death symbol. This is not the place to expatiate on that particularly dark side of German Romanticism which Thomas Mann, speaking of himself, referred to as *Todesvernarrtheit*. The national-political implications of the Romantic death cult are as well known as they are controversial. Clemenceau, his perceptions sharpened by hatred, said that it was a cultural threat without parallel. The fateful effects of such a work as Ernst Jünger's *In Stahlgewittern* need little more than a bare mention. Hofmannsthal's account of the death of a heroine who died in a truly heroic manner was a quietly effective counterblast to the irrational cult of *Heldentod fürs Vaterland* and mystic worship of great national leaders. In her death Maria Theresia was simple, rational, clearsighted and Christian:

The accounts of the days and hours before her death tell of her great composure and strength of soul. She is said to have asked that she be kept awake; for she did not want to be taken by surprise—she wanted to see death approaching. She died . . . fully conscious, her mind quite unclouded. . . . Meanwhile she is said to have reflected and to have spoken the following words in which the union in her of complete Christian and great secular monarch is revealed with greatest simplicity: 'I have worked all the time so as to be able to die like this, but I was afraid I wouldn't manage it. Now I can see that with the grace of God you can do anything.'[1]

As was his custom in these historical studies of his chosen Austrian preceptors, Hofmannsthal attempted in the final phase of this essay to sum up not only Maria Theresia's character and significance for her age but also to connect her as a living force with the Austria of his own day.

It should perhaps be stressed at this point that Hofmannsthal was not in any accepted sense an historian. In this connection a very terse note dated 'X. 27' in *Ad me ipsum* is of some interest in relation to Hofmannsthal's attitude to living history and to the creation of a live mythology:[2]

A minimum of verbal memory.
History-myth Bachofen.
Feeling for places: Attempt to encompass. Symbolic attitude.
Spanning great and distant epochs of time.
Buckle–Gibbon.—Rome's succession alive in Austria (Riegl, Wick-
hoff).[1]

It was, indeed, this preoccupation with historical analogy that
caused Rudolf Kassner, a lifelong friend, to criticize him quite
sharply:

Just as to my mind his preoccupation with history, which began in
boyhood and lasted right through his life, . . . led him astray much too
easily into seeing all sorts of analogies with present-day circumstances,
relationships. . . . He was therefore always ready with a comparison.[2]

There is certainly justification enough for this criticism which is,
in effect, a variation on a fairly common criticism of Hofmannsthal—criticism, namely, of his penchant for *Bezüge*. It is difficult
to generalize in this matter, however, if only because Hofmannsthal did not pursue this historical aspect of his talent beyond the
essay or short study—beyond, that is to say, what could be
regarded as suggestive introductions to a full-scale work. There
was, moreover, a seer-like quality in these historical summaries.
Hofmannsthal brought to them his feeling for the liquid frontiers
of past history and present experience, of time remembered and
time present. As a young man, it will be recalled, he wrote the
famous lyric *Manche freilich*. . . . The fourth stanza has often been
used to illustrate the life-weariness of the young poet, the oppres-
sive, crushing burden of the past on his shoulders:

> Ganz vergessener Völker Müdigkeiten
> Kann ich nicht abtun von meinen Lidern,
> Noch weghalten von der erschrockenen Seele
> Stummes Niederfallen ferner Sterne.

The fifth and closing stanza tells of the past deeds and thoughts,
the blood of ancient races living on unseen in present-day man:

Viele Geschicke weben neben dem meinen,
Durcheinander spielt sie alle das Dasein,
Und mein Teil ist mehr als dieses Lebens
Schlanke Flamme oder schmale Leier.

In the conclusion to the essay on Maria Theresia these visionary ideas, uncanny and even frightening, were modified and brought together into the realm of practical wisdom:

When she closed her eyes in death Frederick the Great wrote to his minister: 'Maria Theresia is no more and therewith a new order of things begins.' It is the order of things which began with her and still lives on today which is of supreme importance to us. She is...an immortal educator. What we call Josephinism is...easier to define, but Theresianism is stronger...by far. She embodied the essence of Austria's social character, and this has remained decisive for all that has come after her.[1]

At this point in the conclusion Hofmannsthal introduced the polarity of Austria and Prussia into his theme. This was, as noted on pp. 89 and 91–2, one way of realizing his implicit aim of defining Austrianism as a vital component in the German heritage. He was on occasion quite forthright in his exposition of this polarity, as for example in the schema *Preuße und Öster-reicher* (1917).[2] In this, however, he was always careful to discriminate between his own national (Austrian) political allegiances on the one side and, on the other, his awareness of cultural and historical relationship in a common ancestry. In the essay on Maria Theresia the distinction was made quite clearly, and by implication distinctly to Austria's advantage:

If the kings of Prussia sharply defined the concept of the estates, divided according to rank, way of life and function in the state, Maria Theresia, on the other hand, had a great and naïve conception of the people, to which we owe an infinite amount, because it is intuitive and therefore inexhaustible. What powers she believed in—or did not believe in—is a question which will not be found in any catechism and yet it has been treasured unspoken by generation after generation: how she scarcely distinguished between justice and propriety, and between propriety and what was natural—so natural was her moral sense...completely without vainglory or longing for recognition; how she never tried to curry favour—neither the favour of the people nor that of history;...her mistrust of theoretical concepts and her trust in human beings—all this has passed into the blood of succeeding generations. Her glory lies rather in those she moulded than in words. If a special light hovers over our national life—which the Germans feel when they come from their world into ours—then this is her doing, and in a way more intangible than can ever be detailed by the pen of the historian.[1]

And in the final paragraph the historical perspective widens still further to span the Roman Imperium to which Hofmannsthal looked again and again as the ancestor of the Holy Roman Empire of the German Nation and thus of his own Austria. And so his gaze took in the chief architect of that distant yet ever present empire, Caesar Augustus. He characterized the emperor in a terse phrase which was his watchword for all true rulers: 'A master-builder of the living spirit.'[2]

Thus imperial Rome, Empress Maria Theresia and her realm fall into vast perspective with the Habsburg empire in the last year of its existence, which fact, although of course unknown to Hofmannsthal in 1917, he was nevertheless endeavouring to prevent from becoming reality:

Looking along the ranks of the great figures in history one would place her near Augustus who, like her, does not owe his fame to war and who, like her, was a master-builder of the living spirit. Admittedly she was an Augustus without a Virgil or a Livy. Nevertheless her rule did not remain without voice. Wherever abundance is gathered together its inner richness must find expression. The Theresian system was full of courage in achieving natural order and it was full of dedication to God. It was close to nature and when it was proud its pride was genuine with nothing of hardness or stiffness about it. Haydn, Gluck and Mozart are its content translated into immortal spiritual form.[3]

The evocation of Maria Theresia was neither the longest nor the most important of Hofmannsthal's wartime essays. But in its depiction of a sovereign who was patriotic in the true sense, who ruled her polyglot territories with tolerance, humanity and essential humility, it can be seen as an early but integral part of a campaign.

Hofmannsthal's idea of postulating a *raison d'être* for Austria was certainly part of this campaign. This chapter has tried to show how he tried at the personal level, as it were—through the medium of great individual, national figures—to justify Austria in her own eyes. The chapter which now follows deals with some of those works of a more general nature which had the same object. Hofmannsthal's campaign, however, aimed ultimately at the realization of a morally rejuvenated and united Europe in which, for example, the practical and conciliating qualities in Maria Theresia's achievement could serve an entire continent. The two *Festspiele* which are the subject of the later part of this study are advanced and vitally important stages in the campaign: the *Große Welttheater* primarily in its depiction of society's way to reform, and *Der Turm* in its depiction of the problem of the state. Seen from this point of view the essay on Maria Theresia, as also the other two historical studies discussed in this chapter, fall into their rightful place and perspective.

CHAPTER 4

THREE CULTURAL-POLITICAL STUDIES

THE historical portraits discussed in chapter 3 were essays in creative interpretation. No less noteworthy, though necessarily more general, were two essays of similar intent: *Österreichische Bibliothek* (1915)[1] and *Österreich im Spiegel seiner Dichtung* (1916).[2]

In 1915 Hofmannsthal undertook the editorship of a new project for the Insel-Verlag.[3] This was designed to be a series of books by various hands and from many epochs. It was to cover a wide range of subject-matter. All books included were, however, to have one thing in common. Each volume, and in all there were twenty-six, was to bear witness to some glorious aspect, physical or intellectual, of the Austrian empire's mission and achievement. Hofmannsthal was constantly depressed—and then stimulated to action—by the sense of Austria's seeming ignorance of her latent spiritual power and mission. He regarded this ignorance as an almost traditional deficiency in Austria. In the *Österreichische Bibliothek*[4] he saw the possibility of stating the defect and of making a modest contribution towards its elimination.

While preparing the series he lighted upon one of those examples of historical continuity and repetition that excited and stimulated him. He discovered that a hundred years earlier, when resurgent Austria was gathering her forces to hurl them against Napoleon, a great predecessor had shown him the way. In 1809 Count Philipp Stadion had founded his *Vaterländische Blätter* in order to achieve 'closer human contact between the provinces of the monarchy as well as collaboration of those many men who, separated from each other by great distances, are working for the public good'.[5]

Stadion further expressed the hope, Hofmannsthal added, that foreign countries, especially German-speaking states, could be brought by this journal to a higher conception of Austria. Hofmannsthal lamented that Austria's memory for essentials was so short:

Austria's memory should not be so short that at every turn in her history she loses sight of those who in earlier generations desired and achieved great things for her,...and not so...ignorant of herself.[1]

This historical ebb and flow fascinated Hofmannsthal and he characterized it in a typical sentence. Again and again he demonstrated this ability to catch and hold a visionary idea— especially one containing the time element—in prose where his sprung rhythms, concealed and half-concealed alliterations, give an effect of space and of the inevitable:[2]

Aber es muß ja im Bereich des Lebenden alles immer wieder aufs neue getan werden, Geschlechter gehen in Halbheit hin, und dann muß eines wieder seine ganze Kraft auf den gleichen Punkt richten wie die Urahnen.

(But in the realm of living things everything must always be done again: generations pass away in only dim awareness of things, and then the time comes when some new generation has to apply its entire strength at the same point where its ancestors began.)

The interpenetration of past and present, a highly sentient awareness of oneself and of the ancestral generations from which one is sprung, awareness of and participation in one's environment—social, cultural, physical—these are familiar themes in Hofmannsthal. An *Österreichische Bibliothek* was to call these things before a generation which had forgotten them:

It is as if each part of our empire deliberately tried to forget that its destiny is to be a part...in these phases between our great historical moments our existence is all the poorer and the real stream of life ebbs away...[our way of life]...which should know about itself and should stretch its roots back into the...past while at the same time asserting its place in the present. Only, however, in our hours of destiny are we imbued with a...feeling for our present and with a sense of our mighty past, and the knowledge that they are one. Only at these fateful moments do we have that belief in ourselves which alone guarantees human dignity. Again and again these things have to be bought back again with our life-blood.[1]

In this essay there emerge, along with the Austrian ideal, the beginnings of the European ideal which, steadily clarified during the war, became the dominant idea of Hofmannsthal's last years. He noted other federations, other multilingual communities, and then defined Austria's mission. As might be expected, he did this in a manner which opened up to the reader the entire sweep of time and history since Marcus Aurelius was in Carnuntum and Vindobona and since Charlemagne united Europe under the sceptre of the Emperor of the Romans:

The blood of the Swiss flows freely through their veins and in their past as in their present they heed what they have in common although they speak different languages. It is the same in the great American state where one people has been formed out of many peoples and these men of many strains all love one and the same soil and happily acknowledge a constitution which is scarcely a century old. Our destiny is harder, our mission different: our inheritance is ancient European soil and on it we are the heirs of two Roman empires. This has been laid upon us and we must bear it whether we want to or not.[2]

For many years criticism's reflex reaction to Hofmannsthal was in many cases the vision of a youthful prince of aesthetes. It is therefore particularly interesting to read what the ageing Hofmannsthal postulated as the ideal 'Austrian library'. He longed to cut through the surface layer of urban culture, professional intellectualism, self-conscious criticism and commentary. There was probably a good deal of self-admonition in his mind when he wrote:

We should aim at collecting in this series not what an individual great figure may have said about certain things and their relationship to one another. Rather should we try to assemble those real expressions of life which seep out naturally in so many places like resin from the incision in a tree.[3]

And Hofmannsthal suggested in a few words these 'many places' which, drawn together and seen *sub specie aeternitatis*, make up a unique web and tissue of life. How, after all, can a country or its inhabitants be characterized? The popular idea of a 'typical' German, Austrian or Frenchman, or of something 'typically' this or that, is fortunate if it contains a quarter-truth. Hofmannsthal saw the dense and sometimes formless mass of contradiction and variation which can yet make up an harmonious whole:

Innumerable and unconscious forces work in the twilight making up the richness of our lives. We could speak about all of them but it is better that they speak for themselves. In the same way it is the unspoken word which is often the most precious thing in human relations and especially where Austrians are concerned—and what is said is not always the best.... The inmost being of a people speaks forth in its customs and sayings, its everyday expressions, and its venerable forms at times of solemn joy and in the hour of death.[1]

One notes here a close connection in mood and subject-matter with Hofmannsthal's most consciously Austrian creation, Hans Karl Bühl in *Der Schwierige* (1918, published 1920), the character and drama in which Hofmannsthal tried to capture the essential mood and spirit of a most characteristic section of Austrian society, the Viennese city aristocracy, at a moment when, as Hofmannsthal realized, it was breaking up and about to disappear for ever. As one reads in the above passage 'it is the unspoken word which is often the most precious thing in human relations and especially where Austrians are concerned—and what is said is not always the best', one recalls Hans Karl's words:

Of course you can't understand me. I understand myself a lot less when I speak than when I keep quiet. I can't even try to explain to you, it's just something that I learned at the front: that there's something written on people's faces.[2]

One also recalls here Hofmannsthal's schema *Preuße und Österreicher* (1917)[3] in which the Austrian individual (*der Einzelne*) is described *inter alia* as 'apparently unable to voice his inner self...prefers to have things left unclear'.

It is fairly clear from these various references that Hofmannsthal believed in and attached great significance to the natural decency and instinctive culture of his countrymen—a decency all the more admirable (or so Hofmannsthal seems to suggest) for its being unaware of itself and unable or unwilling to express itself coherently. Where, however, *Der Schwierige* expresses such views through one section of society, the *Österreichische Bibliothek* essay ranges from the most exalted of the captains and the kings to the salt workers and wood carriers, in attempting to depict an ideal Austria and thus an ideal 'Austrian library'. At the same time Hofmannsthal conjured up an evocation of his land at all times through the ages:

the mountain would have to speak and the water and the forest, the ores of Styria and the salt at Hallstatt and the glass of Bohemia: the Carpathian huntsman[1] would have to speak and the Tyrolean marksman in his mountains watching for the eagle.... The voice of olden times must be heard, as in the old town chronicles such as St Pölten or Steyr or old Hagecius' chronicle of Bohemia, and a single, delicate voice such as that of Marianne Willemer must not be left out.... Here too we must have one of those family or house chronicles such as was recorded by the head of a family in bygone centuries—this alongside the wisdom of half-forgotten but great men: the magicianly spirit of Theophrastus Paracelsus must glow forth again here and the spiritual wisdom of Amos Comenius must cast its gentle light. Reports of the early travels of our missionaries and holy men should be mingled with the bloody and glorious deeds of our armies. Here old tales of commerce and trade...should stand alongside an array of glorious regimental histories; Raimund and Nestroy alongside Abraham a Sancta Clara; the spiritual heritage of Nicholas Cusanus, Abbot of Brixen, alongside the diaries of Feuchtersleben.... Here the pure, pious voices of the Bohemian and Moravian Brethren must sound forth, and there will be no discordant note if at their side the pure, stern soul of a Habsburg prince speaks out from the autobiography of Archduke Charles.[2]

The word 'evocation' was used above to describe this passage. This was done quite designedly. The passage is neither a portrait nor a description in the customary sense. It is really a conjuring up of a 'mythical' landscape (perhaps *Märchenlandschaft* best conveys the idea)—an idealized mood-picture in which all time past and present, human being and natural environment are seen as existing for the inward eye at one and the same time. Hermann Broch seemed to suggest this line of approach when he wrote:

In their totality these essays describe a vast ellipse of landscape which, rich in heroic culture and heroic nature, stretching from northern Italy to southern Bohemia and encompassing the Austrian Alps, has its focuses in Venice and Vienna. It represents the mirror for Hofmannsthal's Austrian-ness (or more correctly, his Old Austrian-ness); although this seems at first sight to be a purely geographical localization, it takes little to discover that the history-bound attachment to the native land is here but the starting point for something more essential. For, deeply involved in Austrian culture...contributing to it, taking a share in its preservation, Hofmannsthal experienced unceasingly the anonymity of culture-forming factors, the anonymity of the folk-song, ...of the many builders who had helped shape the landscape; and the more absorbed he became in this development the more did this unfolding of culture appear to him as a natural process.... The artificial flows into the natural, but this in turn into the artificial.... The planes of reality cut across one another, leaving man to wander between everchanging dream-like settings which, derived from an anonymous somewhere, have nevertheless been erected by himself. He wanders, stripped of his 'I', yet recognizing it everywhere: man's reality lies in the anonymous, and whatever he creates becomes real only when he, like the folk-artist, has plunged into anonymity, returned to nature.... The native land, the native city, the native landscape were the everpresent elements of Hofmannsthal's sentiments.[1]

In holding up the mirror thus to this 'mythical' landscape Hofmannsthal wanted to hold up a mirror to the face of the nation and to make it aware of its own reality. His attempts, as he realized and admitted, were insignificant; 'the sympathy of my contemporaries is everything'.[2]

The essay *Österreich im Spiegel seiner Dichtung* (1916)[3] had as its object, in common with *Österreichische Bibliothek*, the depiction of Austria's true being. In the case of the *Österreichische Bibliothek* essay this was treated as a family matter, that is to say, it was designed for Austrians and, as Hofmannsthal said, for those who loved Austria. *Österreich im Spiegel seiner Dichtung* is rather more polemical in intent and strongly emphasizes a *leitmotif* of the ageing Hofmannsthal, already briefly encountered in the previous chapter. This is the specific Austrianism of his homeland and people within the supra-national German-speaking area. In other words Hofmannsthal wished to express the polarity of Prussia (and Prussianism, which reached beyond state borders) and Austria. He did not want to separate 'Austrianism' from 'Germanism' as a separate idea. He wished to establish Austrianism as an essential part, perhaps the most essential part, in the German heritage. Since 1871 the authoritarian power state constructed by Bismarck and imposed by him on all other German states, to the exclusion (already in 1866) of Austria, had come to be accepted more and more as the genuine and only voice of Germany and of Germanism. Hofmannsthal regarded this as a deception and a danger.

As long ago as 1907 in *Die Briefe des Zurückgekehrten* Hofmannsthal had depicted in quietly terrifying terms the essentially *brüchig* quality in the new German empire—the brittle façade and its strangely ghost-like, shifting, even shifty interior:

for in actual fact nothing that they do really speaks for their whole character; their right hand truly does not know what their left hand is doing; what they think in their heads does not correspond to what their hearts say, . . . the façade does not correspond to the back stairs . . . nor their public affairs to their private lives. That is why I am telling you that I cannot find them anywhere, neither in their gestures nor in their actual speech; because their whole being is not in any one of these things . . . .[1]

In the present essay Hofmannsthal was determined to establish Austria's inalienable rights as part-bearer of the German heritage. He realized the dangers in this and the probable misunderstandings which would arise. He was careful to define his position quite clearly:

We must know how to preserve this dualism of feeling—our allegiance to Austria and our cultural allegiance to Germania—in the midst of this critical...cultural and political situation in which we find ourselves. I see no danger here for the German spirit—in which we have a part—is, in its great richness...based on dualism.[1]

Hofmannsthal seems to have been well aware of the ever-present danger in such a topic of falling into comprehensive concept and generalizing slogan. His remark on this danger has—after two propaganda-bedevilled wars—a pointed significance. In the same paragraph he observed:

It is not a matter of ideas and concepts becoming ever more simple and manageable but rather that they should contain within themselves as much as possible of the actual quality of a community's life.

And what was the Austrian part in the German heritage? In Hofmannsthal's view it was at least of equal standing with that of any other. This is revealed in his rapid and factual, yet picturesque, summary. Characteristically he saw things within a framework of tradition and as an achievement in the round: the deeds of the conquerors were, as in the case of Prince Eugene (see chapter 3), set alongside and seen as one with the works of culture, trade and law. The note of proud imperialism and of unselfconscious superiority was mingled with that of humility in the face of a high ideal. The *Reich* German claim and the Austrian share were at the same time effectively differentiated:

That German spirit which once conquered the world, which prevailed in both east and west, which sent across the Lower Rhine and the Oder and down the Danube its master-builders, its merchants and scholars, its races of peasants which have lasted through centuries; this spirit which carried on commerce and education, which brought enlightenment and prosperity, which colonized without conquering, led without governing; which brought with it the values and the methods of the German peasantry, German civic law, German cathedrals...where has this spirit been preserved if not in us?[2]

There was again an echo of *Die Briefe des Zurückgekehrten* as Hofmannsthal posed the question which in reality pointed to the contradiction between Austria and Prussia, to the fundamental difference between them:

Where is this old form of the German spirit—revealed in the German *Reich* but never fully realized—where is it reflected if not in us?... The fact that we exist and the way we exist, what we can claim for ourselves and what we have to achieve as we stand here amongst polyglot peoples—and what we owe to these peoples for the sake of bygone centuries and because of the superior place amongst them which we assert in fulfilment of our mission here: all that is an historical and holy German heritage.[1]

The florid tone of the closing sentence is markedly rhetorical and the passage itself is more than tinged with tendentiousness. These qualities could be explained by the occasion for which the essay was written. In the *Anmerkung* to *Prosa*, III[2] we are told that the essay was published in a version based on the shorthand text ('erschien nach dem Stenogramm'). The bibliography in the same volume records that the essay appeared in *Die Presse* in 1916 and in *Rodauner Nachträge* in 1919.[3]

The note on the shorthand version leads one to conclude that *Österreich im Spiegel seiner Dichtung* was written as a speech, and in addition to the rhetorical tone of various parts of the essay there are other indications that this was so. An investigation confirms such a claim, and together with the actual occasion on which this speech was delivered throws interesting light on Hofmannsthal's development.

The most obvious proof that *Österreich im Spiegel seiner Dichtung* was indeed a speech is in Hofmannsthal's enigmatic reference, 'here in this very place of learning where I am now speaking'.[4] In the following line he noted how 'an eloquent man' had from the same platform 'often' treated the concept of *Mitteleuropa*. It is virtually certain that this 'eloquent man' was Friedrich Naumann.[5] In the opening paragraph of *Hugo von Hofmannsthal: Eine Rede* Theodor Heuss refers to a letter of Hofmannsthal addressed to Naumann:

while looking through the posthumous papers of Friedrich Naumann I came across a long letter from Vienna—I think it had been written in 1916. In this letter the writer expressed eloquent thanks for Nau-mann's evaluation of the Austrian spirit and of Austrian history in his book *Mitteleuropa*. I was not unmoved when I read the signature: Hugo von Hofmannsthal.[1]

Heuss draws attention, moreover, to an enigmatic note in Hofmannsthal's correspondence with Bodenhausen: 'Today I have an appointment with Naumann.'[2] It is clear from Josef Redlich's diary that Naumann was in Vienna on various occasions during the war[3] and that his concept of *Mitteleuropa* was the subject of a public address in the Hochschullehrer-Verein on 6 November 1915.[4] Redlich's diary also provides the necessary information about the occasion for which *Österreich im Spiegel seiner Dichtung* was written. His diary for 21 October 1916 reads:

I decided to miss Hofmannsthal's lecture in the *Urania* this evening. I did not feel up to listening to talk about 'Austria mirrored in its poetry'. I am afraid that is not the right mirror.[5]

That the milieu for the speech was the *Volksbildungsverein Urania* is interesting and rather significant. The *Urania* has its central hall and headquarters near the centre of Vienna (at the south-eastern junction of the Ringstraße and Donaukanal) and has branches in many Viennese suburbs. Founded several years before World War I it was (and still is) an attempt at high-level adult education on a considerable scale. That the one-time aesthete should write one of his most important wartime works for such an institution speaks eloquently of his development.[6]

This detour leads thus to an understanding of Hofmannsthal's mind and outlook at this point in his career and of the probable influences involved. The somewhat tendentious and imperialistic note observed is the more understandable when the occasion and the time are recalled. It might in any case be worth noting that for Hofmannsthal, a citizen of the Habsburg empire, Austria's mission in eastern and south-eastern Europe was just as real, historically necessary and benevolent, as was for others the British mission in India (or Ireland, Malaya, Malta or Gibraltar). Or, to bring the matter on to ground nearer and more familiar to

Hofmannsthal, it was at least as genuine and disinterested as France's traditional drive to the Rhine and beyond, and her historical mission in Alsace.

Hofmannsthal spoke forcibly, however, against any facile or emotional interpretation of either the inheritance of Austria or her mission. Only with hesitation did he dare a definition: 'These things are not easy and simple.'[1] His words on simple-minded nationalism, from whatever quarter, are a salutary reminder to two generations, German and others, which have too often been prone to 'think in the blood':

They are not palpable and obvious like the chauvinism of Bucharest, and they are not as simple as the heightened national consciousness of the French. They are venerable and in order to recognize them for what they are one needs insight and piety, love for the destiny which has been laid upon us.[2]

The reproach and warning to the extrovert, egocentric nationalism in the Wilhelminian *Reich* was clear. Hofmannsthal's German ideal was scarcely recognizable in Bismarck's creation, still less in the Germany of Emperor William II:

And therefore the ultimate definition of this spiritual Austrianism is difficult to put into words: there is something reserved about it, and because of this trait of character it is very German.[3]

In the stigmatization of un-German methods Hofmannsthal's language took on an unwontedly harsh, metallic quality as he noted just those things which became more and more evident in the *Reich*:

Hard, shrill assertion, the arrogant attempt to define in clear, precise terms the frontiers of the venerable German spirit, to express in words what is German, to put a name to the genius of the German centuries present and future—this is un-German.[4]

In *Die Briefe des Zurückgekehrten* Hofmannsthal had noted in the *Reich* a moral uncertainty, a steady undermining of character best expressed by the almost untranslatable *brüchig* and *innerlich mürbe* (see p. 120). This was a telling observation which had practical confirmation after both wars. These sad qualities were doubtless a major factor in the bottomless misery, cynical hopelessness and distressing self-pity which beset the *Reich* in defeat, especially after the National Socialist collapse. Hofmannsthal seems to have been darkly conscious of these possibilities as he insistently stressed the *traditional* German reaction to good fortune and sorrow, attitudes which, he hoped and maintained, had been preserved in Austria:

The German spirit reveals itself through modesty in good fortune... and by...resilience in misfortune. The idea of persuading itself is repugnant to the German character.[1]

Twentieth-century Germany prior to 1945 was not taught 'modesty in good fortune'. Moderation was out of season. If Hofmannsthal's categories are reversed, then, as he feared, the actual truth is seen rather than his historical ideal.

Hofmannsthal's view of Austria's dual relationship to the *Reich* was a compound of dignity, generosity and self-awareness. The balanced expression is striking:

Our intellectual attitude to the German national state, from which we can accept a limitless amount and to which we have inestimable things to give, is clearly prescribed. It is an attitude which must not be lacking in dignity and beauty, an attitude derived from a feeling of equality and strengthened by the bands of familiarity. A delicate, purified feeling of self-reliance, far removed from any complacency, is its foundation.[2]

Hofmannsthal was a grand master of technique: it is almost trite to emphasize how every subtle turn and visionary effect submitted to his hand. But he was aware of the dangers of this gift and only rarely in his later years did he express himself in the 'grand manner' or in an unashamedly lyrical vein. When he did so the flow was carefully controlled. The closing sequence of the present essay is such an instance. It consists of one vast paragraph. In it Hofmannsthal praised his land and praised its famous men and women, but he knew that the pillars of society and the piers supporting the state were not as firm in his day as of old:

Our cultural heritage is sacred and we know its value. But for us it does not consist in venerable buildings and old institutions, nor in an ...aristocracy rich in glittering memories, nor in the diversity of our landscapes and the rich variety of their customs.[1]

This was Hofmannsthal's formulation of the time-honoured reproach, so often justified, which saw a mouldering Austrian empire living on the crumbling foundations of a nostalgically recalled and ever glorious past. Hofmannsthal added significantly: 'We want to define our cultural heritage in a deeper and more vital way.'[2] His definition was revealing. In his time the term *Kultur* and especially German *Kultur* had assumed certain unpleasant and even aggressively exclusive associations from which it is still not entirely free. In venturing on a definition of *Kultur* Hofmannsthal was thus on dangerous ground. He approached it, however, with the same determined clarity that characterized his discussion of the 'German character'. His conception of *Kultur* was wide, unaggressive, a kind of higher existence:

For us culture is not something dead and rounded off but something vital and alive. It is the interaction of life's activities and forces, of political and military things, it is the association of the material with the moral.[3]

This was the essence of liberal conservatism. The voice of the *Ausgleichpolitiker*[4] could be heard clearly as Hofmannsthal defined 'politics' and castigated the essentially unpolitical nature of Austrians under the later Habsburgs. This, he added, was not in accord with the deeds and heritage of Austria's greatest historical figures:

And because we here cannot easily talk about these things without a little criticism creeping in, we might mention a traditional Austrian error which has been perpetuated over several generations and which is so out of tune with the spirit of our greatest Austrian figures—the great Empress or Prince Eugene—the error, namely, of separating politics and administration, administration and culture.[5]

In the German nation of poets and thinkers, idealists, humanists and musicians, politics had often been regarded as something commonplace, even hypocritical and on the whole untouchable. Latterly, in Bismarck's time, they were often regarded as frankly treasonable. Hofmannsthal could thus not take 'politics' for granted. And so he paused and posed the rhetorical question: 'Politics! What is it exactly?'[1] Slogans and generalizations on politics were pushed aside:

What is politics if it is not reaching an understanding about where the things that matter are to be found—whether they are in the material of commerce and industry, or whether they are in the spiritual realms of faith, and belief in one's motherland?[2]

One notes here how Hofmannsthal developed a definition already foreshadowed in the Grillparzer essay (see pp. 89–90).

It is perhaps some measure of Hofmannsthal's wish to be clear-headed and realistic when it is realized that the above words presage comparable sentiments of Thomas Mann, voiced at a time when Mann, in his role of polemical *Kulturpolitiker*, was the centre of the most violent controversy of his career. In a broadcast talk (June 1947) Mann said *inter alia*:

Politics has been called the art of the possible and it actually is a realm akin to art in so far as, like art, it occupies a creatively mediating position between the spirit and life, the idea and reality, the desirable and the necessary, conscience and deed, morality and power.[3]

These ideas may be a commonplace for the Anglo-Saxon: we know how Hofmannsthal respected 'the political sense of the English, their spacious way of seeing things, their trust in their own sure instinct, their natural, untheoretical way of thinking, untrammelled by any logical method'.[4] But in the absolute monarchy of Francis Joseph I these ideas were no more obvious than they were in the Hohenzollern empire across the frontier. They were certainly not a commonplace in the mouth of a so-called conservative intellectual who was politically a layman and socially a patricianly *Bürger*.

From these considerations it was a short step to a definition of the real strength of the land which is in the common people. The aristocracy and the court were the façade, helpless and hopeless without the people behind and beneath them. Traditional class distinctions had in Hofmannsthal's time long outlived any historical *raison d'être* which originally called them into being. They had, to use a favourite phrase of Hofmannsthal, become 'rigid formulae' (*starre Formeln*). It was but one of the tragedies of the declining Austrian empire that these ludicrously exaggerated cleavages in society existed right through to the bitter end.

An entry in Redlich's diary dating from the same period as *Österreich im Spiegel seiner Dichtung* is typical of the attitude prevalent in liberal-conservative quarters. Redlich himself was, moreover, also an activistic *Ausgleichpolitiker*. On 26 November 1916, a few days after the death of Francis Joseph, he wrote:

Is it not strange that it is the chance outcome of physiological acts which determines in the last resort who is to be the maker of decisions and the bearer of ultimate responsibility? And is there any antique curiosity to be compared with the modern education prescribed for a future ruler? ...Has the entire course of world history from 1750 to 1900 really changed either things or people—here and in Berlin?[1]

The derogatory associations of 'the common people', 'the bourgeoisie', 'worker' and 'peasant' were sadly real in the Habsburg realm.[2] Thus, as suggested in the Introduction, when nationalism, socialism and personal individualism were rising on all sides, little was done even as a palliative, let alone as thorough reform. Many possibilities for true solidarity and communal strength as a nation were lost. Hofmannsthal spoke as much of lost chances as of still present possibilities when he said:

Perhaps the war has given us a pointer as to where the real values are. Reality is surely where the greatest, most absolute, most innate and purest strength is to be found. And that is in the people. That is what this war has made us understand.[3]

Hofmannsthal had in *Österreichische Bibliothek* already indicated his trust in the latent, unspoiled strength of the common people. In the above passage he stated it quite bluntly. He seems to have held this belief with particular conviction. It is apparent not only in such 'public' forms as these 'patriotic' essays but also in his private correspondence where, notably in his letters to Boden-hausen, he expressed himself with complete freedom. His letter of 31 May 1915, for example, illustrates this:

Italy's declaration of war has had a most unexpected effect in Austria: a tremendous surge of confidence...a great wave of enthusiasm through the entire people, such as I should scarcely have thought possible after ten months of war. The common people are simple and magnificent in their conception of things...whereas officialdom—the ministries and the authorities—is always petty and purposeless.[1]

But for Hofmannsthal this posed a very significant question: how was this vast and fresh potential to be used? *Österreich im Spiegel seiner Dichtung* appeared shortly before the death of the aged emperor whose reign had begun in the year of Liberal revolutions. It appeared a year before the October Revolution in Russia. Adolf Hitler's time had not yet come, but his fatal amalgam of cynical expediency, blood mysticism, and irrational appeal by simplification was brewing. 'The spirituality of the people', said Hofmannsthal, 'is a wonderful and clean tablet on which are written only a few...perceptions, which survive the centuries. In the tremendous experience of this war the people have engraved just a few new signs and symbols on this tablet.'[2]

With these considerations in mind it can be appreciated that extreme possibilities for good and evil were in Hofmannsthal's mind when he wrote: 'Great will be the responsibility of those who are intellectually mature enough to interpret these signs for the people.'[3] It is a sad fact that probably only the totalitarian demagogues of the twentieth century have realized and translated into reality the full truth of:

In the unsophisticated depths of existence in which the common people have their being, just as in those dark depths of the individual where there is only a vague and shifting frontier between spiritual and bodily things, you will find not reflection and perception but the wish and the belief.[4]

Hofmannsthal weighed thus the possibilities, and at this point it may be useful to look ahead for a moment to the creation of the work in which Hofmannsthal showed very clearly that he realized just how those 'unsophisticated depths of existence' and 'dark depths of the individual' were to be used by those who perceived and understood them. In *Der Turm* (1925 and, second version, 1927) he demonstrated, as shown in some detail in chapters 6, 7 and 8, on which fearsome side the balance was falling: one thinks especially of the dictator and rabble-rousing leader Olivier and his followers.

As Hofmannsthal wrote *Österreich im Spiegel seiner Dichtung* the future was still open, and as a climax to this urgently pursued study he advanced strenuously, even movingly, the concept of the Austrian Idea. The Austrian Idea, Hofmannsthal said, had to be revitalized; far-reaching reform and experiment would be necessary to make it work:

The Austrian Idea can only be comprehended if we desire and believe in it. And without the light of an ideal we cannot walk the path which now opens up before us. Many aspects of practical...radical... Austrianism will be necessary...and without a breath of spiritual universality no future Austria can be desired or believed in.[1]

Hofmannsthal looked ahead here to the idea which dominated his last years; to the idea of a universal Austria, of Europe as a greater Austria. The phrase (which is not Hofmannsthal's) is ambiguous and tendentious. By it one means, of course, not the attachment of Germany, France and the rest to a grand federation led by Austria; but Austria revitalized, *ausgeglichen* politically and socially, could be seen as a model on a fairly large scale for a European union. It would be extremely rash to suggest that this was in Hofmannsthal's mind at the conclusion of *Österreich im Spiegel seiner Dichtung*. This speech was nevertheless a stage on the road, a fact which becomes clearer in the light of a study of *Die Österreichische Idee*, which was published in 1917.

The Austrian Idea has been mentioned at various points in the preceding pages and before Hofmannsthal's essay of that title[2] is considered here, a brief digression is necessary. This is so because the ideas embodied in Hofmannsthal's essay were to a considerable extent not original and were indeed part of an historical and political approach to the problems of Austria which was to be seen in various of his contemporaries and immediate predecessors. Thus a brief account of these tendencies may assist in keeping Hofmannsthal's own contribution in true perspective. It may also suggest the political-historical atmosphere in which he was working.

According to Francis Ferdinand's plans the various territories in which each of these peoples form the traditional and permanent population were to be clearly demarcated.... The inhabitants of each territory would then enjoy full autonomy. Under the constitution their national freedoms would be limited only in so far as to enable everyone to market the fruits of his labour quite freely in all parts of the monarchy—and in like manner to obtain...all commodities with equal freedom. In this way every citizen of the United States of Greater Austria would enjoy *vis à vis* foreign countries those advantages which come from belonging to a...powerful, international, economic and customs union. No frontiers for trade and traffic between the individual and united states of Greater Austria...a unified railway system, unity *vis à vis* foreign countries, and—for this latter purpose—military unity![1]

The above passage summarizes some of the most important features of a draft prepared in April 1914 at the request of Archduke Francis Ferdinand by Baron J.-A. de Eichhoff of the Ministry of the Interior. The uncompleted draft was ultimately published in *Die Reichspost* (Vienna) on 28 March 1926 under the title *Die geplante Gründung der Vereinigten Staaten von Groß-österreich. Das vorbereitete Thronmanifest des Erzherzogs Franz Ferdinand. Ein tragisches geschichtliches Dokument.*[2]

It could scarcely be suggested that the heir-apparent to the imperial throne was either liberal by conviction or of a tolerant disposition. He was nevertheless a realist and, as the work of Franz and Kiszling shows, he had been keenly engaged for a decade or more prior to 1914 on plans for a reorganization of the monarchy and empire.[1] Ideas of *Ausgleich* and reform were keenly espoused by diverse groups in various parts of the imperial territories[2] and it was indeed not for nothing that the Archduke himself earned the name of *Slawenfreund* ('Friend of the Slavs').

Such ideas were therefore in the air, so to speak; and, as is often the way with political ideas of this kind, the war gave them greater impetus and urgency. This immediate background should be borne in mind when *Die Österreichische Idee* is considered.

The more distant perspective is, however, also of importance in placing Hofmannsthal in his correct position as part of a developing historical tradition. In some cases these ideas—as quite explicit statements—can be traced back to the middle of the nineteenth century, and any history of reform ideas in Austria would be vast and varied.

Such a history would have to include, to name but a few examples, extremes as great as that represented by Prince Schwarzenberg's *Groß-Österreich* plans and Karl Renner's *Das Selbstbestimmungsrecht der Nationen* (1918). It would have to include Aurel Popovici's *Die Vereinigten Staaten von Groß-Österreich* (1906) and Heinrich Lammasch's *Europas elfte Stunde* (1919).[3] Another great study in extremes would be offered by Crown Prince Rudolf's *Große Denkschrift über die innere und äußere politik Österreich-Ungarns* (1886)[4] and Otto Bauer's *Die Nationalitätenfrage und die Sozialdemokratie* (1907). Perhaps, in the present context, most important of all, it would have to include Ignaz Seipel's *Nation und Staat* (1916) and *Der Kampf um die österreichische Verfassung* (1930)—notably the first part, 'Verfassungsreformpläne im alten Österreich'.

As noted in connection with *Österreich im Spiegel seiner Dichtung*, Friedrich Naumann probably had some influence on Hofmannsthal. Naumann would inevitably have roused Hofmannsthal's enthusiasm when, for example, he referred to the central power in Austria in the following terms:

If Austria uses this favourable opportunity she can create anew and extend what Maria Theresia accomplished: national consciousness! Nothing will be of greater help to her than her participation in the common task of building *Mitteleuropa*.[1]...As long as the responsible representatives of the ruling house can think of nothing better than maintaining the *status quo* by small reforms they can scarcely hope to grip the imagination of youth....But as soon as they hoist the standard of a new age, then the capable spirits will crowd round their doors. Austria-Hungary possesses—in all her varied provinces—fine and capable talents, but hitherto there have been too few long-term tasks in the machinery of state to attract them....New enthusiasm for a new form of state is created through compulsion and necessity. It is in the hands of the crown to awaken these spirits with the watchword *Mitteleuropa*....It is in the hands of the crown to decide whether after this war there shall be spring or autumn.[2]

However, as Robert Kann remarked:

In all probability the empire would have become merely an annexe to Germany's world power. This power could have been sustained only by forceful repression of the national movements. This in turn would have led to a greater and continued dependence of the Austro-German nationalists on Germany....Unaffected by these internal shifts, German imperialism would have ruled supreme.[3]

It seems highly probable, in view both of Hofmannsthal's ambivalent attitude to Germany and of his own conscious Austrianism, that his own version of the Austrian Idea owed more to the idealism and practical wisdom of Lammasch[4] and Seipel. The following discussion, taken from the conclusion to Robert Kann's chapter 'Catholicism's National Philosophy', may help to confirm this opinion. The extract is very long, but in its comprehensiveness reveals a good deal of Hofmannsthal's cultural-political background. It accounts too, perhaps, for his apparent nostalgia for the years prior to 1848:

Seipel, though he was by no means blind to social and cultural issues connected with the problem, merely tolerated nationalism, believing that it was, on the whole and beyond very narrow limits, a detrimental factor in the social order of mankind. In this respect some inkling of Seipel's real objectives is given in the following lines:

'The greatest period in Austria's history was the era between the Congress of Vienna and the year 1866, not only because she stood at that time as the leading Great Power in fullest external splendour, but also through the richness and value of her ideas. She was during that time close to the solution of the nationality problem. Thereby she might have shown to mankind the path to a more perfect organization, which might really have vouchsafed eternal peace. It was Austria's intention at that time to unite the Germans as well as the Italians . . . without shaking the foundations of the states which had created the two nations. The old imperium should have been revived in a twofold federation, the German on the one hand, the Italian on the other. . . . Austria would have belonged to both of them and easily might have represented the starting point for further national unifications. After all, what are national splinter groups seeking . . . but security of their possessions and further free developments? This security would have been offered to the Austrian Germans fully through the German *Bund* and to the Italians through the Italian union. At the same time they would have preserved all the advantages . . . for instance, in the economic sphere, from which they had learned to profit through their position in the Danube monarchy. This could have served as an example to the southern Slavs and likewise to the Rumanians, the Ukrainians and the Poles. . . . The old imperium is dead and will not be restored. The modern form, in which it can and must be realized if the ideal of eternal peace on earth is ever to be fulfilled, can consist only in a system of alliances.'

Seipel's statement concludes with the hope that the alliance of the central powers—Austria-Hungary and Germany—may result in fulfilment of this goal. This could very easily be interpreted as a bow to Naumann's 'Middle Europe' confederation project under German leadership, which was then much in vogue. Yet the meaning of Seipel's remarks probably goes deeper. Certainly, when he refers to the period from 1814 to 1866 as ideologically the greatest in Austrian history, the conservative scholar and statesman does not mean the revolutionary inheritance of 1848. Schwarzenberg's and Bruck's concepts of central European federation under Austrian leadership, which in politically changed form had been revived by Naumann during the First World War, certainly appealed more to Seipel. Nevertheless, Seipel's ideas were not focused primarily on the organization of an imperialistic central European power block from Heligoland to Baghdad.

Seipel conceived the medieval Holy Roman Empire of the German Nation, the great predecessor of the Utopian central European union, of the German and Italian confederation, as the centre of occidental secular power. When he spoke longingly of the eternal peace which might have resulted from a central European union, he did not mean the 'German peace' of Ludendorff and the 'Kaiser'. In all probability he thought of the peace guaranteed by the medieval emperor, who was crowned in Rome by the Pope, and, on the basis of the medieval two-sword theories, of the ultimate subordination of secular imperial power to ecclesiastical power. In other words, he longed for the great supra-national peace organization under the sponsorship of the Church; the *Pax Romana*.

In this great peace community the national question is relatively insignificant, but the claims of the nationalities are not directly renounced and certainly not forcefully suppressed. Yet they are definitely subordinated to a more comprehensive and greater religious idea. In this sense Seipel does not recognize full-fledged autonomy, even in the limited sphere of cultural affairs. Here too the national group is not only subjected to the centralistic control of the state but, according to Seipel, to the supreme centralized power on earth, the Church. One of the chief contributions of Catholicism to the Austrian nationality problem is based upon this subordination of the idea of nationalism, not to the state, but to the religious concept of the international and supra-national eternal peace community.[1]

To impose a rigid political or ecclesiastical interpretation on Hofmannsthal would be absurd. But the above account can suffice for present purposes to show the antecedence of the Austrian Idea and these considerations are an important factor in Hofmannsthal's intellectual and spiritual cosmopolitanism. If this importance be recognized, then the 'European' Hofmannsthal of the years between the war and his death becomes a comprehensible and even logical development; and *Die Österreichische Idee* takes its place in that development.

It is difficult to specify which of the works named in the foregoing section had any direct influence on Hofmannsthal. It is quite easy, of course, to demonstrate his interest in the ideas of *Ausgleich* represented by Josef Redlich.[2] One can also point to

Hofmannsthal's friendship at this stage in his career with Rudolf Pannwitz: it is clear from his correspondence with Bodenhausen that Pannwitz's *Krisis der europäischen Kultur* (1917) and *Formenkunde der Kirche* (1916) were much in his mind at this time.

On the other hand it cannot be asserted that Hofmannsthal even read Seipel's *Nation und Staat*, for example. In view of his lifelong preoccupation with history, however (see Kassner's stricture, quoted on p. 110), it is likely that he did and that he was well aware of Seipel's ideas. It is difficult to be more precise than this. The question is more one of the cultural-political atmosphere about him, of which he was clearly aware, as well as himself contributing to it.[1]

Seipel's name has been emphasized in the above discussion. It is to be hoped that a discussion of *Die Österreichische Idee* will now justify this. But before proceeding to this discussion it may be helpful—in arriving at a thorough understanding of Hofmannsthal's aims in this essay—if we consider for a moment the historical context in which it appeared. It is now perhaps half forgotten, but in 1917, when *Die Österreichische Idee* was published, it was widely assumed that as far as Austria was concerned the war was over. The crushing victories on the eastern fronts, the humiliation of Italy at Caporetto, the revolutionary chaos in Russia—all these things indicated that the time had come for Austria to terminate the war and, under the impetus of victory and newly won security, to cut loose from the Prussian-German line of policy and set her own house in the order which was sorely needed.

Stefan Zweig summed up the situation in his autobiography *Die Welt von Gestern*.[2] His account simplifies the position to a considerable extent. It is valuable, however, because it tells not only of Emperor Charles's secret intentions and ultimate failure, but also conveys admirably the general mood of the time. Zweig's narrative is authoritative in that owing to a remarkable coincidence (which he describes) he gained, in 1917, the confidence of Heinrich Lammasch. Redlich, a strong critic of the Austrian empire during its lifetime, has summed up in a temperate and comprehensive fashion a train of events in which judgment can easily be obscured by emotional prejudice one way or the other:[1]

Unfortunately, too, the young emperor did not possess either the far-reaching insight or the truly heroic forces of will which alone could have enabled him...to retrieve what, even at this late stage, might have been retrieved from the errors and crimes of the war dictatorship, by giving to the peoples of Austria the well-founded hope of the ulti-mate transformation of the Habsburg Empire into a free union of peoples based on their political independence and economic co-operation.... Whether the task could have been accomplished, in face of the wide-spread destruction war and war government had wrought in the solidarity...of every nationality...in the Empire, is a question that cannot be answered today, and can perhaps never be answered with certainty.[2]

At this point in the discussion of Austria's destinies that remark of Hofmannsthal's which stands at the head of this study comes to mind: 'Spiritual and intellectual forces are seldom lacking in Austria. But more frequently the will to make use of them is absent.'

When Hofmannsthal wrote *Die Österreichische Idee*, however, these 'forces' were apparently still intact and he hoped that they could be used. He wrote this essay at what seemed to be the moment of victory. At the outset he referred specifically to the fact:

But from the very beginning one should perhaps have thought more of spiritual things—as we are actually beginning to do now, at the end of the war.[3]

The essay falls clearly into two parts. The first, if not of wholly ephemeral importance, is of more historical than actual interest. Hofmannsthal praised and interpreted an achievement whose reality was illusory. He wrote of 'a force...which made its presence felt in ever-renewed waves'.[4] Referring to the war effort of the multi-national peoples of the Austrian empire he wrote:

Behind this simple and lasting dedication on the part of so many and various elements there must be something of vast appeal and extent which can be as little explained by the usual concepts of organization and artifice as by the contrary accusations of indolence and force of habit.[1]

Hofmannsthal was here refuting traditional criticisms of the Habsburg empire and in 1917 fact seemed to be on his side. He went on to interpret these facts in the light of a lofty conception of the nation:

People spoke of an admirable regeneration, but it is perhaps more correct to speak of...an historical concentration of power which has regained its natural balance and strength.[2]

Little more than twelve months passed before these assertions were seen to be vain and empty. It is not possible to say to what degree Hofmannsthal actually believed in what he wrote in this instance. This is in no way meant to question his integrity. It may well be that Hofmannsthal was interpreting facts in an idealized way, hoping that the statement of a possible ideal as a reality would encourage people to see it as such and to act accordingly.[3]

That such was indeed the case and that Hofmannsthal knew the real situation only too well is indicated by an anguished letter to Bodenhausen which he wrote four months before *Die Österreichische Idee* and immediately following a visit to Prague:

Rodaun, 10.7.17. By courier....It was almost too much for me. The determined hostility of these people towards us...the almost wanton anticipation of a future—which will never come in the form they dream of...You have no idea in the *Reich* what...is going on— people against people in the midst of common, grave danger, the reckoning for the past century is presented—and with it the accusations of centuries...This...is the real agony of the thousand-year-old Holy Roman Empire of the German Nation, and if from this cataclysm nothing emerges...save a clear-cut national state—and the old Empire was never that, it was...the only institution that was based on something higher than power and stability and self-assertion—then...the aura of sanctity will have gone which—however weak and pallid it was— still shone above the German spirit in the world.[4]

Apropos the postulating of an ideal and regarding it as if it were a reality, a single sentence written several years after the war provides a clear lead to Hofmannsthal's method and belief. In 1926 he answered a short questionnaire from *Paneuropa*:

1. Do you think the creation of a United States of Europe is necessary?
2. Do you think that it is possible?

1. The one thing which I believe to be necessary is to create new supra-national relationships and to find the political form for them.
2. What is necessary is always possible. Historical events take place when something which most people scarcely believe in is treated by a few people as if it could be realized immediately.[1]

The early part of *Die Österreichische Idee* was at all events more for the day than for posterity. And when Machiavelli was pressed into service to speak for Austria and her permanence, Hofmannsthal's thoughts seemed to be tending towards *Realpolitik* if not downright reaction:

one should not have forgotten those words of Machiavelli... 'As far as the state is concerned the form of government is of very little importance, although half-informed people think differently. The great aim of statecraft should be permanence, which makes up for everything else.'[2]

This point is developed and modified in a rather laborious fashion and had the essay ended there one would probably have treated it as a wartime lapse in a moment of patriotic exuberance. But Hofmannsthal's purpose was something quite different. Suddenly he changed course: Machiavelli was pushed aside as a lofty conception of Austria's situation, significance and lasting purpose opened up in Hofmannsthal's imagination: age is an uncontrollable fact; geographical situation is a physical constant. But from these two, in two short paragraphs, Hofmannsthal created his noblest vision of Austria and what he saw as her European mission. Suddenly the reader's imagination is held by the timeless perspectives and inevitable, effortless continuity of Austria's past:[3]

Es ist nicht gleichgültig, ob man von gestern oder als Mark des Heiligen Römischen Reiches elfhundert Jahre oder als römische Grenzkolonie zweitausend Jahre alt ist und seine Idee in dem einen Fall von den römischen Kaisern, im anderen von Karl dem Großen, ihrem Nachfolger im Imperium, her hat, und dies in der Form, daß das Wesentliche dieser Idee nie abgebogen wurde, sondern sich als ein Unzerstörbares im Vorbeirauschen von zehn und zwanzig Jahrhunderten erhielt.

(It is not a matter of indifference whether we are of yesterday or whether, as one of the marches of the Holy Roman Empire, we are eleven hundred years old, or as a Roman frontier province two thousand years old—and in the one instance have inherited our basic *raison d'être* from the Roman emperors and in the other from Charlemagne, their successor in the imperium—and this, moreover, in such a way that the essentials of this idea were never vitally modified but were preserved indestructible as ten, twenty centuries flowed past.)[1]

Stylistically alone the paragraph—one long sentence—is interesting. As an instance of the vital interplay of form, style and content it is doubly so. The choice of words is notable: *Mark, Heiliges Römisches Reich, Grenzkolonie, römische Kaiser, Imperium*—all these have with the passing of centuries taken on layer after layer of meaning and association. One recalls Hofmannsthal's words:

the dark...splendour, comparable with the sombre gleam of old weapons, which much use in great affairs can confer on the solemn and venerable words of great nations, and which creates an aura of greatness around the simple designations of imperial offices, around the most matter-of-fact titles and inscriptions of ancient Rome—a greatness which makes our hearts beat faster.[2]

In the present instance the words cited set off in the reader's mind a series of 'explosions'.[3] The cumulative wave-like effect achieved by the repeated *oder...oder, und...und* is enhanced by the long-drawn-out onomatopoeia of *vorbeirauschen*. *Vorbeirauschen* suggests in itself not only sound but also the inevitable flowing past of time in which ten and twenty centuries flow into one great whole, one ever-present time. The Roman emperors and the *Pax Romana*, Charlemagne and the unification of western Europe in the name of Christianity, these were for Hofmannsthal the spiritual godfathers of Austria. These were the essence of the Austrian Idea. These enabled her to come into being. But they alone could not justify her existence forever. Something else was needed. It was here that the geographical factor, seemingly prosaic and unchangeable, came to the fore:

The essence of this idea, which enabled her not only to outlive the centuries but to emerge from the chaos and cataclysms of history with an ever-rejuvenated countenance, lies in her polarity, in the antithesis within her: the power to be a frontier province, a frontier fortress, to be the last outpost which divides the European imperium from a geographical complex of mixed peoples, half Europe, half Asia, forever at Europe's doors, forever chaotic and in flux; and the power simultaneously to be a constantly shifting frontier, a point of departure for colonization, penetration, for the waves of cultural influence spreading eastward; and receptive too, forever ready to receive the opposing waves which roll westward.[1]

Colonization, penetration—even culture—have, since the above was written, become terms of doubtful propriety in these matters. Hofmannsthal stressed, however, the ambivalent nature of his words. On the one hand there was the defence of the west against a succession of invaders which began with Attila, continued with the Hungarians and the centuries-long Turkish threat, and which has in the twentieth century lost none of its significance. On the other hand there was the steady expansion to the east: by the sword and with the cross in Charlemagne's time; to demonstrate and introduce superior standards at the invitation of Ottokar of Bohemia; or, under the Habsburgs, to build a powerful and secure *bloc* against either the czar or the sultan.

Hofmannsthal emphasized the mixture of political realism and cultural-political idealism which was in his view part of the Austrian Idea. The associations with ancient Rome and with the universal spiritual-cultural power of the Catholic Church were drawn logically into his synthesis:

In common with all those elements in the spiritual-political heritage of the Romans which have come down to us, this idea transcends mere practical, political things, and in this it is related to the Catholic Church, the great continuation of the essence of the Roman empire. In its spiritual strength and capacity this idea outstrips everything which the various national or economic ideologies of our times have been able to produce.[1]

When he spoke of national and economic ideologies Hofmannsthal was clearly referring to Great Britain and France. He distinguished sharply between the 'synthesis' of Austria and the clear-cut, self-centred character of the two Entente powers. He saw the latter as a consequence of the forces released by the French Revolution and Napoleon. In a revealing paragraph Hofmannsthal characterized the opposing tendencies and stressed Austria's primarily reconciling nature:

This fundamental and fateful disposition towards compromise with the east—let us be more precise and say towards compromise between the old European-Latin-German world and the new European-Slav world—this sole task and *raison d'être* of Austria was in something of an eclipse during the period 1848–1914. Whilst the world at large applied itself consistently to the national problem—which, indeed, in the case of England and France was a supra-national and European (and even more than European) problem, cleverly concealed by them to the point of self-delusion—*we* were compelled as a result of 1859 and 1866 to liquidate the remnants of an old supra-national European policy which had become incomprehensible to contemporary ways of thinking. Then, over decades of difficult internal development which the rest of the world was unable to understand, we had to prepare for the present moment...we had to work out the basis of a new supra-national European policy which took the national problem into account and was able to integrate it into the scheme of things.[2]

It is a pity that Hofmannsthal did not attempt a full study of the historical character and lasting significance of Prince Metternich. The managing director of the Congress of Vienna and lifelong Imperial Chancellor naturally comes to mind when 1848 is mentioned. When Hofmannsthal wrote of 'an old supra-national European policy' in the above context he must have realized that his readers would inevitably think of Metternich. The name alone has long since been associated with reaction and the upholding of the *status quo*. Hence in the absence of a concentrated study by Hofmannsthal, either of the *Vormärz* period itself or of Metternich personally (in whom, incidentally, were mixed such elements of visionary foresight, original idealism and cynical realism as to have fascinated Hofmannsthal), one's initial reaction must be one of suspicion.

It might be as well, however, to recall that for an Austrian of Hofmannsthal's convictions events since 1918 would indicate that Metternich's judgment and ideal of balance of power were correct, even if his methods were as out of keeping with the spirit of the age as they were short-sighted and narrow-minded.

In the absence of a detailed opinion of Metternich any indication as to Hofmannsthal's views on Friedrich von Gentz (1764–1832) is of enhanced interest. Gentz was of course closely associated with Metternich during the first half of the *Vormärz* period. Evidence of Hofmannsthal's attitude to Gentz is admittedly rather slight. It appears, however, that he had a high opinion, although he expressed himself with marked restraint. In the second, enlarged edition (1926) of the *Deutsches Lesebuch* (which Hofmannsthal edited and to the first edition of which he contributed his notable foreword, 'Vorrede des Herausgebers')[1] Hofmannsthal wrote *Gedenktafeln* for each of the twenty-eight additions. One of these was devoted to Gentz:

Austria's famous manifestos of 1809 and 1813 against France were written by him. His *Fragments* and his letters to the political scientist Adam Müller are unsurpassed in form and content. In Austria Gentz's memory lives on in many anecdotes. In Germany he is scarcely remembered, or at most only in the distorted image of him which Young German liberalism bequeathed to posterity. Friedrich Hebbel, however, closes his review of the correspondence mentioned above as follows: 'The same feeling which drove Lessing (to undertake his *Rettungen*) has guided my hand on this occasion: my aim has been realized if by my illumination of the work before us I have aroused some doubts amongst friends of truth as to whether the case against the man who was perhaps our greatest political talent was judged in a really objective fashion.'[1]

Gentz's own summary of Austria's situation and potential significance might easily have been written by Hofmannsthal himself and could be incorporated into *Die Österreichische Idee*:

By virtue of its geographical situation, the uniformity of its manners and customs, of its laws and requirements, its way of life and its culture, all the states in this part of the world form a great political union which has with some justice been called the European Republic. The various members of this league of peoples exist in such a close and continuous community that no significant change that takes place in any one of them can be a matter of indifference to the others.[2]

An interesting study of Gentz which, although not by Hofmannsthal himself, is very much in the line of his later thought is that by Carl Burckhardt. During the last years of Hofmannsthal's life Burckhardt probably stood closer to him than anyone else—with the possible exception of Rudolf Alexander Schröder. In his study[3] Burckhardt quotes one of Gentz's last letters. Its mood and outlook seem to reveal those elements in the *Vormärz* period which interested Hofmannsthal:

World history is a perpetual transition from the old to the new. In the constant cycle of events everything finally destroys itself, and the fruit which has ripened to maturity drops from the plant which brought it forth. If, however, this cycle is not to lead to the rapid decline of established institutions—and therefore of all that is just and good— there will always be, alongside the great and inevitably superior number of those who are working for the new ideas, a smaller number of people who try with moderation and purpose to assert the place of the old and, even if they neither can nor want to stem the rising tide of the age, attempt to channel its course along regulated ways.... I was always conscious of the fact that in spite of the power and majesty of my masters and our cause, and irrespective of the individual victories which they won, the spirit of the age would ultimately prove stronger than we ourselves.... But this was no reason for me to refuse to carry out loyally and perseveringly the task which fell to my lot. It is a poor soldier who deserts his flag when fortune threatens to frown on it; and I also have pride enough to say to myself even in the darkest moments: Victrix causa Diis placuit, victa Catoni.

In the penultimate paragraph of *Die Österreichische Idee* Hofmannsthal asserted that 'Austria's language' was 'too great for the post-Napoleonic age'. He seemed here to be struggling against the current of an historical opinion which thinks of Austria in this period largely in terms of the Holy Alliance, the Carlsbad Decrees and the *ancien régime*. To understand Hofmannsthal aright it is often necessary to distinguish very clearly between idea and execution. In the present instance, for example, one must distinguish between the concept of Metternich's 'middle force and balance of power' and his often petty and cynical methods. It has probably been easier to do this since 1945; since the final destruction of the last traces of Metternich's attempted creation.

Hofmannsthal realized that the war meant the end of an epoch which began with the French Revolution. It seemed to him that the catastrophic events of the war—the inevitable results of nationalistic ideologies—taught a moral which, for the first time since 1848, could be expressed in Austria's political language. When he wrote that Austria was better prepared for the inevitable consequences of the war than any other nation, he was thinking of Austria as an example of European union. She was, as he well realized, far from perfect. For Hofmannsthal, however, Austria's aims and ideals were the only ones possible, if Europe was to learn from the war and arrest her descent into the chaos of ideologies forever at war with each other and forever sterile:

Stronger than any narrow party system and stronger than any ideology —both of which are mistakenly regarded as the only true expression of politics—is the element of destiny. In our case this means drawing together the threads of divers European elements and uniting them in our German spirit in order to effect a compromise between this now no longer narrowly national German spirit and the spirit of the Slav world.[1]

The conservative revolutionary along with the earlier and allegedly decadent Hofmannsthal fell under National Socialist disfavour in Germany. He is likewise unacceptable to Marxist interpreters. The following sentence would alone have been sufficient to justify both, irrespective of Hofmannsthal's partly Jewish origins or of his patrician background:

The ideas of reconciliation, of synthesis, of the bridging of great and gaping differences, have a constant force and spontaneity of their own. These ideas are nourished by actual situations,...by genuine experience; not by slogans, whether they be nationalistic, Socialist, or parliamentarian.[1]

Perhaps it is permissible to note here the absence of an analogy with Great Britain's colonial policy. It is rather strange that Hofmannsthal, who on divers occasions expressed admiration of Britain's practical, empirical wisdom, should in this instance have ignored her example. The conciliatory South African settlement and the attitude of the British empire during the war were—by comparison with the Austrian empire—practical and ideal examples of what could be achieved. Hofmannsthal must have known, moreover, of Britain's experiments in colonial self-government. Probably the stress of war made such allusions unseasonable. This is the more likely when one recalls Hofmannsthal's complimentary references to two neutral powers (Switzerland and the United States of America) in *Österreichische Bibliothek*. There he mentioned the success of those countries which have been 'formed out of many peoples',[2] and pointed to them as an example for Austria.

Hofmannsthal, however, ended *Die Österreichische Idee* with a reference to 'Europe, which wants to shape itself anew', and to Austria's indispensable place in it. But Europe has its eastern and its western aspects, however much, during the past fifteen years, the terms 'Western Europe' and 'Europe' have come to be regarded as synonymous—synonymous, at least, when a European union or community of interests is under discussion.

Eastern Europe beyond the bounds of the Austrian empire had been traditionally inchoate, a meeting-place or battle-ground for Austrian, Russian and Turkish interests; hence, in one sense, Hofmannsthal's reference to the 'polymorphous east'. But in another and far more bodeful sense Hofmannsthal was thinking of the many-sided aspects of the east. At the time when he wrote this essay the future of Russia was completely obscure. Whatever the outcome in Russia was to be—together with its inevitable impact on the rest of the Slav world—Hofmannsthal maintained that Austria alone had the experience, the geographical situation and flexibility of approach to solve the problem and to maintain the new balance. This new Europe, he asserted

needs an Austria, a structure of genuine elasticity, but a structure— a true organism—which is suffused by an inner belief in itself. Without this no association of living forces is possible. [Europe] needs Austria in order to comprehend and contain the polymorphous east. *Mitteleuropa*[1] is a concept much in vogue at present, but in the highest sphere—and this affects the whole of Europe, if we are agreed that a true Europe ought to exist at all—in the sphere of supreme spiritual and intellectual values, a sphere in which decisions will be taken which affect the culture of several millennia, Austria is indispensable.[2]

With these ideas in mind one might suggest that the suicidal policy of National Socialist Germany in rousing nationalism against nationalism on all sides—and bringing the entire continent to the edge of the abyss—has not proved Hofmannsthal wrong. Neither, on the other hand, has the piecemeal absorption and removal from Europe by Soviet Russia of various erstwhile Central European states, including most of the 'succession states'.[3]

At this point one realizes just how much this essay, with its fears and hopes for Austria and Europe, looks forward: to the *Gottesstaat*[4] of *Das Salzburger Große Welttheater* and to *Der Turm*, in which the present and the possible future of Europe constitute the main theme. As we say *Gottesstaat*, however, and as we speak of the state and future of Europe, and Austria's place in Europe, we think back to the historical stream represented by Ignaz Seipel. If this theory be accepted and if we recall the example of Seipel's thought quoted earlier then Hofmannsthal's predilection for the *Vormärz* becomes comprehensible; and then one realizes what he meant when he wrote that 'Austria's language was too great for the post-Napoleonic age'.[1]

The six essays discussed in these last two chapters do not of course give an exhaustive account of Hofmannsthal's activities during the war. They provide, however, a fairly representative impression of his tendencies as he progressed from *Jedermann* to the two remaining festival dramas which are discussed in the following chapters.

As one reviews in retrospect these six essays, however, a query arises. Hofmannsthal's intention in these works was avowedly popular. He was trying to reach the people, to tell them of their own *raison d'être*. As has been seen he was trying to hold a mirror before the face of the nation in the hope that the nation would see therein its somewhat idealized reflection, and be encouraged to change the ideal into reality. This was his purpose: one recalls Requadt's comment, quoted on pp. 13–14. Whether, indeed, Hofmannsthal's *method*—his style, allusiveness, generally high level of thought—made this altogether possible is less certain. It is clear that this doubt would apply especially to *Österreich im Spiegel seiner Dichtung* and to *Die Österreichische Idee*. It is as well to note this doubt before passing to a consideration of the two remaining 'festival dramas', for in them also—as in *Jedermann*—Hofmannsthal tried to reach the broad mass of the people. On his ultimate success or failure to do this may depend to some extent our ultimate judgment of him as an artist, or at least as an artist in the particular part which he chose for himself.

But one thing is fairly obvious. These essays show the constancy of Hofmannsthal's artistic technique as he used and reinterpreted the past—both its individual figures and its ideas—

in order to rejuvenate the present and make it aware of possibilities still alive within itself. One recalls Hofmannsthal's comment which stands at the head of chapter 3. The 'festival dramas' are indeed quite capable of standing alone on their own merits. Perhaps, however, their place in the broader picture of Hofmannsthal's development will become somewhat clearer in the light of the preceding discussion.

CHAPTER 5

'DAS SALZBURGER GROSSE WELTTHEATER'

What a world we have stumbled into! The very beams burst through the floor and the whole edifice trembles to its foundations. Will people go on studying history? Will people need history?[1]

The individual personality of today is no longer the limited individual of old with his dull aching want. Today another kind of distress weighs men down: we now have too much freedom, just as previously there were too many ties. But in this very distress there is new hope.... Again and again our nation seems to have no real soul—and so it lies there like a sick man, incapable of real existence and with strange confused thoughts. But individual people are mindful of the high ideal: in an unprecedented situation, amidst the dissolution of everything firm and seemingly permanent, they draw from their very distress, their very loneliness, a courage which has something of the courage of despair....[2]

...if I could raise the money to produce...an almost private journal, and if I had the full moral support of five or seven people—including you—then I might be able to breathe new life into the concept of Europe.[3]

I N his memoir of Hofmannsthal Carl Burckhardt remarks how the Catholic dramatist Paul Claudel once said of Hofmannsthal: 'Il pesait une terrible fatalité sur lui.' A terrible fatality: by this one might understand that the war and its outcome were a crushing blow to Hofmannsthal. This is an obvious comment.

It would seem to draw attention, as if to something unique, to a reaction which was common enough after both great wars in this century. Claudel, however, used the word *fatalité*. For Hofmannsthal the war was of course the personal tragedy that it was for millions. For him as an Austrian it was the brutally sudden end of a culture and a society—the foundations of his existence. But these considerations are relatively unimportant compared with the greater development within him; for Claudel's word was carefully chosen. Hofmannsthal realized what the war, irrespective of victor and vanquished, meant for the decades that were to follow. It was in no vainglorious sense that he took upon himself the present and future of Europe as a personal and ultimately fatal care.

In the closing decade of Hofmannsthal's life it is impossible to separate man from artist. It is in fact often difficult to separate from one another any one part or aspect of his creative work during these years (1918–29). A remark to Burckhardt, a sentence in a book review, a paragraph from one of the large-scale set speeches of those years, a diary entry, a rhythmic prose sequence from *Der Turm*, a chance comment by a friend on his appearance, even a portrait photograph: all show how he lived in himself a favourite saying of his earlier years—'The whole man must move at once.'[1] In *Die Briefe des Zurückgekehrten* (1907) he had used this phrase with mordant effect to point the moral bankruptcy of Hohenzollern Germany, to stress the violence done to the nation's soul by the promoters of the new *Reich*. Now, in the last strenuously dedicated years of his life, he was himself the embodiment of his own ideal.

It was not as if the realization of Europe's spiritual plight came slowly upon him, allowing time for absorption and reflection. Burckhardt recalls his first meeting with Hofmannsthal, in the middle of December 1918, barely a month after the end of the war. Hofmannsthal remarked on this occasion: 'All that is over and done with and will not come back again. In this war a revolution has become visible which in the course of this century will jeopardize everything we represent and everything we once possessed.'[1] Burckhardt himself has described with particular felicity the plight of soul and mind in which Hofmannsthal passed his declining years. This was the intellectual and spiritual state of mind with which he grappled and out of which his last works were written:

he stood in the midst of a...fateful train of events; he stood, so to speak, at their focal point, and something...uncanny hovered around him at certain moments; because he was perhaps one of the few men in that generation who were completely at one with those intrinsic things which...were about to disappear; and because he constantly sensed the approach of new destructive forces as if they were rolling towards his own spiritual plains and chasms.[2]

The impact of disaster and the sense of greater catastrophe beyond it did not, however, crush him. The comment concerning a new periodical, quoted at the head of this chapter, is sufficient evidence of that. And yet while Hofmannsthal's work in the period 1918–29 can be seen as a corpus of the intellect directed to one purpose, it represented, in one sense at least, no break with the past. The plunge into past ages and cultures has been seen at various points in the present work as Hofmannsthal's most characteristic artistic habit. We have also seen how as the years passed Hofmannsthal varied and developed this practice. It was therefore no surprising mutation when, for the two 'festival dramas' written during the last phase of his career, Hofmannsthal turned once more to the past for his models.

He turned to the seventeenth century, the age of the Thirty Years War and of the Spanish and Austrian Baroque. The atmosphere of the Baroque was of course natural to Hofmannsthal.[3] What Fritz Martini has written of Grillparzer can be applied, save in one respect, to Hofmannsthal:

His intellectual roots were deep in the baroque-Catholic traditions of Vienna, the imperial city, and in the historical folk traditions—drama and poetry—of his race. He had a sovereign grasp of an enormous universal culture, he lived amongst and was of his countrymen, and he was an intently alert—if taciturn—observer of his turbulent age.[4]

Grillparzer, like Hofmannsthal, had turned to Calderón.[1] His *Der Traum ein Leben*, based on *La vida es sueño* (and a tale of Voltaire!) was a bold mixture of the Spanish baroque theatre with elements of the traditional Viennese folk-drama which survived in the suburban theatres of the capital.[2]

This is not the place for a detailed study of Austro-Spanish influence and counter-influence. The subject is huge and has many aspects. The dual role of the Habsburgs, who were so long kings of Spain and emperors of the Holy Roman Empire, meant wave after wave of influence and exchange.[3] The aspect which is particularly significant here is the Counter-Reformation whose spiritual centre was in Spain. The Counter-Reformation and the Thirty Years War overlapped each other, and not only in time. Hofmannsthal turned to the age of the Counter-Reformation and the Thirty Years War for inspiration in the years of Austria's downfall, when all accepted values had seemingly disappeared. In a letter to Burckhardt Hofmannsthal expressed himself on this social and moral collapse in truly baroque terms: 'We can scarcely sense how deeply this crisis has cut into our spiritual world, revealing almost everything as an illusion. Our situation is really tremendous if one can endure it, look it in the eye.'[4]

Martini's description of the spiritual mood of the seventeenth century can perhaps help to explain why Hofmannsthal, in an age of parallel confusion, disillusionment and doubt, turned to the Spanish Baroque and its greatest playwright to serve him as preceptors:

The Thirty Years War...was the decisive experience of the century. It was a human and national experience suffered by all in common with all, in spite of the murderous religious divisions. It also gave to the literature of the opposing camps a similarity of mood which transcended the narrowness of religious difference. But the baroque style was essentially an import from the south-west. Spain had become the centre of modern spiritual and artistic life. The baroque style loved adornment and multi-layered allegory, mystic sensuousness, pomp and pathos. It developed first of all in Spain under Arabian influence. It revelled in a most ingenious and antithetic play of the intellect.

...The Jesuit drama portrayed the grandiloquent and high festive style of the old Church which was now once more on the offensive and victoriously triumphant. Powerful propaganda for the Catholic faith began in all countries.

Here we can give only very general indications of the extremely complicated intellectual situation of the Baroque, in whose development the whole of Europe participated, together with important influences from the ancient classical world. As a result of the war, as a result of the counter-reformers' warning about the infinite power and mystic eternity of God, that joyously earthbound awareness, characteristic of the humanistic Renaissance, was lost. Chasms now began to gape open everywhere, dividing God and the world, eternity and mortality, soul and body, death and earthly happiness, asceticism and worldly pleasures, knowledge and faith. The whole of existence presented itself to seventeenth-century man as an irreconcilable division. The Goddess of Fortune, who is appealed to again and again, hurled man into a chaotic, unpredictable world which was always changing its aspect. This world, in spite of its seductively attractive colours, appeared only as the embodiment of transience, as *vanitas*. For man in the Baroque Age it became a dark, uncanny dream. In his aspiring and simultaneously terrified attitude to life, death is always present. A deep sense of pessimism lies upon this age and at the same time a mystic fervour...which attempts to fathom the mystery of God and the world.[1]

Both *Das Salzburger Große Welttheater* (1922) and *Der Turm* (1925; stage version 1927)[2] owe their dramatic theme and framework to Calderón. Josef Nadler coupled these two dramas together as part of the seventh and final example of the categories into which he divided Hofmannsthal's work. He asserts that in them 'Hofmannsthal created the two highest representatives of his theatrical style'.[3] Nadler stresses the essentially complementary nature of these two plays:

An early notion, widespread in the western world, saw creation as a divine drama. Hofmannsthal's *Welttheater* continues the tradition of Calderón's play on this theme and establishes the modern mystery play. *Der Turm* is a unity made up of three typically 'western' dramatic forms: the mystery play, the baroque drama, and the classical drama. These two plays, by reason of their aim and meaning, are a complementary pair. The *Welttheater* demonstrates the essential meaning of social order....*Der Turm* takes up the idea of mixed peoples in one state and makes it into a drama.[1]...The *Welttheater* and *Der Turm* are social works of art arising out of the historical climacteric during which they were written.[2]

Nadler's practical approach seems to be justified by the impressions of those close to Hofmannsthal in his last years, notably Carl Burckhardt in his memoir already referred to at several points, and Erika Brecht in her *Erinnerungen an Hugo von Hofmannsthal.*[3]

Despite their complementary nature these two plays do present, however, an interesting contradiction. If the *Große Welttheater*, especially in the light of *Jedermann*, is one of the most accessible of Hofmannsthal's plays, *Der Turm* is certainly the most difficult. To some extent, perhaps, this can be explained by the nature of the respective ideas embodied in each play, a point which may become clear in the discussion which follows.

It should also be remembered, however, that the plays were written for different audiences. The *Große Welttheater*, designedly a festival drama, had to make a direct, simple effect. Curt Hohoff said of this play (and of *Jedermann*): 'They are no longer dramas for the humanistic intelligentsia, but mimetic and symbolic theatre, played in front of the doors of Salzburg Cathedral. And the idea is that the modern "masses" [*Masse*] are to be transformed —changed back into the "folk" [*Volk*].'[4] This factor is discussed in more detail later in this chapter.

Der Turm on the other hand, although having many characteristics of the festival-spectacle play, is also its author's last will and testament, the *Alterswerk* into which, Goethe-like, he tried to pack all that he had to say, even at the risk of obscurity.[5]

These various considerations seem, therefore, to make separate discussion of the *Große Welttheater* and of *Der Turm* particularly desirable.

The basic structure of *Das Salzburger Große Welttheater* is relatively simple. Reference was made in chapter 2 to the way in which Hofmannsthal used an ancient symbol as a vital feature of *Jedermann*. In that instance the symbol was the medieval Dance of Death. For the *Große Welttheater* Hofmannsthal took up a comparable ageless symbol of at least equal spiritual dimensions. Concerning this he wrote:

There is a certain timeless European mythology—names, ideas, figures—and these things are bound up with a higher meaning: they are the embodiment of various forces in the moral order. These star-strewn mythological heavens span the entire face of old Europe.[1]

The 'world as a stage' is one of these all-European symbols and Hofmannsthal insisted that it was neither the invention nor the sole property of Calderón:

Everyone knows that there is a sacred drama by Calderón which is called the *Great World Theatre*. The metaphor on which my entire play is based has been borrowed from Calderón's play: that the world is a stage on which men act the parts in life which are assigned to them by God. In addition to this I have taken over the title of the play and the names of the figures who represent mankind—nothing else, how-ever. But these various elements were neither invented by nor are they the exclusive property of the great Catholic poet. They belong to that treasure-house of myth and allegory which was built up by the Middle Ages and bequeathed to the centuries which followed.[2]

A further factor, however, drew Hofmannsthal to Calderón's play. In a century which, notably in German lands, was marked by religious and political dissension, Calderón's vision of the universe took in God, heaven and earth in a great unity. In a conversation with Carl Burckhardt Hofmannsthal remarked: 'Calderón lived in his own country secure within an all-prevailing and undivided faith. There he built up his own world as firmly and as clearly defined as that of Johann Sebastian Bach.'[3]

A word of caution may be necessary here. It has sometimes been suggested that in turning to Calderón and in writing his own *Große Welttheater* Hofmannsthal was either forcing Catholicism on his generation or campaigning for a modern version of the *Ständestaat*, a society where each has his appointed place and stays in it. This would be a somewhat crude and rather superficial view. Hofmannsthal was neither a reactionary clericalist nor an unpractical dreamer. Evidence of his own view of this kind of criticism is found in a letter to Richard Strauss. Strauss had referred to a certain 'specific dogmatic limitation' in the *Große Welttheater*. Hofmannsthal replied:

There is a religious quality in the poem just as there is in *Faust*. There is also a Christian quality, for we all have our origins in Christianity and in the ancient world. But it is no more specifically Catholic than *Jedermann*....Its innermost substance is the glorification of that exalted quality in us, that inner freedom which is...a reflection in us of the supreme Creator.[1]

Hofmannsthal makes here substantial claims for the content of *Große Welttheater*. Before, however, discussing these claims, it may be as well to give an outline of the play's action. Hofmannsthal's treatment of the theme, together with his particular interpretation of various characters, can then, perhaps, be more easily debated with this background in mind.

The action of the *Große Welttheater* is simple enough. It falls into five fairly clear sections which to some extent correspond to the five acts of an orthodox drama. The play begins with a Prologue in Heaven[2] in which the Master (God) announces that he wants to see a play and the play shall portray man's earthly progress. The World offers to put on a mighty show of earthquakes, fire and flood. She pours scorn on man who 'runs all over the place like so many ants, building cities, founding empires, knocking them down again, leaving no stone on the other. There's more sense in a swarm of wasps than there is in them.'[3]

This provokes the Master to defend men who, after all, are created in his own image and likeness, and whose actions are a worthy spectacle for the play now to be performed before God and the assembled holy men and women, prophets and sibyls. Why, the Master is asked, should the play take place at all? What is the point of such a drama when the beginning and end are pre-destined by God down to the last detail? The Master replies that man has choice between good and evil and that the Adversary (a rather mild Devil compared with his fulminating cousin in *Jedermann*) may prompt as he wishes. But he has breathed a 'spark of the highest freedom'[1] into man so that he can decide for himself.

This actually ends the prologue proper. The prologue-like action continues, however, in a somewhat less elevated tone. Stage clothes and properties are brought in, Death is appointed stage-manager, and the name of the play is announced: *Do what is right! God is above you.*

The unborn souls now move on to the stage. They wear cowls and their mask-like faces are all alike with no distinguishing marks as to age, sex or rank. Each soul is given a scroll on which is written the part to be played. One after the other they take their scrolls and are given clothes for the various parts: King, Wisdom, Peasant and Beauty.

Suddenly there is a commotion. One soul, designated to play the Beggar, refuses his role. In a mighty outburst against the misery and inequality of life he justifies his refusal. The presiding angel insists that he take the part but sympathizes with him; and in this sympathy we begin to see something of the special importance of the Beggar in this play: 'Brave soul! What terrifies you is not that you must suffer for the short hour of this play, but you shudder to see the darkness in which the children of Adam dwell.'[2]

The Beggar now demands a part which will give him freedom —freedom, at least, not to suffocate in the world—but the angel tells him: 'The man who has freedom and is worthy of it asks: "Why have I been given freedom?" And he does not rest until he recognizes the fruit it brings. But there is only one fruit of freedom: to do what is right.'[3] The angel goes on to tell the Beggar that deeds alone are 'creation over creation' and that he must see what a tremendous privilege is given to him in the opportunity to play this part.

The Beggar cannot understand how this miserable part can give him the opportunity for even one single deed. 'Play the part', says the angel, 'and you will see.' He reminds the Beggar of Jesus' symbolic words on Calvary and on the Mount of Olives: 'My God, my God, why hast Thou forsaken me?... Not my will but Thine be done.'[1] With this hint of glory to come if he submits to the divine will the Beggar accepts the role and the second main part of the play begins, the 'play within the play'.

The King and Beauty perform the orthodox parts traditionally expected of them. Wisdom, no less beautiful than her earthly sister, is portrayed as a nun, and she longs for the silent remoteness of prayer and contemplation. Then the Rich Man and the Peasant appear. The King addresses himself first to the Peasant. The latter, who speaks a very broad and comfortable-sounding dialect, asks only to be left alone to do his job. The King then speaks to the Rich Man whom he acknowledges as the principal pillar of the state. The Rich Man replies with an *ex cathedra* statement of his own indispensable place in society (this speech is considered in some detail later in the present chapter). The King appoints him chancellor of the realm. The Rich Man almost betrays his own purpose: forgetting his lines he is prompted by the Adversary into saying how the King's sword will if necessary leap gleaming from its scabbard to protect him. When the King questions him he hastily corrects himself, inserts 'we' and 'our' and 'might and honour'.[2]

These various exchanges are punctuated by comments from Wisdom who sees the vanity and falseness of the world and begs God to have pity and not to desert man. At last, the essential features of each character having been sketched, the Beggar enters. The fact that he makes a special entrance, so to speak, long after the others and quite alone, is a further suggestion of his importance. He is depicted as an embittered, homeless peasant, a widower who has lost everything—wife and farm—in a frontier raid. With searing irony he tells his tale. The Peasant, safe, solid, secure as ever, remarks that it is no life out there on the frontier:

poor people and poorer wine, much better to live safe and sound in the heart of the country. The Beggar questions providence and in a half-crazed whisper asks why this had to happen. He describes how his motherless children died one by one and how he himself attended their 'quiet funeral' as relations, pall-bearer and grave-digger all in one. And he pours scorn on Wisdom who, while all this happened, had been safely praying behind her cloister walls and bars in an odour of incense and sanctity.

Wisdom makes the Beggar take his woe to the King. But whom is he to accuse? His main complaint, Wisdom says, seems to be that this happened to him and not to someone else. In a long speech the Beggar summarizes the situation as he sees it: 'You have and I have not':

> Ihr habt, und ich hab nicht — das ist die Red,
> Das ist der Streit und das, um was es geht!
> Ihr habt das Weib und habt das Kind,
> Und habt das Haus, den Hof und auch das Ingesind,
> Ihr habt das Feld und habt die Kuh,
> Und habt das Kleid und auch den Schuh,
> Und habt ein warm satt Blut im Leib,
> Und habt die Zeit und noch den Zeitvertreib,
> Ihr habt den Tag und habt als zweiten Tag die Nacht
> Mit Fackeln, Kerzen, Glanz und Pracht.
> Ihr habt den Wein und noch ein Lautenspiel zum Wein,
> Und habt das Ding und noch den Schein,
> Und habt das ganze Erdenwesen
> Und noch das Buch, worin recht schön und faul zu lesen,
> Darin wird eure Welt beschmeichelt und bewitzelt,
> Damit euch, was ihr habt, noch einmal traumweis kitzelt.
> Das alles habt ihr und woher? weil ihrs gestohlen,
> Gebaut das Haus auf Bruders schmählichem Verderbe!
> Jakob, du sitzest in gestohlenem Erbe,
> Und Esau kommt, das Seine sich zu holen!

The threat in the last two lines is clear. Jacob sits on his stolen inheritance and Esau comes to claim what is his.

The King, basking in awareness of his rank and what he regards as the divine order of society, refuses to lower himself and deal with such a problem:

> Weh, käm der Tag, da Rang und Ordnung wankte,
> So wie dem Leibe, dem das Herz erkrankte,
> So widerführe dem gemeinen Wesen,
> Dessen zu wahren wir von Gott erlesen.

The King makes the Rich Man responsible and tells him to use his undoubted skills of intellect and fair speech to guide the rebel along the right path.

At this point a moving little episode ensues. The Beggar, dejected and dispossessed, catches sight of Beauty at the King's side. The King, he says, has *her* too, the gift of gifts, whose merest ray pierces the poorest heart and transforms night into day, raising up the lowly to the heights:

> Die! die ist auch bei dir!
> Ist dies da, Gabe unter alle Gaben,
> Wovon ein Strahl das ärmste Herze durchfährt,
> Unten in oben, Nacht in Tag verkehrt,
> Ist dies auch eingeschlossen in dein Haben?

Wisdom, sympathetic and understanding, sees hope in this, for it means that the Beggar still recognizes in Beauty the reflection of divine creation. Beside himself with grief that the mighty have exclusive right to everything, even this 'crown of life', the Beggar shouts aloud: he will break in upon them all, this is the end—and he calls for a new world order:

> Ich brech in dein Geheg! Ein neuer Wohlstand her!

The Rich Man now approaches the Beggar and talks to him in a cunning man-to-man way. You, he says, are a good sort of man who can take a bit of advice. We are, he goes on, all workers. But the Beggar interrupts him with a flaming vision of an apocalypse and a new world rising up beyond:

> Der Weltstand muß dahin, neu werden muß die Welt,
> Und sollte sie zuvor in einem Flammenmeer
> Und einer blutigen Sintflut untertauchen,
> So ists das Blut und Feuer, das wir brauchen.

The Beggar refuses further sophistry from the Rich Man, refuses to parley with him or the King and stands silently laughing when the King turns away from him. Wisdom begs God to avert the dreadful deed which, she feels, must follow this silence. The Beggar makes as if to leave the stage. There is a long and tense silence as with much dumb-show and tableau-like effect he walks slowly towards the Peasant. The Peasant, who has been deep in his work of sharpening his scythe (a rather obvious touch perhaps), ignores him. There is another silence. The Peasant, having stopped work, is now chewing away steadily at his bread and bacon. As the Rich Man looks across at him he hastily pushes the rest into his mouth and goes on sharpening his scythe. There is a neat touch of dramatic irony and tension in his comment on the scythe: it has become jagged, he says, it must have come up against a thorn. In the same breath he asks what this fellow (the Beggar) can want of him. The Beggar asks him for work. Complacently describing his possessions the Peasant offers the Beggar a job as wood-chopper in the forest nearby, which he owns. He also demands that the Beggar should act as forest-policeman. There has been a good deal of wood-stealing, mostly by widows and their children. With unfeeling crudeness the Peasant tells the Beggar how to deal with them:

Und Kinder gar, daß d' mir nit viel 'rumschreist,
Richt' einer nix beim G'lumpert mit an G'schrei,
Anzeigt wird nix, das macht nur Schererei.
Hau drein, jags aus, dös Schandpack soll mein Wald respektieren
Und anderswo herumvagabundieren —
Verstehst?

The Beggar obviously has something else on his mind. Then his intention becomes clear. The similarity between himself and those whom he is now called upon to punish proves to be the last straw. He rushes to the middle of the stage, swings his axe and threatens everybody. He shouts his agreement: he will see that order is maintained—but not only in the forest.[1] It is clear that he is about to destroy the *existing* order of things in the shape of

its representatives on the stage. With savage humour he twists
the Peasant's appeals to law and right to suit his own meaning:
the Peasant threatens to use his legal rights as house-owner and
as employer, but the Beggar says that might is right and he now
has the felling-right.[1]

The climax is reached when all the characters in unison call
upon the Beggar to strike and destroy the whole world at one
blow. A remarkable tableau is held for a few moments as the
figures cower before the Beggar while he, staring rigidly ahead,
unseeingly, axe raised on high, stands opposite them, holding
their fate in his hands. This *coup de théâtre* is sustained in a striking
way. Wisdom throws herself to her knees and speaks to God:
how easy it would be for him to solve everything in a moment;
but, she goes on, he prefers to let men go their way and then to
swoop down like an eagle, taking his prey and with a terrible
sign bringing the human play to a sudden end. Wisdom raises
her hands in supplication, begging God to look on her before
the play sinks into the shadows. That she is praying for a moment's
respite becomes clear when she turns and addresses the others.
She tells them that as they step out of the play a short moment
is given to them all in which they must find their true selves.
And she adds that the Beggar too, who is God's messenger sent
to call them all away, must descend from the stage with them, for
his part also has come to an end.

As she speaks, and as the others remain transfixed, the Beggar
moves towards her. As he comes she conquers her terror and
speaks more strongly. The Beggar's countenance undergoes a
tremendous change. His hand, with the axe, sinks down. Wisdom
calls on God to take pity on the Beggar when he appears for
judgment, stained with the blood of his victims. For his fearful
destiny, she adds, was to be the bearer of God's will, testing men's
charity and suffering himself under this fate. His was the only
part in God's play which was too hard:

> Gnad ihm, ihm war von Deines Spieles Rollen
> Die eine überschwere auferlegt!

The Beggar now speaks of a light he has seen and of a voice
from the treetops speaking to him. It is apparent that like St Paul
on the road to Damascus he has been struck by divine light and
is a changed man. A dramatically antiphonal effect is achieved as
the Beggar, Wisdom and the presiding angel question and answer
each other:

> *Beggar.*   — was geschah?
> Daß ich nicht auf dich schlug! Du tratest nah —
> *Wisdom.* Brach da ein Licht hervor? — und —
> *Angel.*   War das nicht
> Des Saulus Blitz und redend Himmelslicht?
> *Beggar.* Du hobest deine Händ und betetest für mich?
> *Wisdom.* Für dich!
> *Beggar.*   Verstehend mich und mein Gericht?

The Beggar now turns to go into the forest. Reproached for
his submissiveness by the Adversary, he replies in a long speech
which, it would seem, goes to the heart of the play's content.
What, he says, would be the use of my snatching riches from
the Rich Man and power from the King? Were I to sit on
the throne, he continues, things would be the same: one idiocy
would have been exchanged for another, and the world would
be violated as in the past. On the contrary, he concludes,
if this play is not to be a poor, petty puppet-play then a
radically changed and quite new state of things must come
about.

The Beggar leaves the stage and goes into the forest. As he
goes Wisdom hands him the axe which he at first refuses. But,
she tells him, he must not be idle in his contemplation—for the
Beggar wishes now to live as a hermit. In a quiet, autumnally
beautiful verse Wisdom says how the sound of his axe must ring
forth to the village, telling of peaceful days:

> Sanft wie der Hirtenstab im Schattensaal,
> Wandle die Axt voraus dem Himmelsstrahl,
> Und wie die Glocke tön ihr voller satter Schlag
> Ins Dorf und melde Herbst und friedereichen Tag.

As the Beggar goes a signal (presumably a horn or trumpet) is heard. The next phase in the action begins. The World sets the mood with an ode to Time which in sentiment and form recalls the *sic transit gloria mundi* of the seventeenth-century Baroque:

> Der Boden gibt einen toten Schein,
> Da wirst du meine Herrin sein!
> O Weh!
> Und ich deine Magd, schwach und verzagt,
> Gott seis geklagt!

As the World sings the light changes: a dismal, grey evening takes the place of day. One after the other the characters realize that time has taken its toll of them and the play is nearly through. The Dance of Death begins. As it ends the angel, obeying a summons from the Master, calls Death and orders him to call in the players. And now, in turn, the players see the bright image of their worldly life collapse. Only Wisdom is unafraid.

There is a mildly comic interlude as the Peasant tries to persuade Death that he has too much work to do, that perhaps Death wants the Beggar. But Death insists, and in a touching little speech the Peasant hopes that in his case hard work will make up for his lack of prayer:

> Hab allweil gemeint, es kommt an Enderl Zeit
> — Ausrasten — zuwasitzen auf die Bänk,
> Daß i an Aichtl auf mein Herrgott denk
> Und Reu erweck für meine Schlechtigkeit;
> Jetzt reißt mich so dahin. Du laßt an ja ka Zeit,
> Jetzt tuats mi g'reun, daß mi so wenig g'reut!
> Gschafft hab i viel, bet' hab i net recht viel,
> Nimm halt der Meister vorlieb mit dem G'spiel!

And finally comes the Beggar. Gently he bends over the cowering Rich Man, helps him to his feet, comforts him in his terror and leads him out. The stage is now in semi-darkness. A curtain is drawn across the lower part and the scene is set for the final tableau which introduces the last phase in the action. The World is on one side of the stage, the Adversary on the other. The lower part of the stage is now revealed, clear of all stage properties (tree, rocks, etc.) and bathed in pallid green light. In the distance the requiem sequence *De Profundis* is heard.

The souls, stripped of their players' robes, now appear, all dressed in white shrouds. The upper part of the stage remains empty. Each soul voices an ejaculation which tells of its joy or hope, its fear or terror:

> *A Soul (formerly the King).* O Zagen!
> *Another Soul (formerly Wisdom).* O Freude!

The King, Beauty and the Peasant quail at what is before them; the Rich Man is terrified; Wisdom and the Beggar are full of joy. Then comes the judgment in which the Beggar and Wisdom go to their eternal rewards and the Rich Man is cast into darkness. With this the play ends.

Any discussion of the *Große Welttheater* must probably be based on the significance of the Beggar. Hofmannsthal himself gave a clear lead:

Such new qualities as I have added to the traditional material are to be found in the figure of the Beggar. In my play he is the central character and is a lone individual in contrast to all the others. Instead of the passive, resigned beggar of the old mystery plays—instead of the 'poor man' in the Gospel who is one of the chosen simply because of his earthly fate…who has been placed on earth only to test the sanctity of others—instead of this figure I have put the active Beggar, deprived, disinherited, the Beggar who longs for his place amongst those who have inherited the good things of the earth: a figure, therefore, which could perhaps be perceived with such clarity only at the present time—the threat of chaos to an ordered world.[1]

This seems to illuminate the essential distinction between Calderón and Hofmannsthal. It might be summed up thus: Calderón's beggar, after initial protest, is happy in the knowledge that Blessed are the poor in spirit for they shall see God:

> *Rich Man.* How shall I make ostentation
>   Best of all my wealth?
> *Beggar.* My woe
>   How shall I best endure?
> *Law of Grace.* Doing well, for God is God.
> *Rich Man.* Oh, how that voice wearies me!
> *Beggar.* Oh, how that voice me consoles![1]

But the Beggar in the *Große Welttheater* is not only a malcontent. Potentially he is the most powerful figure of all. Hofmannsthal expressed himself very directly on this:

I make my disinherited Beggar raise his axe against everything that opposes him: King and Rich Man, Peasant—who over here represents the conservatism of the secure, small property-holder—and Beauty and pious Wisdom: that is to say, against everyone and everything. And it is quite clear from the situation and the preceding dialogue that if he attacks he will be stronger than all of them and that the edifice of an ordered society which has lasted a thousand years—and this synthesis of Christianity and half-Roman, half-German rule of law under which we live is indeed as old as that—will collapse under the blows of his axe.[2]

The sense of the Beggar's Saul–Paul conversion remains a matter for dispute. Outwardly it recalls those sudden transformations—*Wandlungen*—so popular with some expressionist dramatists. One can compare it, for example, with the idea of individual, personal regeneration put forward in Kaiser's *Die Bürger von Calais*: 'I have seen the new man. He was born this night.' This idea may well have been in Hofmannsthal's mind. He referred specifically to expressionist doctrine in connection with an alleged similarity between O'Neill's hero in *The Hairy Ape* and his own Beggar. But he added:

It is chaos's mocking question to order.... The same question, asked in various ways and in all tones of voice, is the entire content of Expressionism in all countries. Or—if you like—not its content but the fermenting agent which drives it on. But Expressionism presupposes the answer by the way in which it puts the question.[3]

The last sentence here is open to a variety of interpretations. With *Jedermann* and the *Große Welttheater* in mind one might perhaps deduce that the urbane and cosmopolitan Hofmannsthal was somewhat repelled by the extremes of some expressionist dramas: the tendency to see things in terms of black and white; little attempt at psychological credibility in characterization; the so overtly 'engaged' tone. Possibly the very vehemence of this kind of drama, together with its more than occasional rawness and immaturity of tone, seemed rather provincial to Hofmannsthal.[1] He seems, moreover, to have noted a certain loveless quality in Expressionism's approach to situations comparable with that confronting the Beggar. In a characteristically terse note, probably dating from about the same time as the letter cited above, Hofmannsthal referred again to *The Hairy Ape* and went on to define the polarity of that play and his own *Große Welttheater*. At the same time he gave a valuable indication of his own attitude to Expressionism and of his own interpretation of the Beggar: 'A figure of our time, the threat of chaos. Thus *The Hairy Ape*—an optimistic answer; my answer was not pessimistic but religious. As the Beggar raises his axe he is stirred by love. Transformation: Saul–Paul impossible in drama on the stage... (Expressionism: transformations without love).'[2]

Hofmannsthal's own views on problems of the day were certainly strong—as strong as those of many Expressionists—and he too developed the use of 'representational' figures in his plays. But aware as he was of the ambiguities of life, the shades between black and white, he often managed to give his 'representational' characters at least some quality of psychological depth, some hint of the contradictory qualities which make up real people. Jedermann, the Peasant and Julian (in *Der Turm*) are cases in point.[3]

An expressionist approach to the Beggar in the *Große Welttheater* ignores, moreover, the possibility of divine grace. For belief in the never-ending and even (in human terms) illogical generosity of God is basic to the Christian code. It can scarcely be eliminated from a discussion of the later Hofmannsthal. Reflecting upon the works of Hofmannsthal's last years Ernst Robert Curtius seems to develop this view to its logical conclusion:

His deepest insight was 'that life can only be lived by means of valid ties'. His appointed task was to purify and transfigure these ties... the tie between the people and the rulers in the state; between man and God and time and eternity. On this road the wisdom of Asia[1] could only be a station and a symbol, not a homeland and a solution. These could be found only in the revelation which had gone forth to both orient and occident: in Christianity. The traditions of his fellow-countrymen and their native-soil showed him the way....The works of his last seven years are Christian not only in their symbolism but in the inclination of his heart with its great and silent 'sursum corda'.[2]

There is not necessarily any discrepancy between Curtius's Christian view and Hofmannsthal's comment to Strauss (see p. 157). Hofmannsthal was after all merely emphasizing that the play could appeal to those who had no denominational ties, perhaps no Christian affiliations at all, a claim to which we shall return presently. But it seems that Curtius might well be representing Hofmannsthal's own personal views. A good deal will turn on how one interprets the notion of 'inner freedom' which plays such a large part in the play and which is mentioned in the letter to Strauss.

Hofmannsthal's stage directions emphasize the fact that his characters are unborn souls. They depict, as it were, the possibilities. The Beggar *would* smash the world *if* the Rich Man were allowed untrammelled freedom, *if* the Peasant looks after himself and lets the rest of the world go by. All the characters are equal in the sight of God, a fact strikingly stressed by their exact similarity in features, form and dress before and after the 'play within the play'. All, as is shown to the Beggar, must accept their lot without overthrowing order. Early in the action it is emphasized that God creates all and knows the end of all things. But equal emphasis is given to the fact that man has free will to make or mar his earthly state, an idea which is equally acceptable to devout

Catholic and scientific humanist. This is the lesson of the Rich Man and to a lesser extent of the King, the Peasant and Beauty.

This view is confirmed in the final scene of the play. The characters, led by Wisdom and the Beggar, move towards the palace of the Master. Beauty is last in the line and stretches out her hand to the Rich Man who has been left alone. She begs the angel not to condemn him to *eternal* damnation:

> Ihm nie? O sprich nicht aus das fürchterliche Wort!
> Weis ihm den einsam kalten finstern Ort,
> Doch sprich kein Nie!

The stage direction describes now how the angel points to a place lower down where the Rich Man kneels. The final tableau shows the angel leading Wisdom and the Beggar into the palace. Beauty, the King and the Peasant kneel at the side of the entrance. Below in the darkness kneels the Rich Man. Thus assigned to purgatory the Rich Man is not damned for eternity to Hell. Though far below in the darkness he is still in the sight of God. He can, in a word, still reform.

Seen thus as a whole the play represents a polarity. The Beggar is the one violent extreme who is cautioned and saved from the sin of anarchical violence. But the other extreme, equally violent and no less so for being less obvious, is the Rich Man who brings the world to the brink of catastrophe. On him everything depends. If the Rich Man does not try to bring about on earth the reflection of the kingdom of God then the Beggar's anarchy is justified.

Why did Hofmannsthal concentrate to such an extent on the Rich Man? The King, the symbol of secular power, is lightly dealt with and at the end kneels with Beauty and the Peasant at the threshold of heaven. But Hofmannsthal seems to have realized (as clearly as Bertolt Brecht or Upton Sinclair and other such polemical contemporaries) where the real power lay. A mildly worded extract from his notes for *Reden in Skandinavien* (1917) indicates this:

Everyone's ego rejoices in the knowledge that he is necessary to the community at large. If he can be proud of the community then his pride in himself increases. On the other hand, however, it must be admitted that the idea of belonging to the system of cosmopolitan industrialism can in the breasts of innumerable worthy people evoke only a sense of shame at belonging to a collective of this kind....

the call for intellectual authority; this authority should rise up from amongst the people. Even the most untutored, most childlike of men would gladly submit to intellectual authority, if it seemed firm and reliable.[1]

This seems to answer the question concerning the Rich Man and the King. The king-figure, as a symbol of responsible authority both spiritual and temporal, was an important feature of Hofmannsthal's artistic constitution. This fact, as shown in chapters 6 and 7, is fundamental to an understanding of *Der Turm*. Hence in the *Große Welttheater* the ruler-symbol might be admonished and urged to live up to his calling. He could scarcely be condemned *per se*. But the Rich Man is wholly destructive.[2] In his present-day form, as the product of contemporary conditions, he is culpable and probably unregenerate. This is clearly brought out in the Rich Man's address to the King:

> Viel mehr ist vorbereit,
> Wenn dies erhabne Schwert mir weiter Schutz verleiht.

The figure of the Rich Man together with the criticism to which Hofmannsthal subjects him are probably based on ideas which had been expressed six years previously in *Die Idee Europa* (1916). Two extracts may illustrate Hofmannsthal's purpose here. The first explains by implication the symbolism of the Rich Man: 'The stigma of Europe: seeking the means and not the end of existence...being concerned with illusory freedom we have forgotten the law.'[3] The second extract embraces the ideal function both of the King and of the Beggar:

A new European idea: new reality. Not a Utopia, not a confederation of states, not a permanent council of ministers, although all this might well come about—but a new European self, a different relationship between self and life, between self and money. Socialization of the state: the realization here and now of the tendencies of 1830.[4]

Paul Requadt tells how 'even during the war he [Hofmannsthal] had, in various neutral countries, spoken up for the idea of a Central European community—and not always as the authorities intended'.[1] The authorities' apprehension seems to have been justified! For Hofmannsthal, and this is one lesson of the *Große Welttheater*, Christian Socialism and enlightened monarchy were mutually reconcilable. Bithell is probably right when he says that the argument in the *Große Welttheater* 'transfigures Communism'.[2]

The above discussion has brought forward some of the points which Hofmannsthal was trying to make in this play. In a word the 'what' has been considered. The 'how', which includes the degree of effectiveness in portraying these ideas, will be the ultimately decisive factor in a final judgment of the play as a whole. Reflecting upon Hofmannsthal's intention in plays such as the *Große Welttheater* Curtius writes:

But this experiment, which Hofmannsthal had first attempted with *Jedermann*, had tremendous significance: it meant nothing less than bridging a chasm which during the past few centuries of Europe's development had become wider and wider; the chasm between on the one hand the enlightened world of culture and education and on the other the elemental urge to play a story on a stage; between philosophical discussion of problems and timeless symbolism.[3]

This is a good point of departure for a consideration of the ultimate merit and effectiveness of the *Große Welttheater*. Such a consideration demands that we now look at the play from a more specifically artistic and theatrical point of view.

The *Große Welttheater* presents a rather unexpected duality. Its general tone, especially in the language of the characters, is subdued by comparison with *Jedermann*. Its dramatic structure, on the other hand, is rather more complex than that of the earlier play. *Jedermann* is divided into 'acts' (see p. 38), but with the exception of the sacred prologue and the scene between Jedermann's mother and her servant the actual *locus* of the action does not change.

In the *Große Welttheater*, however, full use is made of the baroque-type stage-setting stipulated by Hofmannsthal—with its various levels and stage within a stage. One might say that the *static* visual spectacle in this play is on a greater scale than in the case of *Jedermann*. But the overall impression of colour, movement and variety radiated by *Jedermann* is not so marked in the *Große Welttheater*.

In the theatre—or, more correctly, in church, cloister or castle-court—the *Große Welttheater* has always made a considerable effect. Hofmannsthal himself referred to its direct effect on its first audience and at the same time he gave some indication of the kind of public for which his work was planned and the purpose he wished to achieve:

I cannot say that on these fourteen evenings the public was in any way reluctant to let itself be captured by this religious or allegorical play. Neither did the play itself have any difficulty in overwhelming the sensibilities of those present. Everything 'went' without one having to think how it all happened. And yet it was the most mixed audience imaginable. It was not only that for the first time since the war we had assembled in one place in Central Europe a completely international audience; but the various parts of our own nation—I mean the German and Austrian elements in the audience—were socially very mixed indeed. Many simple folk—peasants or people from our small country towns in the Alps—sat alongside the 'newly rich'. Priests and nuns were likewise to be seen amongst Americans, Scandinavians, French and Berliners. Reinhardt's setting and production must take the credit for fusing this extraordinary mixture...into an audience—yes, a completely unified audience which let itself be 'captured' in an almost childlike way.[1]

Outwardly the play seems to have retained much of the Spanish Baroque typical of Calderón.[2] The Spanish element is in no way minimized if one asserts that Hofmannsthal had another, wider aim in view. He was determined to graft his play on to the folk- and peasant-theatre tradition discussed in chapter 1 in connection with *Jedermann*. The success of the *Jedermann* experiment encouraged him. In a short essay which appeared in the *Salzburger Festspiel-Almanach* for 1925 Hofmannsthal recorded how he came to create the *Große Welttheater* in this particular way:

But the man who may regard himself as the creator of the play performed,[1] and as the renewer of an ancient yearning for the theatre so firmly rooted in these parts could not help being moved—more deeply, even, than by the reception given to the play by the great throng...
when, here and there in the streets, he came across people of all ages who were telling each other the content of the play, emphasizing the essentials with a wonderful assurance typical of our peasants, and encouraging others from further afield to come and see it.

The encouragement thus received by the author in this attempt to reach back into the past...and to take up a half-forgotten form of folk-art, together with the rarely granted permission to put up a stage in a Catholic church, a great honour and an equally great responsibility —all these factors led to the second attempt: to give a new content to that old traditional theme of the World Theatre. In this way the spirit of our own times would be expressed without departing from the folk style which manifests itself in appropriate pictures.[2]

Hofmannsthal's wish to join his work to a tradition of this kind was only a variation on the method used in his cultural-political essays of the war period (particularly those discussed in chapter 3). But in the present instance he was well aware that the six figures representing mankind were part of a European rather than a specifically Austro-German tradition. The evident impact on his cosmopolitan audience seemed to fulfil his hope that the 'spirit of our own times' could be poured into these ancient, timeless figures. These figures in their turn, he hoped, would bring to the contemporary problems of the *Große Welttheater* the visible weight of a long European, Christian tradition:

You see, this goes back a good deal further than Calderón and the seventeenth century. These figures, each one by itself in a niche surrounded by Gothic foliation, belong to that world which we encounter in Flemish and northern French tapestries of the fifteenth century. The *World Theatre* is a mystery play or a theatrical allegory.

This is a very old dramatic form which has had its golden age in all European literatures: in pre-Shakespearian England just as in France before she handed over her literature to the imitators of the ancient world. But down here, at least, this form has never quite died out. In Catholic southern Germany and Austria there was until towards the end of the eighteenth century a folk theatre whose themes were taken just as frequently from the Bible as they were from the old treasure-house of allegory left to us by the mystery-plays; and Oberammergau with its passion-play is simply the remnant of this naïve theatrical world, the last tip, as it were, of a sunken island continent. All this was only swept away when, in the wake of the French Revolution, a spirit of rationalism blew across Europe.[1]

The most striking dramatic use of these ancient figures is at the climax of the play. For this climax Hofmannsthal not only reached back into the archaic past but also into his own past. The climax brings to life once more that characteristic folk-symbol embodied in the Dance of Death. Hitherto in Hofmannsthal's dramas this symbol had been implicit in the action, notably in *Der Tor und der Tod* and in *Jedermann*.

By the time Hofmannsthal wrote the *Große Welttheater*, however, the developments he had feared had become reality. And so in the post-war mid-twenties he deliberately brought the actual Dance of Death to life on the stage, confidently trusting that his audience would find its symbolism credible. The scene itself is only a few lines in length but is so constructed and tersely spoken that to the imagination it is ever-present. Each 'type-figure' save Wisdom (the Beggar is off-stage) fades and ages. Beauty laments that time, the murderer and robber, has come amongst them and done violence to them. As she speaks of time, Hofmannsthal introduces two ageless symbols of time: the stark and rhythmic beat of the drum, stipulated in his stage-direction, is echoed in the onlooker's mind by the beat of heart and pulse, by the swing and sound of the pendulum and by the eternal beat of the waves on the shore. This is the first symbol and is quite literally elemental.

Simultaneously a wind arises. The wind as a symbol of time and destiny, of past and future, would be a study in itself. In Hofmannsthal's work it made an early appearance. It recurred again and again in the lyric poetry of his youth; in the *Ballade des äußeren Lebens*, for example:

> Und immer weht der Wind, und immer wieder
> Vernehmen wir und reden viele Worte
> Und spüren Lust und Müdigkeit der Glieder.

Perhaps best known of all is *Vorfrühling* with its strange song of destiny:

> Es läuft der Frühlingswind
> Durch kahle Alleen,
> Seltsame Dinge sind in seinem Wehn.

Less well known, however, is *Regen in der Dämmerung* where the wind is also the main image of the poem and carries the bittersweet longing and wild nostalgia which rise up as the rain falls at twilight:

> Der wandernde Wind auf den Wegen
> War angefüllt mit süßem Laut,
> Der dämmernde rieselnde Regen
> War mit Verlangen feucht betaut....
>
> Der Wind in den wehenden Weiden,
> Am Wasser der wandernde Wind
> Berauschte die sehnenden Leiden,
> Die in der Dämmerung sind.

In *Weihnacht* the wind bears the sound of Christmas bells, stirs up memory of the past and raises brooding doubts about the future:

> Weihnachtsgeläute   Die kommenden Tage,
> im nächtigen Wind...   Die wehn da vorbei.
> Wer weiß, wo heute   Wer hörts, ob Klage,
> Die Glocken sind,   Ob lachender Mai,
> Die Töne von damals sind?...   Ob blühender, glühender Mai?...

At the climax of the *Große Welttheater* this lyrical device is translated into theatrically realistic and yet symbolic sound, against which the voices of the various figures are heard. As the wind rises the figures begin to move. The stage direction calls up yet another association: 'The figures, as if waking from rigid lifelessness, leave their places and move amongst each other, but like people in a dream.'[1] The image here is of those ancient clocks, such as the astrological clock in the Minster at Strasbourg, with their stiff, carved allegorical figures who come forward at the passing of each hour.

Hofmannsthal's own reference to the medieval origin of his figures has already been noted. Some years before writing the *Große Welttheater*, however, the association between the Dance of Death and a clock such as that described above had occurred to Hofmannsthal. This is confirmed in a rather unexpected place. In the notes for *Reden in Skandinavien* (1916) Hofmannsthal referred to *Jedermann* and discussed its significance.[2] Introducing *Jedermann* he wrote: '*Jedermann*: the Dance of Death as in those old chapels, the simplest motives...an old clock, cleaned up, cobwebs brushed away, so that it can strike again and let its figures move in and out.'[3]

One might therefore say that in this short scene there is a threefold symbol of time and destiny: the drum-pulse, the wind and the clock. It is small wonder that Hofmannsthal, writing of this scene at the first performance (1922), was able to relate that

the most powerful or—if you like—most vehement moment in the whole play was the Dance of Death which preceded the fading and farewell of the six allegorical figures, approximately at the beginning of the last third of the play. He [Reinhardt] directed that this episode should be accompanied only by a drum, but in a rhythm which sent a kind of solemn terror pulsating through the audience, evoking a sombre sigh from many people, of a kind quite different from and much more powerful than anything you would ever hear in the secular theatre.[4]

The puppet-like quality of the scene is enhanced by the stark rhythmic quality in the speech of all the figures. The sharp, angular character of the verse reflects the brusque, unadorned, proverb-like speech of the five stricken characters as they move around one another. The whole sequence abounds in antithesis as each human spirit feels God's hand hovering above:

King. Macht ist Ohnmacht! Das geht mir ein
Und schneidet mir durch Mark und Bein.
Rich Man. Ich kannte Zwang nicht, noch Gesetz,
Allein ein Etwas zwingt mich jetzt!

The climax is reached when all five intone in unison and bemoan the shadowiness of life, while the drumbeat pulses behind, above and around them:

Ein fahler Schein, ein hahler Wind,
Weh, daß wir Kreaturen sind.

It is noteworthy that in these lines Hofmannsthal takes the traditional German rhyming couplet, the *Knittelvers,* with its associations—memories of Hans Sachs, the traditions of Shrovetide, mystery- and passion-plays—and transforms it. This feature of Hofmannsthal's style was discussed in chapter 2, notably in connection with Faith's words to Jedermann on the mercy of God. In the present instance the repetition of sound in *fahl* and *hahl* brings with it the moan of the winds of time. The short, sharp *Weh* with the abrupt pause that follows gives the sense of sudden, poignant realization. The vocabulary itself is simple; the lines themselves have the direct, aphoristic quality of those couplets still to be seen, for example, in a Tyrolean cemetery on a gravestone or above a row of skulls in the charnel-house.

It is no accident that one tends to consider the action of the *Große Welttheater* in terms of dramatic 'highlights'. The main impression left by the play considered as a whole will probably be of a series of effective dramatic interludes or insets. This is not in itself a bad thing. But one misses the kind of unity which in *Jedermann* is provided by the principal character and by the sustained build-up to the appearance of Death at the banquet, which is the theatrical climax of the play.

The alternation in the *Große Welttheater* between prose for the spectators of the 'play within the play' and verse for the characters themselves is skilfully done and serves to set off the inner action in a convincing way.[1] The speech of the characters themselves is as finely differentiated as one would expect: the flowing, hypocritical phrases of the Rich Man; the tender simplicity of Wisdom; the direct, manly, dialect-tinged idiom of the Beggar; the very broad rural speech of the Peasant with its ring of parochialism, self-satisfaction and omniscience on a small scale.

But the periodic interruptions by the Adversary and the World become a little tedious, while the chattering and rather unfunny wit of *Vorwitz*[1] is distracting and sometimes irritating. Vorwitz, indeed, often breaks the mood and tension of the play to no good purpose. This character seems to be one of those cases where a stock figure, in this instance the Spanish *gracioso*, has been taken over without being fully 'absorbed' into the action and intention of the play. The effect made by Vorwitz is at times uncomfortably reminiscent of the more conventional and less humorous antics of some Shakespearian Fools.[2]

Bergstraesser says that Vorwitz 'acts as a counterpart to serious significance through the shortcomings of his judgments and the sentimentality of his emotions. He has the quick and superficial mind of impertinent curiosity.'[3] Brenan (see note 2 above) tells how in Lope de Vega's plays the *gracioso* parodies the actions of the principal characters. One's reaction to Hofmannsthal's Vorwitz, as with the Devil in *Jedermann* (see chapter 2), will probably vary according to the tradition to which one is accustomed.

On the other hand it must in fairness be said that the remarks of Vorwitz do cause the issues of the drama proper to stand out in relief: the effect is, perhaps, not unlike the Brechtian *Verfremdungseffekt*, and irrespective of traditions, audiences do not seem to have any difficulty in accepting the latter.

It will have become obvious that in assessing the *Große Welttheater* a comparison with *Jedermann* constantly suggests itself. The literary backgrounds of the two plays are indeed far apart from each other. The austerity of the English *Everyman* has little in common with the baroque spectacle of Calderón's *auto*. Moreover, the upheaval of World War I, with all the changes and developments brought about by it, separates Hofmannsthal's two plays from each other, and not only in terms of chronology. Nevertheless, *Jedermann* and the *Große Welttheater* are frequently coupled in association and not without reason.

First, they are the only two dramas of Hofmannsthal's which are of directly religious inspiration and in which divine characters take part. Secondly, as shown in chapters 1 and 2, Hofmannsthal made *Jedermann* a baroque spectacle-drama and so brought it into the same sphere as the *Große Welttheater*. Thirdly, because of the Salzburg tradition of performance (Domplatz for *Jedermann*, Collegienkirche for the *Große Welttheater*) they are associated with each other in the minds of Hofmannsthal's audiences, and this is not merely by chance. Hofmannsthal designed these two dramas first and foremost as 'festival dramas' and such, on the whole, they have remained. Comparisons are therefore inevitable, especially when the connection in Hofmannsthal's own mind (see p. 174) is taken into account. A comparison is to some extent fruitful in that it demonstrates Hofmannsthal's developing purpose.

As noted earlier, the *Große Welttheater* has not the varied, visual brilliance of *Jedermann*. Perhaps, moreover, it does not make the immediate appeal and impact of *Jedermann*. When one considers the 'models' for the two plays, especially the lavishness of Calderón's *auto*, this might seem surprising. But it is in fact explicable, for where *Jedermann* spoke to society in terms of and through the individual, the *Große Welttheater* is not only more deliberately allegorical but is also wider in intent.

When one says 'more deliberately allegorical' one means that in the *Große Welttheater* Hofmannsthal has formalized or typed his figures to a greater extent than in *Jedermann*; and this formal quality is already very apparent in the earlier play. In *Jedermann*, it will be recalled, Hofmannsthal added certain human touches to characters in order to rouse and hold the audience's interest or sympathy. In the *Große Welttheater* Hofmannsthal's 'wider intent' makes this practice less necessary. The Beggar is the leading figure in the play, but the significant moral is distributed throughout all the characters in the 'play within the play'. Hofmannsthal addresses society through a society, rather than the individual through an individual.

Jedermann and the *Große Welttheater* therefore complement each other and should be regarded as necessary variants of the same basic idea. It was suggested earlier that in the *Große Welttheater* Hofmannsthal attempted to bridge the gap between 'philosophical discussion of problems and timeless symbolism' (Curtius). The extent to which Hofmannsthal was successful is as debatable in this case as in that of *Jedermann*. Because, however, of its frequently austere concentration on the moral essentials the *effect* of the *Große Welttheater* on an audience may be considerable, even though the play is in a theatrical sense less spectacular than *Jedermann*. The problem of its ultimate success and general value probably depends on the extent to which the use of these ancient religious symbols finds an instinctive and sympathetic response in the audience. This was no problem for Calderón. As Curtius has written:

Calderón was able to create his figures in a world whose monarchical and Catholic structure still stood firm and seemed unshakeable. The incipient decay of state and nation was covered over by dynastic and ecclesiastical pomp. Hofmannsthal's historical situation is exactly the reverse. He found himself in a decaying world. He had...to be present at its dissolution right up to the catastrophic end.[1]

Curtius's statement sums up the problem by implication: the response to the *Große Welttheater* will probably be forthcoming in countries and communities which have a virtually unbroken religious tradition and where in consequence the symbolism can have the effect of recalling the onlooker to something which, however weakly, is still within him and in his environment. That is to say that the *Große Welttheater* can reawaken and rekindle the religious, moral sense. Whether it could ever create it is a matter of doubt. In joining his play so deliberately to a tradition

Hofmannsthal has virtually assured success in one sense—and has simultaneously limited it in another.

Bergstraesser discusses this problem with insight. He refers to an article by Leopold Andrian on *Große Welttheater*, and continues:

he indicated the 'more primitive way of developing religious ideas' which Hofmannsthal, compared with Calderón, had to choose. He expected that by such plays an atmosphere of culture could be created which both intellectuals and believers might have in common. Thereby he defined indirectly the position of the play which neither is 'merely a work of art' nor an illustration of dogmatic convictions, but the product of an experience which is poetical as well as religious. The drama is Christian in a general understanding. It contains social criticism but not a social doctrine. Therefore it is at the same time more and less than an 'image of the social doctrine of the Church. . .'.[1]

Bergstraesser seems to take an optimistic view of the play's actual effect but is careful not to confuse ideal with reality.

The extent to which Hofmannsthal has bridged the gap between 'philosophical discussion of problems and timeless symbolism' is therefore questionable. The main achievement of the *Große Welttheater* may on the other hand be—in a sense—the reconciliation of 'the enlightened world of culture and education and . . . the elemental urge to play a story on a stage'.[2] Hofmannsthal does seem to have solved the problem of satisfying simultaneously the intellectual and the common man, in a theatrical sense at least. The combination of homely idiom and clear-cut dramatic situation with sophisticated cunning in the art of linguistic suggestion and traditional overtone seems to be the chief factor in this.

All in all the *Große Welttheater* is in many ways a notable achievement. In the final consideration its principal importance may well lie in the fact that in an age marked by secularism, materialism and a turning away from the 'outworn' religious conventions, Hofmannsthal succeeded in making these things at least a matter for theatrical enjoyment and serious discussion.

The developments elaborated in this chapter complement to some extent the concepts of people, nation and continent which were advanced in the wartime essays discussed in chapters 3 and 4. These various discussions may now help us to reach an understanding of Hofmannsthal's last *Festspiel*, *Der Turm*, a consideration of which concludes the present study.

CHAPTER 6

'DER TURM': BACKGROUND AND PLOT

IN a fairly recent vignette Reinhold Schneider recalled the initial reception given to *Der Turm*.[1] His comments are instructive both from an historical viewpoint and because they give some idea of the essential content and import of the play itself. Schneider, a Catholic of many varying phases, was well qualified to interpret from within, as it were, what was in Hofmannsthal's mind:

I still have a copy of the first edition of *Der Turm* (1927). The price on the cover has been crossed out and reduced by more than half. In the early thirties whole piles of the book could be seen lying around the second-hand bookshops....A bitter reproach to the reading public. I have never been able to forget the sight. The word[2] which unmasked our time (and with it the future) more effectively, perhaps, than any other, lay there amongst all the dead, outworn...pratings of bygone times. This truth was quite clear, wholly of the present, but its language was not that of the world which it had been called upon to combat, the 'sober reality' of the visionaries. It was an inexplicable but nonetheless 'joyful sign', and it waited for the few. And even those few, perhaps, took it up without wholly comprehending its terrible, prophetic consistency.

The external action of *Der Turm* is based on Calderón's *La vida es sueño* (c. 1636). The seeds of the play had been germinating in Hofmannsthal's mind for a long time.[3] In 1902 he had written a free adaptation of parts of Calderón's drama. In the following years he seems to have been thinking about the theme a good deal[4] and in 1907 and 1910 he published fragments of his work. On the latter occasion the appearance of Calderón's play in the repertory of the *Burgtheater* provided the appropriate moment for publication. In his introduction to the fragment of 1910, however, he remarks that he has found it impossible to finish the adaptation. He speaks of a central difficulty which is not so much artistic and technical in kind as intellectual (*geistig*).[1]

The catastrophe of the war and the spiritual chaos following it gave the necessary reality and creative impulse for the completion of the play. Hofmannsthal himself was quite unambiguous about this. Not only was it constantly apparent in his conversations with Carl Burckhardt[2] but he stressed the fact quite unequivocally in a letter to Hermann Bahr in 1918. Here he observed that Calderón's play and his own work on the theme 'became comprehensible in the final instance only through the experience of the war'.[3]

The theme and action of Calderón's play constituted, as Burckhardt pointed out, one of those eternal symbols 'which he liked to call the hieroglyphs of a secret, inexhaustible wisdom'.[4] Allardyce Nicoll has summed up the dual nature of Calderón's play very clearly:

Outwardly this play is but another romantic tale set this time in Poland with a heroine, Rosaura, and a miserable captive, Sigismundo; but what gives the whole action its distinction is the way in which the author has as it were imposed a theme upon his plot. Sigismundo is being kept in durance because an oracle has declared that he, the true prince, would prove a fatal enemy to his father and his country. As the King his parent grows old, however, remorse comes to him, and he determines that his son shall be granted a trial. Given a potion, the young man is brought drugged to the palace, and when he opens his eyes he finds himself surrounded by the trappings of royalty. Almost at once, however, he betrays ungovernable brutality of spirit, even while he wonders in his mind whether all of this may not be merely a dream. His actions are so savage and arbitrary that once more he is returned to his dungeon and there he reflects with regret and horror on what he is convinced must have been an hallucination....[5]

It is not necessary here to outline the remainder of Calderón's action.[6] It has quite evidently a symbolic quality which offers great possibilities for exploring the depths, meaning and illusoriness of human existence. Allardyce Nicoll quotes aptly a sequence which gives some idea of the scope of the symbol. Sigismundo, alone in his cell, reflects:

And though none are rightly ware,
all are dreaming that they are
in this life, until death ends.
I am dreaming I lie here
Laden with this fetter's weight,
And I dreamed that I of late
did in fairer sort appear.
What is life? A frenzy mere;
What is life? E'en what we deem;
a conceit, a shadow all,
and the greatest good is small,
nothing is, but all doth seem,
dreams within dreams, still we dream.[1]

Ernst Robert Curtius has given a summary of the symbol which is particularly relevant for present purposes:

This awakening to the world...is one of the typical situations in Calderón's theatre. How rich is the symbolism in this situation. It is already indicated in Plato's cave myth, and the conception of the body as the prison of the soul is also Platonic. But this cave existence, this prison tower is at the same time the pre-existence of the soul before birth. And this idea is expressed in Calderón's *Gran teatro del mundo* as well as in Hofmannsthal's *Große Welttheater*. And finally Prince Sigismund's awakening to the world, his liberation from the tower, his failure in the test—all these are only an allegorical disguise for the destiny of the human soul as it passes from pre-existence to birth, original sin and redemption. Calderón himself indicated this allegory when he followed *La vida es sueño* by a sacred drama of the same title. This drama elevated the action of the former play on to a theological plain.[2]

It will therefore be apparent that in drawing on Calderón's theme, as Calderón had in his turn drawn on the past, Hofmannsthal was at the last stage in his career adopting a familiar technique.[3] He recreated and reinterpreted a timeless theme in such a way that it brought into his play many of its own associations and overtones.[4] At the same time, however, the theme was exposed and interpreted in the light of modern ideas and problems. Hofmannsthal himself wrote of his intention in *Der Turm* as follows:

Der Turm: here I have to demonstrate the essential pitilessness of our reality into which the soul stumbles as it emerges from a dark and mythical realm....[1]

He also emphasized the specifically contemporary force of his drama:

The individual and his epoch seen as a myth, *sic*: whatever, since Kant, lives on as a changed attitude to the world is somehow mirrored in Sigismund.

No myth comes into being without the actions and sufferings of individual people. Therefore events since 1914 had first to take place before the forces could be formulated as a myth.[2]

Der Turm is set in Poland but the author hints immediately at a symbolic significance. He is careful not to bind his scene to historical fact or environment. The Polish kingdom referred to in the prefatory directions to the play is 'more of saga than of history'. It is set in a bygone century similar in atmosphere to the seventeenth. This period in Poland's history was in actual fact sadly marked by decadence and steady decline; and it soon becomes apparent in the play that Hofmannsthal's Poland is a huge dramatic symbol for the modern decline of the western world. Grete Schaeder's assessment of Hofmannsthal's purpose goes straight to the point:

The action takes place in a world out of joint, in which all human qualities have gone rotten.... The society of *Der Turm* is nothing but a great distortion of all divine order. But it still claims the hallowed rights of this order.... In *Der Turm* Hofmannsthal calls man's original sin by its proper name: it is the force and abuse which arbitrary power inflicts on the human soul.[3]

In point of fact Hofmannsthal hints at this symbolic aim in a rather unusual manner. There are in the fifth act two distinct references to important features of the Roman Imperium. On the first occasion Sigismund (now a crusading king) is talking to the Doctor:

I have read that biography in Plutarch which you had left open for me. Despite the difference in the times there are in it great and relevant resemblances to us and our situation.

A short while later he remarks to the Doctor: 'Let one of our cavalrymen fetch that book of which you spoke. By the Emperor Marcus—.' The Doctor replies: 'Marcus Aurelius—', and Sigismund continues:

Meditations—or whatever you called it. A great monarch, and full of noble thoughts and far-reaching plans to guide the future of Europe along certain paths for centuries to come. But he also was the victim of circumstances and he dies in his tent in the midst of his plans.[1]

The first quotation is a clear instance of Hofmannsthal using an historical analogy (some unspecified depiction of Rome and/or Greece by Plutarch) within his own symbol (Poland in decline). A discussion of the detailed significance of this unnamed biography, together with some reasons for believing that Hofmannsthal had the Alexander-Caesar biography in mind, will be found on pp. 263–4.

The second quotation is of deeper if less obvious significance. Marcus Aurelius, most philosophical of the Roman emperors, spent much time in Noricum and Pannonia (which covered the area of what is today Austria)[2] and actually died in Vindobona (Vienna) in A.D. 180. He is held in particular esteem in Austrian history, being regarded almost as a national possession. His reign marked the end of an epoch in the development of the Roman empire. Much of his reign (A.D. 161–80) was spent in warfare against the Dacians and Germans. Peace was only secured at the cost of concessions which admitted to imperial territory large numbers of barbarians. His death was a turning-point in the destinies of Rome, a *Wendepunkt* in the tragic sense with which this term was used by Hebbel. Following his death the shadows of decline began to gather over the empire, a decline whose reality was only obscured by the prowess of Aurelian and Diocletian, Constantine and Julian the Apostate.

The significance to Hofmannsthal of Marcus Aurelius—a philosopher-statesman of high quality, wise, enlightened, far-seeing, but frustrated and defeated by the material world—is clear enough. The analogy of his times with those in which Hofmannsthal wrote *Der Turm* is likewise apparent.

Hofmannsthal thus doubles the effect. First there is the symbol of Poland in decline. Within that symbol the leading character adopts the same technique and draws an analogy with a still earlier and even more catastrophic turning-point in history. As shown at various points in chapters 3 and 4 Austria was the self-conscious bearer of the tradition of the Roman Imperium. The analogy with Marcus Aurelius was thus designed to make a striking effect. Sigismund's comments on Marcus Aurelius are actually spoken a matter of moments before he receives his fateful wound, an apparent triviality of dire consequence, rather in the manner of the chance wound received in battle by another great reformer, Julian the Apostate.[1] The unexpected consequences, however, altered the entire course of history.

The portent and force of the symbolic setting of *Der Turm* are thus clear. But before embarking on a thorough survey of the play itself, it may be as well to consider fairly briefly the action of the drama. The detailed observations to follow may then fall into perspective against the overall outline of the plot and its development.

The play opens darkly amid rumours of Jew-baiting, wars and uprising. It is a time of growing disorder when 'all are against all'. Evil portents seen by the soldiery of the tower's garrison set a mood of mystery and foreboding, and give warning that more than rational forces are at work.

Prince Sigismund is imprisoned in the tower as the result of a prophecy that he will do violence to his father King Basilius of Poland. Here in the tower he lives a completely sequestered and animal-like existence. His guardian and teacher is the ambitious, unscrupulous and rather unstable Julian, who seems later in the action to have had a hand in the risings or at any rate to be using them for his own purposes.

It is soon clear that Julian intends to use Sigismund for his own ends as soon as opportunity offers. The Doctor who visits Sigismund persuades Julian to initiate a plan designed to restore the Crown Prince to the court. The Doctor himself is a man of great insight and humanity with a marked neoplatonic outlook. He has perceived the essential nobility of Sigismund's soul, which remains untarnished by outward degradation. Through the perception of the Doctor, Sigismund becomes at this early stage in the play a dual symbol. On the one hand he is a symbol of suffering humanity as a whole. At the same time he is established as a symbol of redemption.

News arrives of rising chaos around the King. The King's nephew and heir-apparent has been killed in an accident.[1] The Grand Almoner, Chancellor of the Realm and sworn enemy of Julian, has withdrawn from all his offices. Under the simple name of Brother Ignatius he has entered a monastery.

The impending arrival of a great potentate and emissary from the King is announced. The Woiwode (Duke or *Statthalter*) of Lublin is coming to confer with Julian. Julian gradually reveals that he is planning a great test for Sigismund which aims at no less than his re-establishment at court. The Doctor, at Julian's request, promises a potion which will render the prince unconscious and make possible his unknowing removal to the royal palace. It becomes clear that Julian will propose this test to the Woiwode.

Meanwhile the King, in great anxiety of mind, makes a pilgrimage to the monastery where Ignatius, the former Chancellor, now lives. In this scene some of the forces which condemned Sigismund to the tower become apparent. The kingship of Basilius is seen at once to be arbitrary and decadent. He confesses himself impotent in the face of the troubles which beset the country. He has that strange mixture in his character which was often apparent in certain late Byzantine emperors and Turkish sultans: an inflated, egoistical power-complex, moral supineness, together with physical and mental cowardice.

The King's courtiers are self-seeking time-servers, while his confessor aids him in finding pious justification for his inhumanity towards Sigismund. Ignatius, his former adviser and confidant, is embittered and indifferent to the King's distress. He holds up a mirror to the hypocrisy and cynicism which characterize the King. He prophesies destruction and ruin from the war which was started in defiance of his advice.

Julian arrives in response to the summons from the King. Basilius agrees to the proposed test. He honours Julian; and the courtiers quickly seek the good graces of the new favourite.

In the following scene the potion is given to Sigismund. In the few seconds before a death-like coma overwhelms him, the Prince takes on the bearing and speech of a redeemer. Unconscious and attired in princely dress, Sigismund is carried off to the court.

The scene at the court is long and extremely varied in style and action. Here it is sufficient to note that Sigismund impresses his father with his natural princely qualities. A reconciliation is almost effected, with Basilius very much the master. Then the King surprisingly orders Sigismund to get rid of the new favourite, Julian. Together, he tells his son, they will create a new era, with Sigismund as his father's executive instrument. The Prince, who has throughout shown signs of bewilderment and fear at the King's evident violence, now attacks and humiliates the King.

The prophecy is thus fulfilled and Sigismund seizes power. Julian is quick to hail him as King, but Sigismund is immediately overthrown and condemned again to the tower. Julian is likewise committed to the tower as Sigismund's keeper. He is charged to make good his promise to convince Sigismund that all was a dream in a deep slumber. Julian himself, under pain of death, may henceforth never venture from the tower's walls. The Doctor alone is unperturbed by what has happened and sees the true nature of the situation: 'Mighty is the age which will renew itself through a chosen one. Chains will be broken like straw and towers blown away like dust.'[1]

News now comes of an uprising amongst the people who are

lying in thousands before the churches, praying for a beggar-king, a nameless boy who will be their leader. In chains he will bring about a new kingdom. Back in the tower Sigismund is persuaded that the whole affair was a dream. Julian now tries to woo the Prince into leading a rebellion which he has roused up as the result of much clandestine journeying. He admits openly that he has trained Sigismund only to this end. Sigismund, however, is no longer the helpless, questioning figure of the early scenes. He has meanwhile come to a full realization of his purpose and he now asserts his independence. With a clear-cut rejection of Julian he renounces violence in words which lie at the spiritual heart of the play: 'All is vanity save speech between spirit and spirit.'[1] He refuses in equally uncompromising fashion to become a figurehead for the brutal rabble-rouser Olivier, a renegade from Julian's cause. Instead he goes forth as the long-awaited King of the Poor and promises to bring in a new age of peace and justice.

The golden age, however, is not yet. In the final act Sigismund is seen in the field amongst his victorious forces. The reader senses from the events and developments reported that a considerable time has elapsed. Sigismund is now a simple, austere and kingly figure, firm in purpose and practical in its execution. A remarkable scene follows in which the action passes into the supernatural sphere. A prisoner—a gypsy woman from Olivier's camp—is brought in. During her interview with Sigismund she slits his hand with a tiny poisoned dagger. In the course of this scene, in which with vision and voice the forces of hell well up through the ground, the simulacra of Basilius, Julian and Olivier are all seen. Sigismund's final victory now seems assured.

The visions vanish, the atmosphere lightens, and Sigismund is rejoined by his staff. The Doctor sees his wound and notes the cut across the palm which runs athwart the life-line. And so the doomed monarch, unconscious of his fate, receives the homage and gratitude of his people, while standard-bearers, representatives of the old court, his own rebel forces and his Tartar allies kneel before him in a new-found harmony.

Although he is about to die, however, it is clear that Sigismund's ideals may yet be fulfilled. Down from the hills come the Children's King and his boy attendants, unarmed and dressed in the white of innocence. They will carry on the work of Sigismund. He, although a *'quinta essentia* of the highest human powers',[1] is sprung from an earthly race of evil, cynicism and despair. Unwittingly he is tainted and can be no more than an intermediary between the old and the new. The Children's King assumes command by virtue of his purity and proclaims a new age based on the ideals of love and justice towards which Sigismund has been struggling. He pays tribute to Sigismund as a guide on the way and looks forward to a time of peaceful, constructive activity. This is epitomized in one sentence: 'We have built our huts and light fires on the hearth and forge our swords into ploughshares.'[2]

Der Turm is obviously a play of ideas. The formulation, depiction and resolution of these ideas were a burden which darkened the closing years of Hofmannsthal's life. The way in which this drama consumed its author has been described by Carl Burckhardt. At the same time he demonstrated that particularly supra-personal quality in Hofmannsthal which became so marked during the decade after 1918, that quality which helped to make him a *Praeceptor Europae*:

At that time he wrote…'for six years I have been stuck here like a dog on a chain, at first in terrible fear (not for my own person), then in a dull stupor,…despair, resignation, horror, disgust,…in a world slowly decaying and collapsing.'[3]

This, as Burckhardt pointed out, was the foreground, the façade of his situation in a world visibly crashing in ruin around him. The actual substance was something deeper; it

was the complete change in and reorientation of a productive human being, a kind of deep-sea earthquake in his nature, which jeopardized everything he had been before and everything he had done. And this was a necessary condition for the later work which culminated in the tragedy *Der Turm*, the drama which proved to be all too difficult for him and over which—when to all outward appearances it was finished —Hofmannsthal died.

Burckhardt goes on to say how Hofmannsthal 'took everything bravely upon himself; in the end he freed himself completely of his personal origins, he made no further claims on those elements which had sustained his whole system. He weaned himself away from these things, but only with difficulty'.[1] Burckhardt characterizes this effort of the will in a complex and powerful antithesis:

And yet perhaps the very severity of this sacrifice strengthened even more his wish—no, more than that—a deep, innate, decisive, compulsive will to create something abiding and permanent...something rock-like and absolute...and he always had in mind that idea of Laotse that in...*world* time—the growth of humanity—the son is older than the father and therefore one step nearer the temptation to abandon his duty to the traditions of the past.[2]

Hofmannsthal tried to put aside the narrower homeland, the personal and subjective, in order to concentrate on the wider homeland, that of Europe, and Europe's destiny. The extent to which he was successful in this will be seen, in the closing stages of this study, to be an important factor in determining his ultimate place in world literature. But there can be no doubt as to the tremendous effort which he made to reach *Europe* during those last years. And literally his most strenuous effort was the creation of *Der Turm*. Concerning Hofmannsthal's actual approach to his work there is in the *Buch der Freunde* a poetic aphorism which not only summarizes Hofmannsthal's attitude to past and present at this period in his career but also prepares the reader for his growing tendency to speak *sub specie aeternitatis* and through the medium of 'mythical' figures:

There must be a star on which the things which happened a year ago are in the present; on another, what happened a hundred years ago; on yet another, the time of the crusades; and so on, all in a continuous chain. Thus to the eye of eternity all things appear alongside each other like flowers in a garden.[3]

A consistently realistic summary of Hofmannsthal's attitude to the times and particularly to the notion of a conservative revolution is found in his appraisal (1926) of Freiherr vom Stein (1757–1831):

The very strange figure of Freiherr vom Stein holds Germany's two worlds together—the old and the new—as though by a clasp. For just as he took an active part in the great affairs of the world, which brought about a turning-point in history...in the same way the current of intellectual change, which transformed German life, flowed right through his way of thought....While the world fought for stability on the one hand and revolution on the other, he found in himself syntheses for which Germany is still struggling in vain today: between, for example, the tendencies towards patient conservatism and progress, between moral and economic laws. His syntheses were often too bold for his contemporaries and he often seemed to be a revolutionary when in reality he was preserving old values, and a reactionary when in fact he was far ahead of his time.[1]

Hofmannsthal could have been speaking here of himself and his own artistic character and purpose. His attempt to realize this purpose is found not only in the content but also in the form of *Der Turm*, both of which are discussed in the following sections.

In mood and structure *Der Turm* is as mixed a hybrid as any mature Shakespearian tragedy. It has elements in it of the Spanish-Austrian baroque spectacle-play of the seventeenth century, of which a grandiloquent example was noted in chapter 2 (see pp. 319–20). There is also marked evidence of the influence of the Jesuit drama tradition, not only in the external splendour of the play but also in the liturgical language, notably in the scene with the Grand Almoner. There are distinct reminiscences of Andreas Gryphius's (1616–64) dramas, especially *Horribilicribrifax* (1663). This play seems to have made a considerable contribution to Hofmannsthal's depiction of the rebel-leader Olivier, particularly to his mode of speech. This is illustrated in more detail later, in connection with the actual significance of Olivier in the play itself.

The traditional figure from the folk-theatre of the loyal servant, humorous, somewhat coarse and speaking an incurable dialect, lives on in Anton. The antecedents of Anton in the Viennese *Volksstück* are very numerous and too involved to detail here. Nestroy's part, for example, is obvious. Grillparzer's *Ein treuer Diener seines Herrn* is certainly in the tradition, as is the bird-catcher Papageno in *Die Zauberflöte*. One comparatively little known but important source is Josef Stranitzsky, whose part in the tradition is perhaps especially relevant here. In 1713 Stranitzsky, an extempore player (*Stegreifspieler*) of great talent, rented the new *Kärntnertortheater* which, on the recommendation of the government of Lower Austria, had been built as a permanent house for theatrical troupes. During his thirteen years' occupancy (he died in 1726) Stranitzsky achieved a great reputation. Franz Farga writes of him as follows:

He took *Hanswurst*,[1] dressed him up as a cunning peasant in Salzburg costume, and made a real character of him who intervened decisively in the action and showed up the trickery and roguery of the fawning courtiers. His wit and often splendid satire scourged the weaknesses of the times very effectively.[2]

The family likeness with Anton will be quite apparent.

There are also traces in *Der Turm* of the traditional Viennese 'magic play' (*Zauberspiel*) which formed a vital constituent element of *Die Zauberflöte*. Hofmannsthal takes this tradition and modifies it to suit his purposes in the depiction on stage of supernatural forces (and constant references to others), combined—in the fatal scene with the gypsy woman—with an almost Kafka-like action which virtually transcends the possibilities of the stage. It seems scarcely necessary to say that in this magic-supernatural interest Hofmannsthal was following in Raimund's footsteps. *Der Alpenkönig und der Menschenfeind* (1834), for example, indicates this.

There is in addition a musical-operatic quality in several scenes of the play. This is not the kind of operatic style discussed on p. 60. In that case it was a matter of the dramatic force of certain visually static, aria-type speeches in *Jedermann*. In *Der Turm* the musical-operatic quality is more a matter of the overall structure of several of the big scenes in the play, notably the court sequences culminating in the meeting between Basilius and Sigismund, and in the carefully constructed rising climax to the final scene. Here especially, a comparison with Grillparzer's *König Ottokars Glück und Ende* is fruitful. One thinks of the formal, almost symphonic-operatic structure of the mass scenes in Grillparzer's play: the opening with Ottokar at the height of his power; the meeting with Rudolf on the island of Kaumberg in the Danube; the closing scene, with the victorious armies of Rudolf, the funeral oration over Ottokar's corpse, and the visionary patriotism of the final panegyric on Austria.

This same quality in *Der Turm*, which is of course related to the baroque element already mentioned, is to be found not only in language or actual music—organ, trumpets, choral voices. It is seen particularly in the orchestral grouping of the crowd scenes, in the dramatic build-up to the big dramatic moments, and in the operatic technique of drawing the action to a standstill, not only for a summing-up and comment (as in *Jedermann*) but also for an effect of static panorama and peroration in the manner, for example, of the finale of the first act of *Lohengrin*, the opening of the final scene in the same work, or the moment at the end of the third act of Verdi's *Don Carlo* when, following the rebellion, the Grand Inquisitor and the King descend amongst the kneeling people. To bring the subject closer to the matter in hand, there are distinct reminiscences of the two Grail scenes in the first and third acts respectively of *Parsifal*.

It will be recalled that in the first of these Parsifal, as prospective initiate, witnesses the sacred mystery. But while he, the 'pure fool', feels Amfortas's wound intuitively in himself and darkly senses its meaning, he is ignorant of the full importance of what he has seen. In the later scene he is a different man. For now, through suffering, compassion with others and the wisdom of experience, he has won through to full insight. Thus he takes the place of the old order represented on the one hand by the ascetic but spiritually sterile Titurel and on the other by the emotionally sensual Amfortas.[1]

A certain correspondence may be noted, moreover, in the development of the characters of Sigismund and Parsifal.[2] There is also a correspondence in the elaborate panoply of their two 'big' scenes. For Sigismund these are the meeting with Basilius in the royal palace and the final scene in and before the great field-tent. For Parsifal they are the two scenes in the Hall of the Grail, in the first of which he (like Sigismund) fails the 'test'. In the second (again like Sigismund) he is seen in triumph.

These correspondences cannot be carried too far. But one might nevertheless assert that there is enough matter to warrant a detailed study and comparison of the two strictly 'occasional' festival dramas *Parsifal* and *Der Turm*.

In this account of characteristics and influences mention should be made of a pronounced 'eastern' or Byzantine element in the staging and setting of the play. The almost barbaric splendour of some scenes and the ritualistic ceremonial owe a good deal to Byzantium and there are divers references to Asia, the Tartars, Constantinople, the river Borysthenes (Old Greek name for the Dnieper), which establish this atmosphere of the European East.[3] This element is especially important in creating the essential mood of the play which is partly historical but, to a much greater extent, imbued with the spirit of myth and saga.

Finally, in a general survey[4] must come the Shakespearian quality. Hofmannsthal's lifelong preoccupation with Shakespeare has been summed up by Carl Burckhardt:

at the same time, however, he rejected [English] puritanism, respect-fully but without any really deep feeling for it. What attracted him was the England which was repressed by the beheading of Charles I, the England which found its most complete expression in Shakespeare.[5]

In *Der Turm* the main impact of Shakespeare is felt in the opening scene. Shakespeare's finest openings are frequently those which begin *in medias res*, where the action itself moves rapidly onwards as the situation is revealed in fragments. No time is wasted on static exposition. The audience is caught up in a train of destiny before it knows completely what it is all about. In this way an atmosphere of uncanny suspense and excitement can be achieved. The scene on the battlements at Elsinore ('the coldest place in English literature')[1] provides what is probably the finest example of this genre. It is worth noting that in many such instances the appearance of the principal character is delayed until the curiosity and suspense of the audience have been thoroughly aroused. The carefully prepared entrance of Julius Caesar (*Julius Caesar*, Act I, scene 2) is a further example of this technique.

In *Der Turm* information is conveyed skilfully and naturally through the conversation of the soldiery, and various references are made to a mysterious prisoner. At the same time the scope of reference broadens to include fragmentary remarks on the troubled state of the land and on various supernatural occurrences (*Hamlet* comes to mind again). Thus the tension mounts steadily and the mysterious prince, clad in a wolf's pelt, is by implication connected with the spreading evils and chaos which are afflicting the land.

These various qualities in *Der Turm* have been detailed here for a specific reason. The drama was Hofmannsthal's last will and testament. There is hence a danger that it may be regarded *solely* as a play of ideas. First and foremost, however, it is, like Hofmannsthal's other plays of ethical or polemical content, a drama calculated to make its point before a community or audience through the medium of eye and ear.

The theatrical merits and shortcomings of *Der Turm* are discussed in the analysis of the play's content which now follows. This analysis, therefore, is designed to help us judge not only what is in the play but also to aid us in arriving at an opinion as to its ultimate or absolute value as a work of art.

CHAPTER 7

'DER TURM': STRUCTURE
AND MEANING

ACT I

THE opening lines of the first scene establish one of the main characters. Olivier, a corporal and new officer of the guard at the tower, soon reveals himself as a type. His name is an obvious reminiscence of Simplicissimus's evil companion in Grimmelshausen's novel. The mere mention of the name and then the situation in which Hofmannsthal's Olivier is found bring into the drama the analogy of the chaos of the Thirty Years War. This Olivier is on the one hand the kind of crude, lively and brutal *Rottenführer*, familiar to any student of the period. One recalls, moreover, another figure—or rather figures—who must have served Hofmannsthal as models for Olivier: the fantastic 'reformed ex-captains' in Gryphius's *Horribilicribrifax* (1663), Don Daradiridatumtorides and Don Horribilicribrifax! The similarity in the vocabulary and generally fantastic, overblown style of Olivier and these two heroes is most marked in the fourth act of *Der Turm* and is discussed later in the context of that particular act. For the moment it is sufficient to recall that in the first act of Gryphius's play Daradiridatumtorides indulges, like Olivier, in violent, exaggerated speech, freely spiced with foreign words, as befits a veteran campaigner. His oaths, moreover (*ce bugre, ce larron*), are identical with Olivier's *bougre, larron*.[1]

Olivier, however, also reveals himself as a peculiarly and fatefully contemporary figure. He is that kind of rabble-rouser, a mixture of forceful and even magnetic personality, who has become so familiar in the mass totalitarian movements of the twentieth century. Two remarks of Olivier catch the essential quality both of such a man and of the times which make him possible. In response to a caution from one of the soldiers he replies: 'The times are not such that they can put a man like me in his place.'[1]

It is soon apparent, despite the ornate historical-mythological setting, that reader and audience are confronted with the decline of the western world in symbol. A further short sequence confirms the impression of chaos, prejudice and declining moral standards. Signals are heard in the distance, evidently a well-known code-sign for smugglers:

Andreas. We ought to do the rounds. After all we are on frontier duty here.

Olivier. Leave 'em alone. Whatever they're smuggling's all right by me...arms, gunpowder, lead. Halberds, pikes, spikes,[2] axes. Bringing them up from Hungary, across from Bohemia, down from Lithuania.

Pankraz. Damned Jews! God knows where they get it all from.

Olivier. They sense what's up. They can sense blood in the wind, smell the red cock on the roof.[3]

Concerning the last line it may be worth recalling that a song about the 'red cock' was the *Marseillaise* of the Peasants' War in Germany (1525). The use of the phrase in the present context is a good example of Hofmannsthal's way of suggesting associations and analogies in the minds of his audience. It is done, moreover, in a quite unobtrusive fashion, the reference being absorbed into the text as an integral part of the action. Even if the allusion escapes the audience the phrase is dramatically striking in its own right.

It is interesting to note here how in a few lines the implications widen from the personal to the general, and how the climax is contained in the violent folk-symbol of the cockerel with flame-red comb (suggestive of fire) leaping along the roof of a stricken house.[4]

This leads to an important aspect of the impression caused by this scene. The chaotic situation is obviously suggested by the crudeness and violence of the characters and the action discussed. More striking, however, is Hofmannsthal's language here, an amalgam of the *argot* of the licentious soldiery and folk-dialect of distinctly corrupt flavour. This factor enhances the impression of a world whose foundations are adrift. Particularly alarming is the colourful vulgarity of Olivier's attack on Julian, governor of the tower.[1] This might seem to typify one special aspect of the kind of oratory which one has come to associate with political demagogy of the *Führer* variety:

He can slide down my hump. He's a court fawner. He's an oily louse, he is. Stinks of muscatel and louse ointment, so they say; and washes his hands in a silver washbowl. You just see, inside a month I'll swipe that little courtier over the ear with his own silver washbowl. I'll string him up and polish my boots with the fat off his belly.[2]

These linguistic considerations are given further point as the play develops. For each scene and for each character Hofmannsthal uses an individual style and vocabulary. Thus he ranges from the type of idiom just noted to the precise and sober clarity of the Doctor, the inflated sophistication of Basilius and the court, the liturgically-inspired mysticism of the Grand Almoner, and to the various developments in Sigismund's speech which culminate in the rhythmic tread and biblical imagery of the final scene.

This ability to change mood and to adapt language to character is probably one of the marks of a natural dramatist. It is clearly demonstrated with the entrance of the Doctor. The Doctor rarely speaks more than three or four lines at a time and his speech is a subtle combination of clinical brevity and terse generalization or prophecy. To his sharpened perceptions the captive prince appears in a dual aspect: as symbol of suffering mankind and as symbol of the pure spirit of inspired, reforming leadership.

This initial depiction of Sigismund is effective in a curiously complex way. A moment before he sees the prince the Doctor observes: 'the burden of the whole world lies upon him. I see now how all the threads come together.'[3] This contains both aspects of Sigismund: the sorrows of the world as a stricken individual representative of it, and the responsibility for the world. This second quality is evident in an exchange between Sigismund and the Doctor:

Sigismund. Light is good, goes inside and makes pure blood. Stars are light like that. There is a star in me. My soul is holy.[1]

Sigismund expresses himself here in the accents of a children's rhyme. Hofmannsthal is at this point close to the ancient tradition in which the fool or simple-minded idiot was regarded as being innately innocent and mysteriously closer to his origin in God. Throughout this sequence one must sense rather than trace a marked Russian quality. One thinks of the tradition of the Holy Idiot, of the peculiar prominence and significance of the idiot in Pushkin's *Boris Godunov* (and in Mussorgsky's musical-dramatic setting). Reading Sigismund's childish rhyme one recalls the pathos and dramatic power of the nursery scene in *Boris Godunov*, where a comparable effect is gained by contrasting the apparent *naïveté* of the child's prattle with the rising anxiety of the Czar.

Together with this Russian association the *Parʒival* legend again comes to mind. Thus at this early stage in the action three important features are linked in Sigismund: princely character and qualities, the wisdom born of experience and suffering, and the strength of spirit which rises from innate innocence. The Doctor alone sees Sigismund's true character: 'O more than dignity in such defilement! That is a princely being,....'[2]

The qualities embodied in Sigismund were necessary for the expression of Hofmannsthal's ideas of individual, personal regeneration. From these arises his stress on personal reform rather than the reforms to be effected by wholesale change in class-structures and groupings.

The dualistic character of the Doctor's observations corresponds to a dualism within him. In his outlook on life he has the features of a Christian humanist and humanitarian. His 'second sight'—his ability to see through the veil of the world of appearances—

has qualities of that neoplatonic mysticism which was an important feature of Hofmannsthal's intellectual constitution. This mysticism permeates the revealing self-analysis *Ad me ipsum*, already quoted at various points and particularly with reference to *Der Turm*.[1]

The Doctor's contribution to *Der Turm* is mainly spiritual and ethical: Hofmannsthal was apparently aware of the danger that the neoplatonic element might swamp the action. As it is, the shadowiness of the Doctor's character and the brevity of his speech give a sense of impersonal, universal truth to the Doctor's words. This allows him to carry out his purely dramatic function with great effectiveness and without diverting attention from the main action and character. In a letter to Burckhardt Hofmannsthal discussed this aspect of the Doctor together with the function of Count Adam, Sigismund's companion during the 'test' and, in the fifth act, his aide:

So as not to overload the atmosphere and to prevent the whole thing from becoming an overpowering nightmare I have deliberately given Count Adam a purely functional role rather than a character of his own. The same applies to the Doctor who always remains a shade outside and above the action.[2]

Thus a remarkable composite effect is achieved in this first meeting between Sigismund and the Doctor, for the speech of each character stands in vivid contrast to that of the other. The Doctor's role has already been described: Sigismund's speech is a combination of monosyllabic, vacant terror with fantastic, highly coloured aphorism and prophecy. Anton's speech is that of the folk, naïve and shrewd at the same time, led or driven in all directions, but having limitless reserves and wanting only guidance. In the interaction of the trio, Sigismund–Doctor–Anton, the entire situation is depicted. The sharp contrasts in speech, moreover, give to this depiction a marked quality of depth.

At this point an important aspect of Hofmannsthal's dramatic technique should be noted. As the Doctor utters his heartfelt cry ('O man! O man!') Sigismund, on his knees with hand stretched out, does not speak but utters only a cry of woe. This tableau-like effect, a further feature common to Hofmannsthal and Grillparzer,[1] is an eloquent yet reticent way of handling a complex situation, heavy with emotion which could easily become embarrassing. The complementary technique of meaningful silence is also developed in this play. In the present instance the Doctor holds a flaming torch, presses Sigismund—who is leaning against his knee—towards him, and throws light from above into the Prince's face. The symbolism of the grouping and the significance of the Doctor as guide and spiritual adviser are immediately apparent. This becomes more obvious still when, in response to the great, empty silence on the part of Sigismund, the Doctor says: 'Nothing of the madman's fixed stare here, no murderous eye, by God: only a fathomless abyss. Soul and torment without end.'[2]

This scene of the group with the Doctor's torch flaring from above is meant to make a deep impression on the audience. It is symbolic of the whole relationship between Sigismund and the Doctor. For the Doctor is in effect Sigismund's mentor throughout the play. It should be emphasized, moreover, that it is he who, as a result of what he sees in the Prince at this point, suggests to Julian the fateful idea of the return to court. Thus one recalls this tableau periodically as the action moves on and Sigismund's destiny runs its course to the moment in the final act immediately before he receives the wound, the moment where he is at the peak of his worldly fortunes. There too the Doctor is at his side as adviser and spiritual mentor.

This tableau is also important because it establishes what the text indicates, namely that while Sigismund is a symbol of suffering mankind, he is also the saint-king, inspired by the spirit of God and destined to lead travailing mankind out of its woes.[3]

At this early but climacteric stage in Sigismund's development it may be helpful if we interrupt the detailed examination of the text as such in order to concentrate in some detail on the actual constitution and relevance of the play's main character. This will necessitate the introduction of certain background matter—matter, however, which is indispensable to an understanding of Hofmannsthal's purpose in creating this unusually complex figure. Walther Brecht attempted this understanding with great penetration. Writing of *Ad me ipsum* he asked

how the two later dramas would have looked in the light of *Ad me ipsum*. Perhaps the way in which its questions are phrased would not have been quite enough for them. This would not apply so much to the *Große Welttheater* in which the Christian-Catholic element and the modern problems consequent upon the social revolution are so clearly depicted. But it would apply much more to *Der Turm* which deals with the entire political, social and cultural problem.[1]

It is, incidentally, a pity that Brecht was evidently unable within the framework of his essay to detail further what appears to be a clear and practical insight into the situation in the *Große Welttheater*, and its place in Hofmannsthal's overall view of life, as represented in these two dramas. The above passage certainly defines the respective and mutually complementary fields of the two dramas with incisive brevity. Brecht goes on to say how in the light of his remarks on *Der Turm* 'one realizes...to what an extent the ideas of his entire earlier work—especially that of his youth—are based on the individual personality...'.[2]

In his discussion of *Der Turm*, however, Brecht seems to emphasize that increasingly formal-objective quality, the tendency to speak of and to the generality which was noted in connection with the two earlier 'festival dramas':

[the play] is concerned...with the totality of things (hitherto only *Jedermann* with its antique and objectivizing form had been universally significant in the same sense). Sigismund's absolute isolation of soul is all the more moving and terrible (especially in the first version)—Sigismund, the Saviour who has come to bring peace to this world of horror. He is not so very much involved in those problems of personality and personal destiny which figured so largely...in the earlier plays. In spite of the extreme isolation apparent in his Caspar Hauser beginnings,[3] Sigismund was depicted by Hofmannsthal as an essentially social being, and so, dedicated only to the salvation of others, he goes through the world like a crystalline being, solitary, inexpressibly pure, ...secluded and closed-up within himself, but shining forth to others. The stern and noble core of his being cannot be damaged; it can only be crudely smashed from outside. Unlike all those around him (and also unlike Hofmannsthal's earlier characters) he has no desires of his own. He wants nothing but the execution of good and he is always certain of this because he is always in contact with the... Divine. Thus he scarcely needs any transforming development, any purification, any difficult detour through life in order to...win through to a realization of his higher self and to a deeper perception of life. He already has this when he emerges from his...cave.... But in him it has become ethical and active. For this reason alone he can finally become a ruler.[1]

These last two sentences contain the core of the matter. There is a tendency in criticism of Hofmannsthal to attach overmuch significance to his philosophic conception of 'pre-existence'. Hofmannsthal's mysticism and his neoplatonic sympathies are a very delicate subject indeed. It is only too easy for the most positive critic to lose himself in all manner of subjective-aesthetic-philosophical and basically unrealistic considerations. This can soon become a kind of esoteric *Glasperlenspiel*, especially in view of Hofmannsthal's aphoristic terseness in writing of these matters. Curt Hohoff's sharp comment is not altogether unjustified: 'Hofmannsthal research ties itself up in *Der Turm* and in a whole lot of sketches and projects which were never carried out.'[2]

Herbert Steiner, editor of the first complete edition of Hofmannsthal's works, has some very consequential things to say on precisely this theme of neoplatonism and its dubious position in criticism of Hofmannsthal. He writes—explicitly concerning *Ad me ipsum*—

Literature on Hofmannsthal has taken over many of the concepts used here: pre-existence, for example, ... But in all this it is an open question to what extent these same terms should in their turn be regarded as Hofmannsthalian creations [*ihrerseits wieder als Dichtung zu fassen sind*].[3]

Steiner goes on to describe the arrangement of the various fragments, sheets, notes, etc., and comments:

What they contain cannot be summarized systematically, touching as they do upon ideas of other poetic thinkers, and—as Hofmannsthal himself ever more clearly realized—on concepts which can be found in the Neo-Platonists and since. They *touch* on these things, no more than that, and indicate that point where the beautiful and the moral seem to grow from *one* root.

Hofmannsthal's works and utterances, together with the recollections of his close associates, show that in the final reckoning he assessed the significance of his life and work by the influence they had, or could have, on the nation. It was to this end that he toiled in order to finish *Der Turm*. It was for this that he became a 'guardian of the German spirit',[1] not only in the dramas but even more explicitly in the series of university addresses, book and programme introductions, and comments on the intellectual and spiritual situation of post-war Europe. Hofmannsthal's subjectivism, his self-scrutiny and mysticism were important to him only in so far as they enabled him to realize his larger purpose to his own satisfaction and to make it comprehensible to the outside world.

It is clear, moreover, that Hofmannsthal cared very much about his reputation and effect. This was not in any vainglorious sense. He was concerned rather that he be understood and interpreted aright. Hohoff observes:

During the last ten years of his life Hofmannsthal himself made various pessimistic observations. He felt that he was not appreciated and Max Rychner reports how he said sadly: 'Does anyone really want anything more from me at all?' Similar testimony is found in [the writings of] R. A. Schröder, Walther Brecht and E. R. Curtius. These remarks date from the time when the *Kulturpolitiker* Hofmannsthal was in actual fact...a kind of guardian of the German spirit, acclaimed by the great writers and scholars of his time.[2]

Hofmannsthal's correspondence with Carl Burckhardt, probably the closest friend of his last years,[3] is revealing in this connection, as in so much else. Constantly it is apparent that Hofmannsthal looked out from his own personal dilemma (which in heightened, clarified form was that of his century) to the world outside, where his personal strivings and their product could be (to use Brecht's words) 'ethical and active'. Hofmannsthal's letter to Burckhardt of 10 September 1926, for example, reads as follows:

The vast and distant horizons of the Catholic Church constitute the only really great antiquity which remains to us in the western world. Nothing else is really big enough, scarcely anything else is left to us. And I can see the time—it is actually there already—when our entire eighteenth and early nineteenth century German humanism will seem to have been nothing but a Utopian episode, really nothing more than an episode.

I love my own destiny, however. The older I get the more I love it. And the fearsome severity, the violence of this turning-point in everything, make me rise above the temptation to brood on what was destroyed when Austria was shattered, and thus to waste the rest of my life in sterile bitterness. I have kept my homeland but I no longer have a fatherland, other than Europe. I must impress this upon myself, for clarity alone protects one from gradual self-destruction.[1]

The above details demonstrate, then, how much was embodied by Hofmannsthal in the most important figure of what was the dominating work of his last years. They demonstrate, moreover, that in the final consideration Hofmannsthal was intent on the public effect of the work (and its main character) designed to crown his life's achievement. As he observed in *Ad me ipsum*: 'The individual and his epoch seen as a myth, *sic*: whatever, since Kant, lives on as a changed attitude to the world is somehow mirrored in Sigismund.'[2]

It will be clear, therefore, that in Sigismund Hofmannsthal meant to create an individual figure of far-reaching and deep implication. His innate purity and naïve goodness are contrasted with his instinctive kingly qualities; and the reader feels that both will be fused to form the ultimate ideal. These initial scenes are really the formal introduction to the play, the *es kann so sein* in Hebbel's sense.[3]

A sharp distinction is drawn between Sigismund, the natural ruler, and Julian, arbitrary, opportunist and ambitious. Julian is a man of some fine qualities, hopelessly entangled in base motive and the hope of personal gain. A comparison with the historical Wallenstein suggests itself and, of more actual interest perhaps, one thinks of that particular *Realpolitik* which Albert Schweitzer saw as a major threat to the civilization of the twentieth century.[1]

This comes out clearly in the conversation between Julian and the Doctor. The Doctor returns and finds Julian transformed by the news of the sudden death of the King's nephew; for Julian sees how, with Sigismund as his tool, he can make use of the chance thus presented to him. 'What', he asks the Doctor, 'do you see in my face?' The answer sums up the terrible, complex mixture of heroism, weakness and baseness:

Doctor. Tremendous, hopeful excitement! Far-reaching plans! Great plans embracing a whole kingdom. Your Grace is made of heroic stuff.

(*Julian cannot help smiling but suppresses it immediately*)

But. . . the source itself is polluted. The deepest root has been gnawed into. In these commanding features good and evil wrestle with each other like snakes in fearsome combat.

Julian. . . . Great agitation lies ahead of me—I need different nights. . .

Doctor. . . . But you are denying your heart. Heart and mind must be one. You have consented to a Satanic division, you have suppressed your noble parts. And hence these lips curled in bitterness, these hands which deny themselves the touch of wife and child. . . . Your gait reveals heroic ambition. . . . [But] your nights are full of raging desires and powerless yearning. Your days pass in boredom and you are consumed with frustration. You doubt the Supreme Being—the wings of your soul are bound in chains.[2]

The above sequence recalls Requadt's assessment of Julian's character and the reasons for his downfall. Requadt's account is particularly valuable as it places these things in perspective against the implications of the play itself. He writes:

The poor hope for deeds from the King. They hope that with the dissolution of an order no longer legitimated by the spirit a new kingdom will be founded, based on justice—here Hofmannsthal takes up the *Witiko* theme. 'The world is conditioned by deeds' says Julian, Sigismund's guardian and teacher. And yet this same Julian meets with disaster because his actions do not spring from the Theresian unity of heart and mind, but, on the contrary, he intentionally plays off the classes against each other.[1]

Requadt associates here the ideal of kingship in *Der Turm* with that depicted in practical terms by Hofmannsthal in his essay on Maria Theresia. Hofmannsthal's view of the 'Theresian unity' was discussed in chapter 3. In the present context a brief extract from the essay itself seems to illustrate Requadt's point:

The special secret of this strength, the individual signature of her being, lies in the unity of her person in every situation; it is never merely her head, her statesman's will that is at work; she cannot arbitrarily leave aside her heart and conscience. The whole woman is in everything she does.[2]

With the above considerations in mind it can be said that Hofmannsthal makes the premises clear in this first act, and the three leader-types are established: Sigismund, Julian and Olivier. They are drawn against the gathering gloom of growing chaos in a civilization and society which has ground itself into incoherence and disintegration. Simon the Jew, servant to Julian, depicts the madness and violence of this crumbling system. In his description one feels much of what has happened since 1914. The character of Simon is another good example of Hofmannsthal's skill in creating a special language and vocabulary for each figure. In this depiction of disorder, dishonesty and impending doom, Simon speaks the Yiddish-influenced German of the traditional *Ostjude* (eastern Jew, usually from Poland or White Russia) which, rightly or wrongly, carries with it the associations of *Liederlichkeit*, *Schieberei*, *Schlamperei*, etc., characteristic of the times described.[3]

It is of course difficult to look at this sort of thing objectively since the anti-Semitic terror and wholesale murder of the Jews in Germany, Poland and elsewhere. The *traditional* effect of a dialect or *argot* and the instinctive reaction of the hearer cannot be denied, however, and morality plays no part:

When the war started the soldiers and the suppliers were paid in silver. But when the war'd been goin' two years the metal was mixed, an' in the third year 'twas jus' silvered copper. But folk took it. Then the King saw that y'can make money by printin' 'is face on tin, on muck, 'n then the big men get the idea too; then the townfolk and then the little 'uns. So the King makes 'is own money, 'n the lords make theirs. 'N who doesn't make it?—Until the 'ole place is swimmin' in the stuff...Ah, but they won' let yer use the new stuff for taxes 'n duties. An' the soldiers and the miners are s'posed to take the cheap stuff. An' so wot 'appens? The miners won't go down the mine no more, 'n the bakers won't make no more bread; 'n the doctors just run away from the sick 'uns, 'n the students play the wag, 'n the soldiers just clear out. And nobody takes no notice of the King no more. An' then there ain't nuthin' what's right and proper in the 'ole world,...'n wot's everybody talkin' about? They're talkin' about a whoppin' big rope, that's wot they're talkin' about: a great big rope as long as from 'ere to Cracow. An' this rope, they do say, is rubbed with soap every night.[1]

The hangman's noose, a huge and realistic symbol of rising rebellion, murderous violence and summary, bloody justice, is suddenly and boldly introduced. It sums up in one phrase what Simon has described. Thus vivid detail and an apocalyptic picture of general doom are brought together in one whole.

ACT II

The first scene of the second act of *Der Turm* is a theatrical *tour de force* and is for its greater part a good instance of Hofmannsthal's ability to take varying traditions and motives and shape them together into an harmonious and purposeful whole. The contrast between this immensely long first scene and the act just concluded is a baroque antithesis of the 'earthly time–eternity'

(*Zeit–Ewigkeit*) type. Whereas the opening scenes are wholly in and of the world, its materialism and madness, the scene at the monastery is wholly devoted to things spiritual and eternal.

If the scene is baroque in purpose and position, its setting is Gothic, not to say Romantic in an almost Udolphian sense. It takes place in the cloisters in the hour before dawn. There is a royal party, a poor pilgrim, a saintly ancient of great powers who sleeps only at this hour, and then in his own coffin. There is an unseen monastic chorus which at intervals intones in a *Dies Irae*-like manner; and there are readings from Guevara.

From these disparate traditions, which have all the appearance of being mutually inimical, Hofmannsthal constructs a sustained piece of dramatic bravura whose content is solemn and austere. It makes a singular impression. Briefly described this impression may be likened to the still, sure point at the centre of a whirlpool —a place of calm amid the storm raging on all sides.

This dramatic effect is achieved in a simple manner. The scene is virtually a dramatic triptych. The first picture is dominated by the brilliantly erratic figure of the King with his accompanying *motifs* of disorder and ruin. The central picture is dominated by the motionless, exalted figure of the Grand Almoner. The final picture is dominated by the energetic, ruthless figure of Julian, with his great ambitions and basically unsteady plans. The scene closes on a note of hectic excitement and uncertainty.

In the figure of King Basilius are seen the gesture and emblem of outworn majesty, the form without the substance, the institution which lingers when the historical necessity has passed away. The speech of the King has a luscious, overblown quality which expresses the essential hollowness of the character. Hofmannsthal seems here to draw on biblical rhythms and associations of a notably voluptuous kind:

Today is the feast of St Aegidius. And the stag goes rutting. A fine clear evening: the magpies fly in from their nests in pairs and have no fear for their young. And the fisherman rejoices...and mighty, princely, the stag steps forth from the wood and his lips part so that

he seems to laugh, and he cries out mightily so that the animals amongst
the new young trees press their trembling flanks against each other in
terror and yearning desire. And we were like him and enjoyed majestic
days, before the weather broke and changed, and at the sound of our
coming the limbs of beautiful women parted, and wherever we chose
to enter, the silver candelabra or the rose-red torch shone upon the
wedding of Jupiter with the nymph. . . . And of this there was seemingly
no end, for our strength was regal.[1]

One notes how the transition to the biblical style is effected.
In order to conceal his intention Hofmannsthal allows the King
to speak one or two fairly commonplace sentences. The change
in style is then carried out steadily but gradually, until it reaches
its effulgent climax in the final lines.

Hofmannsthal contrasts the façade-like glories of the immediate
past with the nameless and hopeless terror of the present. The
reader inevitably thinks of the apparently sure and settled state
of Europe before 1914, and then of Europe between the war's
aftermath and the violent outbreak of Fascism and Communism
in the thirties and forties. The old systems have ground themselves
into the sand, but a new solution is not yet in sight. The King
continues in a mood of 'façade–reality' antithesis:

Now, however, hell has long since been let loose on us, and a conspiracy
against our happiness lies in wait, beneath our feet and above our head . . .
and we cannot seize the ringleaders. We want to go hither and thither,
and fortify our power, and it is as if the ground became soft and our
marble limbs sank into nothingness. The walls tremble from their very
foundations and our path has become impassable.

Various courtiers now amplify and detail the familiar situation,
emphasizing particularly the failure of the monetary system and
the resulting distortion and reversal of customary practice. This
leads inevitably into a prophetic passage in which all blame is
laid on the Jews. The familiar search for the scapegoat makes its
appearance. The bold young fops of the court, representatives of
those classes and cliques which have brought the country to
disaster and moral ruin, now offer to ride forth against the Jewish

usurers and swindlers and wreak vengeance on them (and also work off their own frustration).

The technique is familiar and was of course in the process of further refinement—preparatory to direct use—even as Hofmannsthal wrote this play. *Mein Kampf*, begun in 1924, was already in limited circulation by the time *Der Turm* appeared. The gross simplifications, coarseness and question-begging of the courtiers have a quality in their language which was a few years later to become a commonplace of cynical, political opportunism:

and over everything the Jews, those stinking vampires: they have sucked the marrow out of the country's bones. They have taken the silver out of the money and left the stinking red copper in our hands . . . their foul fox-den is papered with pawn-tickets from the nobles. Put iron gloves on your hands and then take hold of ten thousand of them and squeeze them hard until they are all squeezed out— then blood and sweat will flow on the ground and the fields will become fertile again and silver and gold will fall out of the ears of corn.[1]

In other words the poor, innocent fatherland, which wished no harm to anyone, now lies bleeding from a thousand wounds. It is so simple and good-hearted, misunderstood by all:[2] so simple and well-meaning, in fact, that a few wicked Jews have contrived to get the entire country into their power. All that is needed is to dispossess the *Schieber* and all will be well. The argument is childish, but it has cost many million lives. Hofmannsthal's awareness of what was in the air around him might have served as a warning to others, especially in view of the colourful simplicity with which he draws this scene.

In point of fact the depiction of anti-Semitism is so accurate and emotionally realistic that the reader may for a few moments think that Hofmannsthal himself was violently anti-Semitic![3] The whole court, together with the King, are, however, depicted continuously as so unsavoury and immoral that their anti-Semitism serves only to damn them still further.

This entire episode, however, can be seen as an example of the controlled and applied use of an ancient tradition. Anti-Semitism was a feature of much medieval drama. Hofmannsthal's absorption of the practice, language, structure and themes of medieval drama was seen earlier in this study. It would seem likely that here— and also in the figure of Simon discussed earlier—Hofmannsthal is making use of a traditional theme (anti-Semitism) and an ancient type-figure in order to adapt them to his own dramatic purpose.

The climax of this first triptych is reached as the King recalls the terms of the mysterious prophecy that his own son would destroy him. Things which could only have been meant symbolically are, he says, now coming to pass.[1] The sun over a great city is extinguished in broad daylight; darkness, disease, famine and rebellion cover the face of the land.

The recurrence throughout the play of sun, moon and stars in the imagery is very noticeable. Examples are too numerous to give in detail; but it is quite evident that this use of cosmic imagery was deliberate. It underlines the supra-personal, supra-national, even supra-temporal validity of this drama. Julian, for example, tells Sigismund that he will see the host of rebels 'as the moon on the day of judgment will see those who rise from the dead'.[2] This leads in turn to yet another characteristic feature of the play: the apocalyptic note in many of the utterances. This is seen, for example, in Julian's description of the rebellion which he later stirs into action:

Rebellion, open rebellion bares its teeth tonight like a bear on top of a sheep-pen. Dungeons...burst open and yield up their living entrails and violence rages at violence.[3]

The Grand Almoner now makes a silent processional entrance which divides the scene effectively and is in itself one of those operatic, baroque tableaux typical of the traditional court spectacle of the seventeenth century with its concentration on protocol and court ceremonial. The effect of the Almoner's entrance is greatly enhanced by the sound offstage (presumably in the monastery church) of one intoning voice:

Ecce ego suscitabo super Babylonem quasi ventum pestilentem. Et mittam in Babyloniam ventilatores et ventilabunt eam et demolientur terram eius.

(For see, I will send a plague-wind to Babylon. And I will send rebels to Babylon and they will stir up this city and will lay waste to its territories.)

The texts for both solo and chorus, whose chant is heard repeatedly during this scene, are taken from the opening verses (first, second and fourth in the Authorised Version) of the fifty-first chapter of the Book of Jeremiah. This chapter depicts, as its sub-heading observes, 'the severe judgment of God against Babylon'. Hofmannsthal's implicit analogy with the modern European Babylon is in the present context quite obvious.

The Grand Almoner is thus seen immediately as a kind of divine representative, a messenger from an angry God to warn a modern Babylon. This note of divine wrath is sustained throughout the scene as a monastic choir punctuates the action at intervals with the strophe:

> Et demolientur terram eius!
> Et cadent interfecti in terra Chaldaeorum.
>
> (And lay waste to their territories.
> And they will fall dead on the ground of the Chaldaeans.)

The three fragmentary extracts from a work of the Spanish moral philosopher Guevara that precede the Almoner's main conversation with the King are in content reminiscent of many a German lyric of the time of the Thirty Years War.

The reading of the extracts is a very important feature in setting the characteristic mood of the scene, and a brief survey of Guevara's significance to Hofmannsthal yields interesting results. Antonio de Guevara (sometimes spelt Quevara) was born c. 1480 and died in 1545. He was *inter alia* Historiographer Royal to Emperor Charles V. It was in this capacity that he wrote a famous work on Marcus Aurelius: *Libro del emperador Marco Aurelio con Relox de Principes*. Guevara's work is a fantastic and imaginary life of Marcus Aurelius. He asserted that it was genuine history based on a (non-existent) Florentine manuscript. The *Relox de Principes* presents the picture of an ideal ruler and it was soon translated into various languages, including English (Lord Berners's posthumous translation was published in 1534), Italian (1534), German (1599, translated by Aegidius Albertinus, see following paragraph), and Latin (1606).

In view of the influence of both Charles V (see pp. 230–1) and Marcus Aurelius (see pp. 188–9 and 266–9) in the composition of *Der Turm* the above details are worth noting. It is not possible to say definitely whether Hofmannsthal was familiar with Guevara's work on Marcus Aurelius either in the original or in German translation. It seems likely, however, for he was obviously familiar with the work from which the readings in *Der Turm* are taken. This is the *Libro de Menosprecio dela corte y alabança dela aldea* (1539). This was also translated into German by the Munich court secretary Aegidius Albertinus (1560–1620). It appeared (Munich and Amberg, 1599) in the same series as the biography of Marcus Aurelius. Its German title is *Von der Beschwerlichkeit und Verdruß des Hoflebens, und Lob dess Feldtbaues und Landsitzes und de conviviis*.

Of perhaps most consequence, however, in the present discussion is Hofmannsthal's actual choice of extracts from this work. All fragments read at the Grand Almoner's request by the Young Brother are also to be found in the first, third and fourth paragraphs of the very lengthy Guevara extract which forms the twenty-fourth and final chapter of the fifth book of *Der abenteuerliche Simplicissimus* (that is, the final chapter of the novel proper, immediately preceding the *Continuatio*). This, as the sub-heading to the chapter says, 'is the last one and shows why and how Simplicissimus left the world again'.

A detailed comparison of Grimmelshausen's extracts and Hofmannsthal's treatment of them would lead too far afield in the present study. Three relevant things may be noted briefly, however. Hofmannsthal has chosen those lines which contain particularly strong baroque antitheses. He has, moreover, altered and heightened the language, thus transforming Albertinus's impressive but somewhat stiff original into passages of striking rhythmic beauty. Finally, he has made a most characteristic interpolation. He has inserted into the strictures on the world (represented here by Basilius's court) the image of the world-theatre. A comparison of the relevant passages, placed side by side, will demonstrate all these facts and illustrate how Hofmannsthal introduced the world-theatre image without strain and in a completely 'absorbed' manner:

Guevara–Albertinus–Grimmelshausen

i. Farewell world, for one can neither trust nor hope in you. In your house the past has vanished, the present runs away between our hands, the future has never begun, things most constant fall away, the strongest is broken to pieces, the most eternal has its end, so that you are dead amongst the dead, and in a hundred years you grant us not one hour of life.

ii. Farewell world, for in your palace people promise without intent; men serve without payment; men caress with intent to kill; men are raised up only to be ruined; men give aid, only to strike down; men give honour, only to desecrate; men borrow and do not pay back; men punish without forgiveness.

iii. God keep you, world, for in your house the great and the favoured ones are overthrown; the unworthy are given preferment; traitors are looked upon with grace; fidelity is pushed into the corner.

iv. The wise and the capable are sent away and the unskilled are rewarded greatly; the cunning are believed, while the upright and honest have no credit: each one does as he will and no one as he should.

Hofmannsthal

i. Get thee gone world, for we cannot rely on you; you are not to be trusted. In your house the past only lives on as a ghost; the present crumbles beneath our hands like a rotten, poisonous toadstool; the future knocks at the door as a robber's fist at midnight, and in a hundred years you yield us scarcely an hour of true life.

ii. Get thee gone world, in your palace men serve without payment; men caress with intent to kill; men are redeemed, only to be overthrown; men give honour, only to desecrate; men borrow and do not pay back; men punish without forgiveness.

iii. In your festive hall a stage is set up and on it you play four or five wild scenes which are dreary to behold: there men haggle over power and woo for favour; there the able ones are thrown down; the unworthy are given preferment, the traitor is looked upon with grace, and honest men are pushed into the corner.

iv. The upright are pushed into the corner and the innocent are condemned. Credit is only for him who lusts for power; for the honest there is no credit.[1]

This connection, Guevara–Grimmelshausen–Hofmannsthal, might for present purposes be expressed in terms of Spanish Baroque–Thirty Years War and German Baroque–situation and problems of the twentieth century. The connection gives further point not only to the present discussion of the Almoner's scene, but also to the general survey, in the first part of chapter 5, of Hofmannsthal's models and precepts in the final decade of his life.

The Guevara readings themselves, especially in Hofmannsthal's dramatic context, point to the nothingness of the world, whose delusions mean everything to Basilius and his court. The trinity of the world—time present, past and future—is summed up (in the first reading, i) in evocative imagery which is a compound of spectre, decay and violence.

It is interesting to note that as the King's impatience grows, as he obtrudes himself more and more on the Almoner's notice, the readings progress from the universal to the general, and from the general to the personal. The world of the captains and kings is characterized (in ii and iii) in a series of sharp, brief antitheses.

At the words 'honest men are pushed into the corner' the King himself steps forward and is thus directly associated with what has been said. The Almoner contemptuously ignores the King, who makes rash promises which would benefit only the nobility; and the courtiers fawn and kiss his hands and garments. Basilius smiles complacently and basks in the adulation. This silent tableau fixes another picture in the audience's mind; it directly precedes the actual exchange between King and erstwhile counsellor.

The reading continues and reaches its climax as the Almoner calls out with a mighty voice that nothing has meaning, nothing is real save the certainty of the last judgment and the separating of the grain from the chaff. The chant from the church ceases, the courtiers leave, the Almoner sits exhausted and motionless in his judgment seat.

The exchange which follows is in powerful and dramatic contrast to what has gone before. The colour, panoply and song are gone, and the stark words of the aged Almoner remain. His words are essentially a cold and merciless stigmatization of the evils and negligence which have led to the present impasse. The reader sees in symbol the insouciant madness of 1914, together with its terrible aftermath.

Two features in the actual style and language of the Grand Almoner give authority and effect to his words. The rhythm of his speech, even more than the vocabulary, has a biblical ring:

Vain was the war, untimely was the war, feckless and wicked was the war. And when it was lost he who had raised his hands and cried out against this war was chased from the council table.[1]

The effect of the scene is heightened by the ceremonial use of trinities of expression. The King addresses the Almoner in his three titles; the Almoner phrases his condemnation in like manner.[2] A good example of this is the following sequence which also contains a familiar baroque quality of the 'façade and reality' (*Schein und Wirklichkeit*) type. It recalls again the fearsome visions of the age of the Thirty Years War:

King. Cardinal Grand Almoner! Grand Chancellor of the Crown! Lord Privy Seal of the Realm! The exalted kingdom raises up its hands to you.

Grand Almoner. Ah! Say that again! Ah! What is that then? The exalted kingdom? I see a desert waste; an abomination do I see: the towns and markets burn like a torch; in the streets the robbers wait in ambush, and the graveyards have already swallowed up the villages.[3]

A further example of the Almoner's characteristic 'three-piled' expression leads to an additional point of character:

It is written: the bad man loves not him who punishes him. The word 'vain'—mark well—has two meanings. In the first place it means boasting of oneself, to be a spectator of oneself, to indulge in intellectual self-love. In the second place it means worthless, for nothing, lost in the womb. Your thoughts, your deed, your seed, are vain, brought to nothing by you yourself in the womb.[1]

Mention has been made of Hofmannsthal's ability to create a style and language appropriate to each character. In the above instance the Grand Almoner—despite the loftiness of his tone and matter—falls quite credibly into the pedantic exactitude of the practised master of the pulpit and of theological disputation.[2]

At times the Almoner's language takes on enhanced authority by reason of its quasi-proverbial ring: 'For it needed self-control —and this war could have been avoided—and wisdom: and hard it is to tread the path of wisdom for it is full of thorns.' Sometimes his speech has the penetration and conviction of the polished aphorism: 'But it was easy to do the vain thing and to ride forth, instead of recking our own rede.'[3]

As the exchange between the King and the Almoner proceeds, the Almoner takes on more and more the quality of a moral conscience. Superficially there is an inconsistency in the action. It appears that the Almoner was originally in favour of isolating Sigismund, but that now he accuses the King of inhumanity.

In fact, however, the contradiction may not be so great as it appears to be. It will be recalled that in Calderón's play the captive prince was a symbol of awful, unreasoning violence. Hofmannsthal has intentionally retained some elements of this in Sigismund. It is this trait of violence, the fact that he is sprung from an earthly community of pain and cruelty, that ultimately makes it impossible for him to be any more than an intermediary, pioneering figure between the wicked past and the pure, untarnished future, embodied in the Children's King. Violence, in the shape of the apocalyptic war in which Sigismund is to be victorious, and in the brutality which he displays in the meeting with his father, becomes necessary because (and only because) of the weak, wilful and hypocritical evil of the old order. Things *need* not have developed in this way.

Hence, it might be argued, in banning the spirit of potential violence at a time, one would have to assume, when peaceful reform was still possible, the Grand Almoner was probably moved by reasonable motives. In damning the King for continuing to ban this initially (and necessarily) violent figure, the Almoner is also right; for Sigismund's violence is the prelude to peace. The situation, one might argue further, has got out of hand, and Sigismund, with his immense, violent energy and purity of motive, is the only man who can set about the building of a new world on the ugly ruins of the old.

But this is a tortuous argument and its tenuousness must be obvious. Undoubtedly the obscurity here is a weakness of the play. Despite the brilliance of the dialogue in the mutual re-criminations of the King and the Almoner the content is overloaded. The episode requires analysis in the study rather than depiction on the stage. The latter, though superficially effective, can scarcely convey the recondite metaphysical aspect of the situation.

But the Almoner seems to speak with the voice of an avenging God again when, having castigated the King for his fleshly obsessions and misuse of power, he defines ultimate truth; for Basilius hysterically demands the truth which, he says, the Almoner has always concealed from him. And so the Almoner speaks: 'The truth which exists behind all appearances is in God.' The truth of God, in other words, may take on many outward forms but is basically unchanging. The Almoner adds—in words which recall the aphorisms of the *Buch der Freunde*:

Hold on to what your eyes see and enjoy yourself with adultresses and hunting hounds. But I say to you: there is an eye for which today is as yesterday and tomorrow as today. Therefore the future can be fathomed and the sibyl stands with Salome, and the star-gazer with the prophets.[1]

Basilius has wanted truth—God, the counsel of the Almoner—on his own terms. Now he rebels against the unmoving austerity of divine destiny. Divine destiny is unendingly merciful but unendingly just and—as in the Church's doctrine of wilful mortal sin—not of unending patience. Hence the Almoner's final outburst, in which he abandons his relentless self-control, has the tone and authority of one who is inspired by God.

The volubility of his towering onslaught on Basilius is in strong and dramatic contrast to the aphoristic brevity of his earlier comments. In style his homily is rich in antithesis and compelling linguistic rhythms and alliterations. It follows the tradition of the baroque sermon, perfected in Vienna by Abraham a Sancta Clara during the Turkish peril:

God! God! Do you take the Word into your dribbling mouth? I will teach you what God is. You come to me for help and sustenance, and you find something that does not please you. Instead of a familiar being into whom—as in a mirror—you can put yourself as you put yourself into the faces of the tail-wagging creatures about you, you find an impassive countenance and you are seized with horror at it. Something speaks with my mouth but as if from out of you, aiming at you; it does not seize you and yet it will not let you go; instead of your going from one thing to the other, one thing after the other comes to you; nothing new, nothing old, decrepit but not defunct, barren, lame, yet carrying the whirlwind. You can go on no more, do no more, dissolving and yet of stone, in naked want and not free. But then there is still something else! You cry out: it is behind your cry and forces you and makes you hear your own cry, feel your own body, weigh the weight of your own body, perceive the gestures of your body...breathe in your own dissolution, smell your own stink: ear behind your ear, nose behind your nose. There is despair behind your despair, terror behind your terror, and it will not release you to yourself, for it knows you and will punish you. That is God.[1]

This is the grand climax of the scene from the ethical and theatrical point of view, and Hofmannsthal sustains effect and impression. The Almoner sinks suddenly from the heights of inspired eloquence into a death-like trance; and the feeling is conveyed that in him body and matter are as nothing; the pure flame of God blazes through him.

There is a moment of silence. Then the King springs to life with a cry to his courtiers. He orders them to seize the Almoner and compel him to yield up his counsel. The courtiers leap to obey, monks interpose themselves and raise their hands in defence. The Almoner lies there like a dead man. The scene is in dumb-show and the more effective, following the torrent of eloquence.

The tableau thus created, which fixes the visual and intellectual effect in the mind, is reminiscent of that type of highly detailed Gothic altar which is divided into dramatic sections: a flurry of pikes, a phalanx of helmets, a painfully realistic crown of thorns, a face with greed, envy or hatred written across it forever— impressions which meet the observer in German Gothic altars as far apart as Berne, Kalkar and Schleswig.[1]

An English critic thinks inevitably of the immortal picture of the winter day in 1170 when Archbishop Becket and his monks confronted the King's retainers. The picture here in *Der Turm* is as vivid, the intensity as great.

At the highest point of tension the monks' choir in the church breaks the suspense with its *Ecce ego suscitabo super Babylonem quasi ventum pestilentem*. This is a divine voice warning Basilius of the plague-wind which is about to sweep over his modern Babylon. The King turns away abruptly; the moment of tension is past. But the impression, heightened by the visual technique described, remains in the mind.

This is the end of the self-contained scene with the Almoner, but Hofmannsthal allows his audience no respite. While the conflict between divine order and kingly sinfulness is still fresh in the mind, Julian enters and the action springs forward again. The test is arranged and Julian, the arch-plotter, moves into the centre of the picture.

Hofmannsthal closes the scene with a further twist. The courtiers, so ready to assault the physically defenceless Almoner, now fawn upon the new and powerful favourite. In grotesque fashion they invent and remember all manner of relationship, connection and good works. The King, alternately craven, supine and brutal, recovers his official composure, his *illusions de grandeur*. He overflows in a flood of sentiment as he hypocritically embraces Julian and speaks of the 'dear grave' (in the monastery enclosure) of his dead queen.

The scene ends with the various complex situations and conflicts all superimposed one upon the other. A characteristic touch is seen in the final stage-direction. Hofmannsthal's love of dumbshow, expressive silence, gesture, etc., has already been noted. The technique, as Grillparzer had proved (see note 1, p. 205 above), allows the playwright to make a vital impact.[1] In the present instance the onlooker's mind inevitably turns towards Sigismund's fate as Julian, his mentor, goes out with the King. As the mind broods and the retinue leaves the stage, Julian throws a quick glance at Anton. Anton is evidently terrified by what he sees in Julian's face and crosses himself as the curtain falls. This is visual theatre of a high order.[2]

Technically the Grand Almoner's scene (the central episode) is reminiscent of the scene between the Grand Inquisitor and the King in *Don Carlos* (Act v, scene 9). That scene, like the one under discussion, turns the whole course of the play; and the Grand Inquisitor, like the Grand Almoner, is complete master of the King.

It seems likely, in fact, that Hofmannsthal had Schiller's Grand Inquisitor in mind: the Grand Almoner was originally to be called Grand Inquisitor. This is apparent from a letter to Carl Burckhardt. Discussing certain difficulties in the character of Anton, Hofmannsthal remarks: 'he would also introduce a jarring note at the end of Act II (first half, scene with the Grand Inquisitor) if I let him open his mouth there...'.[3]

One can only speculate as to Hofmannsthal's reasons for changing the title of the Grand Almoner. Probably the popular and instinctive associations of the term 'Grand Inquisitor' were

226

the main reason. The term 'Grand Almoner' is quite neutral in this respect. The Almoner himself is a positive and is probably meant to be, in the main, a 'good' character. He must impress the audience as such without the disadvantage of a title which might militate against him before he has spoken a word.

'Grand Almoner' is in any case, however, a more apt choice. The title of Almoner, a monastic office, was originally given to the monk appointed to dispense alms. The term came to be applied to a similar functionary in princely and ecclesiastical households. Hofmannsthal probably took the idea and function of the Grand Almoner from French history. From the fifteenth century the Grand Almoner (the title first appears in 1487) was a high-ranking member of a religious order. He administered the alms monies for the King. Frequently he exerted considerable political influence. Thus Hofmannsthal's character is from this point of view in a definite tradition.

It is not easy to encompass all the implications of the Grand Almoner. In some ways he is, as has been shown, one of Hofmannsthal's most spectacular theatrical creations. Simultaneously the obscurity of his language sometimes prevents him from being dramatic in any dynamic and lucid way. But there is a further feature, one which has bearing on his intrinsic significance: it can of course be asserted that he is an essentially positive, 'good' character. He stigmatizes the King, he acts as a kind of divine conscience, he is evidently a man of great holiness and austerity of life. But it is scarcely to be denied that he is also most unlovable. He may be—and almost certainly is—right. But his rightness is expressed with a chilling cruelty which seems to indicate spiritual arrogance of rare degree. His rightness seems to be of a peculiarly sterile kind.

These considerations are perhaps of some interest because Hofmannsthal, while probably unaware of the obscurity mentioned, could scarcely fail to realize that he had created an essentially unlovable character. But Hofmannsthal, although pronouncedly Catholic in his cultural-political sympathies, was seemingly well aware of the fact that one can be right in judging a situation while at the same time remaining clerically obscurantist and uncharitable in one's outlook. One would hate to think of the Grand Almoner as regent of the realm.

The second scene of the second act is effective in a quiet, contrasting manner. As is already evident, Hofmannsthal arranged the action of *Der Turm* so that it would swing alternately from the 'big' scenes—at the tower itself (opening scene), the cloisters, the palace, Sigismund's camp—to the more confined, less colourful but no less purposeful scenes such as that between the Doctor and Julian, the present scene in Sigismund's room, and (after the test) the scene in the tower between Julian and Sigismund.

In this way the necessary contrasts of mood and spectacle are achieved; the great spectacle-scenes themselves gain by their position and stand out in relief, as it were. The general effect is thus of an uneasy, disturbed action, moving at varying speeds but nevertheless inexorably forward.

The symbolic significance of Sigismund in the drama as a whole has already been discussed to some extent in another and more general context (see pp. 205–9). Here it need only be added that the Sigismund who is carried off to the court in princely garb is already half-developed, and in him are seen the joint characteristics of crusader and saviour. In the final sequence, moreover, the dualistic nature of the play—that of a passion-play allied with that of an ideological drama—is firmly established. Sigismund's words and gestures at the end of the scene recall the liturgical symbol of the King of Sorrows, exemplified in the garden of Gethsemane:

Sigismund. Angel and devil are one: they have the same secret thought. (He steps forward a pace.) Are you looking at my mouth so that I can tell you what it is? Man is a unique glory and he does not have too much sorrow and pain but too little.[1] That is what I say to you. (In a changed voice.) I am raised up. Gone is all fear. But all at once my feet are so cold. Warm them for me, Anton.... Put them into the fiery oven where wander singing the young men, my brothers. Lord God, we praise Thee, from face to face! Chosen forth! (He throws up his hands.) Father, now I come! (He collapses. The two masked servants come forward.)[1]

ACT III

The third act is one long scene and is built on the same basis as that of the scene in the cloister. In fact the three large-scale scenes in cloisters, palace and camp are, as will become apparent, similar in structure. If the second (palace) is on a vaster scale than the first, the third (camp) outdoes the second in sheer size and brilliance of spectacle.

This is a baroque feature which is probably best explained in architectural terms. In many large baroque churches one sees three distinct dome-cupolas, the first above the nave, the second, higher and larger, above the chancel. The highest and largest of all is above the high altar and is often decorated with a vision of heaven.

The third act, then, is larger than the scene in the cloisters. It consists principally of a central episode, the vital exchange between Basilius and Sigismund. This sequence, which begins and ends as incisively as its opposite number in the earlier scene (Grand Almoner and Basilius), is flanked by episodes of introduction and conclusion. Where the scene with the Grand Almoner was markedly ecclesiastical in setting and ceremonial, the palace scene has all the secular glitter of the formal Spanish-Austrian court procedure of the sixteenth and seventeenth centuries. Again Hofmannsthal achieves a good deal by stage direction and in silent movement.

The setting itself is elaborate and complex: the death-chamber of the Queen, with a window overlooking the Court Church. There is an oratory with a secret door and a small passage with another window which overlooks the death-chamber itself. The impression made by the scene itself—the macabre gesture of

Basilius in holding the rest in the death-chamber—is mixed. On the one hand the effect is of a ritualistic ceremony which is superfine, sophisticated, automatic and utterly lifeless: what Hofmannsthal would call a *starre Formel* (rigid formula) in fact. On the other hand there is a note of emotional and almost sensuous religiosity. This kind of fanatical piety (noted in the Romanov and Wittelsbach families, for example) is often quite independent of life itself, of behaviour and morals. It is a true sign of inner decadence. Basilius has already given a sign of this in his short speech about the 'dear grave' in the monastery. The King's attitude to his pliant confessor is yet another confirmation of the Grand Almoner's taunt that Basilius wants God and truth on his own terms. The confessor himself is a notable example of Hofmannsthal's critical attitude to conforming clericalism in alliance with the Establishment.

Thus before a word has been said (apart from the stage-setting words of the castellan who tells the audience that this is the death-chamber) the onlooker has received a considerable and complex impression. The castellan himself provides the clue to the situation:

The death-chamber of the thrice-blessed Queen! This main entrance has been untrodden for twenty-one years. The venerable Sisters of the Visitation, two of whom watch here in prayer from midnight until the grey of dawn, enter by this little door, which leads down to the sacristy by a spiral stairway hidden in the pillar.[1]

This is somewhat stilted, but in addition to giving information it leads to an important point. There are distinct reminiscences here of the Habsburgs, especially the Spanish line. One thinks of the egocentric grave in the Court Church at Innsbruck, commissioned by Maximilian I, and of the brooding death-meditation of Charles V who, according to legend, caught a fatal chill while lying in his own coffin, savouring a foretaste of his own requiem. The Escorial, built by Philip II, and Philip's own attitude to the religious-emotional aspect of death, are a comparable manifestation of the same strain. This aspect is brought out by Schiller to some extent, but more obviously by Verdi. In, for example, Act II, scene 1 of the opera (original version) Don Carlo has taken refuge in St Juste in an attempt to forget his misery. Monks pray before the tomb of Charles V and tell of the vanity of expecting peace in earthly life. Verdi makes use of the legend (rather like that concerning Barbarossa) that Charles did not die but lived on quietly as a monk. He even introduces a character (a monk) in whom Carlo sees and hears a resemblance to his grand-father. A considerable climax of the 'death-in-life' type is achieved when the King and his new Queen pass in procession before the tomb in the presence of Carlo.

That both Charles V and Philip II were in Hofmannsthal's mind when he wrote this scene is confirmed in an interesting manner later in the scene itself. Basilius says to Julian:

Those words of my thrice-blessed uncle, Emperor Charles V, appear before my soul: the words with which he handed over his crown and lands to his only son Don Philip. 'If', he said, 'my death had given you possession of these lands, such a precious inheritance would have given me great claims on your gratitude....'[1]

A few lines later the presence in Hofmannsthal's mind of the withdrawal and death of Charles V becomes even more apparent: 'Perhaps I too shall withdraw to a monastery for the rest of my days: may a worthy son pay my subjects....'

The scene proper begins with the panoply of the processional entry, in which the full extent of the rigidly formal court cere-monial, already noted, is seen:

From below are heard the organ and the chant of nuns. The castellan steps up to the alcove, sprinkles the bed with holy water from a silver bowl at the entrance to the alcove, and respectfully draws the curtain. Outside the sound of approaching people is heard, then the thrice-repeated sound of a halberd striking the stone floor. At a sign from the castellan the servants hurry across and throw the doors wide open. The court enters: the life-guards,[2] staff-bearers, pages with lanterns: then the standard-bearer of the realm with the silver eagle: then a page who bears a crimson cushion on which lie the King's prayer-book and gloves. The King enters, his Polish hat in his hand, curved sabre girded on. Close behind him comes his confessor: then gentlemen of the court, at their head Julian, alone. Behind the gentlemen are four chamberlains.[1]

The stage movement now begins. It is marked by an even greater sense of protocol and ceremony:

The King takes his gloves from the cushion which is proffered by a kneeling page. He draws on the left glove and tucks the right into his belt. The life-guard and the staff-bearers have meanwhile circled the chamber and have gone out through the main doorway: likewise the castellan and the servants. The doors are closed. Two staff-bearers take up their positions immediately inside the doorway. The gentlemen of the court stand on the left in front of the oratory, Julian on their extreme right....The King approaches the alcove; a chamberlain hurries forward and raises the curtain. Another chamberlain hands the King the holy-water brush. The King sprinkles the bed, kneels down and remains there praying for a moment. The confessor kneels with him. The King rises, steps into the middle of the chamber, his confessor a short distance behind him. The chant and the organ have ceased.

Carl Burckhardt seems to have drawn Hofmannsthal's attention to an alleged lack of balance in this scene. He asserted that 'the direct, overt element seems to prevail over the indirect—the actual mimetic quality in the speech of the characters'.[2]

It is odd, however, that he appears to have made no such criticism of the particular obscurity noted in the scene with the Grand Almoner. In the present instance his critique seems for once to have been somewhat forced. Hofmannsthal's reply shows that he felt this to be so. His comments also reveal his full intention in the depiction of the King. At the same time he made some general, marginal comments which are of value in an understanding of the play:

However, as far as the speech of the main characters is concerned, I should be very grateful if you would mark...those passages in which the mimetic, concealed element seems to you to have been dissipated too much. As a matter of fact, when I go through it in my own mind I cannot find anything which seems at first sight to justify your point.

The act, represented as a theatrical action—not just read as a text[1]—contains a good deal that is very palpably mimetic: on the one hand the ceremonial, on the other the...violent action which lies in wait from the beginning and finally breaks forth. As to details: I am sure that in the case of the King at least, I have not weakened at any point his conscious, regal allure. Indeed, he is almost terrifying because one cannot guess at all what sort of man breathes behind this mask. But that is as it should be.[2]

Hofmannsthal has here summed up his intention with Basilius. He has also summed up the direct impression which Basilius makes on mind and eye. Probably the most terrifying aspect of a very unlovable character is that he has no definite character, not even a bad one. At no time in this scene does the onlooker feel that here, for better or worse, is the real Basilius. Tear-stained sentiment, egocentric narcissism, whining self-pity, sickening religiosity, lush eloquence, rapid changes of mind: these alternate with one another. But neither in whole nor in part do they actually present the moral petrifaction and putre-faction that is Basilius behind his own façade.

In setting the atmosphere for the entrance of Sigismund, Hofmannsthal makes use of that Shakespearian technique, noted in chapter 6, in which the entrance of the main character is delayed until curiosity and suspense have been roused to a considerable pitch.[3] Here in the palace Hofmannsthal telescopes exposition, the rousing of curiosity and the appearance of the major figure into one scene.

It may seem puzzling that the author has adopted this technique for the middle of the play. In effect, however, this scene, while logically and dramatically connected with preceding events, is a new beginning. The audience knows that Sigismund is to be a new and different figure in appearance and action, however much his inner character and state of soul may remain unchanged. The curiosity and excitement arise from the fact that the audience has no idea what form this difference will take. There are numerous possibilities.

Hofmannsthal plays on this curiosity by advancing various ideas, fears and hopes from the King. A characteristic example of this is seen when the King receives news from the stable-master of Sigismund's taciturnity and cold, princely bearing ('a look like cold steel'). The King looks questioningly at Julian:

Julian. Never in his life has he mounted a horse. I was always mindful of Your Majesty's stern edict.

King. Mastery of himself without parallel. I must surely fear the terrible power of the disguise?[1]

The episode is one of considerable suspense. It begins with the report of a chamberlain: 'In a few moments the Prince will ride into the castle courtyard.'[2] Then come the eyewitness accounts. The structure of the scene at this point recalls that of *Egmont*, especially the minutes preceding the arrival of Egmont himself at the summons of the Duke of Alba (Act IV, scene 2):

Alba. (He looks up attentively as if hearing something and goes to the window) It is he! Egmont! And did your horse bear you here so lightly without shying at the smell of blood. . . . Dismount! So, now you have one foot in the grave. And—now—both!

It will be recalled that this symbolic image of the horse runs through the entire drama: for example, Act II, scene 2:

Egmont. As if whipped onward by invisible spirits the sun-horses of time bolt away, pulling the frail coach of our destinies behind.

This fate image recurs at one of the most tense and tragic moments in the play: the brief, matter-of-fact conversation between Ferdinand and Egmont, while Alba pretends to read the letter which is the signal that all is ready for Egmont's arrest (Act IV, scene 2):

Ferdinand. That is a fine horse which your men have brought to take you home.

Egmont. It is not the worst by any means. I've had it for quite a while. I'm thinking of giving it away.

One must not be dogmatic here; but it is more than possible that Hofmannsthal had this horse-and-rider image in his mind when he was preparing the scene for Sigismund's entrance.[1] This idea is supported a few lines later when the image of Sigismund entering masterfully into his destiny is introduced into the King's hopes and fears:

King (quietly to Julian). The supreme concept of authority has been impressed upon this boy? The concept of unconditional obedience?
Julian. Let my King remember that the youth is ignorant of this world and of his position in it. He knows one Supreme Thing; he raises his eyes to the stars and his soul to God.
King. We will hope that this is sufficient. (Very audibly) For the world is out of control and we are determined to put out this spreading fire—if necessary in rivers of blood.
(The courtiers, who are standing at the back near the window, are looking at something down below. The pages crowd round the window and, with a good deal of scuffling, try to look down into the courtyard. The King notices this and looks across.)
Chamberlain. The prince dismounts. Count Adam tries to hold his stirrup, but the Prince anticipates him. He turns towards the main doorway and enters the castle.[2]

What L. A. Willoughby wrote of the central image in *Egmont* might be applied here in a modified manner:

Goethe's confession that he was a visual type, for example, cannot serve as a ready-made key which automatically unlocks all the doors of his poetic imagery. The effect produced by an image within a complex of related thoughts and images may well not be predominantly visual or tactile at all, whatever he himself may have said. It is obvious, for instance, that the meaning of the central image in *Egmont*, the famous image of the horse and charioteer, is not to be exhausted solely by dwelling on its visual and tactile aspects. Its very essence is the feeling of movement in the plunging horses—a kinetic image—and the effect of control in the charioteer as he reins them in—a kinaesthetic or muscular image. Only inasmuch as the visual recedes, and gives place to these much more intimate bodily sensations, do we appreciate that relation between unconscious and conscious direction which Egmont is here trying to communicate, and which is the main theme of the play. Only through a close examination of the immediate and the wider context can we determine the nature and significance of this particular play. And we must be bold enough to let the context decide, and to acknowledge the objective existence of the poetic impression, independently of its relation to the poet's conscious intention.[1]

This kind of subterranean allusiveness cannot be directly proved. But such suggested relationships—*Bezüge* to use a much-quoted Hofmannsthalian category—are at least in harmony with Hofmannsthal's known manner of writing. The existence of various such more or less specific *Bezüge* has been suggested fairly frequently throughout the present study. Others follow in due course, notably in connection with the fifth act of *Der Turm*. But it might be stressed at this medial point in the consideration of the play that they are not necessarily a virtue of Hofmannsthal's style. They can indeed be rather puzzling in that they sometimes have the air of lending further ranges of significance which, however, cannot always be properly detected. For a polymath of superfine and uncannily rapid perceptiveness they would probably mean a good deal, even in theatrical performance. But for the great majority of men they present at first sight an obscurity, and on reflection a somewhat recondite historical-literary chase.

This chase can be fascinating and sometimes rewarding. It scarcely adds to the direct dramatic effectiveness of the drama, however, and Hofmannsthal was anxious to be judged as a dramatist. In all probability the appearance of these *Bezüge* in his dramas—and especially in *Der Turm*—is a product of that interest in history which constantly tempted him to see analogies with present conditions. Kassner noted (see also p. 110) that this process was sometimes all too facile. But this habit is doubtless part of Hofmannsthal's unitive tendency in thought.

It was asserted in chapter 3 that Hofmannsthal did not pursue this historical aspect of his talent beyond the essay or short study. This is true in that he never wrote a full-length historical biography nor a philosophy of history. But perhaps we should modify this assertion where *Der Turm* is concerned. For the technique of parallelisms, noted so often in studying the wartime essays, is actually developed—or at least modified—in this drama: once we have the 'key'—Don Carlos, Marcus Aurelius, or Egmont, as the case may be—we certainly seem to glimpse a wider range of significance.

Whether this somewhat tortuous technique is a virtue is therefore debatable. One can at least say that Hofmannsthal was in this matter both subtle and, on the whole—when one surveys the chronological sweep of his essays and later dramas—consistent.

In the particular instance under discussion—the horse-and-rider image—Hofmannsthal certainly makes his point, even if the reader has never heard of *Egmont*. In this scene the contrast is made between the feverish excitement within the palace and the cold, contained power of Sigismund. This is expressed in his absolute mastery of his horse and his anticipation of the King's agent (Count Adam) who wishes to hold the stirrup, that is to say, to guide and direct him. This recalls in turn the cool and instinctive ease with which, after initial failure, Sigismund—now master of his own destiny—swung himself into the saddle and turned a look 'like cold steel' on his retinue. These incidents, expressed in terms of Hofmannsthal's horse-image, tell the reader that whatever immediate frustration Sigismund may suffer, his ultimate mastery is assured.

Hofmannsthal was successful here in realizing an ideal which he described as follows:

It is important in this play that one should always have something tangible, something in the visible foreground, as it were—an action . . .of quite concrete nature. Simultaneously and behind this action something more exalted, something of the mind and spirit, something *generally* valid, difficult to put into words, must likewise reveal itself, step by step and keeping pace with the action; . . .this something is not perceptible in rational terms but in one's imagination.[1]

This impression of an action moving on two levels of comprehension is heightened by the puzzled excitement which continues to rise in anticipation of the entrance of Sigismund. For every speculation on the part of the King, Julian has an opposite. In contrast to the King's crazed preoccupation with material violence, Julian emphasizes the spiritual purity of Sigismund's character. The theme of Sigismund's entry into the world of evil is expressed in an image of complex beauty:

King. What speech may we expect from him?

Julian. The most respectful, but not, indeed, as spoken at court.

King. But?—

Julian. Perhaps like the speech of angels. His speech is like an underground spring emerging into the light of day—like the tree which has been pierced and releases balsam through its wound.[1]

In the first part of chapter 6 the tower in which Sigismund is held captive was noted as a symbol of complex possibilities. In the above passage the tree as a symbol of unspoiled, pure nature, close to the earth and to its original source of existence, is equated with the tower.

This equating of two seemingly disparate notions becomes credible in the light of a particularly acute observation by Requadt, who defines the tower-symbol as follows:

If one thinks only of Calderón, the actual inventor of this fable, then one sees the tower only as a dungeon in which humanity is defiled. On the other hand, comparison with the course taken by the Madman,[2] whose goal—the citadel—is a precursor of the tower, shows that the tower is simultaneously core, heart of the world...point of origin.... The Madman, having stormed through the world, leaves its empty husks behind him, eager...to cast off life; and in the citadel he touches upon the secret of the world. Sigismund goes the opposite way: from the isolation of the tower into the world.[3]

Julian's tree-image ('an underground spring emerging into the light of day—like the tree which has been pierced and releases balsam through its wound') can be interpreted quite credibly as suggesting Sigismund's emergence from the 'tower' of his own isolation and innate spiritual purity. The 'pierced' and 'wound' in Julian's image tell of the violence to Sigismund and hint at the violent way he must go in the world on his progress from primal purity to inspired and ideal ruler.

But Requadt seems to have missed the combination of violence and mildness in this image. These conflicting qualities are fundamental to Sigismund and are summed up by the opposing ideas of 'pierced' and 'balsam'.[1] Just as Sigismund comes forth from the tower and ultimately develops the speech of the world—in order to reform the world—so does the healing balsam imprisoned within the tree flow forth, with violent and even pointless waste: this is quite a significant point in view of Sigismund's savage treatment of his father and the devastation caused by his victorious war. Requadt, however, expresses the ultimate development of Sigismund as indicated in this symbol: 'Sigismund must progress from using the language of angels to that social language which brings men together.'[2]

Thus the approach of Sigismund is heralded. Hofmannsthal's treatment of Anton demands comment at this point. The King dismisses the court, preparatory to receiving his son. He paints a vivid word-picture of the silent tableau which will announce peace and accord between father and son:

If, however, I step out on to the balcony with my young guest and—as a sign of our cordial understanding—lay a fatherly arm on his shoulder, then let the trumpets sound: for then a great moment for this kingdom will have come.[3]

Immediately after this patronizing and hypocritically sentimental outburst, Anton observes to Julian as he goes out: 'I dreamt about dirty water and teeth falling out! No good can come of all this: it's bound to go wrong!' This piece of cheerfully peasant-like Freudianism serves a good dramatic purpose in that it deflates abruptly the effect of the King's rhetoric. But it also reminds the audience of the presence, in this sink of scented corruption and decay, of the embodiment of sturdy sanity and naïve-instinctive strength. This element constitutes one of the most significant differences between Calderón's play and Hofmannsthal's interpretation of the same symbolic situation. Max Kommerell's comment is applicable here:

Master and servant: what a delightful theme in world literature. But unfortunately in German literature, if one disregards Austria, only

Lessing treats it appropriately.... This universal humour establishes a unity where the gulf between the ruling and subject classes threatens to tear mankind into two halves. It gives the lower rank a kind of superiority in so far as the *privileged* social form is also seen in terms of limited vision or absence of directness.... But it is beyond all humour when the relationship of servant to master becomes a dedication of the soul and thus recalls that kind of exalted friendship which almost makes a nobleman of the servant. How great are these features in Shakespeare; they are completely lacking in Calderón, who as a general principle rigidly preserves the distinctions in rank.[1]

Kommerell expressly excludes Austria from his stricture on German literature. With Anton in mind one can perhaps apply to Hofmannsthal part of his tribute to Shakespeare and Austria. Requadt's remarks are relevant here:

Anton is Sigismund's bridge to the world. In his mouth the ordinary language of the world would have repelled the prisoner. The dialect, however, makes a more sympathetic approach possible. It permits—in the words of the *Buch der Freunde*—not a personal language but a personal voice.[2]

The appearance of Anton in this scene together with his constant closeness to Sigismund are part of the trust and belief in the people, the *Volk*, which Hofmannsthal developed during his middle years and especially during the war.[3] As he observed in *Österreich im Spiegel seiner Dichtung:*

Perhaps the war has given us a pointer as to where the real values are. Reality is surely where the greatest, most absolute, most innate and purest strength is to be found. And that is in the people. That is what this war has made us understand.[4]

Curt Hohoff has summarized this aspect of Hofmannsthal's development. Apart from a somewhat one-sided preference for the comedies his general conclusion seems valid. He concentrated on Hofmannsthal's last work, *Arabella* (1927–9), and thus on the more patriarchal aspect of this folk interest; for Mandryka, the very embodiment of the unspoiled rural provinces, owns villages and forests and has four thousand subjects. But Hohoff's essential point is not affected by this:

Together Mandryka and Arabella find a patriarchal paradise: close to the people—who are still people and not mass,[1] the Slavonic folk, still rooted in their old customs and remote from the town...close to what is holy.... That is Hofmannsthal's progress: from the Paris-scented decadence of his youth...to the Slavonic folkishness of the Danube lands, to those real forces of life which Goethe sought amongst the Mothers.[2]

Hofmannsthal takes advantage of every dramatic possibility in the situation before Sigismund's entrance. With the exit of Anton and the courtiers the scene is actually set for the meeting between father and son. By a bold dramatic ruse Hofmannsthal enables the audience to see both on the stage simultaneously, that is to say at the same moment of anticipation. This is done without undue artificiality or over-theatrical soliloquy.

The King withdraws with Julian through the oratory to a window whence he can see and hear Sigismund.[3] Sigismund enters the death-chamber with Count Adam. The audience thus gains a double impression. The one is direct, that of Sigismund, as yet mute but every inch a princely figure. His appearance and monosyllabic speech suggest great potential power. At the same time, in the low-toned conversation between Basilius and Julian, the audience can see Sigismund through the sentimental yet egocentrically calculating eyes of the King.

Count Adam obediently plays his part and tries to imbue Sigismund with submissive respect for Basilius. The audience meanwhile searches Sigismund's face for a sign, simultaneously searching the King's face and weighing his words for some indication of what will happen.

Hofmannsthal's purpose here is plain. The difference between father and son must be established to the very point of becoming grotesque. The audience must feel implicitly what becomes explicit in the following dialogue. The King and Prince are incompatible. It is impossible for the pure strength of Sigismund to ally itself with the hopeless corruption of Basilius. Amelioration or compromise are both impossible.

In the encounter between Sigismund and the King there is another marked but completely 'absorbed' reminiscence of Schiller's *Don Carlos*: the dialogue between Philipp and Carlos (Act II, scene 2):

Carlos. Now, then, or never!—
 We are, for once, alone—the barrier
 Of courtly form...
 Has fallen! Now a golden ray of hope
 Illumes my soul...
     and Heaven itself inclines
 With choirs of joyous angels to the earth,...
 My father, let us be reconciled! (He falls on his knees before
 him.)
Philipp. This trickery grows too bold—
Carlos. A son's devotion too bold?
Philipp. And all in tears! Unworthy sight! Away, leave me!
Carlos. Now, then, or never! My father—
 Let us be reconciled.[1]

Carlos is of course eloquent throughout. Sigismund is for the greater part monosyllabic. The following sequence from *Der Turm* illustrates the point, however, as Sigismund's passionate feelings are expressed in tortured words:

Sigismund. Yield up your secret! Let your face dawn before my eyes! Reveal yourself to me!—I have never kissed another human being. Father, give me the kiss of peace....
King. Enough. I do not like this mask. Control yourself, Prince of Poland. Remember the place whence I have called you and the place to which I have raised you up. (Sigismund stands there helplessly.)[2]

The meeting between Basilius and Sigismund thus takes place. The dialogue—mainly a monologue from Basilius—runs on; and it is clear that Basilius, the old and effete régime, merely wants the fresh vigour and unspoiled name of the Crown Prince in order to bolster up his own sagging fortunes. It is a realistic comment on Hofmannsthal's part, when, confident of success with Sigismund, the King orders his son to liquidate Julian, the recently installed but now (he hopes) superfluous prop of the throne.

This command is the external motivation for Sigismund's violent attack on the King and his own consequent downfall. The real reason, however, is to be found in the sudden insight brought about by the King's words:

Let each of your steps be terrible...decisive. Overthrow those of evil intent before they can recover from the shock and plan rebellion. Drive class against class, district against district, home-dwellers against the homeless, peasant against nobleman. Let men's weakness and stupidity be your allies, gigantic and never-ending.[1]

Sigismund, as yet unversed in the ways of the world, sees instinctively the way he must go. His must be the reconciling mission which brings just these classes and elements together. Therefore, despite all purity of motive and ultimately peaceful intention, there is only one solution to the problem symbolized in the unregenerate Basilius.

The situation might perhaps be expressed in simple theological terms. A merciful and patient God allows for a purgatory in which, in divine terms, amends may be made for sin and preparation made for eternal peace in Heaven. Cynical and wilful mortal sin, however—the persistence in sin—is unforgivable, and eternal damnation is the only solution. There is no possibility of regeneration and reform. Sigismund will conserve and transfigure what is of proven good and potential, unspoilt value in the society about him. But Basilius is hopelessly lost. This is the *quinta essentia* of Sigismund's 'conservative revolution'.

Hence Basilius is thrust violently from Sigismund and the Crown Prince takes command. The scene is richly dramatic with two distinct operatic-type tableaux. The first is when Sigismund sets his foot on the King. The second is when, with the state banner in his hand, he casts away the King's sword; for the sword is the symbol of arbitrary violence:

My deeds will satisfy my will.... My power will reach as far as my will... (he throws down the naked sword at their feet). There! I do not need it! I am the master![1]

Requadt summed up Sigismund's experience in this episode in a precise manner:

Therefore Sigismund expects to find in Basilius's countenance the face of the son of God; but he finds instead a...wily, scheming and arbitrary ruler.... What Sigismund now experiences is a radical break with the world: hence his distraction.[2]

Requadt, however, is so obsessed with the (undeniable) force of the personal symbolic world of *Der Turm* that he seems to miss the point of the climacteric moment when Sigismund casts the sword from him and is overpowered. He remarks merely:

After the clash with his father, Sigismund violently takes possession of the regal cloak. But the servants have no difficulty in tearing it off from behind; for by throwing away the sword he has left himself defenceless. With this gesture Sigismund wanted to establish power-without-force. In this we see the difference between him and the King.[3]

This is of course quite unexceptionable. It is strange, however, that the actual point of the incident eluded Requadt, because his tracing of the 'cloak-symbol', as a symbol of power and awareness of the world, is both subtle and convincing.

Hofmannsthal must have emphasized this startling episode, the sudden reversal of fortune, for a specific reason. Idealism, individualism, measureless desire for good are not enough. Of themselves they can of course achieve much for the individual, and individual regeneration is a potent force in the world. However, if ecclesiastical terminology be permissible here, for every Cistercian and Carthusian there must be both Jesuit and Capuchin. And they must have around them an active and devoted laity. Sigismund is not yet mature for command. He must proceed—keeping his inner allegiance pure—from the realm of the individual to the world outside. He must, as Alewyn said in a general sense of Hofmannsthal himself, go out into the crowded street.[4]

In other words Sigismund and what he stands for must go to the people; or the people must come to him and become one with him.

The particularly ominous words at the close of *Österreich im Spiegel seiner Dichtung* come to mind again here:

Great will be the responsibility of those who are intellectually mature enough to interpret these signs for the people. In the unsophisticated depths of existence in which the common people have their being, just as in those dark depths of the individual where there is only a vague and shifting frontier between spiritual and bodily things, you will find not reflection and perception but the wish and the belief.[1]

It is clear that Sigismund's path must lead down to the people, where 'the greatest, most absolute, most innate and purest strength is to be found'.[2] This is to become visibly apparent at the end of the next (fourth) act where, after time for recollection and peace back in the tower, Sigismund is sure of himself and of his methods. Necessary forcefulness and pacific idealism are there united in him for the well-being of all. With this in mind, defenceless purity and sudden—even though necessary—violence are seen now to be characteristics of the immature, inevitably self-centred youth who in the palace scene tries to alter the course of destiny by one terrible blow.

This is here implicitly apparent. What is explicitly clear is that Julian and what he stands for are spent forces. The truth of the Doctor's words in Act I now becomes terribly clear: 'the source itself is polluted.... In these commanding features good and evil wrestle with each other like snakes in fearsome combat.'[3] Julian has subjugated idealism and steadfastness to personal gain and glorification. Such men may achieve much. But to serve Basilius and Sigismund and what they represent, though credible (Talleyrand's was no greater *volte-face*), is a course which must and should bring its own retribution. That in Hofmannsthal's time, as in others, this has not often been apparent—either in individuals or in the causes they serve—does not invalidate the argument. That Julian is personally attractive to some extent, that his decline is depicted with feeling and quiet pathos, only heightens the sense of waste and futility.

The scene, which is about to end quietly with the disappearance from court of the disgraced Julian, flames into unexpected excitement in the closing lines with the news that the roads are impassable and that a new turn in events is imminent. Count Adam's account, coming after the elegiac exchanges between Julian and the Doctor, is of great force:

The mob has gone mad. They are lying before the church-doors in their thousands, praying for a Beggar-King, a nameless boy who is to be their leader and who, in chains, shall bring about a new kingdom.[1]

This sudden interpolation serves two purposes. Hofmannsthal again leaves his audience no respite. Should attention or receptivity be flagging, as this long, complex and colourful scene draws quietly to a close, then, with this new vital interest, the mind is sent questing onwards into the next act. It is a dynamic touch in Hofmannsthal's attempt to bring unity and continuity to a widely spaced action. For the action of *Der Turm* is in the main a mixture of the panoramic and the episodic. Without such life-charged links as this closing description of the uprising it could easily fall apart.

In the second place the news draws Sigismund and the people of the country together in spirit. It is the first spoken intimation of the ultimate course and climax of Sigismund's career. The broader significance of this union between prince and people is shortly to become clear.

ACT IV

The fourth act is the shortest in the play and, like the preceding act, consists of one scene only. Otherwise, in mood, structure and language it has nothing in common with the scene at court. It is in fact a further and bolder development of the technique of dramatic contrast between the various phases and *milieux* of the action in this play. It is bolder because in the scene itself Hofmannsthal runs through the entire range of mood from the massive calm and lofty moral superiority of Sigismund, through the hectic violence and last frenzied threshing of Julian, to the fantastic and vulgar mouthings of the new self-styled leader Olivier. All three are at one point apparent simultaneously.

The scene is in fact a greatly heightened reminiscence of the second scene in Act II when Sigismund was carried off to the palace. The implicit contrast between the 'then' and the 'now'— on what is virtually the same ground—enhances the dramatic effect and helps to impose some sense of unity on the play.

Perhaps this point is best illustrated by the example of *Egmont*. Goethe's action in that play is also frequently episodic, even panoramic. In at least two instances, however, he imposes a certain unity on this action and thereby achieves a tragic ironic effect. The first is in the contrast between the initial appearance of the Regent (Act I, scene 2) and the ghastly parody of this, on virtually the same ground, at the first entrance of her successor, the Duke of Alba (Act IV, scene 2). The second is in the contrast between the Egmont–Oranien scene (Act II, scene 2) and the Egmont–Alba scene (Act IV, scene 2). These two scenes are structurally similar and the situation in the latter—Egmont's blindness to his own danger—is a heightened version of his situation in the first. There are even certain similarities in character between Oranien and Alba. Both are men of immense willpower, drive and ruthlessness. Both have a clear, decisive faculty, great reserve and self-sufficiency. In both men these qualities conceal depths of passion which are only occasionally allowed to break forth. How alike are the scenes—and yet how tragically different!

In the present scene in the tower Hofmannsthal achieves a comparable if less intense effect by use of a similar method. Sigismund is now back in the tower. Hofmannsthal gives the scene a setting worthy of the ripest 'Gothic terror' tradition. This is not to diminish the example taken from Calderón, but Hofmannsthal's beginnings were partly rooted in the Romanticism of the nineteenth century, and the prisoner of noble birth, immured and in chains, was a stock situation. But these are only peripheral considerations which may help to explain the sense of familiarity experienced when confronted by this scene.

In *Der Turm* the underground vault is hewn out of the rock; it has a spiral stairway; and Anton, the faithful servant, breaks the gloom with a lamp in the traditional Romantic manner. Hofmannsthal, however, avoids melodrama and the obvious. There is no whispered conspiracy, no mystification. The action moves forward at once. The opening exchanges depict the final distinction between, and inevitable separation of Sigismund and Julian.

A special use of language is here the main guide to the situation. At once it is apparent from Julian's immoderate, excited tone, his violent imagery and urgent persuasiveness, that he has lost control over himself. The quality of his speech is in marked contrast to the self-conscious coldness and self-sufficiency of the early scenes in the tower. His language now has the ring of a megalomaniac:

I have brought all things under my sway. I have woken and stirred to life the very earth, what dwells in and is born of her. . . . I have breathed life into the peasant, the clod of earth. I have stirred up the beast with teeth and claws; the snout of the swine and the throat of the fox bellow your name, and the beadles and bailiffs are strangled by earthy hands.[1]

In this very violence, however, there is a sense of strain, the sense of a crazed, would-be leader gathering his faltering strength for a final, desperate, perhaps despairing fling.

Sigismund is almost pedantically exact and academically calm by comparison. Immediately a new and decisive note is heard in his speech. For the first time in the play Sigismund speaks rationally and with decision. Requadt hinted indirectly at the logic of this, though in an unnecessarily obscure and meta-physical way, when he observed:

and in the same way Sigismund wanted to preserve the origin of his tower-existence when he went out into the world. But this was only possible if the world which he encountered was in substance identical with himself, that is to say identical with Sigismund interpreted as the world-ego [*Welt-Ich*] of the tower, i.e. if it [the world] was symbolic.[1]

What this presumably means (or, at any rate, what it should mean) is that Sigismund, the isolated individual, found that his own inner picture of the world did not correspond to external reality. In other words he and the world spoke two different languages. He spoke what Julian called a language 'perhaps like the speech of angels. His speech is like an underground spring emerging into the light of day.'[2]

Sigismund's experience is analogous to the contrast between the perfect world striven for and realized within the mind and soul of the contemplative monk, and the physical reality of material corruption in any worldly guise. Sigismund's developing insight is symbolized by his originally childlike speech in the tower, which was a mixture of innate innocence and holy wisdom, by his sentient yet inchoate exclamations in the presence of the King, and now—his insight complete—by the combination of his innate qualities with the practical, 'external' language of the world. 'To talk is to be human', says Anton.[3] Requadt equates the two processes and one is symbolic of the other—'these processes of becoming capable of speech and of becoming human'.[4] Thus Sigismund does not suddenly learn to speak. All the prerequisites are there. Experience merely arranges things in true focus. Hence there is no real struggle between Sigismund and Julian in this, their final scene together. Sigismund has now consciously outgrown Julian, and two brief aphorisms really summarize his present standpoint. In the first Sigismund turns the sense of Julian's urging:

Julian. Your soul had to suffer in order to be uplifted: everything else was vain and empty.

Sigismund. You have taught me how to grasp that. All is vanity save speech between spirit and spirit.[5]

This is more significant than the fairly obvious retort a few lines later:

Julian. You utter the truth, my son; for this time you are safe.
Sigismund. Yes, I am. Lord and King forever in this fortified tower (he strikes his breast).

To isolate this latter sequence, as has sometimes been done to prove a critical point, is to simplify to the point of misleading. Certainly this line goes to the heart of one aspect of the symbolism of the tower itself. But it does not imply Sigismund's decision to turn his back on the world. Even such a sensitive critic as Requadt seems to have missed or to have ignored the point here. Requadt treats this section of the play in some detail. He remarks merely of this particular point in the action:

Because Sigismund experiences the complete destruction of the symbolic world, he is reluctant to leave the tower again. He refuses Julian's request to do so, and the latter is brought low by the rebels, led by Olivier. Sigismund finds himself in a new situation only when the poor in their eschatological faith beg him to assume power.[1]

This begs the question. A critic cannot have it both ways. Either Sigismund resolves firmly to leave the world or he does not. To attribute his change of mind solely to the urging and eschatological faith of the oppressed is to contradict Sigismund's alleged decision without explaining it.

The key to the situation seems to lie in Sigismund's second aphorism spoken as Julian commands him to put on the emblems of power:

Julian. Put on the royal robe! Buckle on the belt!
Sigismund. I will not do it.
Julian. You will not do it?
Sigismund. You have laid me in the straw like an apple, and I have become ripe, and now I know my place. But it is not where you would have me be.[2]

Requadt remarks of this:

completely in accord with his organically involuntary existence (language = the flowing forth of sap from a pierced tree) he now refers to himself as an apple which has become ripe; he decides to remain in the 'worldlessness' (*Weltlosigkeit*) of the tower.[3]

Sigismund is now mature, certainly; but this maturity does not lead him to the contemplative inwardness of the tower. Secure in himself and sure of his purpose, he is actually waiting for the right moment, the call from the one quarter—the poor, the oppressed, and other men of goodwill who know and hate their plight. This is the meaning of 'I know my place. But it is not where you would have me be.' Sigismund will lead a revolutionary movement, but not at Julian's behest nor as his figurehead. The symbol of the ripe apple, one of life and fruitfulness, must in any case lead away from the idea of seclusion.

As if to substantiate this interpretation, the conversation with Julian ends abruptly as Anton brings in the messenger. This is the first glimpse of the outside world since Sigismund's awakening to life. It is the world of the people. With the entrance of the messenger, hard on Sigismund's last words, this decisive theme is visibly introduced. Its climax is the assumption of kingly power by Sigismund.

Julian's castles in the air collapse abruptly as the messenger tells how the risings threaten to sweep their instigator away. Again the contemporary note, constantly implicit, is here explicitly apparent. Hofmannsthal may well have been recalling the avalanche unleashed by the recent Russian Revolution after its initial, comparatively peaceful and controlled stage. There is of course no exact correspondence with Julian (certainly not Alexander Kerensky, although Grand Duke Michael is a possibility!). It is more the phenomenon as such: the apocalyptic vision of an order of life, an entire society, suddenly and utterly swept into chaos and apparent madness, with the wheels of revolution grinding to and fro over their own inventors.

In the resulting disorder, when Julian vacillates between fearful belief and *illusions de grandeur*, when even Anton is bewildered and frightened, Sigismund preserves his glacial calm. He will leave the tower when his hour has come, and then with decision and purpose. His answer to Anton's fear-stricken persuasion further substantiates the foregoing essentially positive interpretation of his attitude:

Anton. Look, boy, you follow me right now, you obstinate—, or I'll—
Sigismund (looks at him calmly). I will not. But if ever I do say:
I will—then you shall see how gloriously I go forth from this
tower.[1]

As voices are heard from above calling his name, Sigismund,
eager for the decisive action, actually instructs Anton to show the
murderous rebels the way to him: 'Come here, point to me and
cry aloud: here he stands.'[2] There is an obvious symbolic overtone: Sigismund's determined calm, the noise of the rabble and
the fear of the servant recall the scene in the garden of Gethsemane
when the soldiers came to arrest Jesus.

Hofmannsthal follows this bold identification of Sigismund as
a saviour-figure with a powerful reminiscence of an early moment
in the drama. The stage-direction says that as Sigismund speaks
the above words the torchlight from above (shining down the
spiral stairway) becomes stronger. Olivier, the new leader-
personality, enters and is seen for the first time in his new role:

Olivier. Bring him to the light (Two men with torches move across).
Now, is he going to open his trap? Where is my *Passauersegen*[3]
(reaches under his jerkin).

It is of perhaps more than incidental interest that Hofmannsthal,
although ostensibly setting his play in a saga-like Poland, achieves
—in this scene particularly—a vivid local colour and idiom which
should make a direct impression on a German-speaking audience.
Earlier in this scene, for example, the messenger-boy's narrative
is distinctly reminiscent of the Peasants' War (1524–5):

The peasants have come up out of their holes in the ground. . . . The
masters are all in the woods and they won't be coming out again. Their
feet are *that* high up in the air (laughs distractedly). The peasants got
'em and hanged 'em from the trees.[4]

In Olivier's speech the allusion to the *Passauersegen* suggests
the religious wars of the seventeenth century. The effect here is
not anachronistic. Hofmannsthal, like Shakespeare, preferred his
audience to have the illusion of reality, something which might

evoke a direct, even automatic response. The Polish equivalent here would be meaningless. The extent of the *direct* response from an audience is an open question. But the word has a *familiar* ring.

Sigismund does not respond to Olivier's threat and for a few seconds a vivid tableau is held in which the situation is visually impressed on the audience's mind. It recalls the tableau of Sigismund and the Doctor in Act I when the idea of Sigismund as man of destiny, saint-king and symbol of suffering humanity was first suggested. Inevitably the audience must feel the contrast and development as the torch shines on Sigismund's face, now set with decision and regal calm.[1]

The principal interest in the remainder of this episode is not so much that it depicts the actual sorry end of Julian. More important is the terrifying picture of the rabble-minded dictator which Hofmannsthal creates in a few lines. Here is not only the irrational power-craze, the egocentric and commonplace mind, the ruthless and loquacious violence. Here also is perhaps the most terrible and depressing characteristic of modern dictatorship —that incredibly petty vengefulness, the lascivious vulgarity which is not content with beating its enemy and rendering him harmless or dispossessing him; it must humiliate him in his own eyes and before the world. It must hunt him down, deride, cheapen and leave him with no rag to his back nor vestige of self-respect.

At the same time, while it degrades humanity to such depths, it degrades itself infinitely more. It is remarkable how Hofmannsthal contrives, without strain or any sense of dragging in a characteristic, of scoring a point, to depict and even prophesy the terribly familiar phenomenon. Several short extracts from Olivier's rantings will suffice to indicate this:

Come here, animal. Are you in your right senses and ready to drink a silver bumper of your father's blood?...Have they castrated your brains out of your skull?...What are you staring at? *Bougre,, larron, écoute.*[2]

Of the overthrown Julian he says:

Bring him here, that Judas, that maleficent court toady—even if he is bleeding from ninety-seven wounds. Bring His Excellency here, dead or alive....Worthy brethren, we'll hang the lot, but before we do it I want a confession and I want to see him there at our feet, whimpering for pity and begging for his life.[1]

At Julian's death he orders, 'Hang the lackeying sow from the window-frame'.

The markedly modern note of Olivier's fulminations needs no further stress. With the elimination of Julian the contest of wills between Sigismund and Olivier becomes straightforward. Again the distinction is expressed less in the actual discussion between them—which is not real discussion—than in the highly differentiated language of each character.

The significance of Hofmannsthal's language technique in this scene (as in the entire play) seems to be virtually ignored by much criticism which is more intent on establishing Sigismund as some other-worldly symbolic ideal, unfortunately dragged into fatal, contaminating contact with the world. Grete Schaeder, for example, otherwise quite consequential in her approach to *Der Turm*, is not free from this unwillingness to face the full implications of Sigismund and his situation. She says of him somewhat regretfully:

But when man acts, the eternal element in him is subordinated to the exigencies of the age in which he lives: no one can escape the blood which begot him, nor the mind which educated him. Even the speech between spirit and spirit is conditioned by the moment.[2]

This is indisputable but no cause for regret. Sigismund 'acts' in this scene with Olivier, and is neither intimidated nor mystified by the extreme worldliness and coarseness of his language. His deftness in turning Olivier's points indicates his own essential practicality. Olivier's language itself shows Hofmannsthal's real grip on the language and outlook of the mob: 'Are you opening your gob against my almighty person?—I'll sew you up in a dogskin and toss you on the dung-heap.'[3]

Where Olivier speaks in the crass extremes of the street-corner, Sigismund is cool and precise. He sees the inevitability of the rebellion and the inevitability of violence. Olivier tries to coerce him into service as a royal figurehead who will please the women and so buttress Olivier's power. Sigismund's answer is:

There is no need for any women, for you will storm through like the east wind. You will gather up prisoners like hay, and every tower and fortress will be just a joke for you.[1]

Sigismund's last words to Olivier demonstrate the true humility of dedicated majesty: 'Make no mistake, for with me no one thing is better sheltered than another.'

Then Sigismund is silent. He does not speak again until he accepts the crown from his true equals and comrades, the poor, the oppressed and the innocent. The episode closes with a violent spoken tableau as Hofmannsthal sums up Olivier and what he stands for in a few brief exchanges. This is the last time (in this first version of *Der Turm*) that Olivier is seen alive, and his image must remain in the mind throughout the final act of the play.

This tableau is vividly effective. The English critic, however, bred on Shakespearian conflict visible and audible (Macbeth and the royalists, Hamlet versus Laertes and Claudius, etc.) may find this fresco-like treatment of certain characters somewhat disconcerting. In this respect the second version of *Der Turm* (1927) is probably superior in that both characters (Sigismund and Olivier) remain visible in the action until the climax and end of the play.

The fresco-like technique in character depiction—it is also a characteristic of both *Jedermann* and *Das Salzburger Große Welttheater*—is another indication that Hofmannsthal became more and more deeply aware of traditional folk-practices and their values. This same technique was, for example, a marked characteristic of fifteenth- and sixteenth-century drama; and of particular relevance to Hofmannsthal is the fact that it was also a very marked feature of the traditional Austrian folk-theatre—of Sterzing, Bozen, Brixen, Hall, etc.

In the present instance Hofmannsthal uses this technique with dramatic brevity as Olivier, surrounded by his rabble of staff officers, answers their queries. As he does so the prophetic nature of Julian's dying words is felt: 'I have raised up the lowest of the low, but it has availed me nothing.'[1] Olivier's final words could easily have been transferred to a National Socialist meeting of the mid and late twenties:[2]

Third Officer. And the priests? The teachers and clerks? The tax-collectors? The lackeys?

Olivier. Blot 'em out like flies. Law and order shall vanish. Wolves and vultures shall come after us, and they shall not say that we've left the job half done. But now I have been sufficiently incommoded and importuned, and everybody knows just how he's got to watch himself. And now my throat is dry.... Quick march! For my withdrawal.... Everybody shall know that my Almighty Person is betaking itself to dinner. Torches, advance! And you there, form up behind my Regal Magnificence. (Goes off with his retinue... preceded by torches and beating of drums.)[3]

As already noted, this is the last occasion on which Olivier is seen alive in this first version of *Der Turm*. With the violently colourful impression of his exit still fresh in mind it may be appropriate to add some general remarks on Hofmannsthal's presentation of this character.

The seventeenth-century models for Olivier were noted at the beginning of the present chapter. It was pointed out there that Hofmannsthal's indebtedness to Gryphius's *Horribilicribrifax* is particularly obvious in the present scene. The most marked similarity (other than the coinciding oaths!)[4] is found between Olivier's speech and the fantastic jargon talked by both the old soldiers in *Horribilicribrifax*. The latter is highly coloured, rich in fanciful allusion, which indicates much travel, some education and a good deal of imagination. These features are perhaps best observed in the bloodthirsty clash and hilarious reunion between Horribilicribrifax and Daradiridatumtorides. The latter, for example, proclaims himself unafraid even if Horribilicribrifax were 'Roland himself, brother of the great Charlemagne, and had done more and mightier deeds than Scanderbeck and had crept into the very skin of Tamberlaine'.[1]

It is in this scene too that Horribilicribrifax threatens to smash Daradiridatumtorides 'into two hundred and seventy thousand pieces so that you will suffocate in a sea of your own blood'. Both heroes, moreover, are fond of referring to themselves in a very grandiloquent third person.

Now all these features are in Olivier. Not only is his language spattered with foreign words (this was noted in the opening scene of the play) but he is also a great and fantastic boaster who, like the two old warriors, is fond of numerical detail: one remembers Julian's ninety-seven wounds! Moreover, Olivier's street-corner idiom alternates with inflated polysyllabics which probably justify Andreas's question as to whether Olivier was at one time a university student![2]

It is not necessary to pursue the trail further. Hofmannsthal's purposes here are poles apart from those of Gryphius. And if, as seems very likely, he did borrow from *Horribilicribrifax* he did it only to draw on atmospheric vocabulary and not to 'borrow' a character. There need be no question of linking the respective dramatic personalities in any way.[3] If, as suggested at the beginning of this chapter, Olivier does bring some of the chaos-ridden atmosphere of the Thirty Years War into *Der Turm*, so much the better.

But Hofmannsthal obviously intended Olivier to be the embodiment of the popular leader. He sees him as a demagogue, tyrant and cynic. This might seem to indicate a certain narrowness in the author's political views, for such a conception of this pheno-menon, accurate enough in itself, by no means exhausts the problem. It might tentatively be suggested that Hofmannsthal's idea is rather similar to the baroque idea of the demagogue. Such a similarity could not cause any surprise. It may also be that Hofmannsthal's own social—and eminently civilized—background made it difficult for him to imagine such a figure as originating anywhere else than among the lower orders of society. It is interesting to recall the great significance which he attached to the Rich Man in the *Große Welttheater*. One wonders whether the total impression of Olivier might not have been all the more terrifying and 'contemporary' had he had at his elbow, as a kind of Grey Eminence, such a figure from the higher, more 'civilized' and wealthier reaches of society. Olivier leaves a great impression on the mind as he leaves the stage for the last time. The picture lacks, however, the ultimate comprehensiveness.

It is significant for an understanding of Sigismund's role that the great turn in the drama which is now announced comes from an anonymous man of the people. He says merely the words for which Sigismund has been waiting. He does not say 'Come to us' or 'help us'. He says simply 'We are with you. Speak to us.'[1] They are there with Sigismund. He needs only to speak, to acknowledge them, and they and he will be one. There is no doubt in their minds.

The short scene of self-identification is beautifully constructed and is another spoken tableau. It is intended as powerful contrast to the tableau which precedes it. The situation is externally similar. Sigismund, now named as the King of the Poor before whom the sword and the scales will be carried, stands in the middle. Around him are the people, similar in appearance and speech to Olivier's rabble-officers, but they speak with a simple folk-dignity. In its stark, rhythmic, repetitive quality their speech achieves an austere, psalmic effect:

An Old Man (pushing his way to the front)
> Look at him, our King, how he stands there.
> As if bathed in the living water of the river,
> Thus he shines from head to foot.

A Man. He is afraid of us!

Several. Are you afraid of us, master?

A Man. Speak to us.

Another. If he cried out our souls would burst like sacks....

The Old Cripple. A cleft opens up and the kingdom of this world will plunge into it.[2]

The idea of Sigismund as a Saviour is enhanced by the liturgical structure of this short episode. The repeated 'Stay with us! Endure with us! Let us not die, O Lord!' conveys this. The *De Profundis* is perhaps the most obvious reminiscence: 'Out of the depths I have cried to Thee, O Lord; Lord, hear my voice.'

At the chant-like climax, Sigismund speaks, as if to himself, awed by the immensity of what he is doing, although he knows that it must be. His unspectacular assent has none of the fervour of sudden impulse: 'But I will go forth with you.' He will go forth from the tower in reality and in symbol. He will go into life and lead them to a new existence. This is expressed in one vigorous image: 'I sense a wide and open land. It smells of earth and salt. There will I go.'

And so, as people's King, he is clothed in garments in which, as Requadt pointed out, 'spirit and power are symbolically united'.[1] These are 'a dalmatic, golden shoes—a golden crown'.[2] With moving demonstrations of affection and solicitude for him and with rising enthusiasm the scene moves to its close. The ritualistic structure is preserved and is felt in the language. The image of Jesus entering Jerusalem on Palm Sunday rises in one's mind as the calls are repeated:

Voices. Stay with us! Endure with us!
Another. Let us not die, O Lord!
A Man. The women want to come in and kiss his feet.
Another. Chase the old mares away. They are not worthy to see his face. (The women outside cry out.)
A Man. Are you hungry? The women cry out that we are letting you go hungry.
Others. Bring everything! Set up a mountain before him! Bring meat, bread and milk. Bring honey and cream....
Many Voices. Bring! Bring! Bring!
Several. Stay with us O Lord....
A Man....When you have tasted all this, will you still think that it is all a dream?
Anton. Ah! Don't you believe it! Now he'll wake up straight away.[3]
Voices. Awake here, amongst us.
Others. Do not go away from us.[4]

Sigismund breaks the mood with an image of vast scope and implication, symbolic of the great deeds ahead: 'Like the rooster in the farmyard I can smell the dawning day and the hour when the stars leave their watch-towers.'

Thus the dawn of a new day, the dawn of a new age, and the cosmic extent of what is to come, are brought together in the mind. The brief scuffle between Sigismund's followers and Aron, Olivier's adjutant, brings the new King to his first *ex cathedra* statement. He tells of the qualities on which the new realm will be built, of the personal integrity, responsibility and self-discipline which will be its triple pillars: 'Where we are going, we obey before we are commanded and we reap without hoping for supper at eventide.' With this promise, now about to become reality, the play moves into its final phase.

ACT V

The fifth act is not only the vastest scene in the play both in sheer length and in splendour of mass spectacle. It also completes a unity of setting. It will be recalled that the play began in the open air in a warlike setting and a mood of mystery. It then moved inwards, not only into the minds of the characters, but into the tower, the cloister, the palace and the vault. Now, at the climax, the play moves into the open again as mystery and conflict are resolved. The scene is still of war, much more so in fact. But the mood is now one of successful striving towards an age of security and peace.

The setting itself indicates many obvious antecedents and possible influences on its composition. The scene on the island of Kaumberg in Grillparzer's *König Ottokars Glück und Ende*, showing the King by divine right and popular choice amongst his soldiery, is the most obvious. Superficially there are echoes of Wallenstein's camp with its polyglot soldiery and wheeling activity; of Brutus in his tent, book before him, on the eve of Philippi; of Richard III and the apparitions in his tent on the night before Bosworth Field.

The action, set in the royal tent, begins in the romantic suspenseful hour before dawn. The opening itself, with its carefully casual and matter-of-fact conversations, has the pent-up excitement and feeling of unity with the King which the audience senses in the conversations of 'the poor condemned English' round their watchful fires a few short hours before Agincourt.

It is obvious that much time has passed and that the conflict is near its climax. Throughout the early part of the act the excitement is maintained by fragmentary pieces of information from friend and foe, all building up a huge picture of total war, in which at least three parties are involved: Sigismund's crusade, Olivier's nihilistic rebels, and the court.

With the entrance of King Sigismund it becomes apparent that the fusion in him of spirit and world is now accomplished. He is the complete leader—just, stern and kindly, as the occasion demands. Some German critics seem to find this essentially practical figure altogether too earthy. They explain him away accordingly in that vague terminology which probably came into being when Hofmannsthal was found to be something of a symbolist. Grete Schaeder, for example, has the courage not to ignore this development, but explains it away in the following pious manner:

Sigismund's actual tragedy lies in the fact that with the possession of power he becomes more and more a stranger to himself...and his true greatness; while on the other hand everything in him which is disputable...rises more and more to the surface. In his field-camp Sigismund remains locked in the tower of his own inner life, but no longer in the purity of a contemplative spirit, rather as a man who must dream where he ought to act. The world which he wants to create from a fusion of eastern and western humanity is a fanciful dream and not a real new order. There is thus far no order, yet the mere thought of it intoxicates him: he sits in judgment and ordains violence in the name of order, just like his father Basilius. Does not he too begin to succumb to the corruption of power when, without a tremor, he has people hanged? Does he not also—like Julian—summon up the underworld when, to the terror of his followers, he allies himself with the heathen Tartars?[1]

This is really rather priggish. What should Sigismund have done? Grete Schaeder wishes perhaps that he had withdrawn into his personal tower of inner emigration, secure in the knowledge that he knew what was right and that he himself was completely innocent. He might even have published his own *Meditations* (after someone else had rid the land of Olivier), pointing out how superior his own vision and moral methods were—both to those of Olivier and to the crude practicality of the liberator.

It seems indeed as if Grete Schaeder were unfamiliar with Hofmannsthal's ideas of German–Latin–Slav *Ausgleich* and as if the wartime essays had never been written. The time-dishonoured traditions that the races beyond Germany's eastern borders are still subhuman (and heathen too!) seem implicit in Grete Schaeder's pious horror. As to 'acting' (*handeln*), even the most idealistic leader often has to deal with the given situation and not shun it if it does not suit him: Hofmannsthal had not, for example, celebrated Prince Eugene, the *practical* idealist, for nothing.

In Sigismund there is, indeed, nothing of the secluded visionary with world-destroying thoughts. Just how opposed this idea was to Hofmannsthal is apparent from a comment reported by Carl Burckhardt. It has special relevance here because Hofmannsthal was discussing certain German features:

He was just to every great German figure. But he never let himself be led astray by greatness. There was something there which to him seemed pernicious. Sometimes he encountered it in Luther...in certain expressions of Romanticism, in certain aspects of Hegel. On one occasion he read Fichte's *Reden* with a good deal of distaste; afterwards he talked about a blind and boastful ethos, feverishly heightening the sense of self. He called it false—and provincial.[1]

Reading Burckhardt's account of Hofmannsthal's views, one is tempted to think that had Hofmannsthal lived to read criticism such as that just discussed, he might well have sharpened his comments even more. 'False and provincial' seems to be particularly apposite.

Sigismund is in fact the explicit contrast to a German failing often noted by Hofmannsthal. Hofmannsthal's critique, incidentally, applies equally well to Grete Schaeder's elevated thought-game:

Once, in 1929, he wrote from Germany—quite shocked by the 'recrudescence...of a dark Protestantism, based on the gloomiest form of Pauline Judaism'. A new publication of Einstein had appeared at the same time, so complex that a layman could only just about get a vague idea of its contents. And he added: 'There is too much tension in this world. However, it is much easier for the good old Germans, because they do all these uncanny things with only half their personality—or one assumed for the purpose. And all along they go on living as cosily as ever—most of them, that is. But those few who feel within themselves the necessity for absolute standards are sometimes driven mad.'[1]

Sigismund, *pace* Grete Schaeder, has just this much needed sense of 'the necessity for absolute standards', and attempts rather to realize it than to think about it. He himself is depicted as unarmed,[2] and his threats of hanging follow the burning of monasteries by the Tartars. He directs that no force is to be used in making the gypsy captive, Olivier's mistress, yield up what she knows.

Sigismund himself clearly realizes the differences between his present state and his ideal, individual world of the tower. He says to the Doctor: 'You are surprised that I have learnt the language of the world so quickly? Good friend, my place is a terrible one and even in broad daylight I live under the stars....'[3] The life 'under the stars', symbol of his pure, inward, ideal world, must now be carried into the light, into the affairs of common day; and all things which come upon him must be dealt with.[4]

The supra-personal significance of the ensuing conversation between Sigismund and the Doctor on the unnamed Plutarch biography was noted on pp. 187–8. Regarding the mention of Plutarch, however, it is of course impossible to say which of the *Parallel Lives* was in the author's mind. There are good reasons for believing, however, that it was the Alexander-Caesar biography. There is in any case the covert reference to Julius Caesar when, later in the scene, Sigismund collapses: one of the lords asks 'Has he the falling sickness, like his father?'[1] This recalls Caesar's debility and Shakespeare's (as well as Plutarch's) depiction of it.[2] One might also, perhaps, argue certain similarities between Caesar and Sigismund. But this in itself would not necessarily prove anything. More apparent, however, are the distinct Alexander-like features of Sigismund in this scene. His vision of a new universal order imposed by himself—'You small peoples I will mix anew in a great melting-pot'[3]—and his vision of the East both recall the figure of Alexander the Great.

This is no chance reminiscence. Although Hofmannsthal never completed a work on the great Grecian conqueror, the figure and symbol of Alexander had a large part in his early formative development. Two fragments are of interest here; one is a dramatic sketch, the other is in the form of a diary entry: *Alexanderzug—Fresken* (1893) and *Alexander—Die Freunde* (1895).[4] Requadt has discussed the place of Alexander in Hofmannsthal's growing conception of the 'world ruler' (*Weltherrscher*)[5] and it should be recalled that the first sketches for *Der Turm* date back to 1899 at least.

Hofmannsthal, moreover, was sufficiently impressed by Wassermann's *Alexander in Babylon* to recommend it to Bodenhausen in a special book-list which he sent (at his friend's request) in his letter of 7 June 1906.[6] In this context it is perhaps worth recalling that Hofmannsthal's fragment *Der Gefangene* was published in 1907.

It is therefore likely that Julius Caesar *and* Alexander were in Hofmannsthal's mind at this point in the drama. Hence the imaginative perspective of the reader widens to a vast extent, once he realizes the force of this rather involved *Bezug*.

As Sigismund proceeds with his affairs one notes how his speech 'fits' (the German *sitzt* is again the only exact expression) his developed character in a special and very human way. He has, as noted, the tone and directness of authority. Over and above this, however, there is apparent the reticent warmth, a quality of manly kindliness (*herbe Wärme* is the exact quality of feeling), which one feels to be characteristic of a seasoned field campaigner and leader of men—where the trust on both sides is silent and automatic. Again the figure of Prince Eugene comes to mind. Sigismund says, for example, to the Doctor:

I envy you your learning. No, I love you for it. You are not a rent-paying tenant in your own body. You live in your own palace.[1]—Do not leave me, unless our way of life becomes too much for you.[2]

In the midst of state and military duties he finds time for a gruffly sincere word to his ever-faithful servant: 'You must eat better, Anton, and get more rest. Take double rations: I want to see your old well-upholstered face again.'[3]

At this point it should be noted how the first mention of the Children's King is introduced. There is talk of chaos in Olivier's ranks, of the ruination of Basilius's cause, and the fact that a recent war devastated the frontier provinces. This war is not specifically the present one, but the very vagueness here increases the effect of time having passed. Into this sad picture of decline and fall Hofmannsthal introduces the hopeful symbol of innocent youth, a fresh start, a return to the state of initial purity:

Count Adam. The Counts Palatine and Lords of the Realm,[4] those of them who are still alive, have been let in past the sentries, with a bodyguard,[5] and are waiting outside. The shooting was down by the river, between our advance posts and the Greens. . . . But they have declared themselves neutral, and the shooting has stopped.

Sigismund. The Greens are marauders, dispersed remnants of Basilius's army, deserting cut-throats from Olivier's rabble. . . .

Count Adam. They are children from all three provinces, and they have a Children's King over them.

Sigismund. What do you mean by that, Adam?

Doctor. You will find suchlike everywhere in the woods, ever since the four years' war under Basilius devastated the frontier provinces. They are waifs and strays from the villages where there are no houses. . . .

Count Adam. There are nearly ten thousand of them. They have special laws and customs, and over them they have an elected King who is said to be a strong and handsome boy whose glance is like a young lion's. They plough and have gone back to living like the people of old. They work with their hands and sing as they toil.[1]

The reference to the four years' war, and the devastated frontiers is naturally a superficial allusion to World War I which was still fresh in the minds of Hofmannsthal's first audiences and readers. More important, however, is the fact that this is the first occasion on which it has been hinted that Sigismund's regime will be anything other than permanent. This is thrown into greater relief by the fact that the conversation immediately swings to the mysterious gypsy woman to whom the King is about to speak. The former thus assumes in advance an ominous character, in addition to the aura of strangeness with which she is surrounded.

This episode is immediately followed by the discussion of Marcus Aurelius. The importance of this to the whole drama was discussed at some length on pp. 188–9. Here it is necessary to draw attention to one line only: 'But he also was the victim of circumstances and he dies in his tent in the midst of all his plans.'[2]

It seems that Kleist's *Robert Guiskard* (1803–4 and—rewritten, surviving version of ten scenes only—1807) was much in Hofmannsthal's mind during the composition of the fifth act of *Der Turm*.[3] Allowing for the difference between the idealized symbol-figure of Sigismund and the tough, ambitious warrior-duke, it is probably true to say that there is a certain similarity between the two figures in their actual aspirations. Like Sigismund the historical Guiskard died in his tent when victory was in sight. It is to be presumed that Kleist's character suffered this fate in the original (destroyed) version. The fact that Guiskard succumbed to the plague, as opposed to the fatal wound which causes Sigismund's death, does not vitiate the comparison to any significant extent. An additional point of some relevance is the fact that Guiskard died within sight of his goal—Constantinople. It may well be that the thought of Guiskard and the Byzantine capital

266

influenced Hofmannsthal in the evocation of that 'eastern' atmosphere which was discussed in chapter 6.

The other obvious reminiscence at this point in the drama is that of Julian the Apostate. Like Sigismund, Julian was a ruler of great individualistic powers who felt the 'necessity for absolute standards'; he was forced, not to sacrifice personal idealism, but to make it work in practice and to limit his own flights of thought (and expression) to the fugitive hours of leisure in his field-tent. As hinted on p. 189 the similarity between the chance but fatal wounds of Sigismund and Julian when victory seemed assured suggests that Hofmannsthal had the ill-fated apostate in mind at this point.

He was of course familiar with the historical figure of Julian. This could in any case be assumed from his vast reading knowledge of classical antiquity.[1] More particularly, however, there are various interesting references to Julian, as the hero of Ibsen's *Emperor and Galilean* (1873), in Hofmannsthal's early essay *Die Menschen in Ibsens Dramen*.[2] Hofmannsthal wrote *inter alia*:

Before they began to suffer under such circumstances, almost all these people lived through a confusing, half dream-like childhood—like being in a fairytale forest from which they emerge with an unallayable homesickness and some curious quality which cuts them off from everyone else: like Parzival who rides into the world in a fool's motley and with the experience of a small child. Parzival's childhood in the Forest of Brizljan has for me always had a very symbolic quality. This awakening in twilit solitude with dream-like questions about God and the world....All of them [that is, Ibsen's characters]...grew up in such a forest....Julian in the stuffy atmosphere of a Byzantine monastery...from this childhood some peculiarly dreamlike quality remains in them; they are apparently always thinking about something different from what they are saying; in fact they are all poets....They believe in the infinite possibilities of the 'marvellous' which human beings have in them; they believe in the creative, transfiguring power of pain.

Later in the essay Hofmannsthal asserted:

All Ibsen's characters represent nothing but a scale of mental states,... Julian has them all in embryo and lives through all of them....And to my mind the basic problem here is always the same and is basically undramatic. How does an Ibsenian character behave in life—this artistic egoist...lacking in will-power and with a great nostalgia for beauty and simplicity?...If one [Hofmannsthal lists here the personal situation of various of Ibsen's characters]...or has all the power in the world like Julian?...I think that the answer is very simple: actually he [the Ibsenian character] has no proper place amongst human beings and can make nothing of life. Therefore he often goes to his death—like Julian...or he cuts himself off, which is almost the same thing.

It is a matter for argument as to whether Sigismund's dying words—'The soothsayer has said it: there is no place for me in this age'[1]—are an echo of 'actually he has no proper place amongst human beings' in the above quotation. The whole passage, however, with its singling-out of Julian the Apostate as the embodiment of all the characteristics discussed, reads like a youthful sketch for the fully developed, complex and somewhat contradictory figure of Sigismund as encountered in the final versions of *Der Turm*. (This assertion may be the more tenable in the light of a study of Sigismund as he is portrayed in the version of 1927. This is treated in chapter 8.) The first sketches of *Der Turm* were, as noted earlier, made in 1899, that is to say only a few years after the Ibsen essay had been written. It is also interesting to note that Hofmannsthal alludes in the above extract to the Parzival-symbol, already discussed in connection with Sigismund.[2]

Thus Sigismund's thoughtful words to the Doctor take on a dual significance—Marcus Aurelius and Julian—and the picture of the former dying 'in his tent in the midst of all his plans' pervades the scene with a sad foreboding. And then, immediately following this speech, the gypsy is brought forward and Sigismund speaks the words which became for Hofmannsthal the motto-motif of the drama:

The Olivierian spirit in the world exerts its Satanic power in two ways: through women and through Mammon. (He touches the piled-up objects with his foot.) Take the ropes off her.[3]

In threefold progression and suggestion of disaster (Children's King—Marcus Aurelius—the 'Olivierian spirit' and the freeing of the gypsy's hands) Sigismund goes to his parley with the mysterious prisoner as a man doomed in advance.

The fantastic scene which follows seems to have been a late interpolation into Hofmannsthal's scheme. A letter to Burckhardt of 13 October 1922 discusses the role of Basilius and remarks: 'He does not appear in the play again, except in the fifth act—in order to fall down dead.'[1] This letter was, as noted, written in 1922. Hofmannsthal was therefore referring to the first version of *Der Turm*, at present under discussion. The simulacrum of Basilius does indeed appear during Sigismund's dialogue with the gypsy woman. He assumes alternately his own form and that of a fox. At Sigismund's command he collapses 'as a writhing fox'.

It seems likely, however, that in 1922 Hofmannsthal had something more straightforward in mind; for the note in the above letter indicates no supernatural action. It is of course possible that Hofmannsthal simply omitted to go into detail as to what he had in mind regarding Basilius's appearance and collapse. His note is certainly terse, and he may have had the supernatural staging in mind from the beginning.[2] Erika Brecht, on the other hand, places the origin of the supernatural scene in 1925. There seems to be no reason why her account should not be believed, even though on occasion she does appear to overstress the close personal contact between her family and Hofmannsthal. She writes:

The gypsy-scene had its origin in the direct impression made on Hofmannsthal by a strange book: Ossendowsky's *Götter, Tiere und Menschen*. Round about 1925 Hofmannsthal was full of this escape story by a Pole who had fled from Bolshevik Russia. He talked to us about it for a whole evening, especially about the author's experience in the Asiatic steppes, where he met Baron Ungern-Sternberg and took part in the latter's fantastic reign over the wild Mongols there. There were, for example, ghost-scenes in a tent, in which a host of uncanny apparitions were seen, amongst them 'a man with a head like a saddle'.... The scene in *Der Turm* is quite different from that in Ossendowsky's book; only the tent and the wild, Asiatic atmosphere are the same, full of demons and terrible ghosts.[1]

This account may also help to explain the presence in Sigismund's forces of the allied Tartars who, according to hearsay, have played an important and violent part in Sigismund's campaign. Erika Brecht remarks with some justification that the gypsy-scene was 'rather tedious but poetically unique.'[2]

Hofmannsthal's purpose in this involved and fragmented scene is certainly difficult to follow. It may well be considered a mistake to introduce such a markedly supernatural element so late (and so illogically) in the play. This magical element is—as it stands here—never absorbed into the play's texture.

The most likely reason for the scene is that Hofmannsthal wished to deal with several outstanding problems and characters—all interrelated—at one and the same time. He wished to show those characters and forces against which Sigismund has been fighting. He wished to show how Sigismund, in defeating them, must also realize that he himself is sprung from the same earthly community of woe and wickedness, that he himself has been unwittingly but inevitably tainted by contact with it. He wished, it may be assumed, to show that Sigismund was the true tragic figure in the sense postulated by Friedrich Hebbel: he is the great man of deeds and purpose, born just before his time in an age destined to be a turning-point (*Wendepunkt*)—the beginning of the Christian era, for example, or the breakdown of the medieval order. This great man, Hebbel says, rises up with good motives against his age. He must sometimes resort to violence, even cruelty (Herodes, for example). He is submerged and destroyed by his age, but not before his deeds and reforms have ensured either final victory or ultimate progress after his death.

Hebbel's theory did not specifically include the tragedy involved in the hero becoming contaminated by the evil of his age. This is perhaps Hofmannsthal's original addition to the idea, original in that tragedy forces itself on Sigismund from the outside. Thus, in the few moments before what should be his ultimate triumph, Sigismund sees not only what he has conquered but, paradoxically, what must prevent him—through violent contact with it—from being more than an intermediary pioneering figure.

The barbaric, nightmarish scene takes its course, and Basilius, Julian and Olivier appear before the King. The scene is unfortunate not only because of its strained language and (at this juncture) unconvincingly fantastic content, but because it shows too that seemingly wilful obscurity of symbols which occasionally marred Hofmannsthal's work.[1] One's irritation rises when Hofmannsthal's mastery over language and suggestion is recalled—when, moreover, his proven ability to create a mood and make a point in a few lines is summoned as evidence against this scene.

Gerhard Meyer-Sichting has given what is probably the most consequential and positive reading of the episode. He writes:

One can only sense it, not 'understand' it....If we try, not so much to analyse but to enter into the gypsy-scene, in which Sigismund's tragic entanglement with earthbound powers is depicted, and if we experience the gypsy in her wild demonism as the representative of those very powers, then the poetic force will rouse in us an elemental terror.[2]

Meyer-Sichting's view has in itself much to commend it. He explains perfectly what the scene *does*. Whether it is effective, either poetically or dramatically, is quite another matter.

William Rey, in a brilliantly argued essay,[3] seems to regard this scene as evidence of Hofmannsthal's own uncertainty about the optimistic and visionary end which he gave to this first version of the drama:

There is, for example, that peculiar twilight in the conjuration scene... in which reality and vision, strategy and magic, are mixed in a strange fashion. The military defeat of Olivier is presupposed, and then confirmed and justified during the conjuring up of his ghost...by the superior strength of Sigismund. Here it is shown that Sigismund has not completely left the 'inner world' of the tower and come into the world of reality, and that, moreover, even in his field-marshal's tent he still believes in the magic power of the spirit. (For this reason, under the spell of the conjuration, he is powerless against the malignity of objective reality, and succumbs to the poisoned knife of the gypsy.) ... The figure of Olivier is lost in a ghostly realm of the underworld: he does not, as in *Turm II*, represent sober political reality and historical law. Therefore the actual severity of the struggle...is obscured.

The comparative merits of the two versions of *Der Turm* are discussed in chapter 8. One does not necessarily have to agree completely with Rey's fairly clear preference for *Der Turm II* in order to concur with his views on the gypsy-scene and on the problematical state of mind which it reflected in the author himself. One feels, moreover, that Rey might strengthen his case even further by stressing the artistic, dramatic and (from the standpoint of the drama as a whole) structural deficiencies of the scene.

The episode ends at any rate with a fine *coup de théâtre* as the gypsy leaps into the air (presumably she has just given Sigismund the fatal scratch); Sigismund calls his men, who appear with a lantern as the grey dawn light comes through the walls of the tent.

The grey dawn light has its own dual significance. It heralds the new day of victory, just revealed to Sigismund in the apparitions, and the coming of a new age. But it is also, for Sigismund, day in the sense of 'Tag! Ja, es wird Tag! der letzte Tag dringt herein!'[1]

From this point onwards the drama's structure is tight and cohesive. Events now move rapidly and clearly. The short scene before the final pageant gains much from its tense, unsentimental brevity. In the Doctor's clinical terseness the tragedy is felt to be well-nigh consummated: 'How did Your Majesty come by that wound? It is a sharp cut across the palm and right down through the lifeline.'[2]

With the entrance of the repentant representatives of the aristocratic estates the scene moves on to another plane. It is a further variant of the baroque, tableau-like spectacle scene which has been such a marked feature of the play. There is, however, mingled with this a reminiscence of the savage barbaric splendour which the western critic knows mainly from such things as the camp in Borodin's ballet-opera *Prince Igor*,[1] the procession of noblemen in Rimsky-Korsakov's *Mlada* and the Coronation Scene in Mussorgsky's *Boris Godunov*. The pageant is noteworthy for the sustained, deliberate manner in which it is built up. The operatic quality here is more marked than at any other stage in the play:

At a sign from Adam the curtain at the main entrance is raised. There enter: an officer who bears the standard of the realm, an armed peasant with the rebels' standard—a black pole to the top of which is fastened a bundle of broken chains—and a Tartar captain with a standard consisting of a gilt half-moon and a stallion's tail. The three standard-bearers take up position along the short left-hand side of the tent. Indrik moves across and takes the standard with the broken chains. The lords of the realm enter from the left, led by Adam. They immediately kneel down opposite Sigismund. Simultaneously Sigismund's field-captains enter: five or six men from the lower classes, clad in armour. They take up position back left, close to the entrance. Adam, who has come in again, takes the Sword of State, handed to him in its silken scabbard by a page, and stands on the left behind Sigismund.[2]

This complex process takes place in complete silence, and the impression of immense restrained power in Sigismund is enhanced thereby.

The contrast between Sigismund's dry, practical tone and the inflated, outworn formulae of the noblemen is indicative of the changed times and of the new régime:

The Oldest Lord. . . . Invincible One! Exalted King! Sovereign King and Lord of us all!

Sigismund. Stand up, cousins, stand up![3]

In the addresses of the Oldest Lord, Hofmannsthal allows his vein for lyrical, rhythmic prose to flow full and stately. The effect is the greater, because in this play the lyrical strain is on the whole carefully controlled. In these speeches, especially the second, Hofmannsthal mingles picturesquely depicted fact, apocalyptic vision and abstract idea at one and the same time:

Just as the rays of dawn greet the shipwrecked mariner after a storm-tossed night of terror, so does the mild speech of our gracious King shine on us, healing us, who have been tried and tested!—And after what a night of horror!...Towns swept off the face of the earth as if by a broom, castles and monasteries become gaping, burnt-out ruins, and the fields a swamp of blood....But our hereditary King speaks graciously to us and with...pious emotion we see...the venerable banner of our old kingdom and gaze on this alone.[1]

In this first speech Hofmannsthal achieves the necessary effect of vastness, of ruin and universal disorder yielding before the King. Hofmannsthal is aware, however, of the danger of mere rhetoric. The repentant noblemen are in any case in a mood to be extravagantly loyal. Sigismund, characteristically, keeps the spokesman to the point and pricks the bubble of his eloquence: 'You had better look at all three of them, gentlemen; wherever we ride, they will be fluttering and rattling in the wind.'[2]

The second speech of the Oldest Lord is therefore less rhetorical in tone, more direct, but of wider implications. Dramatically it fits in perfectly with the sequence of the action. It is also a valuable summary of events. Essentially, however, it is Hofmannsthal's view of his age and his warning to it. This speech was his artistic formulation of the contemporary time of which he had written: 'What a world we have stumbled into. The very beams burst through the floor and the whole edifice trembles to its foundations.'[3] Here, in the words of the Oldest Lord, he formulated what in another context he called that

something in this age that does not so much seize and shake the treetops as grasp at our very roots. Often the ground we stand on seems to have turned to water...yet the way to become master of such a situation must be found in ourselves.[4]

At the present advanced time in the twentieth century it is a truism to assert that the suicidal conflicts and mutual throat-cutting of the various European nationalisms and imperialisms have reduced the continent to a battlefield, in both moral and physical senses. This, for the first time since the Ottoman power was halted before Vienna, has rendered the entire continent helpless against the incursion of hostile and alien influences from outside. The following was—in 1925—Hofmannsthal's prescient warning against this self-slaughtering policy and its consequences:

but still more fearsome was the discord which tore our hearts asunder. Force and the law, these twain pillars of the world, in monstrous conflict before our very eyes! Son against father, ruler against ruler, violence against violence like fire against water—but there came yet a third, as when on the day of judgment the earth opens up and engulfs fire and water: along with the fools and evil-doers, the heretics and fanatics,...Asia itself broke in across our frontiers and tried to be overlord as in the terrible days of our fathers.[1]

The picture of Sigismund's victorious power is conjured up in a boldly effective union of the rebels' symbol of the sundered chains with the phrase (used of himself by Attila) 'the scourge of God':

And then, terrible above the chaos, the standard of the sundered chains was raised by one mighty hand—and to us with heads bowed low in defeat it sounded like the scourge of God.

It is perhaps interesting to note that Stefan George uses the identical images of 'chains' and 'scourge' at the climax of his vision of the leader who is to found the new kingdom:

> Der sprengt die ketten fegt auf trümmerstätten
> Die ordnung, geißelt die verlaufnen heim
> Ins ewige recht wo großes wiederum groß ist
> Herr wiederum herr, zucht wiederum zucht, er heftet
> Das wahre sinnbild auf das völkische banner
> Er führt durch sturm und grausige signale
> Des frührots seiner treuen schar zum werk
> Des wachen tags und pflanzt das Neue Reich.[2]

> (He breaks the chains and sweeps aside the rubble,
> He scourges home the lost to lasting law,
> Where lord again is lord, the great is great
> Again, where poise again is poise. He fastens

18-2

The true device upon the nation's banner.
Through tempests and the dread fanfares of dawning,
He leads his tried and faithful to the work
Of sober day and founds the Kingdom Come.)

The inspiring rhythm of George's poem may well sweep the reader along. It leaves him, however, with heroic but rather imprecise concepts. Hofmannsthal does at least try to give some definition to his aspirations. For the noblemen, kneeling before Sigismund, provoke him into an *ex cathedra* proclamation. These noblemen, like Ottokar in Grillparzer's play and like the ruling aristocracies of Russia or Italy, East Germany or Hungary in Hofmannsthal's own time, do not—will not—realize that their time is past, that the 'hallowed power of our forefathers'—which Sigismund has overthrown—covered a multitude of sins. The violent and wholesale destruction of which they complain was really set in motion by themselves. Sigismund soon makes them aware of this and in his final speeches the essential qualities of the new age are detailed. He is their King, not from power-lust, not for violence and the wish to oppress, but 'from strength and necessity'.

Sigismund promises to be 'just and great, mild and mighty'. And then at last comes his conservative revolution, no dictatorial illusion of grandeur, but sober recognition of what has proved outworn and ruinous. Co-operation and agreement are needed, rather than force and factional intrigue: 'It is my intention to unite both in one existence: to bring order and to set aside the old order. And for this I need you: your consent...which is more to me than your subjection.'

Sigismund's next words take on the rhythms of inspired vision as he speaks of the eternal principles which must govern individuals; and his implications widen to include whole societies and nations:

What you call peace is your power over the peasants and over the earth. What you call justice is only your justice, that the wolves should rule instead of the dogs. Can you not put away this desire? Can you do nothing but sit on your possessions and brood about your rank?

The voice of the reformer and *Ausgleichpolitiker* is heard as Sigismund promises to build from the foundations and demands sacrifice and moderation from all:

I bear within me the spirit of the founder and not the spirit of possession, and the order which I understand is rooted in moderation and self-sacrifice.[1]

(Ich trage den Sinn des Begründens in mir und nicht den Sinn des Besitzens, und die Ordnung, die ich verstehe, ist gefestigt auf der Hingabe und der Bescheidung.)

It would lead too far afield at this climacteric final stage of the drama were the actual style and language of Sigismund's speeches to be analysed in detail. This latter passage, however, provides a good illustration of how Hofmannsthal achieves the singular, compelling quality in this episode. The repeated *Sinn*, in conjunction with the similar-sounding antitheses *Begründen* and *Besitzen*, makes a powerful, aphoristic effect. Then come the firm, strong, mutually complementing sounds of *verstehe* and *gefestigt*, followed by another antithesis—both in sound and sense—the gentle, dark sound of *Hingabe* and *Bescheidung*.

Sigismund's speech could easily degenerate into a set-piece of stylized oratory. Hofmannsthal preserves the essentially dramatic situation by directing considerable movement on Sigismund's part, and by markedly increasing tension in the Doctor. He also introduces changes of tone and approach in the speaker. Following the *ex cathedra* pronouncement, Sigismund's manner becomes personal, almost pleading, as he shows the nobles the path of reason: 'Friends, you think that your fate can be cut off from other fates like a peasant's plot by his fence. But that is not so—'. That this applies to nations as well as to individuals, and that his own destructive violence was necessary and inevitable, is clear from his analogy: 'for the world is about to renew itself, and when mountains move towards each other they do not heed the old church tower in the way.[2]

Sigismund then speaks of a most contentious issue, both in the climax of the play itself and in criticism of it. This is the Tartar alliance. Grete Schaeder sees this as evidence of Sigismund's guilt and moral decline.[1] Requadt says that like Götz von Berlichingen he becomes guilty when his Tartar allies burn the monasteries.[2] Certainly Sigismund must inevitably become spiritually soiled by violence. But Hofmannsthal seems to have had something greater in mind: *Ausgleich* with the forces of Asia. In the later part of his career he continually emphasized the need for *Ausgleich* with the (Slavonic) East; and as far back as *Die Idee Europa* (1916) he had drawn attention to a 'striving towards Asia as a sign of the times'—to the fructifying complement to Europe represented by Asian attitudes to life.[3] This interpretation is supported by Sigismund's words on the Tartar alliance and the Tartars' leader:

he draws together the strength of Asia...and the peoples who obey him are without number,[4] and between him and me he has placed the river down there, the great river Borysthenes...and its broad waves mirror the joy of our concord...because it is time for the great ones of the earth to meet each other in a great fashion.

The time has forced itself upon mankind when it must cast aside traditional modes of thought, traditional barriers and methods:

Your petty kingdoms, your houses which you build in defence against each other: these I do not heed and I wipe out your frontiers. And I will take all you little peoples and mingle you anew in a great melting-pot.[5]

In this last sentence, with its overtones of Alexander,[6] of Charlemagne, of Emperor Frederick II (Hohenstaufen)[7] and of Charles V, there is seen Hofmannsthal's vision of a new European imperium. It would be all too facile to equate this idea with a latter-day Caesaro-Papism, even with any dark Catholic intent such as that allegedly seen sometimes in the 'European' activities of Christian Democracy in some western European countries after 1945: Hofmannsthal's own Europeanism was of an essentially sober, practical and tolerant nature.[8] Sigismund's words are 'a warning to the peoples of Europe...to put all thoughts of division behind them and to keep the peace—as "citizens of the new age"'.[1]

Sigismund refuses the traditional coronation.[2] His realm will be based on new principles. The time will come later when his milder countenance can be revealed. Then crowns may be worn. In other words, the substance of the ruler must come before the outward symbol of his power. The basically unviolent nature of this King 'by strength and by necessity' is seen in his words, which are the negation of all power for power's sake: 'If what I set up cannot last, then throw me into the knacker's yard with Attila and Pyrrhus, those kings who created nothing.'[3] In view of Sigismund's appearance to the noblemen as the seeming 'scourge of God',[4] his deliberate definition and rejection of violence without moral purpose is important.

At the same time, however, a further point arises in connection with Hofmannsthal's portrayal of Sigismund as a would-be ruler. It was suggested earlier that Hofmannsthal did at least try to give some definition to Sigismund's aspirations. But it is striking that, despite the abundance of idealism and the generous concepts which Sigismund puts forward, there is at the same time no precise content to his purpose as a ruler. Reference was made earlier to a certain similarity between Sigismund and the expressionist ideal of the 'New Man'. One notes here a further similarity in that this lack of political precision is common to both.

One should not, of course, demand of an author that he lay down a hard and fast political programme. Nevertheless it must be reiterated that in this play Hofmannsthal broaches problems which are basic to twentieth-century society; and his criticism is sometimes very strong indeed. Accordingly one might with some justice expect that at the ethical-political climax of the play the author would give some rather more detailed indication of the ideas which he sees as possibly redeeming the sorry situation depicted and assailed earlier in the drama. One wonders whether this inability to give precision to Sigismund's 'counterweight' might not have been a contributing factor to Hofmannsthal's decision to drop this scene altogether when he came to create the second version of the play, in which Sigismund dies the death of a passive martyr. This alternative solution, if such it may be called, is discussed in the next chapter.

As Sigismund approaches what is presumably to be the end of his address to the assembled noblemen, he collapses. The protracted death-scene begins. As suggested earlier, the scene is reminiscent of the long drawn-out death in his tent suffered by Julian the Apostate. The tent is opened to admit the daylight, and the serried throngs of the people in arms are seen. All are bare-headed, and the mighty standard of the rebels, the emblem of the sundered chains, rises up from among them.

The scene at this point has a massive, elegiac quality. There is little movement, save in the foreground as Sigismund is carried to a couch. The crowd increases but remains motionless. The tableau of the unconscious Sigismund, with the Doctor, Anton and Count Adam at his side, takes on a movingly sacrificial atmosphere as the great congregation waits in silence.

The true nature of Sigismund's death is indicated in a whisper from one of the noblemen: 'Has he the falling-sickness, like his father?' This is not only an analogy with Julius Caesar[1] but is also the expression of Sigismund's inextricable entanglement with the past.

The use of the falling-sickness as a way of suggesting Sigismund's roots in the old order is a further instance of a characteristic of Hofmannsthal. As has been seen at various points in the action, he seems, while drawing or filling out a character, to light upon an historical figure or analogy. This is at its first appearance dealt with directly or by suggestion, so that the reader sees or at least senses its presence below the 'surface' of the actual character. This habit of Hofmannsthal was discussed at some length on pp. 235–7, and it has been seen that such figures as Don Carlos, Charles V, Marcus Aurelius, Julian the Apostate, etc., are instances of this subterranean technique.[2] The particular figure, however, seems on occasion to stay in Hofmannsthal's mind and appears in another form or variation later in the action, thus confirming, if necessary, the existence of the initial suggestion or hint which the reader may have sensed at its first appearance.

It is interesting to note that the idea is sometimes developed or modified in a way quite different from that in which it first appeared, and is adapted, as here with Caesar's falling-sickness, to suit the immediate dramatic purpose. For the original hint of Julius Caesar (the Plutarch episode) was essentially positive and heroic. Now, however, Julius Caesar's debility, a sign of physical decadence, is used to indicate a complex and wholly negative fact, Sigismund's involuntary but inescapable entanglement with the past.[1] The effect of this is heightened by his delirious reaction to the suggestion that the Grand Almoner, who has miraculously survived the holocaust, should crown him.

Neither Sigismund nor the Grand Almoner, however, who for all his wisdom and (self-centred) sanctity is also linked with the corruption of the past, has the decisive place in the new age. Instead of the Grand Almoner who is expected to arrive at any moment, the Children's King and his followers make their way down the opened ranks.

Erika Brecht claims that the idea for the Children's King originated in a kind of *Wandervogel* group:

After the war our daughter was a very enthusiastic member of a group which was part of the Youth Movement; the young...people formed a 'company of players' and performed old plays and dances. They tried, by their manner of dress and way of life, to rid themselves of everything which could be called 'bourgeois'. They tried to live wholly in accord with nature and above all to cancel out, to atone in some way for the war and what had brought it about. They tried to build a new world...our friend was passionately interested in and sympathetic towards the activities of this new post-war youth. The... touchingly stern figure of the Children's King grew out of this interest. Without this figure, which gives the climax of Hofmannsthal's sombre drama the hope of a new heaven and a new earth, the delicate and subtle point of the tragedy is lost.[2]

The scene itself has a quiet beauty which contrasts with the grief and despair of the people, who are slow to realize the significance of what is happening. The processional movement of the Children's King and his entourage, their white garments, Mass-bell and heightened psalm-like language, bring the presence of God into the action. They bring the peace of divine order, the order for which Sigismund has struggled and against which, in struggling, he has sinned. The paradox of his violence is that in serving God he has forgotten him. There seems to be no way out of this dilemma save by the new, youthful and unstained forces which the Children's King represents.

Grete Schaeder suggests in a wearily disillusioned manner that 'life goes on: the Children's King is the symbol of a new generation which is absolved from the sins of the past by its mere existence and later appearance on the scene'.[1] This is of course all right as far as it goes. Erika Brecht is more positive. She links Sigismund and the Children's King as complementary parts of one progress, and conveys this idea in a suggestive phrase which is a modification of the text itself:

Sigismund is rooted in the criminal deeds of his father. In purity and greatness he is super-human, but he has looked too deeply into the misery of the world. He can only destroy, he can only try to wipe out evil; he 'beats the ploughshares into swords'. After him come those for whom he has cleared space in the chaos of the age. He was only an intermediary king. At his death children appear, unburdened and full of courage and hope; and they 'beat the swords into ploughshares'. They have, once more, a natural awareness of God.[2]

The return of peace and the awareness of all things existing under God's hands are conveyed in the beautiful falling cadences of the boys' canticle:

The light is soft and I hear the sickles sing in the grass and the swathes fall across the scythe...and the sun shines forth from its mighty mansion and all things point to one.[3]

As the scene moves to its end the movements of the Children's King and his acolytes, together with the kneeling crowd, take on an increasingly religious and ritualistic quality. The pace now slackens perceptibly as Hofmannsthal builds up the final tableau. The people cry out, the banners flutter to the ground, and the Children's King, followed by attendants, captains, nobles and the throng, rises with right hand outstretched in blessing. The boys who now enter proclaim the new age, and call upon God to aid and bless it: 'Mitte spiritum tuum, et creabuntur et renovabis faciem terrae!' The Children's King takes the sword of the realm in its scabbard as token of peace. Bearing the body of Sigismund, the crusading, doomed child of evil and despair, the procession leaves the stage, and the drama is over. The Children's King emphasizes that the memory of Sigismund's life and work will be needed to fortify the new security and peace: 'We need his grave to sanctify our dwelling-place.'[1]

CHAPTER 8

A DISPUTED LAST TESTAMENT

OPINION concerning this sunlit and idyllic conclusion to a drama of terror and woe has been necessarily divided. Grete Schaeder is right when she says of the Children's King:

The power which he radiates...cannot be realized in the...reality of *Der Turm*....The Children's King is a figure of faith—but as we look at him we cannot ignore the fact that, historically speaking, he is a Utopian figure: we think involuntarily of the Children's Crusade in the Middle Ages.[1]

Some clarification is obviously necessary, the more so as Hofmannsthal himself was clearly in two minds about the play's conclusions. The situation is therefore best considered in the light of a brief review of the second version of 1927. A short summary of the changes made by Hofmannsthal will be of some assistance.

To all intents and purposes the action up to and including Sigismund's abortive attack on Basilius is unchanged. Certain changes in the dialogue—mainly of a simplifying character, and some actual redistribution of the dialogue—might tend to confirm the idea that the second version is primarily a stage version: a stage-version, moreover, calculated to make a direct and instantaneous effect rather than a deep and lasting one. The changes do not give the impression of springing from organic necessity.

Structurally, however, the alterations in the last two acts are far-reaching. Following Sigismund's failure, he is sentenced by his father to be ceremoniously executed. The black-draped scaffold (similar to that which Brackenburg saw by torchlight, *Egmont*, Act V, scene 3), its sixty steps, the scarlet garb of the patricide, the almost ritualistic summoning of representatives of all states of society—all combine to create a mood which verges on melodrama. Hofmannsthal has in addition introduced some by-play between the King and his court, designed to show him at his most cruel and capricious.

In the fourth act there is a sudden but organized revolt of the mob. It seems to have been organized by Count Adam, fresh from toppling Sigismund as in the version of 1925. Sigismund, rescued quite literally from the steps of the scaffold, is brought to the palace and proclaimed King. The noblemen, named and differentiated, now conduct a State Council in which Basilius is forced to abdicate. Sigismund then dismisses the state councillors with gentle firmness and surprisingly appoints Julian as his chief minister. This seems to have little motivation, save to enrage the noblemen. Sigismund refuses in any case to co-operate in Julian's plans. News arrives of the people rising up in arms at Julian's instigation (as in the version of 1925) and it is evident that they are beyond his control.

Sigismund retires to rest. The final act takes place within the royal palace. It is again the darkness immediately before dawn. The rebels break into the palace to acclaim Sigismund as the King of the Poor. They bear with them the mortally wounded Julian, who has ridden out in the night to attempt to restore his authority. The people implore Sigismund to lead them. This episode follows closely the conclusion of the fourth act in the version of 1925. Sigismund agrees, but remains oddly passive, even timid. On two distinct occasions, immediately preceding Olivier's entrance, he is depicted in the stage directions thus: 'is terrified', 'fearfully'.[1]

Olivier now enters, accoutred in iron and leather, pistols in belt, helmet on his head. This is in deliberate symbolic contrast to the near-naked 'innocence' of those who have beseeched Sigismund to lead them.[2] The people guarantee to guard Sigismund, but are persuaded somewhat forcibly from the room by Olivier's men.

A discussion between Olivier and Sigismund follows. It is marked by passive resistance on Sigismund's part and on Olivier's by an insistence that Sigismund shall allow himself to be used as a figurehead. The attitude of Anton is interesting here, and is evidence of an almost cynical realism on Hofmannsthal's part, a sense of realism which recalls Goethe's bitter depiction of the people in the later stages of *Egmont*. Anton punctuates the discussion with such phrases as: 'Now listen to the gentleman. He can do a lot!'[1]

With the refusal and withdrawal of Sigismund, Olivier determines on his assassination. His adjutants arrive with the news that they have dispatched Basilius: 'Done for him. On the stroke of seven. Up against a cellar-wall with a sack over 'is 'ead. Buried him on the spot.'[2] Olivier briefs them for the shooting of Sigismund. At the same time he orders them to peer at Sigismund, who is standing in the adjoining room at the bed on which Julian's body lies. He tells them to find a physical double of Sigismund. The brief episode has a ring of terrible truth and most cynical opportunism:

Olivier. I've got to have somebody who's as like him as his own twin-brother. And somebody who'll be like a glove in my hands.
Aron. What do you need a double for when you've got the man himself?
Olivier. He himself can't be used. Let's go. I'll give the three marksmen their orders personally.[3]

Carl Burckhardt remarks aptly:

Here Sigismund, the embodiment of all the highest forces in the nation, is to be misused by Olivier—as a means of seducing and deceiving the people....Something is wanted which will make the mob take the one spirit for the other: nothing else.[4]

Burckhardt rightly emphasizes the contemporary power-political force of Olivier's words.

There follows a short but powerful dialogue between the Doctor and Olivier. The Doctor, having overheard the plan, attempts to convince the insurrectionist of the exalted quality of the King whom he is about to destroy. The irreconcilable views of the two men, of the philosophies which they embody, can be summarized in several brief exchanges:

Doctor. Look at the whole world: it knows nothing more exalted than what we encounter in this being.

Olivier. I look at the world which brings forth his sort just as I look at a comic side-show at the fair.

Doctor. And the people recognize it! Far and wide it brings them to their knees.

Olivier. And it's just those very creeping objects who are going to be polished off.

Doctor. The world is not ruled by iron but by the spirit which is in him. He is a mighty being. Take care!

Olivier. Now you have pronounced his sentence. So he's got to be cashiered, knocked off, wiped out. And that's what I'm here for. For I and a few others have sacrificed ourselves, and we are taking the burden of government off the people, so that they won't get dizzy.[1]

On the printed page, as opposed to performance in the theatre, this passage presents some complexity. It seems clear that the Doctor ignores Olivier's words, although Olivier consistently replies to the Doctor. Thus the Doctor's reference to the people recognizing 'it' and being brought to their knees as a result, is a reference not to Olivier's views—which will of course bring them to their knees in one sense—but to the Doctor's previous statement of Sigismund's exalted qualities and the way in which the people are brought to their knees in adoration. Olivier turns the Doctor's words in a crudely witty way ('kneeling'—'creeping'); and his highly unusual choice of words (*kriechende Angelegenheiten*) is like a blow in the face; it emphasizes his contemptuous view of people as animals or insects to be driven about at will.

Olivier now leaves the palace. Sigismund enters and in response to the shouts of the crowd below he goes to the window, ignoring the warnings of the Doctor and Anton. The voices from below acclaim and call on Sigismund to stay with them and lead them. A shot rings out. Sigismund collapses and with Anton and the Doctor at his side he dies.

This revised version has many obvious merits. Theatrically it is as much a *tour de force* as the version of 1925. The tension before the rescue of Sigismund, and the sense of the scaffold and mob below the palace-window are finely sustained. The excitement and confusion of the overthrow of Basilius, the bearing in triumph of the scarlet-clad Sigismund, are likewise scenes of fine dramatic quality. The Council of State and the pathetic abdication of Basilius reveal Hofmannsthal in the sort of Shakespeare–Pushkinian situation which roused his theatrical imagination.[1] The final act, though of low temperature by comparison with the earlier version, has a bitter, remorseless quality, a sense of dread inevitability. An audience may miss the epic sweep of the first version, but the stark thrust of character against character atones in part for this.

The reason for this only partial atonement lies in the remodelled character of Sigismund. No longer is there any clear distinction between the ethics of Julian and his pupil. In the first version, Sigismund is kind and considerate to his ruined preceptor, but there can be no question of following his ideals, even though Sigismund's dying cry 'Here I am, Julian!'[2] is a confession of his own ultimate insufficiency. In the second version Julian, with all that he stands for, becomes Sigismund's chief adviser. His death seems to be much more an unfortunate chance and much less the Nemesis which overtakes those who summon up powers beyond their control. There is no visible or implicit break between Sigismund and Julian in this later version. In fact Sigismund is seen by Olivier's men, bending over the bier of Julian.

Now it is possible to argue that this identification of Sigismund with Julian is only partial. For it might be said that Sigismund owes his liberation of the spirit to Julian and that he must see in him that tragic antithesis which always confuses the concept of a high mission with that of personal ambition. It might be argued, moreover, that the dying Julian can scorn the very people on whose behalf he has unleashed the forces of chaos. But even if these auxiliary arguments are tenable, it should not obscure the fact that the dividing line between Sigismund and Julian becomes indistinct to the point of obliteration.

This is an important consideration which must necessarily weaken Hofmannsthal's intended effect. If Sigismund becomes ethically indistinguishable from his Machiavellian mentor, then the depth and nature of his tragedy ('The Messiah has been caught in the works of the modern power-machine')[1] are necessarily changed too. This obscurity surrounding his moral format, combined with his utter passivity, seems to reduce him in stature and tragic character. One hopes that a protagonist of the second version of the drama will deal with this particular and far-reaching difficulty.

Sigismund's passivity after his assumption of power constitutes a problem in its own right. Watching and listening to this re-formed character one constantly feels that Sigismund is about to do great things, which never materialize. Here, if anywhere, Grete Schaeder's criticism of the earlier version might be appropriate: 'Sigismund remains locked in the tower of his own inner life, but no longer in the purity of a contemplative spirit, rather as a man who must dream where he ought to act.'[2] Characteristically Grete Schaeder praises the passive Sigismund of the second version, who goes to his passive doom with his individual moral purity unbesmirched: 'Here, Sigismund dies within an hour of his elevation to the throne. He dies in the full glory of human purity and without being sullied by power.'[3]

There are of course several ways of looking at the problem. It can be asserted that by removing the Children's King from the action Hofmannsthal forces his readers to focus their entire attention on Sigismund, who in this final and definite shape—with no symbolic, 'pure' continuation in the Children's King—becomes the sole bearer of the Christlike, Messianic mission. It might well be asserted, moreover, that Sigismund embodies the idea that man will always crucify the pure, redemptive force until the end of time—in whatever guise it may appear. This view is both Catholic and consistent with Hofmannsthal's later thought.

Equally Catholic, however, is the idea that the passive martyr who virtually invites martyrdom may at the same time run the risk of falling into grave sin. For the saint there is, after all, a time when inaction may be called for; but there are also times when action is positively blessed! In the present context the analogy of Jesus driving the buyers and sellers from the temple (Matthew xxi. 12–13) might seem to be appropriate.

One is led to the reluctant conclusion that this predominating preference for the second version originates not so much in its more realistic ending as in the high-minded refusal of Sigismund to have anything to do with (to paraphrase Thomas Mann's words) the filthy business of active politics and the necessity of making them work.

It can certainly be asserted that Hofmannsthal's prophetic sense of what was to come and (perhaps more particularly) his insight into the character of contemporary society—especially German society—did not desert him in this dark, bitter ending to his drama.

Compared with the version of 1925, this remodelling presents of course an infinitely more realistic conclusion. That is to say, as suggested above, that Hofmannsthal accurately assessed the spirit of the age, and depicted the downfall, chaos, boundless evil and weak passivity to come. This was in 1927.

Carl Burckhardt recalls, in the closing lines of his study, Hofmannsthal's terrible cry before the cathedral in Freiburg: 'I cannot say what it is, but I feel something rising up against everything that is mine, and pressing in upon me.'[1] The final lines of Burckhardt's study are as follows:

after we had taken leave of each other, he turned round just once more in the carriage, which was already in motion. And then I knew for certain how short was the span of life remaining to him; or rather, I saw that he knew. He actually died as a result of the death of his elder son, before the onsurge of those times whose inevitability he recognized more clearly, perhaps, than anyone else.

This was in April 1929. It seems clear that Hofmannsthal himself did not regard this second version of *Der Turm* as being necessarily definitive. This is apparent from various remarks of Hofmannsthal himself, and especially from Burckhardt's observations.[1] However, the two endings, taken together, do represent a complementary last word. If the second conclusion depicts the short-term reality in its inevitable terror of body and soul, the first depicts the way out into a better future. By its insistence on pure, individual, personal values, it helps to find this way.

Erika Brecht maintained that the second version was the result of pressure from Reinhardt,[2] whose concern was primarily theatrical. She maintained further that great damage was done thereby, that the manner of Sigismund's death does not in depth of significance measure up to the preceding version. She points out with some justice that in the *Gesammelte Werke* (1934) the original ending was restored. It might also be relevant to add that in the other editions which have appeared (the Schulausgabe, 1952, and that printed in *Ausgewählte Werke*, 1957) the first version was used. Before its inclusion in *Dramen*, IV (1958)— part of Fischer's complete edition—the second version was not republished after the first edition of 1927.[3]

But the problem is not so straightforward as these facts might indicate. Hofmannsthal himself seems to have been unaware of undue pressure and to have determined quite independently on the changed ending. Two letters to Carl Burckhardt are important here: in the first, written on 12 January 1925, Hofmannsthal describes his general attitude to Reinhardt:

For it suits your fancy to paint Reinhardt as the demon-king who has me in his clutches, but that is certainly not the case at all. He is nothing but a dedicated, dreamy, very strange, very reticent and very attractive person: and it is at bottom a matter of indifference to him whether I am here at all. And what I have to discuss with him (concerning *Der Turm*) can certainly be done in one evening.[4]

In the second letter, written on 10 July 1926, Hofmannsthal reports progress on the new version of *Der Turm*. His view on Reinhardt's part in the decision to modify the play seems to be quite unequivocal:

the two final acts are going to be completely different. I shall not let the play be performed until then. It is because I occasionally feel that I myself have undergone an inner change that I have such inner freedom towards this material. . . . The final acts of *Der Turm* in the new version will be good. I have a lot to thank Reinhardt for in this matter. Without his initial doubts and then his complete agreement, I should never have been able to make this fruitful decision so quickly. Do you remember that July evening six years ago when we read the last act of *Egmont* together? At that time I had an intimation what the end of *Der Turm* would have to be, but since then it has eluded me, because I was overpowered by the material itself and the apparent possibilities in it. Now it has all come back to me.[1]

The fortunes of the various youth movements, *Wandervögel*, etc., may be of more than incidental relevance here. In the early twenties the enthusiasm and devotion characteristic of these idealistic efforts seemed to many people—and notably to Hofmannsthal (see p. 281)—to promise great progress and social regeneration in the future: the kind of vision which Rudolf Alexander Schröder seems to have in mind when he writes of 'the Children's King...entering over the ruins of a shattered world, adorned with all the insignia of future glory'.[2]

But as such movements declined, were modified, or 'used', so initial optimism declined amongst such hopeful observers as Hofmannsthal. This may well have been a contributing factor in the exclusion from the second version of the Children's King, his retinue and all mention of 'the Greens'.

In a further letter to Burckhardt, Hofmannsthal seems to have been quite clear about his own motives in modifying the drama so radically:

no courage is needed; it seems to me—quite simply—to be a task which has to be done; and how it is to be done is obvious to me. I had given the final act a greater horizon than the theatre can take; I must not leave the royal castle, everything must happen there—in quick succession. Olivier, however, will have to be moved into a higher sphere; but he must remain just as terrible as before: that very peculiar relationship which I always wanted to establish between Essex and one of his judges (the one who feels himself to be the executor of what the exigencies of the times demand)[1]—this relationship now appears between Olivier and Sigismund; he has to get rid of Sigismund, but it all has to happen in a quietly ominous atmosphere.[2]

Hofmannsthal, however, does not seem to have abandoned the Children's King. An entry in *Ad me ipsum* under the date 10 November 1926 (several months after the above letter) reads 'Sigismund the man, of whom his father expects a continuation of himself. He, however, unexpectedly replaces his father and in his turn is continued in the Children's King.'[3]

The fact that the Children's King was still a real and living figure in the author's mind, even as he was working on the version which eliminated the character, seems to indicate at least that the second version was itself not definitive. Requadt wrestles with the problem of the two endings to some purpose:

In the remainder of the action Sigismund's actual assumption of power is prevented by the appearance of Olivier, who...appears as 'world without spirit', dressed wholly in 'iron and leather'. Sigismund soon falls victim to his marksmen. Is the apparently harmonious first version made invalid by his failure?

Sigismund's last words are significant: 'Bear witness that I was there, even though no one recognized me.' It is decisive for our judgment of the two versions that these words appear in both and have due weight as the words of a dying man. This fact alone would exclude the idea of any basic change of emphasis in the final version. Certainly the contrasts now clash more strikingly with each other [that is, in the final version], but the solution is less sentimental and more pure. Above all, Hofmannsthal avoids giving the impression that in the Utopia of the Children's King he is holding out the prospect of a real Kingdom of God. Sigismund recognizes in the first version that there is for him 'no place in this age'...although in this version Olivier is in fact conquered. According to Hofmannsthal's stage-direction Sigismund looks at the Doctor as he speaks his last words. To him, the only one who knows the true situation, Sigismund bequeaths the apostolic office of proclaiming this truth. The Christian faith preserved Hofmannsthal from complete despair, because the shining forth of the divine element as it is about to disappear is also his poetic conviction.

The inexorable nature of the conflict in the final version of *Der Turm* together with Hofmannsthal's determination not to offer any palliatives have been rightly emphasized.[1]

The interpretation here of the Doctor's role is, however, somewhat forced. One would not deny that the Doctor alone sees the real situation and the sense of Sigismund's words. Apart from Sigismund he is, to paraphrase Schröder's words, the only true 'human being' in the play; and as such Schröder contrasts him with the 'animals'—Basilius, Julian, Olivier, etc.[2] But true as Requadt's assertion is, one could scarcely put forward the Doctor as a substitute for or continuation of Sigismund.

In his anxiety to avoid the Utopian idea and a sunlit operatic finale, Requadt seems in fact to be fighting a battle where, perhaps, no real conflict exists.[3] The situation might be expressed thus: the second version is realistic and time-bound, in accordance with the spirit of the age as Hofmannsthal saw it, a world 'above which no heaven soars; the world is here a funeral vault, shut off from above by a great door of bronze'.[4] The first version of 1925, on the other hand, is an ever-present, ever-possible hope whose relevance neither time nor circumstance can change. Thus Requadt's 'less sentimental and more pure, the determination not to offer any palliatives', while partially true (it is hard to see how the second version is more pure), are in the final reckoning beside the point. Viewed at a distance in time the two versions are seen to be serving different ends.

On the other hand it should not be assumed that the dénouement of the first version is wholly satisfactory. To say this need not vitiate the value of Hofmannsthal's expression of hope, embodied in Sigismund and the ideals put forward by him. It is more a question of the *dramatic* form given to their visual realization in the shape of the Children's King. The beauty of this scene is scarcely to be denied. But one or two qualms do arise when one considers its position relative to the act as a whole. In this context the appearance of the Children's King is uncomfortably reminiscent of the *deus ex machina*, so beloved of baroque drama. And the *deus ex machina* traditionally determines the outcome and ties up all threads, but without necessarily *solving* anything.

It is possible to look at the change of mood brought about by the Children's King in two ways. Let us consider the contrast: the experienced, heroic, complex Sigismund—the uncomplicated, 'backgroundless' innocence of the Children's King (a literally *unbeschriebenes Blatt*). The contrast will strike some as moving; to others it may seem crass and poorly motivated. The Children's King, indeed, might seem to be a slender substitute for one of Sigismund's record, however stained by the world he might be. In visual, dramatic terms it might be thought that 'redemption' by figures who, it has been unkindly said, are idealized boy-scouts, is scarcely representative of the mature Hofmannsthal. Whether for Hofmannsthal, as a believing Catholic, *any* redemption in the here and now is possible, must remain an open question. The hope and aspiration *represented* by the Children's King are, on the other hand, a summons to make one *try* to realize the Kingdom of God on earth.[1]

If pressed to a choice, therefore, one would say that the first, vastly more complex version is in the long run more important, though not by any means more immediately effective. There is good evidence to support this plea for the first version. Mention was made earlier in various places of Hofmannsthal's singular affection for *Egmont*. One of the most telling episodes in Carl Burckhardt's *Erinnerungen an Hofmannsthal* is the account of an occasion in 1920 when the ageing Hofmannsthal read aloud to his young friend a long episode from the fifth act of Goethe's drama.[2] What motivated this was a conversation about final acts and *Der Turm* in particular. This conversation explains to a considerable extent why, in the absence of Hofmannsthal's final version of *Der Turm* (in other words, a version that wholly satisfied him), there is some reason for accepting the claims of the version of 1925 as approaching the ideal which Hofmannsthal set himself:

One evening...we talked about last acts, that criterion of reality in a drama, in which its inevitability is made clear, the actual creative victory is realized, and a world-law is made credible and convincing. The poet spoke of *Der Turm*, of the terrible difficulty of the task which he had set himself. 'What I have to do here', he said, 'is to show clearly how chaotic forces break in upon an order which is no longer sustained by the spirit: the sacrifice must stand out...against this dark and threatening background—the captive prince who, utterly alone, fights out the struggle within himself, aided by the strength of soul which he has won from suffering. But what then?' said Hofmannsthal. 'The last act? A spirit of reconciliation, the future, must shine forth out of all the terror and fear. Only then has tragedy any true basis. Hölderlin saw Empedocles like that. In Shakespeare the sense of night, the horror, the complete hopelessness is often too deep. Goethe has been unjustly called undramatic—and all because he is constantly looking for the healing powers. Even in the most terrible situations, fate is for him so meaningful,...always present as a manifestation of a higher plan; if there is no solution in human terms then the redemption is to be found beyond human life, always in the realm of those living forces that hold the world back from the abyss of nihilism. You see, in *Egmont*, for example, the characters are also the embodiment of certain forces, entangled in a terrible and magnificent game. And from their actions and sufferings there always arises, in the final analysis, a spirit of higher morality.'

And then he took a volume of Goethe from the shelf, and began to read aloud the last act of *Egmont*.[1]

Even while admitting the necessity for the ending of the second version of *Der Turm*, Burckhardt has himself summarized Hofmannsthal's basic attitude: 'Deepest tragedy was always for him merely the last step before emerging into freedom and light.'[2]

Thus when Requadt says that 'the Christian faith preserved Hofmannsthal from complete despair',[3] he is right but seems rather mournfully to trust the larger hope in a perceptibly faint manner. For Hofmannsthal the practical Christianity of his maturity was not a vague, semi-despairing, poetic conviction; nor was it a personal refuge. The more Christianity declined in the world of his time, the more necessary it became for him to postulate its maxims in visible form. Otherwise the triple symbol of Sigismund as human individual, saint and ruler becomes meaningless. Otherwise the Children's King does remain a mere humanitarian dream, whereas he should be the symbol of the Kingdom of God, which can be striven for here on earth.

In a definition of drama Bernt von Heiseler, himself an artist of firm Christian (Lutheran) conviction, wrote

For it is the essence of drama that amidst all the confusion and gloom of the struggle, a spirit of reconciliation should shine forth—whether it be merely a premonition of a dying man or only a Promised Land seen in the distance from a high mountain.[1]

This clears the ground for a definitive Christian interpretation of tragedy which reads as if Heiseler had in mind *Der Turm*, Sigismund's fate and the possibility of the kingdom of the Children's King:

It has been said that drama in its true sense—namely tragedy—has been made impossible by Christianity, because when God became Man the reconciliation of the world with God was accomplished; the irreconcilable nature of earthly opposites, it is said, was suffered by Christ at his crucifixion, and was cancelled out by the Resurrection, so that tragic action, as represented in the drama, is no longer necessary.

That would be true if the Resurrection of Christ had been followed by his reappearance as judge of the world, and by the foundation of a new heaven and a new earth. But it is with us as Martin Luther says: 'We are not yet, but we are becoming. It is not yet done and accomplished, but it is coming. It is not the end, but it is the way.'

It would be both misleading and unjust to Hofmannsthal if Heiseler's idea of drama, and of tragedy in particular, were to be applied in totality to *Der Turm*. His theory might well seem to be unnecessarily restricted, even dogmatically exclusive, as, for example, when he continues:

Therefore the entry of Christ into the human story does not mean the end of drama but rather its real beginning. If drama beforehand had been a solemn ceremony in honour of a deity who was but darkly sensed, now it is service in the face of God revealed.

Of principal relevance here, however, is Heiseler's 'Promised Land seen in the distance from a high mountain'. This, incidentally, brings to mind again Hofmannsthal's words on tragedy: 'A spirit of reconciliation, the future, must shine forth out of all the terror and fear. Only then has tragedy any true basis.'

Heiseler summarized his own argument in the words of Luther. These same words are perhaps the most appropriate with which to close this survey of *Der Turm* and the disputed significance of its first, visionary ending: 'It is not the end, but it is the way.'

BIBLIOGRAPHICAL NOTE

The following is a chronological survey of the various versions of *Der Turm* and of fragments which relate to it. These latter include episodes from Hofmannsthal's adaptation of Calderón's *La vida es sueño* (*Das Leben ein Traum*). *All* fragments of *Das Leben ein Traum* are now in *Dramen*, III, pp. 339–438.

1. *Der Gefangene* (from *Das Leben ein Traum*), in *Der Tag*, Berlin, 25 December 1907.

2. *Das Leben ein Traum* (fragments), in *Die Zeit*, Vienna, 15 October 1910.

3. *Das Leben ein Traum* (fragments), in *Blätter des Burgtheaters*, Vienna, June 1919.

4. *Das Leben ein Traum* (fragments), in *Rodauner Nachträge*. Vol. I. Amalthea-Verlag, Vienna, 1919.

5. *Der Turm*, Acts I and II, in *Neue Deutsche Beiträge*. Bremer Presse, Munich, February 1923. Erste Folge, zweites Heft, pp. 18–91.

6. *Der Turm*, Acts III, IV and V, in *Neue Deutsche Beiträge*, January 1925. Zweite Folge, zweites Heft, pp. 9–98.

7. *Der Turm*, first book edition. Privatdruck der Bremer Presse, Munich, 1925 (private and limited edition).

8. *Der Thronwechsel* (parts of Act IV in the second and final version of *Der Turm*), in *Neue Zürcher Zeitung*, Zürich, 21 August 1927.

9. *Der Turm*, second and final version. S. Fischer Verlag, Berlin, 1927.

10. *Der Turm*, first version, as published in *Neue Deutsche Beiträge*, 1923–5, in *Gesammelte Werke*. Vol. 3. S. Fischer Verlag, Berlin, 1934.

11. *Das Leben ein Traum* (fragments), identical with those published in *Rodauner Nachträge* (1919—see 4, above) with the addition of 1160 lines from Hofmannsthal's posthumous papers, in *Corona*, Heft 1 and Heft 2, Munich and Zürich, 1937.

12. *Der Turm*, first version, based on text in private edition of 1925 (see 7, above), *Fischer Schulausgabe*. S. Fischer Verlag, Frankfurt/Main, 1952.

13. *Der Turm*, first version, based on text in private edition of 1925, in *Ausgewählte Werke*. Vol. 1. S. Fischer Verlag, Frankfurt/Main, 1957, pp. 219–335.

14. *Der Turm*, first version, as published in *Neue Deutsche Beiträge*, 1923–5, in *Dramen*, IV. S. Fischer Verlag, Frankfurt/Main, 1958, pp. 7–208.

15. *Der Turm*, second and final version (see 9, above), in *Dramen*, IV, pp. 321–463.

In the present study we are concerned only with the complete versions of the play, that is, the versions of 1925 and 1927. An excellent overall account of the various phases in the composition of *Der Turm* is that in Jakob Laubach's *Hugo von Hofmannsthals Turm-Dichtungen, Entstehung, Form und Bedeutungsschichten*, pp. 38–42. This work, a doctoral dissertation, dates from 1949. I was able to consult a copy kindly placed at my disposal by Professor Wilhelm Grenzmann of the University of Bonn. The work, together with an up-to-date bibliography, was published by the University of Fribourg (Switzerland) in 1954. Laubach's treatise was of great assistance in assembling the material for this bibliographical note.

The first book edition of *Der Turm*, a limited edition published in 1925 by the Bremer Presse, differs somewhat from the first published version printed in the *Neue Deutsche Beiträge* (1923–5). The third act alone remains unaltered, or rather unshortened. Basically the play remains the same as regards acts, scenes, characters, action and main themes. One subsidiary theme was eliminated: in the first printed version (*Neue Deutsche Beiträge*) Count Adam states that the Children's King is an illegitimate son of King Basilius. This statement is omitted in the Bremer Presse book-edition.

Other modifications affect the scene with the gypsy in the fifth act. There is only one gypsy in the Bremer Presse edition (two in the *Neue D.B.* version), and there are also various cuts. Laubach observes shrewdly that they fall into two categories: (1) those which make the work 'more concentrated and suitable for the stage'; (2) those which affect the sense of the text itself. In the Bremer Presse edition passages are omitted which tend to identify Sigismund too closely with the idea and figure of Christ the Redeemer. In like manner passages which are very obviously reminiscent of certain biblical sequences are omitted. The same sentences are, incidentally, not included in the 1927 version, in which the action up to Sigismund's attack on Basilius (Act III) is virtually unchanged. The far-reaching problems connected with the later acts of the 1927 version are of course dealt with in chapter 8 of the present work.

There are further differences between the *Neue D.B.* and Bremer Presse versions: in the latter several passages are omitted which were evidently regarded as being very difficult. Nearly all of them are from speeches of Sigismund. For the most part they are somewhat lyrical in quality and refer to what Laubach calls Sigismund's *magisches Weltverhältnis* (magical relationship to the world).

There is one addition to the Bremer Presse edition as compared with the version in the *Neue D.B.* During the dispute with the Grand Almoner (Act II), one speech of Basilius is lengthened by several sentences.

The version which appeared in the *Gesammelte Werke* of 1934 is in the main identical with that in the *Neue D.B.* Several slight alterations, a word or even a single letter, were made, but the two editions can be regarded as virtually identical.

The Fischer Schulausgabe (1952) seems to have been based on the Bremer Presse edition (1925), although no indication is given. According to the *Fischer Almanach* for 1955 it is *ungekürzt* (unabridged), although close examination and comparison show this to be slightly inaccurate. The same may be said for the version in *Ausgewählte Werke* (1957), which is also apparently based on the Bremer Presse edition.

The first version of *Der Turm*, now in *Dramen*, IV, is the text of the *Neue D.B.* edition. The second and final version, also in *Dramen*, IV, is the text of 1927 (see 9, above). I understand from Dr Steiner that in the *second* edition of *Dramen*, IV the Bremer Presse text will replace the text based on the *Neue D.B.*

It is thus difficult to say which is the 'definitive' edition of the first version. Laubach says very reasonably: 'the text of the private edition [Bremer Presse] shows that the poet regarded the version completed in autumn 1924 as the "penultimate one" [*vorletzte*]. Even at the time when the last three acts appeared in the *Neue Deutsche Beiträge* he was at work shortening and modifying the play. The first result of this is the private edition.'

It can thus scarcely be said that the editions of 1934 and 1958 (*Dramen*, IV)—reprints to all intents and purposes of the *Neue D.B.*—are the only authorized editions. This assertion has on occasion been made. The claims of the Bremer Presse text have at least equal validity.

In the present study all textual references to *Der Turm* are based, unless otherwise stated, on the Fischer Schulausgabe (1952). To complicate still further a complex and irritating situation, I have noted that a later (1956) reprint of this edition begins on the left-hand instead of (as earlier) the right-hand page! Thus if this more recent text were to be consulted, some differences in page-references would be apparent.

Although I personally regard the Bremer Presse version as

having claims superior to that of the *Neue Deutsche Beiträge*, I have not ignored the latter and have consulted it in its various editions (1923–5, 1934, 1958).

Concerning my use in the present study of the Fischer Schulausgabe: it seemed more practical to give page references for this edition as it is so accessible—it has been in general circulation for a number of years and prior to *Ausgewählte Werke* and *Dramen*, IV it was the only text of the play that was anything like generally available.

On the other hand I was able to take the precaution of checking all textual references against no. 90 (in the Birmingham Reference Library) of the limited edition of 1925 (Bremer Presse). I was able to use this copy for a short period. The edition was, however, limited to two hundred and sixty copies, and cannot therefore be regarded as being in general circulation. Even this edition, however, is not flawless despite the fact that (or perhaps because) Hofmannsthal himself saw it through the press. For Hofmannsthal was a notoriously bad proof-reader, a fact recently stressed by Dr Steiner himself (*Zur Hofmannsthal-Ausgabe* I. *Bericht und Berichtigung*, Berne, 1959, pp. 8–9) and by Michael Hamburger in his review of Steiner's book (*German Life and Letters*, vol. 14, 1–2, 1960–1, pp. 101–2). Hamburger, for example, points out how an error in the Bremer Presse edition ('Stürme' for 'Türme') has been incorporated in the text of *Der Turm* (first version) now in *Dramen*, IV (p. 132). This particular error, incidentally, is not made in the Schulausgabe (see p. 66).

To conclude an involved and tedious tale, I should perhaps add that consultation with Dr Steiner confirmed my belief that combined use of the Bremer Presse editions and of the Schulausgabe is justified.

There are fortunately no such bibliographical problems concerning the second and final version of *Der Turm* (1927). There are to date only two complete editions of it, see nos. 9 and 15 above.

CHAPTER 9

CONCLUSION

IN the foregoing pages an attempt was made to show Hofmannsthal's aims in both versions of *Der Turm* and the technical and
artistic means he used to achieve them.

The question may therefore now legitimately be put: did he
succeed? One's first reaction is to enquire after the play's record
in the theatre. Unfortunately this does not tell us a great deal,
although it does give us some significant leads. For *Der Turm*
has had an odd career in the theatre and has never established for
itself a permanent place in any repertoire. It should be added,
however, that social and political conditions were hardly favourable
during the fifteen years or so following Hofmannsthal's death.
An analogy with the fate of Kafka's novels might not be altogether
out of place.

The play, however, has been performed in several places
during the past decade and a half.[1] These performances have
usually been given in a strictly occasional setting and always, as far
as one can tell, the first version has been used. Reception has been
mixed: productions at the Monschau and Hersfeld Festivals seem to
have been well received, while the long-awaited performances at
Salzburg in 1959 evidently made very little impact on the public.[2]

The detailed analysis of *Der Turm* would appear to show,
however, that Hofmannsthal was on the whole successful. The
paradoxical retort to that might be: yes—in the details. Does
Hofmannsthal's series of theatrical *tours de force*—the Almoner
scene, the release of Sigismund, etc.—does his highly differentiated
use of language, does his use of symbolic-historical figures—add
up to a convincing whole?

These questions can perhaps best be approached in a rather
oblique fashion by citing the example of *Faust* II. There is no

intention, especially at this late stage in the study, of comparing *Der Turm* with Goethe's comprehensive last drama. It may be recalled, however, that *Faust* II was the *Alterswerk* (that is, the work of ultimate maturity and old age) in which Goethe ranged freely over form, style, period and ideas in the intention of packing into his play as much of himself, his wisdom and experience as possible, even at the risk, cheerfully taken, of formlessness and obscurity. It will, moreover, be recalled that Goethe was little concerned at the prospect of not being understood. The totality of his work, its comprehensiveness, were what mattered to him.

Hofmannsthal was in a comparable position save in one respect. He did want to be understood in the here and now; and he did, in consequence, want his play to be performed. Both as lifelong man of the theatre and as author of such 'public' works as *Das Schrifttum als geistiger Raum der Nation* or the foreword to the *Deutsches Lesebuch* he was naturally anxious to be of public significance.

It often seems that to some extent he fell between the two stools of comprehensiveness and of immediate effectiveness combined with comprehensibility. In this respect the two earlier festival dramas, *Jedermann* and *Das Salzburger Große Welttheater*, are more successful in achieving his aim of reviving a popular and yet significant theatre, and thus reaching what Requadt called the 'sensuously receptive spectator' (see p. 14).

Carl Burckhardt describes the overall impression made on him by *Der Turm* (the first three acts, that is) as follows:

A question: it refers to the atmospheric elevation, so to speak. Do you not think that the atmosphere is sometimes rather too rarefied for the theatre? I do not mean so much the exalted tone of the ceremonial, nor the sense of remoteness created by the imposing solemnity of the characters,[1] nor the economy with which each one carries out only his pre-determined task within the drama. I mean rather a certain intellectual quality in the choice of vocabulary for all the participants. This suddenly becomes very clear when Julian's servant [Anton] comes on the scene with his folk idiom.[2]

This is at least partly true, in that there is justification for Burckhardt's assertion that the characters fulfil their special function in the play and nothing else. Let us put the situation in a different way: do we—can we—imagine the characters as existing off-stage or prior to the visible action of the drama? With Shakespeare, for example, one is often tempted to speculate on Hamlet's doings at Wittenberg (or, to echo an old and favourite essay question, where he was when his father was murdered!). Shakespeare's characters, with all their universal and 'general' qualities, have full human dimensions and lineaments. One scarcely imagines Basilius and Sigismund as having existed before the rise of the curtain. This suggestion recalls the opinion of Hermann Broch:

Anything that ever delighted the young man's eye, . . . all this is saturated with colour and plastically retained; truly everything is there, only the living human being . . . is missing. And if he is, as an exception, admitted, then he is usually an actor and therefore denatured to a mere puppet, almost as though the self-suppressing author felt bound to be reticent about his fellow man.

Broch goes on to cite the example of Stifter in whose landscape man is

naught but a prop, naught but—in the truest sense of the word—an optical figure, a non-living being whose shadow-existence follows some abstract moralizing, some idealistically romanticized convention, and knows no human desire.

Placing Hofmannsthal in this tradition, Broch then shows how in the novel-fragment *Andreas* the author

created a new type of man, a man completely under the spell of the landscape's magic. . . . Nevertheless, even the most glorious magic succeeds only within the magic hour; the moment this has passed and the clock strikes one . . . as soon as the book is closed—the landscape it's true, remains, but the magic figures disappear. For they possess almost no human existence of their own, much less that street existence . . . with which characters like Robinson Crusoe, Gulliver, Rastignac,

Oblomov...and even Madame Bovary have engraved themselves into the memory of mankind, remaining all but independent of the book and filled, for that very reason, with well-nigh mythical overtones.[1]

It may not be strictly fair to take what Broch writes of Hofmannsthal as a prose artist, and apply it to his drama. But it will be appreciated that Broch, in a more detailed and elaborate way, is describing that 'intellectual quality' of which Burckhardt complained in *Der Turm*.

Perhaps only Anton achieves the full dimensions of real life; one might better say the 'normal' dimensions. On the other hand Hofmannsthal intended no doubt to achieve the 'remoteness' that Burckhardt mentions, as part of the mythical and timeless character of his figures. In this respect, certainly, his figures will be as old and as new a hundred years hence as they are now; whereas the *modern* and symbolic figures of Mr Eliot, for example, who with his reinterpretations of Greek archetypes attempts something comparable but with contemporary figures and idiom, may appear dated—or at least obscured by their erstwhile 'contemporariness'. Hofmannsthal, on the other hand, has deliberately removed his setting and characters from any association with real time and place. He may in consequence be found ultimately to speak *sub specie aeternitatis* the more directly—a paradoxical notion certainly.

Even if this point were to be conceded, however, Burckhardt's stricture on the 'intellectual quality' in *Der Turm* still remains as a reproach to it. There is no denying that Hofmannsthal did not know what to leave out! The play is so *kulturgesättigt*,[2] the characters, their language and its overtones are so complex, as to make full effectiveness difficult. One notes Hofmannsthal's success in the scenes of low life—the soldiers, Simon, Anton, Olivier's rabble, the poor—and one contrasts them with the elevated and infinitely subtle dialogue of the Almoner, Basilius, Julian and Sigismund. Although the latter is frequently of remarkable virtuosity and effect, the contrast is sometimes too great.

This may well be the heart of the matter. Hofmannsthal seems not only to have been unable to decide what to leave out; he seems to have put on the stage—most public of art forms as he well knew—things which are of a most personal nature, fit subjects for artistic depiction in the story form, or—more particularly—in the diary and letter form. That is to say that matters and problems best depicted in a form where the reader has leisure, the sense of being alone with the artist and of being able to see into his mind, are depicted in the form whose very nature is that of instant impact and speed—the more epic and less personal approach.

Hofmannsthal seems to have attempted both at once. In other words he attempted to stage those intricacies of the mind— the mental constitution of Sigismund for example—which are least suited for dramatic effectiveness: one recalls the dictum of I. A. Richards, cited in connection with *Jedermann* (see p. 39). Simultaneously he attempted by a series of effective *coups de théâtre* to create a grand drama in the high tradition. This combination was not attempted in the two earlier festival dramas, and their effect is correspondingly more direct. Rudolf Kassner seems to have put his finger on the point when he tried to define Hofmannsthal as a dramatist:

Hofmannsthal wrote some things for the stage and some things for himself. These latter were not expressions of his convictions and beliefs, but arose dreamlike out of him, emanations of a true, inborn, visionary temperament.... This links him to the twentieth century, which manifests itself through him in the dream. This dream probably originated in the Romantic dream of the nineteenth century, but it continues on into the twentieth. As I said, he—Hofmannsthal—wrote for the stage. In his last drama *Der Turm* it looks as if he wanted to reconcile both the stage and what I should call the dreamlike quality. Many people regard it as a peak of creativeness. But it does not seem to me to be quite that. He himself was more attached to it than to other products of his intellect, just as a mother is often more attached to a sick child than to her healthy ones.[1]

Kassner, indeed, takes this point further, and makes a generalization on Hofmannsthal as a dramatist. He asserts that

Hofmannsthal was lacking in the ability to create a dénouement for his dramas. Kassner calls this quality 'perepeteia, a sudden change of fortune, a sudden change of direction'. He then applies this criticism directly to *Der Turm*:

Dénouement is certainly the most difficult thing to achieve in drama. Actually only one possessed can do it successfully...and it will not be properly achieved if the dramatist tries to encircle a given theme like a hunter stalking his game.

Hugo Garten joins Kassner in seeing Hofmannsthal as deficient in truly dramatic power. His reflections seem to support some of the strictures already put forward in this chapter:

Hofmannsthal lacked the elemental power of the born dramatist; despite the fascination the theatre held for him, he remained at heart what he had been at the outset—a poet. He drew his inspiration not so much from life as from letters;...Moreover, his creative energies were thwarted by a fatal inclination towards introspection and self-analysis. His path is strewn with innumerable fragments, and even his completed works often exist in more than one version.[1]

If one agrees with Kassner and Garten an odd paradox becomes apparent. On the one hand *Der Turm* is the most violent of Hofmannsthal's dramas both from the point of view of change and development in the central character and especially in terms of the physical action. On the other hand it is lacking in 'perepeteia, a sudden change of fortune, a sudden change of direction'. Where, then, does the truth lie? It is again partly to be found, perhaps, in Hofmannsthal's baroque heritage. If we consider *Der Turm* as a drama in the direct baroque tradition—that this is true should be clear from the analysis of the play itself—then it will be clear that Hofmannsthal was not trying to achieve those things whose absence disturbs Kassner and perplexes the contemporary critic.[2]

The strong baroque element in Hofmannsthal has recently been emphasized by Claude Hill, who approaches the problem from a rather different standpoint from those of Kassner and Garten, but reaches essentially the same conclusion even if he phrases it rather more moderately and shows himself to be markedly sympathetic to Hofmannsthal's method:

It is no coincidence that Austria's predominant style of architecture is the Baroque. The show-loving and ornament-studded spirit of Baroque is still alive in the hearts of the population; and Hofmannsthal, who so often preferred Baroque authors and plots for his adaptations, shows himself to be a true son of his native country with the unique contribution he made to modern opera. The same holds true for the Salzburg Festivals which owe so much to the Austrian dramatist. Indeed, the whole relation of a basically musical-lyrical poet to the art form of the drama, for which he was not fitted by inner disposition, is nothing else but the Baroque heritage of a young man who had, so to speak, the corpuscles of the theatre in his blood. Consequently, Hofmannsthal's plays, although often poorly constructed and lacking in plastic skill, nevertheless live on a rich theatricality, on colours, moods, situations, single scenes, aural display, in short—on Baroque ornaments. That Hofmannsthal should also have borrowed from the rich store of Viennese folk theatre of the low classes and suburban playhouses is, therefore, not surprising, and is amply evidenced by the richly humorous servant types he employs in so many of his plays. All said then, it may be stated at the risk of sounding paradoxical: Hofmannsthal, although not a great dramatist, was a great theatrical showman who aimed at reproducing the macrocosm of the world and his dreams in the microcosm of the stage. Rejecting the vision-limiting soberness of the realistic school, he wrote in an essay (1903): 'Let us never forget that the stage is nothing and worse than nothing unless it is something wonderful. . . . That it must be the dream of dreams, or else it is a wooden pillory on which the naked dream skeleton of the poet is disgustingly prostituted.'[1]

A further point arises, however, from this consideration, and here also Hofmannsthal cannot be completely justified. Much mention has been made throughout this study of Hofmannsthal's awareness of the past and of the various forms taken by this awareness in his writings. His use of traditional forms and symbols has likewise been much discussed. The fundamental query is this: how far is a tradition which has become quite conscious a genuine tradition? At what point does a tradition which is forcibly kept alive, however much and however positively modified, become an ideology, kept alive for its own sake?

To phrase the issue in this way is to put it very sharply; but the problem is vital, not only for Hofmannsthal, but for most writers of conservative tendencies. In the case of Hofmannsthal there is no clear-cut answer. Our reaction will depend almost entirely on our reaction to his ideas and ideals: if we can accept or find sympathetic the vision of society seen by Sigismund in *Der Turm I* (of if we can find much that is constructive in such a work as Seipel's *Nation und Staat*), then we will find Hofmannsthal's traditionalism and its artistic exploitation justifiable.

If, however, we cannot accept his views—we may see them as unrealistic or as a piece of downright clerical reaction—then we are unlikely to be able to accept the form in which they are presented, the more so as the form itself then carries associations of an inimical content and atmosphere.

Whichever individual approach we may take, one further basic point becomes obvious. We cannot claim for Hofmannsthal that full validity of his dramatic work which could make it acceptable to peoples of varying traditions and beliefs. *Jedermann* was probably the work in which he most nearly approached this ideal. Hofmannsthal may have 'written for Europe' during the closing phase of his career. In *Der Turm*, at any rate, he wrote for Europe in Austrian terms, and thereby placed a limit to the automatic or immediate appeal which his drama could have. Had he, perhaps, not striven so hard to be a preceptor, a *Statthalter* of the spirit, he might have succeeded rather better in being just that.

This is not so much a paradox as it appears. In seeking so earnestly and conscientiously to set down what in Hofmannsthal's own terms can be called *das Bindende und Bewahrende*[1] he may well have stultified somewhat his own powers of imagination. Could he, however, have acted differently? This raises the whole question—it seems that it is a peculiarly modern question—of self-conscious 'representativeness' of the artist, the degree to which it is genuine, the degree to which an artist can be 'representative' and yet remain true to himself. This is something different from the artist as seismograph, an idea postulated in *Der Dichter und diese Zeit* (see Introduction), for a seismograph moves and reacts involuntarily.

In Hofmannsthal's case the above query seems to need some amplification: could he have acted differently—was it arbitrary choice, a nobly misguided sense of duty which made him become a preceptor, even a preacher? The answer to all these questions is probably in the negative, for his 'Austrianism', of which his 'Europeanism' was a projection, was an integral part of his constitution. In this sense he could not help being representative. This is perhaps best explained in Willy Haas's memoir *Der Mensch Hofmannsthal*:

There was also something Austrian and something historical in all this. With the accession of Maria Theresia it was not only the Habsburg dynasty that came to an end, but also the real substance of Austria as centre of a world-wide power. Maria Theresia rebuilt Austria... within as well as around the...skeleton of a bureaucratic hierarchy which functioned quite mechanically. This hierarchy, which she created and which actually lasted until 1918, was intended to hold the flesh of the country together—simply as flesh, as life....Or, let us put it quite plainly: the attachment of real children to a real mother, without any historical assurances....It is no coincidence that the most beautiful and most accurate words ever written about her come from Hofmannsthal's pen....he too regarded a spontaneous way of life as being of the highest social and political value; and he believed in this as sincerely as in his own existence. For, in the last resort, this was what it came to in Austria, as this childlike love for Mother Austria grew less and less: to leave everything to the inspiration of the moment, in order to keep Austria together for a while longer. Struggles over the constitution...such things as these were but minor occurrences in the routine world of diplomacy with its mundane ideas...which only a real poetic state-genius could have transformed back into lasting... reality. It is almost certain that Austria could have had such state-geniuses: Grillparzer could probably have been one, and here again it was Hofmannsthal who wrote such incomparable words about him. And almost every word which he wrote about Grillparzer as a politician can be applied to Hofmannsthal himself. Yet this Austria, which by the very nature of things was forced to limit itself to the smallest possible combinations and manœuvres...in order not to bring down the whole edifice, could no longer afford men of great character. And so it allowed Grillparzer and Hofmannsthal to vegetate, lonely and embittered.

And just that is the great curse—on Austria and on these great men. The historical existence of a structure, its quality of 'really existing' in the Hegelian sense, shows itself most strikingly in the fact that it produces really living men of its own type and quality. Almost every country has such representative figures as symptoms of its historical consolidation. Austria as well. Sometimes the political activity of these men may be highly questionable; here and there they may be personally unpleasant. But as pure products of the historical structure which has produced them, they represent its viability. And in the mere act of representing—even if in nothing else—they for their part heighten this viability in confirming it. D'Annunzio was one such product and he achieved something for Italy, not as a politician, nor as a character, but as a representative Italian and as a poet. Barrès and Péguy...and they achieved much for France—as representative Frenchmen and writers, not as politicians. Grillparzer and Hofmannsthal were of the same type: representative, genuine Austrians, products, children, mirrors of Austria, which in them demonstrated its fertility. And they died in loneliness, although their political talent was certainly much healthier than that of Barrès or D'Annunzio.

Hofmannsthal, whose poetic perception was almost like an historical map, for whom every province was a province of the old monarchy, whose love refused to yield up any single province....Hofmannsthal died in this helpless little state which calls itself the Austrian Republic. For those of us who also recognized the weaknesses of this doomed monarchy, this would not have been a particularly bad fate. But for him it was certainly the worst fate of all. Not only had he lost his eldest son, he had also lost his oldest mother.[1]

Haas closes his study on a somewhat sentimental and epigram-like note. The point, however, is clear. Hofmannsthal was to an unusual degree the product of his environment and its past. If we take the three festival dramas discussed in this study—and add to them the 'mythical' evocations of Maria Theresia, Prince

Eugene and Grillparzer, and add the 'mythical' evocations of Austria herself—then we are confronted with an artist who is at once embodying his country and guiding it. There are complexities and inconsistencies in this achievement. The strenuous note is on occasion quite audible. One is annoyed from time to time by the 'generality' of it all. One thinks longingly, perhaps, of the personal and so markedly contemporary world of *Der Schwierige* in which Hofmannsthal achieves reality and a certain general validity at one and the same time.

We can agree with Requadt and many others, and maintain that this play is Hofmannsthal's most characteristic and successful achievement. We can agree, but at the same time be aware that *Der Schwierige* could be so successful because, perhaps, it deals with personal values, values which do indeed have general validity but which are depicted dramatically in a limited section of society.

Could Hofmannsthal have applied this technique to the matters which absorbed him in his festival dramas? It is impossible to dogmatize. It seems to be highly unlikely, however, for the following reason: in his 'generality', his 'formality', Hofmannsthal is in line with a tendency of twentieth-century literature which can no longer create in the solidly three-dimensional terms of a Dickens or a Fontane. Man knows so much about himself and has in the course of a few decades experienced so much—his spiritual and intellectual world is so complex, his foundations so unsure—that to depict things in the old 'realistic' manner may be downright (if unwittingly) dishonest.

By creating in this non-realistic manner, then, Hofmannsthal was, paradoxically, creating realistically and honestly. He explains, he admonishes, he sets up his and our precepts. It is sometimes not easy to follow him wherever he leads. It is hoped, however, that the present study has proved that the attempt is in itself a worthwhile venture.

NOTES

PAGE 7

1   *Prosa*, III, 279–89. This essay is discussed in chapter 4.

PAGE 8

1   *Hofmannsthals Wandlung*, in *Über Hugo von Hofmannsthal* (Göttingen, 1958), p. 153.

PAGE 9

1   *Die Welt von Gestern* (Stockholm, 1947), pp. 65–71.

PAGE 10

1   See either 'Hofmannsthals Prosaschriften', in *Neue Rundschau*, II (1951), 1–30, or Introduction (in translation by James and Tania Stern) to *Selected Prose* (of Hofmannsthal) (London, 1952).

2   *Deutsche Vierteljahrsschrift* (*DVjss*), I (1955), 1–19.

3   'Hofmannsthal', in *Hofmannsthal: die Gestalt des Dichters im Spiegel der Freunde*, ed. H. A. Fiechtner (Vienna, 1949), p. 354. This essay, one of several written by Borchardt on Hofmannsthal, was published a few weeks after Hofmannsthal's death and first appeared in the *Neue Zürcher Zeitung*, 11 August 1929.

PAGE 12

1   *Hofmannsthals Wandlung*, p. 154.

2   *Die deutsche Novelle von Goethe bis Kafka* (Düsseldorf, 1956), pp. 284–303.

PAGE 13

1   See Hofmannsthal's correspondence with Bodenhausen, *Briefe der Freundschaft* (Düsseldorf, 1953), p. 87.

PAGE 14

1   'Hofmannsthal', in *Deutsche Literatur im XX. Jahrhundert*, ed. Otto Mann and Hermann Friedmann (Heidelberg, 1954), pp. 38–9.

2   *Prosa*, II, 289. The final metaphor is striking. It is perhaps worth noting that shortly before this essay was written Hofmannsthal had been very impressed by Werner's edition of Hebbel's letters and had recommended it to Bodenhausen. See *Briefe der Freundschaft*,

p. 80, letter of 7 June 1906, in which Hofmannsthal referred very positively to his friend Kassner's essay on Hebbel in Kassner's volume of essays *Motive*. For further evidence of Hofmannsthal's interest in Hebbel at this time see also *Briefe der Freundschaft*, pp. 262–3 (note to p. 90), and *Brief an den Buchhändler Hugo Heller* (to which the note refers) in *Prosa*, II, 233–4.

PAGE 15

1 *Prosa*, II, 281–2. Hofmannsthal actually expresses the idea of the artist as seismograph (*das seismographische Gebilde*) in the final paragraph of the essay (p. 298).

PAGE 16

1 This point becomes clearer, perhaps, if one notes that the method is comparable to—though in Hofmannsthal's case probably not as consistent as—that often used by Wagner, Thomas Mann and T. S. Eliot.

PAGE 18

1 *George* (Berlin, 1920), p. 1.

PAGE 20

1 *Selections from Albert Schweitzer* (London, 1953), p. 45.
2 *Prosa*, II, 268.

PAGE 21

1 Rudolf Kassner has explained how Hofmannsthal came to write *Jedermann*: 'In those years Hofmannsthal wrote *Das Gerettete Venedig*, *Ödipus und die Sphinx*, *Elektra*, and began to think about *Jedermann*. Clemens Franckenstein, who had seen the old mystery play *Everyman* in London, introduced him to this theme.' See 'Erinnerungen an Hofmannsthal', in *Die Gestalt des Dichters im Spiegel der Freunde*, ed. H. A. Fiechtner (Vienna, 1949), p. 240. Hofmannsthal had a very wide reading knowledge of English. Some reference to his attitude to England and to English culture, in so far as it is relevant to this study, is made on pp. 105 and 198. Mary Gilbert's 'Hofmannsthal and England', in *German Life and Letters*, I (1936), 182–93, is an excellent account of the influence of English culture and social forms on the young Hofmannsthal. It also indicates how this influence was a factor in his later development.
2 *Das alte Spiel von Jedermann* (1912), *Prosa*, III, 114–15.

PAGE 22

1 *Op. cit.* pp. 115–16.

2 Hofmannsthal's full title for his version was *Jedermann: das Spiel vom Sterben des reichen Mannes erneuert von H. v. H.* The choice of the verb *erneuern* was probably quite conscious. It means of course more than 'modernized' in the customary sense, or 'adapted for the modern stage'. Hofmannsthal had used this phrase (*für die neuere Bühne eingerichtet*) for *König Ödipus* (1906). 'Renewed and reinterpreted' would seem to come as close as possible to Hofmannsthal's sense and intention.

3 *Prosa*, III, 116.

4 *Ibid.*

PAGE 23

1 *Buch der Freunde* (1922–9), now in *Aufzeichnungen*, pp. 22, 81.

PAGE 25

1 Compare Hofmannsthal's aphorism in *Buch der Freunde*: 'God said: I was an unknown treasure and I wanted to be known. So I created man.' See *Aufzeichnungen*, p. 34.

PAGE 26

1 *Buch der Freunde.* See *Aufzeichnungen*, p. 53.

PAGE 27

1 *Prosa*, III, 444–50.

2 *Op. cit.* 444–5.

PAGE 28

1 *Prosa*, IV, 492–7.

2 *Op. cit.* 524.

PAGE 29

1 This is of course a whole subject in itself. Apart from the various specialized works (Zingerle, Stumpfl, Dörrer, etc.), Nadler gives an account which is particularly helpful for this present study. See *Literaturgeschichte Österreichs* (Salzburg, 1951), pp. 117–29.

2 *Prosa*, III, 441–3.

3 Hofmannsthal intended to write a *Xenodoxus* in order to complete a kind of latter-day baroque trilogy: *Jedermann, Das Salzburger Große Welttheater* and *Xenodoxus*. It was to have been based on the *Cenodoxus, der Doktor von Paris* (1602) of the greatest Jesuit

dramatist, the Swabian Jakob Bidermann (1578–1639). The fairly detailed *Aufzeichnungen zu einem Xenodoxus* (written for the greater part during the period 1922–5) were first published in *Neue Rundschau*, III–IV (1954), 401–23. In the same journal are an excellent account and interpretation of the fragment by Edgar Hederer (pp. 424–36). These *Aufzeichnungen* are now in *Dramen*, IV, 483–99.

PAGE 30

1 *Prosa*, III, 445.
2 *Ibid.*
3 *Ibid.*

PAGE 31

1 This idea, particularly, seems to be a development of Hofmannsthal's interest in Nadler's approach to literature.
2 Hofmannsthal, Richard Strauss and Franz Schalk (joint directors of the Vienna State Opera) and Max Reinhardt were the guiding spirits at the inception of the Salzburg Festival. There are various accounts of Hofmannsthal's ideals in sponsoring the Festival—by himself and by others. A good brief account is *Gespräch über Österreich* by Bertha Szeps-Zuckerkandl. It is an excerpt from an unpublished memoir. See *Hofmannsthal: Die Gestalt des Dichters im Spiegel der Freunde* (Vienna, 1949), pp. 337–8. The conversation as recorded is stilted and rather theatrical but in a very short space links Salzburg with Hofmannsthal's views on the fall and future of Austria.

PAGE 32

1 *Outline of European Architecture* (Pelican, second revised ed., 1951), pp. 179–80.
2 This antithesis was taken from a description of the *Kapuzinergruft*, burial vault of the Habsburgs since the time of the Thirty Years War. See *Das Österreichbuch*, ed. Ernst Marboe (Vienna, 1948), p. 156.

PAGE 33

1 *Die Mozart-Zentenarfeier in Salzburg* (1891). See *Prosa*, I, 43.
2 *Festspiele in Salzburg*, *Prosa*, III, 447.
3 *Prosa*, III, 448.
4 The strangely exciting, ascetic quality of the *Franziskanerkirche*,

with the symbolism of its triple pillars behind the high altar, gives a good indication of Hofmannsthal's meaning here.

5 Hofmannsthal's actual words are *des Jahrhunderts*. 'Of the century' has little obvious meaning in English. The addition of 'seventeenth' seems justified by the context.

PAGE 34

1 *Prosa*, III, 448.

PAGE 35

1 *Op. cit.* pp. 448–9.
2 *Op. cit.* p. 449. Hofmannsthal again cites Nadler.

PAGE 39

1 *Principles of Literary Criticism* (London, 1944), p. 231.

PAGE 40

1 For Hofmannsthal's views on this see also *Das Spiel vor der Menge*, *Prosa*, III, pp. 60–5, in which he discusses Reinhardt's production of the play in Berlin (1911). The conversation between Tieck and Immermann which he quotes in support of his own aims (p. 63) is of particular relevance here.

2 There is no reason for thinking otherwise. Reinhardt's interpretation of the part is felicitous and justifiably renowned. Hofmannsthal seems to have been in complete accord with his production of *Jedermann* in Salzburg (1919)—as also in Berlin eight years earlier. For Hofmannsthal's views on the Salzburg production see particularly *Festspiele in Salzburg*, *Prosa*, III, 448. Although agreement was not always so wholehearted (witness the grave difference of opinion about the production of *Der Turm* in 1928), there are many instances of Hofmannsthal's admiration for Reinhardt. See, for example, *Das Reinhardtsche Theater*, *Prosa*, III, 429–35; *Max Reinhardt*, *Aufzeichnungen*, pp. 325–32; *Reinhardt bei der Arbeit*, *Aufzeichnungen*, pp. 333–49; *Wiener Brief*, *Aufzeichnungen*, pp. 267–80, notably pp. 275–8.

PAGE 41

1 The most obvious association is that of the famous passage, Ecclesiastes iii. 19: 'Denn es gehet dem Menschen wie dem Vieh.'

PAGE 43

1 There is probably a reminiscence here of the legend telling of Emperor Rudolf's encounter with the beggar. The Poor Neighbour, like the beggar speaking to his 'Brother Rudolf', refers to his 'brotherly share'.

PAGE 44

1 See *Dramen*, III, 501; also Walther Brecht, 'Die Vorläufer von Hofmannsthals Jedermann', *Österreichische Rundschau*, IV (1924), 271–87.

2 Hofmannsthal's attitude to money, the interest system and the power of capitalism, is very important in a full understanding of his mind and outlook. It is discussed in some detail later in this chapter, and in chapters 3 and 5.

PAGE 45

1 Hofmannsthal's depiction of Jedermann at this point seems to presage the importance attached to the Rich Man rather than the King in *Das Salzburger Große Welttheater*. This is discussed in chapter 5, pp. 170–2. See also pp. 60–1.

2 *Festspielführer* (1947).

PAGE 46

1 *Duster* (usually *düster*) means 'dark' or 'dusky'. But it has an overtone of 'gloom' or 'mournfulness'. As in the comparable case of *finster* there seems to be no one English word which conveys its full flavour.

PAGE 50

1 See L. Forster, *The Temper of Seventeenth Century German Literature* (London, 1952), pp. 6–7.

PAGE 52

1 Hofmannsthal describes the stage used in the original (Berlin) production as a simple set of platforms on three levels. This was intended to approximate to the old English stage. See *Das Spiel vor der Menge, Prosa*, III, 62–3; also this chapter, note 1, p. 40 above. See *Dramen*, III, 35, for original stage-direction.

2 A remarkable and instructive example of the secular spectacle with its incredible lavishness, allegory and symbol, and highly formal

quality, is given by Franz Farga, *Die Wiener Oper von ihren Anfängen bis 1938* (Vienna, 1947), pp. 26–7: 'Amongst public spectacles of a musical-theatrical kind one should note above all the festive activities which marked the marriage of Leopold I to Margarita of Spain.... The great palace square was enclosed on all four sides by a gallery several storeys high. The allegorical events in the action represented a contest between air and water in order to prove which of them had the greater share in the production of a pearl. The four elements were represented by Juno on her coach of clouds, Vulcan and the cyclops on a cleft mountain, Neptune with his tritons in an ornate tank of water, and Flora in a garden of pleasure. The ship "Argo" floated into the middle of the palace square laden with singers and musicians. A singing-match between the various deities...began. When this proved indecisive, the knights took up the contest and a tournament was started. Suddenly fanfares sounded forth amidst the noise of the fray....A curtain of clouds was drawn back and the Temple of Immortality was seen, with all the gods of Olympus. A shimmering procession went forth from the side doors of the temple. In front was a gondola in which the Goddess of Fame had her throne. Behind her came the benevolent spirits of bygone Austrian rulers; around them in a throng were the cavalry and soldiers of foot. Leopold I himself rode along at their head. After the procession the Goddess of Fame announced to him that as a reward for his virtue the "pearl" Margarita was to be his. Following this a cavalry ballet, in which the emperor and the entire nobility took part, brought the spectacle to a close. More than a thousand people participated....'

PAGE 54

1 'Expressionismus', in *Deutsche Literatur im XX. Jahrhundert* (Heidelberg, 1954), p. 110.

PAGE 55

1 Scarcely a point which could be taken by the peasant and 'man in the street' whom Hofmannsthal was trying to reach—but quite characteristic of his attempt to please intellectual sophisticates and naïvely responding onlookers at one and the same time. The song makes a colourful and abandoned impression even without the learned background!

NOTES

PAGE 56

1 Hofmannsthal took over the procrastinating and realistic notion of the doctor from the earlier versions of the story. See K. Goedeke, *Every-Man, Homulus und Hekastus* (Hanover, 1865).

PAGE 57

1 On the other hand one should perhaps not be too solemn about this particular tradition. Candles and lamps also did rather odd things in the age of 'Gothic terror': witness the return of 'Monk' Lewis's spectral Alonzo to the Fair Imogene—whereupon 'the lights in the chamber burned blue . . .'.

PAGE 58

1 *Selections from Albert Schweitzer* (London, 1953), p. 54.

PAGE 59

1 A rather free rendering of *goldstrotzend*. But *strotzen* ('to teem with', 'to be bursting with') does not seem to have an exact equivalent in this instance.
2 *Prosa*, III, 130.

PAGE 61

1 *Op. cit.* p. 356.

PAGE 62

1 'Expressionismus', in *Deutsche Literatur im XX. Jahrhundert*, p. 127.

PAGE 63

1 *Modern German Literature* (London, 1939), p. 250.

PAGE 67

1 *Hofmannsthal: Selected Essays* (Oxford, 1955), p. xiv. Theodor Rall, on the other hand, was somewhat uncomplimentary about this habit and interpreted it as a Jewish characteristic! See *Deutsches Katholisches Schrifttum Gestern und Heute* (Einsiedeln/Cologne, 1936), p. 65. To judge from the rest of Rall's four-page section on Hofmannsthal the date of publication is also some indication as to its tendency. See also p. 212, note 1 (p. 353).

PAGE 68

1 Author's italics.

PAGE 71

1 The translations, which are rhythmic rather than strictly accurate, are those given in the *Roman Missal*.

2 T. S. Eliot used a comparable technique with marked success in *Murder in the Cathedral* (1935). In two speeches, that preceding the murder of Becket and that which closes the play, the rhythms—even the vocabulary—of the *Dies Irae* and *Te Deum* are very noticeable: (i) '*Chorus*. Dead upon the Tree, my Saviour, / Let not be in vain Thy labour;...' (ii) '*Chorus*. We praise Thee, O God, for Thy glory displayed in all the creatures of the earth,....'. This parallelism of technique is perhaps not surprising. There is a good deal of material for a constructive comparison of the courses taken by Hofmannsthal and Eliot from their original positions as prophets of despair (albeit in differing ways) to their later activities as artists of cultural-political significance, based on a decidedly Catholic viewpoint.

3 The danger is very real and one to which the greatest may succumb. It is a contentious point, but there are, for example, admirers of *Egmont* who find the reintroduction of the private love-interest (Act III, scene 2) irritating and tending to diminish Egmont's stature. Was this, one asks, the reason why he rejected Oranien's moving appeal? Was it really Goethe's *intention* to show how the heroic seems here to tremble on the brink of the irresponsible, while the *Volk* that idolizes Egmont is forgotten? In the present instance a less refined dramatist could have tugged at the heart and irritated the mind and spirit at one and the same time.

PAGE 72

1 See *Festspiele in Salzburg, Prosa*, III, 448–9: 'The great marble statues, between which the actors entered and left the stage, had the effect of something self-evident and appropriate; likewise...the six angels moving into the dusky portals of the cathedral,....' This, of course, refers specifically to Salzburg, but as already indicated the practice is readily adapted to all manner of churches great and small. (The above passage is quoted in full on p. 35.)

2 Letter of 9 November 1923, *Briefwechsel*, p. 140. Hofmannsthal refers to *Der Turm* but his remarks apply equally to the effect achieved here in *Jedermann*.

PAGE 73

1 The free rhythmic translation is again that given in the *Roman Missal*.

PAGE 74

1 Goethe had a comparable difficulty with Mephistopheles. In *Trüber Tag* (*Faust* I) the teeth-gnashing medieval devil is seen— a survival from *Urfaust* and Goethe's earliest 'traditional' conception of him. Goethe's Faust, however, was a figure of the modern age and his familiar had in consequence to be the cynical, witty, post-Enlightenment rationalist seen elsewhere in the drama. (This positive comment is not meant as a contradiction of the particular criticism of Goethe's Mephistopheles noted above.)

PAGE 75

1 'Held fast by mortal time' or 'in the thrall of mere mortality' gives some idea perhaps of Hofmannsthal's meaning here. But the simple directness of the original can scarcely be conveyed in English.

2 *Aufzeichnungen zu Reden in Skandinavien*, *Prosa*, III, 356.

PAGE 77

1 Personal reminiscence would normally be out of place in a discussion such as this. But the following may clarify the point somewhat: a short while ago the author analysed *Jedermann* with a group of Lutheran seminarists. Their positive reaction to the play and its dénouement seemed to be based on Jedermann's 'Ich glaube: Solange ich atme auf Erden, / Mag ich durch Christtum gerettet werden.' This was regarded as much more significant than the 'Catholic' Good Works who was regarded more as the voice of conscience than as the representation of 'merit' in the theological sense.

PAGE 78

1 *Das alte Spiel von Jedermann*, *Prosa*, III, 115. See also p. 21 where the whole passage is quoted.

PAGE 79

1 'Geist des Barocktheaters', in *Weltliteratur: Festgabe für Fritz Strich* (Berne, 1952), p. 32.

PAGE 80

1 Letter of 10 February 1912 and (Hofmannsthal's reply) 26 February 1912, *Briefe der Freundschaft*, pp. 136–8.

PAGE 82

1 'Geist des Barocktheaters', p. 24.

2 Various works on Hofmannsthal by Richard Alewyn are referred to in this study, while others are listed in the bibliography. It is also fairly common knowledge that Alewyn has for many years been working on a critical biography of Hofmannsthal which is, as Fritz Martini noted in his *Forschungsbericht*, very keenly awaited. See 'Deutsche Literatur zwischen 1880 und 1950. Ein Forschungsbericht', *DVjss*, IV (1952), 478–535. The section on Hofmannsthal is on pp. 495–9. A more recent 'research report', by Hanna Weischedel, gives an excellent, comprehensive survey of Alewyn's various essays on Hofmannsthal. See 'Hofmannsthal-Forschung 1945–58', *DVjss*, I (1959), pp. 63–103. The section on Alewyn's works is on pp. 66–9. Hanna Weischedel also refers to Alewyn's 'eagerly expected monograph' (p. 69).

PAGE 83

1 *Deutsche Literaturgeschichte von den Anfängen bis zur Gegenwart* (Stuttgart, 1948), p. 452.

2 *Ad me ipsum*, 30 August 1923, *Aufzeichnungen*, pp. 234–5.

3 *Ad me ipsum*, *Aufzeichnungen*, p. 235.

PAGE 84

1 It is of incidental interest to note that in 1928 Hofmannsthal nominated as one of the three best books of the year Redlich's 'great biography of Emperor Francis Joseph I'. See *Gelegentliche Äußerungen: Die besten Bücher des Jahres, Prosa*, IV, 515. For other references to Hofmannsthal's relationship with Redlich, see also p. 135, note 2 (p. 335).

2 *Das politische Tagebuch Josef Redlichs, 1908–1919*, ed. by Fritz Fellner, 2 vols. (Graz/Cologne, 1954). The entry quoted above is on p. 82 of vol. II.

3 Hofmannsthal refers thus to countries such as Great Britain and France whom he regards, comparatively speaking, as ethnically unified in that they each have one predominating language and culture, relatively uniform customs, etc. He contrasts this implicitly with Austria's numerous 'nationalities'—German, Hungarian, Ruthenian, Croatian, Czech, Italian, Polish, Slovakian and Slovenian.

4 *Antwort auf die Umfrage des 'Svenska Dagbladet'* (*Übersetzt von Friedrich Stieve*), *Aufzeichnungen*, p. 363. This letter of 20 May 1915 appeared in the Swedish newspaper *Svenska Dagbladet*. Hofmannsthal's original has not been preserved beyond the first few lines. The version now in *Aufzeichnungen* is a translation of the Swedish text. See *Aufzeichnungen*, p. 375, also *Prosa*, III, 517, for Steiner's account of this rather complicated story.

PAGE 85

1 *Prosa*, III, 369–83. Herbert Steiner (*Anmerkung, Prosa*, III, 516) notes that Hofmannsthal had asked Rudolf Borchardt to write a draft for the 'Berne address'. He adds that approximately the first half of the surviving notes, now in *Prosa*, III, was written by Borchardt. According to Steiner it is virtually impossible to determine exactly how much influence Borchardt had on the composition of this address. It is worth noting that in a letter to Bodenhausen, dated 23 March 1917, Hofmannsthal remarks that he is to give 'a very fine lecture (written by Borchardt)' in Berne. See *Briefe der Freundschaft*, p. 229. The lecture was given on 31 March 1917. See Max Rychner 'Einleitung: Blick auf die zwanziger Jahre', in *Zur europäischen Literatur* (Zürich, 2nd ed. 1951), p. 13. In a letter to Borchardt, written on Easter Monday 1917, Hofmannsthal remarks that he gave 'your (our) lecture in Berne'. See *Hofmannsthal: R.B. Briefwechsel* (Frankfurt/Main, 1954), p. 123. The Klett (Stuttgart) edition of Borchardt's works is not yet complete. This may ultimately throw some light on the problem, while the correspondence (as yet unpublished save for a few letters) between Hofmannsthal and R. A. Schröder might also yield a clue. Schröder was associated equally with Hofmannsthal and Borchardt.

The problem may of course be of little account. On the other hand one thinks of Gundolf's involuntary part in the notes *Aufzeichnungen zu Reden in Skandinavien*, and reserves judgment. See Bernhard Blume, 'A Source of H.'s Aufz. zu Reden in Skand.', *Modern Language Notes*, LXX, no. 3 (1955), 157–65.

2 *Prosa*, III, 377.

3 Hofmannsthal's italics.

4 *Prosa*, III, 378.

5 *Antwort auf die Umfrage des 'Svenska Dagbladet'*, *Aufzeichnungen*, p. 365.

PAGE 86

1 Gordon Shepherd gives an excellent, brief account of the baleful effects of the Hungarian *Ausgleich* (1867, one year after Austria's ejection from the German Confederation) on imperial affairs generally. See *The Austrian Odyssey* (London, 1957), pp. 58–64.

2 See Richard Alewyn, 'Unendliches Gespräch', originally published in *Neue Rundschau*, III–IV (1954). The section on Hofmannsthal's correspondence with Bodenhausen is on pp. 561–6. Particularly relevant in the present context are Alewyn's remarks on pp. 563–4. This essay was subsequently reprinted in Alewyn, *Über Hugo von Hofmannsthal* (Göttingen, 1958).

3 *Briefe der Freundschaft*, pp. 144–5.

PAGE 87

1 *Briefe der Freundschaft*, pp. 149–50.

2 III, iii, lines 1912–28.

PAGE 88

1 Notably in *Grillparzers Politisches Vermächtnis* (1915), *Prosa*, III, 252–9; *Österreich im Spiegel seiner Dichtung* (1916), *Prosa*, III, 334–5; *Aufzeichnungen zu Reden in Skandinavien* (1916), *Prosa*, III, 360; *Zur Krisis des Burgtheaters* (1918), *Prosa*, III, 422; *Rede auf Grillparzer* (1922), *Prosa*, IV, 112–31. For Hofmannsthal's earlier views see, for example, *Notizen zu einem Grillparzer-Vortrag* (1903), *Prosa*, II, 85–93.

2 *Grillparzers Politisches Vermächtnis*, *Prosa*, III, 254. The last sentence makes an oddly clairvoyant impression. Hofmannsthal might almost have been writing his own literary epitaph for the benefit of those earlier critics who regretted that his lyrical strain, his 'weary violin' (Alfred Roeffler's phrase) was silenced so early.

3 *Prosa*, III, 254.

PAGE 89

1 *Op. cit.* pp. 254–5.

PAGE 90

1 Hofmannsthal had great admiration for this statesman. See *Österreichische Bibliothek*, *Prosa*, III, 279–80. This essay is discussed in chapter 4.

2 *Op. cit.* pp. 255–6.

3 Such a definition presages Hofmannsthal's *Buch der Freunde*

(1922–9) with its many Goethe-like aphorisms, which in their terse comprehensiveness are especially reminiscent of the late Goethe as revealed, particularly, in his conversations with Eckermann.

4   *Eugen Gottlob Winkler* (1936), in *Ahnung und Aussage* (Gütersloh, 1952), pp. 285–6.

PAGE 91

1   *Prosa*, III, 256.
2   *Ibid.*
3   *Hofmannsthal: Eine Rede* (Tübingen, 1954), pp. 12 and 14.

PAGE 92

1   *Prosa*, III, 257.
2   There is much evidence of this. However, two late essays are particularly indicative of it: *Das Schrifttum als geistiger Raum der Nation* (1927), *Prosa*, IV, 390–413; and *Wert und Ehre deutscher Sprache* (1927), *Prosa*, IV, 433–40. Both were written at a time when Hofmannsthal's forebodings about the future of Germany were well advanced. This latter fact is discussed in connection with *Der Turm*, chapters 7 and 8.
3   *Prosa*, III, 258.

PAGE 93

1   *Erinnerungen an Hofmannsthal und Briefe des Dichters* (Munich, 1948), p. 34.
2   Author's italics in order to convey force of *auch uns* in original.
3   *Prosa*, III, 259.

PAGE 94

1   *Bemerkungen*; undated and first printed in *Prosa*, IV, 101–6. Steiner (*Anmerkungen, Prosa*, IV, 522) says that the *Bemerkungen* date from 'not before 1920'. The above passage is on p. 105.
2   *Worte zum Gedächtnis des Prinzen Eugen, Prosa*, III, 204–14.

PAGE 95

1   *Prosa*, II, 269–70.
2   *Österreichische Bibliothek, Prosa*, III, 283.

PAGE 96

1   *Worte zum Gedächtnis des Prinzen Eugen, Prosa*, III, 213.

2 Hofmannsthal was writing several months after the outbreak of a war which seemed for the moment to have set at naught the achievements of Austria against Napoleon, her prowess in the Balkans, even the expulsion of the Turkish power.

PAGE 97

1 *Prosa*, III, 204–5.
2 *Op. cit.* p. 205.

PAGE 98

1 *Op. cit.* pp. 206–7.
2 *Op. cit.* p. 207.

PAGE 99

1 Hofmannsthal's essentially cool and sober attitude to his work is amply documented in his various correspondence. Two comments in letters to Richard Strauss exemplify this. In his letter of 16 September 1916 Hofmannsthal put his view with unusual sharpness: 'We both have good will, together with a serious and consistent approach—and that is worth more than the wretched "talent" which every scoundrel seems to be fitted out with these days.' In one of his last letters to Strauss (16 November 1928) Hofmannsthal defined his attitude thus: 'Clearheadedness, not vagueness, is the right atmosphere for artistic production.' See *Briefwechsel* (Zürich, 1952), pp. 349 and 675.
2 A thrust against rampant chauvinism in any quarter home or abroad. For further evidence of Hofmannsthal's views on this subject see *inter alia* two early wartime essays: *Boykott fremder Sprachen?* (1914), *Prosa*, III, 182–8; *Unsere Fremdwörter* (1914), *Prosa*, III, 195–203.
3 *Prosa*, III, 207–8.

PAGE 100

1 *Op. cit.* pp. 210–11.
2 *Op. cit.* p. 211.
3 *Ibid.*
4 *Ibid.*
5 *Op. cit.* pp. 211–12.

PAGE 101

1 *Op. cit.* p. 213.
2 *Op. cit.* pp. 213–14.

PAGE 102

1 The fact that Hofmannsthal was familiar with and admired Friedrich Naumann's *Mitteleuropa* is discussed in connection with *Österreich im Spiegel seiner Dichtung* and *Die Österreichische Idee*. See chapter 4.

2 See *Die Österreichische Idee*, *Prosa*, III, 401–6. This essay is discussed in the following chapter.

3 *Prosa*, III, 214.

PAGE 103

1 Schulausgabe (Frankfurt, 1952), pp. 93–4.

2 These points can scarcely be suggested in translation, especially when one considers the peculiarly rhythmic quality of Hofmannsthal's prose here. The original expressions are *Asien*; *wollte Herr sein*; *die Hand unseres gebenedeiten Königs*; *dieser einen Gestalt: Eugen*; *vermag ein Mann*.

3 Literally 'father of the country'.

PAGE 104

1 *Maria Theresia: zur zwei hundertsten Wiederkehr ihres Geburtstages* (1917), *Prosa*, III, 387–400.

2 In *Beruhigung*, for example: 'Wir sind Germanen gemütlich und brav....'

PAGE 105

1 *Prosa*, III, 387–8.

2 *Erinnerungen an Hofmannsthal und Briefe des Dichters*, pp. 48–9.

3 *Prosa*, III, 393–4.

PAGE 106

1 *Op. cit.* pp. 394–5.

PAGE 107

1 *Op. cit.* p. 388.

2 The original is 'Sie hatte Ehrfurcht vor dem Lebenden'. Again one recalls Albert Schweitzer—and his celebrated concept *Ehrfurcht vor dem Leben* (1915). See *Selections from Albert Schweitzer* (London, 1953), p. 48 for Schweitzer's description of how his concept came into being.

3 *Prosa*, III, 388–9.

PAGE 108

1   *Op. cit.* pp. 389–90.
2   *Op. cit.* p. 390.
3   *Ibid.*

PAGE 109

1   *Op. cit.* p. 396–7.
2   This particular point is discussed in more detail in connection with *Österreichische Bibliothek.* See chapter 4.

PAGE 110

1   *Aufzeichnungen*, p. 242. Also cited on p. 267, note 1 (p. 365).
2   'Erinnerungen an Hofmannsthal', in *Hofmannsthal: Die Gestalt des Dichters im Spiegel der Freunde*, p. 242.

PAGE 111

1   *Prosa*, III, 399.
2   *Prosa*, III, pp. 407–9.

PAGE 112

1   *Op. cit.* pp. 399–400.
2   The original phrase is *Baumeister des Lebendigen.* The elliptical sense-laden phrase, a combination of concrete (*Baumeister*) with abstract (*Lebendigen*), was a favourite device of the later Hofmannsthal for securing a striking effect in a few words. See, for example, *Der Turm* (1925), Act V, Sigismund's speech ending: 'dann wollen wir...zusammen die *Bürger des Neuen* sein'. Schulausgabe, p. 95, author's italics.
3   *Prosa*, III, 400.

PAGE 114

1   *Op. cit.* pp. 279–89.
2   *Op. cit.* pp. 333–49.
3   Hofmannsthal's purpose and artistic idealism in his connection with the Insel-Verlag are apparent from his letter of 12 March 1922 to S. Fischer. See *Neue Rundschau*, III–IV (1954), 396–400.
4   A good account of this venture is given by Felix Braun in 'Encounters with Hofmannsthal'. See *German Life and Letters*, vol. II, 1 (1948), 1–12, esp. pp. 3–4.
5   *Österreichische Bibliothek, Prosa*, III, 280.

PAGE 115

1 *Prosa*, III, 279–80.

2 *Op. cit.* p. 280. The original is given here in order to demonstrate the stylistic feature referred to above.

PAGE 116

1 *Prosa*, III, 281.

2 *Op. cit.* p. 282.

3 *Op. cit.* p. 287. An interesting development of this image occurs at a vital point in *Der Turm*, Act III. See p. 238.

PAGE 117

1 *Op. cit.* p. 286.

2 Act II, scene 14: conversation between Hans Karl and Helene Altenwyl. *Lustspiele*, II, 261.

3 *Prosa*, III, 407–9. The self-critical aspect of this is discussed by Requadt, 'Hofmannsthal', in *Deutsche Literatur im XX. Jahrhundert*, pp. 58–9.

PAGE 118

1 *Jäger* can of course mean both 'huntsman' and 'gamekeeper'.

2 *Prosa*, III, 287–8.

PAGE 119

1 Introduction (transl. by J. and T. Stern) to *Selected Prose* (of Hofmannsthal) (London, 1952), pp. xiii–xiv.

2 *Prosa*, III, 289. Felix Braun remarks that 'the series...was soon to be given up, on account of the scant interest shown it by readers in Germany'. See 'Encounters with Hofmannsthal', pp. 4–5.

3 Literally 'Austria as mirrored in its poetry'.

PAGE 120

1 *Prosa*, II, 332–3. The title means 'Letters of the man who returned'. Hofmannsthal writes in the first person, but in the guise of a much-travelled businessman who returns to Germany after an absence of eighteen years.

PAGE 121

1 *Prosa*, III, 345–6.

2 *Op. cit.* p. 346.

PAGE 122

1   *Ibid.*
2   *Op. cit.* p. 516.
3   *Prosa*, III, 521.
4   *Op. cit.* p. 344.
5   Naumann's *Mitteleuropa* had appeared in 1915. The subject and its detailed relevance here are huge. Robert Kann gives a very balanced survey and interpretation of Naumann's work as it affected Austria-Hungary. See *The Multi-National Empire* (New York, 1950), II, 246–54.

PAGE 123

1   T. Heuss, *Hofmannsthal: Eine Rede*, p. 7.
2   Letter of 15 January 1916. See *Briefe der Freundschaft*, p. 207. Heuss, doubtless writing from memory, gives the sense of Hofmannsthal's words and not an exact quotation.
3   See II, 71, 73, 97.
4   See II, 73; entry for 8 November 1915.
5   II, 149. Hofmannsthal also gave this lecture in Zürich a few months later. See letter to Borchardt, Easter Monday 1917, *Briefwechsel*, p. 123. See also editorial note, p. 234.
6   I am much indebted to the late Dr Ernst Flaum of Adelaide for a good deal of information about the *Urania*, especially its 'patriotic' wartime programme.

PAGE 124

1   *Prosa*, III, 347.
2   *Ibid.*
3   *Ibid.*
4   *Ibid.*

PAGE 125

1   *Ibid.*
2   *Ibid.*

PAGE 126

1   *Op. cit.* pp. 347–8.
2   *Op. cit.* p. 348.
3   *Ibid.*
4   A term which as a rule applies specifically to Austria-Hungary. It means 'one who favours a policy of equalization and/or com-

promise'. In effect this usually means some kind of Greater Austrian federation. See pp. 131–7 for an outline of some characteristic forms of *Ausgleichpolitik*.

5   *Prosa*, III, p. 348.

PAGE 127

1   *Ibid.*
2   *Ibid.*
3   *Listener*, XXXVII, no. 259 (12 June 1947), 895–7.
4   See also p. 105.

PAGE 128

1   *Tagebuch*, II, 161.
2   In the passage cited in the preceding note Redlich commented on 'the ruler' in the present century: 'What can he possibly understand about things when he does not even know the routine of administration—to say nothing of any knowledge of the material and spiritual needs of the masses? And what a part is played in all this by the court and royal household!'
3   *Prosa*, III, 348.

PAGE 129

1   *Briefe der Freundschaft*, p. 196.
2   *Prosa*, III, 348–9.
3   *Op. cit.* p. 349.
4   *Ibid.*

PAGE 130

1   *Ibid.*
2   First published (in French) as 'La vocation de l'Autriche', in *Revue Autrichienne* (Vienna) on 15 November 1917. The German version ('Die Österreichische Idee') was first published in the *Neue Zürcher Zeitung* on 2 December 1917.

PAGE 131

1   Rudolf Kiszling, *Erzherzog Franz Ferdinand von Österreich-Este* (Graz/Cologne, 1953), pp. 255–6.
2   'Plan for the establishment of the United States of Greater Austria. Manifesto prepared for his accession to the throne by Archduke Francis Ferdinand: a tragic, historic document.' Kiszling had access to Redlich's diaries while they were being prepared for

publication. He asserts (p. 342) that Eichhoff's draft was included in Redlich's entry for 15 October 1915. The published version does not include it, although in the entry for this date (II, 66) Redlich gives an account of a discussion with Milan Hodža, the Slovak leader, in which the plans of the late Archduke were discussed.

PAGE 132

1 George Franz, *Erzherzog Franz Ferdinand und die Pläne zur Reform der Habsburger Monarchie* (Vienna, 1943). Kiszling's more recent biography is extremely interesting and particularly well documented. It reads, however, very much like an official biography, and in its exclusively pro-Austrian, pro-Habsburg tone it tends decidedly to the black-versus-white technique. Redlich's diary is refreshingly frank about Francis Ferdinand and is often downright hostile to him without, however, overlooking his strength and executive ability. See entry for 26 June 1914, I, 234. Robert Kann gives an excellent character-study of Francis Ferdinand which takes into account his many conflicting qualities. See *The Multi-National Empire*, II, 187–97. Kann also draws an interesting distinction between Francis Ferdinand and the other 'lost hope' of Austria, Crown Prince Rudolf. See also character-study of Rudolf, pp. 181–7.

2 As a sign of the contemporary significance of such ideas it may be of interest to recall that amongst the accusations made against the Hungarian Cardinal Mindszenty in 1949 was that of having had a rendezvous with the Austrian Pretender, Otto von Habsburg, and of being involved in plans for a Bavaria–Austria–Hungary federation. That the idea is still alive is also indicated, for example, by the activities of the *Forschungsinstitut für Fragen des Donauraumes* in Vienna. The German (Hamburg) weekly journal *Der Spiegel* gave an interesting account of a lecture given to this Institute on 24 June 1955 by Professor Stefan Verosta, head of the International Law Division in the Austrian Foreign Ministry. See issue of 7 July 1955. At the time of writing Professor Verosta is Austrian Ambassador to Poland.

3 Gordon Shepherd gives an interesting brief summary of the ideas of Popovici and Renner. See *The Austrian Odyssey* (London, 1957), pp. 57–8.

4 Copies of this are not easily accessible. Richard Barkeley gives a

good account of Rudolf's ideas in his biography. See *The Road to Mayerling* (London, 1958), pp. 152–5, also pp. 78–84 for an account of Rudolf's earlier memorandum.

PAGE 133

1 Naumann uses this term in a markedly cultural-political way. In this context, therefore, *Mitteleuropa* (literally 'Middle' or 'Central' Europe) has dynamic, not to say emotive, overtones which make it difficult to render the concept adequately in any one English word. See H. C. Meyer, *'Mitteleuropa' in German Thought and Action: 1815–1945* (The Hague, 1955), for a detailed account of the evolution and aberrations of this concept.

2 *Mitteleuropa* (Berlin, 1915), pp. 25–6.

3 *The Multi-National Empire*, II, 254. Kann's sub-chapter (pp. 246–54) is specially relevant in the present context. It considers Naumann's theories with particular reference to the position of the Austrian Empire.

4 A prominent *Ausgleichpolitiker*, last Prime Minister under the imperial regime, and a very sympathetic character.

PAGE 135

1 *The Multi-National Empire*, II, 218–19. The lengthy quotation from Seipel's book is, as Kann notes, on p. 139 of *Nation und Staat*.

2 Hofmannsthal's relationship to Redlich has been noted at various points in the course of this chapter and the preceding one, notably in connection with the latter's *Politisches Tagebuch*. Further sources are the correspondence between Hofmannsthal and Carl Burckhardt (Frankfurt/Main, 1956), pp. 15, 153, 195–6, 228, 284, 287; and Hofmannsthal's letters to Redlich, selected and edited by Helmut Fiechtner. See *Wort in der Zeit*, VII (1956), 16–30. It is also relevant to note that Redlich served with Lammasch in the last imperial cabinet. See also p. 84, note 1 (p. 324).

PAGE 136

1 Probably the best guide to this difficult problem is Michael Hamburger's excellent and detailed study, 'Hofmannsthals Bibliothek: ein Bericht', *Euphorion*, LV (1961), 15–76.

2 Stockholm, 1947, pp. 297–300. The English translation, *The World of Yesterday*, appeared in London, 1943. The account

referred to is to be found on pp. 198–200. The episode is long and does not submit to any severe cutting (for quotation purposes) which would at the same time preserve its relevance.

PAGE 137

1 A good, non-tendentious account of this difficult subject is given by Robert Kann, *The Multi-National Empire*, II, 266–85. A. J. P. Taylor gives a detailed and very readable account in *The Habsburg Monarchy: 1809–1918* (London, 1948), pp. 241–51. Unfortunately, however, Taylor allows a certain tone of prejudice to come through. This, together with a tendency to resolve issues in terms of 'wisecracking' simplification, means that on occasion one has difficulty in treating his conclusions with complete seriousness. This is particularly unfortunate because Taylor's book is probably the best-known recent English work on the subject.

2 *Austrian War Government* (Yale University Press, 1929), p. 160. The name of the translator is not given.

3 *Prosa*, III, 401.

4 *Ibid.*

PAGE 138

1 *Ibid.*

2 *Ibid.*

3 This technique, a mixture of warning and encouraging idealism, had certainly been used earlier, notably in the memorial tribute to Prince Eugene (1914) and in the essay on Grillparzer (1915). See chapter 3.

4 *Briefe der Freundschaft*, pp. 236–7.

PAGE 139

1 *Prosa*, IV, 508–9.

2 *Prosa*, III, 402–3.

3 The original is given here in order to demonstrate the assertions that follow.

PAGE 140

1 *Prosa*, III, 403.

2 *Der Dichter und diese Zeit*, *Prosa*, II, 270.

3 In the sense used by Gerard Manley Hopkins.

PAGE 141

1   *Prosa*, III, 403.

PAGE 142

1   *Op. cit.* p. 404.
2   *Op. cit.* pp. 404–5. Author's italics.

PAGE 143

1   *Prosa*, IV, 132–41.

PAGE 144

1   *Prosa*, IV, 373.
2   Quoted on p. 104 of *Das Österreichbuch*, ed. Ernst Marboe (Vienna, 1948). The author has been unable to trace the original source of the quotation.
3   In *Gestalten und Mächte* (Zürich, 1954), pp. 195–222.

PAGE 145

1   *Prosa*, III, 405.

PAGE 146

1   *Ibid.*
2   *Prosa*, III, 282. The original is paraphrased here. The entire passage was quoted on p. 116.

PAGE 147

1   See above, p. 133, note 1 (p. 335).
2   *Prosa*, III, 406.
3   See pp. 2–4 for explanation of this term.
4   Perhaps the most meaningful translation would be 'divinely ordained society'.

PAGE 148

1   *Prosa*, III, 405.

PAGE 150

1   Letter to Carl Burckhardt, 11 May 1919. *Briefwechsel*, p. 14.
2   *Beethoven: Rede, gehalten an der Beethovenfeier des Lesezirkels Hottingen in Zürich* (1920). *Prosa*, IV, 29–30.
3   Letter to Carl Burckhardt, 12 February 1920. *Briefwechsel*, p. 28.

PAGE 151

1 This expression, which seems to have originated with Addison, came to Hofmannsthal by way of the aphorist Georg Christoph Lichtenberg (1742–99).

PAGE 152

1 *Erinnerungen an Hofmannsthal*, p. 9.

2 *Erinnerungen an Hofmannsthal*, pp. 11–12. Burckhardt's own account of the atmosphere in Vienna during the period from September 1918 to 1919 is a sensitive and restrained evocation. It forms a valuable background to the phase of Hofmannsthal's development under discussion here. It dates from 1931 (*Sonntagsblatt der Basler Nachrichten*) and is now in *Reden und Aufzeichnungen* (Zürich, 1952), pp. 109–33.

3 See chapter 1.

4 *Literaturgeschichte* (1948), p. 356. The 'one respect' in which Hofmannsthal differed from Grillparzer was of course the fact that the former was scarcely a taciturn observer!

PAGE 153

1 See Walter Naumann, 'Grillparzer und das spanische Drama', *DVjss*, III (1954), 345–72. This is an excellent brief study of Grillparzer's indebtedness to Calderón and (from p. 359 onwards) to Lope de Vega. Naumann treats the subject in a comprehensive perspective, which makes this essay a relevant and valuable background to the present study.

2 'Suburban' is a soulless approximation of *Vorstadt* in this particular sense. But there seems to be no equivalent English institution.

3 E. R. Curtius has summarized this development and its place in Hofmannsthal's artistic constitution with admirable clarity and sense of perspective. See 'George, Hofmannsthal und Calderón', in *Kritische Essays zur Europäischen Literatur* (Berne, 1950), pp. 183–4.

4 *Briefwechsel*, p. 16.

PAGE 154

1 *Literaturgeschichte* (1948), pp. 139–40.

2 Some account of the various versions of *Der Turm* and the history of its composition is to be found in the bibliographical note at the end of chapter 8.

3 *Literaturgeschichte Österreichs*, p. 472.

PAGE 155

1 Nadler's actual expression here is *Völkergedanke*. In this context the word has for an Austrian a particular meaning, which seems to have no precise equivalent in English. It has overtones which recall the kind of ideas discussed in chapter 4, of *Ausgleich*, many different ethnic and cultural groups living as one nation, etc.

2 *Literaturgeschichte Österreichs*, pp. 472–3.

3 Innsbruck, 1946.

4 'Hofmannsthals Lustspiele', *Akzente*, IV (1955), 369–83, p. 381. My inverted commas. *Volk* often bears—as here—associations of something unspoiled, vigorous, unsophisticated, as opposed to the anonymous, urbanized 'masses', the city-proletariat which is regarded as having lost these virtues as well as all other individual features.

5 See also chapter 9.

PAGE 156

1 This striking metaphor emphasizes Hofmannsthal's tendency in his later years to use cosmic imagery. This is, one assumes, a reflection of his effort to express himself, quite literally, *sub specie aeternitatis*.

2 Foreword to *Das Salzburger Große Welttheater*. See *Dramen*, III, 252.

3 'Begegnungen mit Hofmannsthal', in *Neue Rundschau*, III–IV (1954), 356.

PAGE 157

1 *Briefwechsel* (Zürich, 1952), p. 468.

2 One naturally thinks of Goethe's *Faust* here. But Calderón's Prologue in Heaven in *El gran teatro del mundo* did, after all, antedate Goethe by about a century and a half. However, the sequence of influence, Calderón–Goethe–Hofmannsthal, is very interesting. Three excellent essays relevant here are J. Sofer, *Die Welttheater Hofmannsthals und ihre Voraussetzungen bei Heraklit und Calderón* (Vienna, 1934); Stuart Atkins, 'Goethe, Calderón and *Faust, der Tragödie zweiter Teil*', in *Germanic Review*, XXVIII (1953); Heinz Wiemann, 'Gedanken zu Goethes Faust und Hofmannsthals Welttheater', in *Studies in Language and Literature presented to August Lodewyckx* (Melbourne, 1948).

3 *Dramen*, III, 257.

PAGE 158

1   *Op. cit.* p. 260.
2   *Op. cit.* p. 271.
3   *Op. cit.* p. 272.

PAGE 159

1   *Op. cit.* p. 273.
2   *Op. cit.* p. 282.

PAGE 162

1   There is an untranslatable overtone here (*Dramen*, III, 305) which gives the Beggar's words a terrifying sarcasm. *Ordnung* is a much stronger word than the English *order*. To most Germans and Austrians it bears automatic associations of the *Ordnungsamt* (office for compulsory registration), of the peculiarly German conception of unquestioned public order embodied in the phrase *Ordnung muß sein*, a phrase which can excuse any degree of bureaucratic obscurantism. The word is perhaps best summed up by the reaction of a native speaker of German on being asked what immediate response is evoked by *Ordnung*: 'Domestic order, certainly, as a child learns it; then—huge piles of documents and papers and official stamps and superior little officials and waiting-rooms full of depressed-looking people!' It is therefore, perhaps, not an exaggeration to say that the Beggar sees the hated *Ordnung* as something smug, complacent, unquestioned, smoothly functioning, and ignorant of individual needs. He now proposes to introduce his *own* interpretation of the word!

PAGE 163

1   This seems to be the technical term in English, according to the Forestry Office of New South Wales! But the German *Schlagrecht* carries a double sense, that of felling trees, and that of actually striking people—which the Beggar is about to do.

PAGE 166

1   *Dritter Brief aus Wien, Aufzeichnungen*, p. 296.

PAGE 167

1   Translation, evidently original, used by Allardyce Nicoll, *World Drama* (London, 1949), p. 226.
2   *Dritter Brief aus Wien*, p. 297. This letter was addressed to readers of the American journal *Dial*. The striking absence of metaphysical

complexity is surely no accident. The explanation certainly gains thereby. It might be noted in passing how odd it is that Hofmannsthal, who could evidently expose complex and subtle notions with such simplicity, should on occasion evoke such obscurity from some of his most friendly critics, especially in the matter of his later works. One thinks particularly of K. J. Naef's masterly and thorough study (Zürich, 1938), which is the most ambitious single work on Hofmannsthal that has appeared so far. Naef's work, of course, deservedly occupies a unique place in Hofmannsthal scholarship. But it is marred from time to time by an abstraction of thought which makes it difficult of access. Such criticism, moreover, tends to give a one-sided impression of metaphysical obscurity in Hofmannsthal himself. See also pp. 207–8, 248–9, 261.

3   *Ibid.* An excellent study of the Beggar's significance is Arnold Bergstraesser, 'The Holy Beggar. Religion and Society in Hofmannsthal's Great World Theatre', in *Germanic Review*, XX (1945), 261–86. Bergstraesser, however, seems to lean rather heavily on a 'pre-existential' interpretation of the Beggar in the neoplatonic sense (see also pp. 204, 207–8). This somewhat obscures the force of the play as defined by Requadt (see pp. 13–14) and Hohoff (see p. 155).

PAGE 168

1   Hofmannsthal's remarks on Count Harry Kessler's enthusiasm for Becher, Werfel and Däubler might seem to support this view. See letter of 28 April 1916 to Bodenhausen. *Briefe der Freundschaft*, pp. 213–14.

2   *Aufzeichnungen und Tagebücher aus dem Nachlaß: 1922–1929, Aufzeichnungen*, p. 202.

3   This is discussed in chapter 9. See also pp. 63–4, 68, 179–80, 194, 206.

PAGE 169

1   Curtius was probably referring to another work inspired by Calderón, the *Semiramis* fragments. Hofmannsthal worked intermittently on this for many years. See Curtius, *Kritische Essays*, pp. 194–8, and Edgar Hederer, *Hugo von Hofmannsthal* (Frankfurt/Main, 1960), pp. 325–34. For *Semiramis* fragments see *Dramen*, III, 447–55 (*Semiramis*, 1905 and 1908–9) and pp. 456–78 (*Die beiden Götter*, 1917–18).

2   *Kritische Essays*, p. 199.

PAGE 171

1   *Prosa*, III, 366–7. Bergstraesser takes up this idea of authority and remarks: 'Such representative service Hofmannsthal tried to render by "striving to integrate himself into the high order of being". [Bergstraesser's reference is Ernesta Calmberg, *Die Auffassung vom Beruf des Dichters im Weltbild deutscher Dichtung zwischen Nietzsche und Stefan George* (Diss. Tübingen, 1936), p. 135.] A fruit and also a witness of this striving is the Holy Beggar who, in the end, discovered and fulfilled his mission as exemplary figure in the play of life by penetrating to the authority above himself. This authority is beyond the arbitrary and fragmentary authority of any human being and therefore gives freedom to men. What Hofmannsthal experienced as his own basic issue he considered also the fundamental problem of our time: "to recognize authority above one's self is a sign of higher humanity".' [*Buch der Freunde, Aufzeichnungen*, p. 20.] 'The Holy Beggar,' pp. 285–6.

2   'To get round the money system is perhaps the sense of the moral and even religious revolution in which we seem to be engaged.' *Buch der Freunde, Aufzeichnungen*, p. 59.

3   *Prosa*, III, 380. Hofmannsthal's words seem to be a good example of a certain kind of 'conservative revolutionary' thought. Compare, for example, Ernst Jünger's note: 'In conversations about the horrors of these days the question often arises: where do all the murderers and torturers come from who were not seen amongst us before? But they were potentially there....Our common guilt leads to their being set free to harm men: in robbing ourselves of our ties [Bindungen] we released them. And so we must not complain if this evil affects us as individuals. "I am free, I am free"—that was the great theme for strong and beautiful spirits during a whole century or more. Yes: but in the same process quite different spirits were set free as well.' *Strahlungen* (1949), entry for 16 April 1943.

Bergstraesser, who also refers several times to Hofmannsthal's wartime addresses, notably *Reden in Skand.*, emphasizes the concept of law in *Große Welttheater*: 'Although Hofmannsthal presents the Beggar's intuition in terms of a mystical inner experience, he defines its effect as the union of law and individual which is freedom. This equation of freedom and personality is related with that of Goethe. Hofmannsthal interpreted Goethe's concept of law as the idea of the "purified personality" *wo das Ich Persönlichkeit wird* [where the ego becomes personality].' 'The Holy Beggar', p. 280. The reference is to *Reden in Skand.* See *Prosa*, III, 365.

4   *Prosa*, III, 381–2.

PAGE 172

1   'Hofmannsthal', in *Deutsche Lit. im XX. Jahrhundert*, p. 60.

2   *Modern German Lit.*, p. 251.

3   *Kritische Essays*, p. 182.

PAGE 173

1   *Dritter Brief aus Wien, Aufzeichnungen*, pp. 299–300. See also Carl Burckhardt's account of the 1922 performance, *Wissen und Leben* (Zürich), XVI (1922–3), 91–2. One notes how even the European citizen could be a chauvinist on occasion. The coupling of French-men with Berliners as foreigners is particularly delightful!

2   This element was treated very effectively by Curtius, *Kritische Essays*, pp. 191–2. Bergstraesser also emphasizes this aspect: 'Within the monumental structure of the baroque stage, the representatives of mankind perform the play of life, between Time and Eternity, first as social drama, then as a Dance of Death, finally as a scene played before the judgment seat of the Master.' In a footnote he adds: 'To Calderón life is a test of man's obedience, to Hofmannsthal life is a test of man's freedom. Because the meaning of freedom reveals itself to Hofmannsthal through the process of life, his understanding comes closer to that of Goethe.' 'The Holy Beggar', p. 261. This seems to be a precise summary of the difference between Hofmannsthal and Calderón.

PAGE 174

1   *Jedermann.* Mary Gilbert has noted an interesting stylistic point of which this is an example. See Introduction to *Hofmannsthal: Selected Essays* (Oxford, 1955), p. 15. Dr Gilbert comments on the final phase of Hofmannsthal's prose style as follows: 'Finally one of the most noteworthy features of this phase is the poet's avoidance of the first person, and the resultant use of the passive mood or paraphrase in its stead.' In a footnote Dr Gilbert adds: 'But whereas in the earlier period he could trust himself and his audience (*Ich; Sie*), later he talks of *Wir*, giving up his identity and

preferring the anonymous form, but without establishing a true communion.' This, it would seem, comes very close to the heart of the matter. The argument might be taken further. It could be said that having felt the firm ground of pre-1914 Europe slip from under his feet (however much he personally was aware of signs and portents), he tried in his last phase to write oracularly. This is not meant in any vainglorious sense. Hofmannsthal was merely trying to point a way, speak of an ideal, interpret a situation, in a world of chaos. He tried to do this in an impersonal way, as if what he said and wrote were self-evident and, as it were, in the atmosphere.

2   *Prosa*, IV, 269–70. Erika Brecht has told how Hofmannsthal obtained permission from Archbishop Rieder of Salzburg. The Archbishop's answer was, it seems, in the best tradition of 'Church-people-drama': 'Why should not *Frau Welt* make her appearance in church and sing too? After all, David danced before the Ark of the Covenant.' *Erinnerungen an Hofmannsthal*, p. 57. *Frau Welt* is a traditional figure representing secular, earthly things.

PAGE 175

1   *Dritter Brief aus Wien*, pp. 295–6. Hofmannsthal does not refer to the 'progressive' activities of Joseph II. Presumably he was generalizing for the benefit of his overseas readers.

PAGE 177

1   *Dramen*, III, 318.

2   See pp. 60–1.

3   *Prosa*, III, 353. The Dance of Death seems to have fascinated Hofmannsthal from an early age. Its part in the structure of *Der Tor und der Tod* (1893) is well known. It is mentioned directly, moreover, in the closing lines of *Prolog zu 'Der Tor und der Tod'*, *Gedichte und Lyrische Dramen*, 1st ed., p. 178. There is also, for example, a diary entry of 1893, which refers to Abraham a Sancta Clara's *Mercks Wien* (1679) and then, in a striking quotation from Wilhelm Scherer, to the Dance of Death. See *Tagebuchblatt, Aufzeichnungen*, p. 99.

4   *Dritter Brief*, p. 303.

PAGE 178

1   The structure of Hofmannsthal's baroque stage with its three levels helps here, of course. See also Hofmannsthal's remarks on the

staging (in the Collegienkirche, Salzburg) for the first performance, *Dritter Brief*, p. 303. Bergstraesser says: 'the stage represents
the universe.... The plot of the drama develops on the two levels
of the eternal and the temporal, or, as Calderón says, on the level
of truth and the level of semblance.' 'The Holy Beggar', p. 262.

PAGE 179

1 Might be translated as 'pertness, cheekiness', etc.
2 With whom he is related: for an account of the development of the
gracioso, notably in the plays of Lope, Calderón and Rojas Zorrilla,
see Gerald Brenan, *The Literature of the Spanish People* (Cambridge, 1951), pp. 205, 279, 312.
3 'The Holy Beggar', p. 264.

PAGE 181

1 *Kritische Essays*, p. 199.

PAGE 182

1 'The Holy Beggar', p. 283. The article by Andrian is in *Hochland*,
xx (Nov. 1922), 177–80. The final quotation is from K. J. Naef,
Hofmannsthals Wesen und Werk (Zürich, 1938), p. 212.
2 Curtius, *Kritische Essays*, p. 182. See p. 172 of this study.

PAGE 184

1 'Hofmannsthal', *Neue Rundschau*, III–IV (1954), 594–6. Schneider
refers of course to the version of 1927, discussed in chapter 8. His
very general remarks refer to the overall content and ethical aim of
Der Turm. They can thus be applied equally to the first version, at
present under consideration, despite the 'optimistic' ending which
contrasts with the 'pessimistic' ending of the second version.
2 As Schneider uses it here this expression has overtones of such
biblical usages as 'the Word was made flesh', etc. Schneider thus
implies an almost Messianic validity for Hofmannsthal in this play.
3 A list of all fragments, versions and editions of *Der Turm* will be
found in the bibliographical note at the end of chapter 8.
4 Letter to Hermann Bahr, *Dramen*, III, 503.

PAGE 185

1 *Dramen*, III, 503. See also pp. 339–438 of the same volume for all
fragments.
2 *Erinnerungen an Hofmannsthal*.

3   Also cited by Curtius, *Kritische Essays*, p. 187.

4   *Erinnerungen an Hofmannsthal*, p. 41.

5   *World Drama* (London, 1949), p. 235.

6   A good modern translation of the play is that by Roy Campbell, *The Classic Theatre*, ed. Eric Bentley (New York, 1959), III, 407–80.

PAGE 186

1   *Op. cit.* p. 236.

2   *Kritische Essays*, pp. 194–5. Another good account of the cave symbol is given by Max Kommerell, 'Die Höhle' and 'In Felle gekleidet', in *Beiträge zu einem deutschen Calderón*, 2 vols. (Frankfurt/Main, 1946). These items are in I, 49–56.

3   For the idea underlying his play, Calderón drew on the past. The actual fable by means of which he expressed it was, however, his own invention. This fact is also noted by Requadt. See p. 238.

4   An excellent annotated synopsis of Calderón's play is given in Walter Naumann's 'Grillparzer und das spanische Drama', *DVjss*, III (1954), 353–4.

PAGE 187

1   *Ad me ipsum, Aufzeichnungen*, p. 242.

2   *Ad me ipsum*, p. 233.

3   *Hofmannsthal und Goethe* (Hameln, 1947), pp. 76–7.

PAGE 188

1   Schulausgabe, p. 85. See bibliographical note at the end of chapter 8, pp. 298–302.

2   He spent at least three years of his reign (A.D. 172–5) at the Pannonian frontier fortress of Carnuntum on the Danube, a few miles below Vienna, and part of the *Meditations* was written there.

PAGE 189

1   For the relevance to *Der Turm* of Julian the Apostate see discussion of Act V, chapter 7.

PAGE 190

1   Doubtless a reminiscence of the heir-apparent to the throne of Austria-Hungary, Archduke Francis Ferdinand, assassinated at Sarajevo, 28 June 1914.

PAGE 191

1   Schulausgabe, p. 67.

PAGE 192

1   See also pp. 249 and 205, note 3 (p. 350).

PAGE 193

1   Schulausgabe, p. 14.
2   *Op. cit.* pp. 100–1.
3   *Erinnerungen an Hofmannsthal*, p. 18. Full text of letter in *Brief-wechsel*, p. 40.

PAGE 194

1   *Op. cit.* p. 19.
2   *Op. cit.* p. 20. See also *Briefwechsel*, p. 246.
3   *Aufzeichnungen*, p. 40.

PAGE 195

1   *Zum Deutschen Lesebuch: Gedenktafeln, Prosa*, IV, 387–8.

PAGE 196

1   *Hanswurst* (lit. Jack Sausage) is a traditional stock figure of fun in the German folk-theatre. He is related to the English Jack Pudding, the Low German Pickelhering, etc. He is usually a clumsy, crude, greedy peasant. He first appears in the sixteenth century, in, for example, Brant's *Narrenschiff* (1494), Luther, Hans Sachs, Fischart's *Geschichtklitterung* (1575), and by 1573 he is an established stage-figure. In later periods he appears, for example, in the *Possen* (farces) of the young Goethe and, somewhat modified, in Keller's *Zürcher Novellen*. The circus *dummer August* (stupid Augustus) is another form of the same figure. See *Trübners Deutsches Wörter-buch* (Berlin, 1939), III, 327.
2   *Die Wiener Oper*, p. 37. It is perhaps appropriate to note here that various works of Otto Rommel have proved invaluable, not only in the present limited instance, but in arriving at some idea of the background and even the atmosphere of *Der Turm*. Specially important in this respect was Rommel's indispensable and monu-mental *Die Alt-Wiener Volkskömodie. Ihre Geschichte vom barocken Welt-Theater bis zum Tode Nestroys* (Vienna, 1952). See also

C. P. Magill, 'A New History of the Viennese Popular Theatre', in *German Life and Letters*, VII (1953-4), 11-16. This is an admirable full-length review of Rommel's book.

PAGE 198

1 A relevant comparison is also provided by the fragment *Der Priesterzögling* — *Monarchia Solipsorum*, *Dramen*, III, 491-3.

2 This opinion is entirely personal, but has been encouraged by the revolutionary productions (since 1951) of *Parsifal* at Bayreuth under the direction of Wieland Wagner. Wagner has supported his methods and interpretation in a series of essays, vignettes, etc.— notably the *Schema* which appeared in the festival programme, 1952, Heft 7, pp. 8-9.

3 In a letter of 5 March 1928 Burckhardt describes how one of his students attended the first performance of *Der Turm* (second version). He was apparently impressed by Sigismund, Julian and Olivier. But the King was 'too Byzantine'! See *Briefwechsel*, p. 279. Hofmannsthal's interest in the Byzantine empire can be traced back at least as far as *Der Kaiser und die Hexe* (1897). Interesting in this connection is his work during the last decade of his life on a *Phokas* drama (Phocas was Byzantine emperor, A.D. 602-10), for which Calderón was again the inspiration. Hofmannsthal's notes remain unpublished, but are discussed by Hederer, *Hofmannsthal*, pp. 325-6.

   There is also a late reference to Byzantium in *Ad me ipsum* ('Autobiographical, IX, 28') which is enigmatic and interesting, especially as regards Hofmannsthal's thoughts on the decline and fall of Europe, together with her possible renaissance: 'Early effect of that picture: Emperor Maximilian talking to eight of his captains—in their own language. Preoccupation with history. Early (14-17), Buckle: ideas and events in their connection with each other. Alongside this, going to the sources: the *Monumenta Germaniae*, Gibbon, Duncker's *Geschichte des Altertums*, Wattenbach's *Deutschlands Geschichtsquellen*. Significance of Byzantium— artistic plans arising from this.' See *Aufzeichnungen*, p. 243.

4 Some very specific influences—*Egmont*, *Caspar Hauser*, etc., are discussed in chapters 7 and 8 in connection with the text itself.

5 *Erinnerungen an Hofmannsthal*, p. 49. See also, for example, *Shakespeares Könige und große Herren* (1905), *Prosa*, II, 147-74; *Shakespeare und Wir* (1916), *Prosa*, III, 324-32.

PAGE 199

1 The writer was under the impression that this description was almost proverbial, but has been unable to trace its origin.

PAGE 200

1 See *Horribilicribrifax* (Halle, 1883), p. 9, and Schulausgabe, p. 4.

PAGE 201

1 Schulausgabe, p. 5.
2 Very freely translated in an attempt to preserve the racy spirit of the original. 'Morning-stars' (*Morgensterne*) has probably lost its warlike meaning in modern English. A weapon of this name was actually a kind of flail, with a star-like ball of metal at the end of a chain. But it has been suggested that Hofmannsthal had in mind the staff with a ball of wood on its end, studded with spikes. This gave an effect oddly reminiscent of the rising sun!
3 Schulausgabe, p. 5.
4 Evidence of this is plentiful and various. There can, for example (in vastly different circumstances), be few more exciting and ominous uses of this symbol than that in Gustav Frenssen's *Jörn Uhl* (1901), when a farm-labourer, returning late at night to the *Uhl*, sees the 'comb of the red cock' as the fatal and decisive fire breaks out.

PAGE 202

1 Compare *Horrib*. pp. 77–8.
2 Schulausgabe, p. 7.
3 *Op. cit.* p. 11.

PAGE 203

1 *Op. cit.* p. 12.
2 *Ibid.*

PAGE 204

1 The significance of neoplatonism to Hofmannsthal and especially the influence of Gregory of Nyssa's (A.D. 331–94) *Vita Moses* on him has been shown by Walther Brecht, 'Hofmannsthals "Ad me ipsum" und seine Bedeutung', *Jahrbuch des Freien Deutschen Hochstifts* (1930), pp. 319–53. In a particularly relevant footnote (p. 352) Brecht remarks: 'It would not be difficult to show that Hofmannsthal's whole art and thought had a neoplatonic basis. In the present context I will only draw attention to a telling note...in

Ad me ipsum: "that youthful experience (from about 16 to 22) that all the present beauty in nature seemed only to point back to something earlier and quite inaccessible. Compare here the quotation from Gregory of Nyssa, *Life of Moses* in Burdach, p. 400." (This is the motto of *Ad me ipsum*.) In like manner Hofmannsthal writes in *Raoul Richter, 1896*: "All beauty seemed only to remind me of something which had gone before."...In other respects—in art as in life—the neoplatonic anamnesis was for him familiar and very much alive; and he took it very seriously.' The extract from *Raoul Richter, 1896* is in *Prosa*, III, 170. The rather controversial place of neoplatonism in Hofmannsthal's work is noted later in the present chapter. An excellent and brief outline of neoplatonism is that in Jules Lebreton and Jacques Zeiller, *The History of the Primitive Church*, 4 vols., transl. Ernest Messenger (London, 1948), III, 720–9. For Gregory of Nyssa, see IV, 894–6, 898–9.

2 13 October 1922. *Briefwechsel*, p. 99.

PAGE 205

1 Especially in the historical dramas, and in *König Ottokars Glück und Ende* in particular. This, together with the use of eloquent silence noted above, was of course a heritage from the tradition of eloquent—even grandiloquent—mime and tableau in the baroque spectacle-theatre. This elaborate tradition was modified but continued in the characteristic verse-drama of the nineteenth century. The Vienna *Burgtheater* under Heinrich Laube (1849–67) and Franz Dingelstedt (1870–81) was a stronghold of this somewhat florid neo-classical style of performance and declamation.

2 Schulausgabe, p. 11.

3 Cf. Sigismund's words (later in the play, after his return to the tower) to the scheming Julian, whose ambitions are wholly materialistic and who is the quintessence of *Realpolitik*: '*Julian.* Your soul had to suffer in order to be uplifted—everything else was vain and empty. *Sigismund.* You have taught me how to grasp that. All is vanity save speech between spirit and spirit. *Julian.* I gave sustenance to your spirit; for I begot it in you. I created you out of yourself, pouring my innermost being into you. *Sigismund.* But now I, your begotten creature, stand above my begetter. When I lie in solitude, my spirit soars where yours can never go' (p. 69). The detailed implications of this are discussed later in connection with Act IV.

1 *Jahrbuch*, pp. 344–5. 'Cultural problem' (*Kulturfrage*) has a wider implication in German than in English. It often includes religious matters generally. This meaning is obvious in the term *Kulturkampf*. *Kulturfragen*, denoting relations between church and state, was used, for example, by President Schärf of Austria in his inaugural address in 1957.

2 *Op. cit.* p. 345.

3 Hofmannsthal was for thirty years (from 1899) a good friend of Jakob Wassermann (1873–1934). Wassermann gave an account of this productive camaraderie in *Hofmannsthal der Freund* (Berlin, 1930). Wassermann describes (p. 26) how they read their works to each other and that in Altaussee (Styria) after 1906: 'Every year for 23 years I used to see him from August or September until late autumn, after the war almost daily, right into December.' Wassermann's *Caspar Hauser oder die Trägheit des Herzens* appeared in 1908 and was well known to Hofmannsthal whose *Der Gefangene* (see bibliographical note, p. 298) had appeared a year previously. The story is another reading of the basic situation of Calderón's *La vida es sueño*. Wassermann's novel is historical in that it relates the tale of the boy who appeared in Nürnberg in 1828. He could neither speak nor walk. Wassermann saw this as an almost mythical symbol of innocence in an hostile world (cf. Martini's comment: 'symbol of oppressed innocence in a wicked world', *Literaturgeschichte*, p. 491). The novel has the dark tower motive, the motive of the murderous dynasty, and above all the faith in the regenerative power of pure human innocence of spirit. Hofmannsthal's familiarity with the Caspar Hauser tale is further substantiated in an interesting manner. There is an allusion to it in *Der Dichter und diese Zeit* (1906), *Prosa*, II, 276 and also in *Vorspiel für ein Puppentheater* (1906), *Dramen*, II, 496–7, where the poet says *ad spectatores*: 'Now you will hear the click of the dice, now the innocent prisoner rattling his chains; Caspar Hauser will appear, the mysterious orphan.' The proximity in this extract of an innocent prisoner in chains and the figure of Caspar Hauser is scarcely a coincidence. Hofmannsthal also refers to P. J. A. Feuerbach's treatise on Caspar Hauser (*Beispiel eines Verbrechens am Seelenleben eines Menschen*, 1832) in his *Gedenktafeln* for the 2nd ed. (1926) of the *Deutsches Lesebuch*, *Prosa*, IV, 371.

PAGE 207

1 *Jahrbuch*, p. 345.

2 'Hofmannsthals Lustspiele', *Akzente*, IV (1955), 369. Sympathy with Hohoff's view, however, should not mean that one denies the importance of these fragments in the development of Hofmannsthal's views. Various critics have regarded the *Semiramis* fragments, for example, as a forerunner of *Der Turm* and especially of the problems embodied in Sigismund and the Children's King. See especially Hederer, *Hofmannsthal*, pp. 333–4. See also p. 169, note 1 (p. 341). In comparable fashion, although in this case there is no explicit comparison with *Der Turm*, Hederer (pp. 325–6) indicates how in the *Phokas* fragment Hofmannsthal deals with the essential problems of monarchy. See also p. 198, note 3 (p. 348).

3 'Bemerkung zu "Ad me ipsum"', *Neue Rundschau*, III–IV (1954), 381.

PAGE 208

1 Hohoff, p. 369.

2 *Ibid.* He interprets the significance of Hofmannsthal's remark in a rather narrow sense, limiting himself to the comedies. This does not invalidate the significance of the remarks themselves.

3 See, for example, letter of 28 October 1922, *Briefwechsel*, p. 104: 'It was exceedingly fortunate for me that you crossed my path at this point in my life. In May 1918 Eberhart Bodenhausen died. He was the most human and therefore the strongest character in my whole circle of acquaintance. Six months later I made your acquaintance.'

PAGE 209

1 *Briefwechsel*, p. 227. Burckhardt was about to marry and had written to Hofmannsthal, mentioning the fact that his future wife was a Catholic (p. 225). Hofmannsthal's positive comment on this led him to the larger point made in the above extract.

2 *Aufzeichnungen*, p. 233. See also p. 187.

3 The first of Hebbel's three stages in the ideal tragedy: (1) It can be so; (2) it is so; (3) it *must* be so.

PAGE 210

1 See chapter 1, pp. 19–20.

2 Schulausgabe, p. 18. Hofmannsthal's stage-direction ('Julian

cannot help smiling...') is a good example of his technique of visually suggestive drama and of his psychological accuracy: susceptibility to compliments from any quarter is an integral part of the kind of unstable leader-personality represented by Julian.

Translation of *Zweifel am Höchsten* ('You doubt the Supreme Being') presents a problem. It can mean any or all the following: God, the highest principles in life, even the royal command of Basilius.

PAGE 211

1 'Hofmannsthal', p. 60.

2 *Prosa*, III, 398.

3 These are all very evocative words which have no exact English equivalent and flavour. Their meaning embraces inefficiency, sluttishness, black-marketeering, general dishonesty, slackness, etc.

PAGE 212

1 Schulausgabe, p. 15. Translation cannot hope to reproduce the unique colour and flavour here. It can only try to create some atmosphere of quick-tongued and ungrammatical raciness! Curiously enough Hofmannsthal himself has been accused of using *Judendeutsch* (Jewish German). Theodor Rall observed with quite unconscious humour: 'On the other hand the Germanism of these works is not quite so unrestricted as Hofmannsthal's Catholicism and his Austrianism. Sometimes he struggles in vain against his own destiny. "From the weariness of long forgotten peoples vainly would I liberate my eyelids [Lidern]." Not from his songs [Liedern] either. For amid all the verbal glitter and in spite of all the severe verbal discipline, an indefinable something reminds us, and his word order reminds us too, of that race which Hofmannsthal would have liked to forget. Read the sentence quoted above and then continue: "nor ward off from my frightened soul the silent falling of distant stars." It is probably in order to bring the verb forward once or twice—that is, after all, only poetic licence. But when it is repeated a hundred times over, as with our poet, then it is original sin. [There is an untranslatable gibe here. *Erbsünde* means original sin but also hereditary sin, i.e. of his race.] And it is the same with the unending series of rhetorical questions: "To what end are these built?...What use is all this to us?"' *Katholisches Schrifttum Gestern und Heute* (Cologne and Einsiedeln, 1936), pp. 64–5.

Quite apart from Rall's pedantic tone and solidly *bieder* pun, the criticism demonstrates the sort of insentience which would blame the Swabian Schiller for rhyming *frei* with *treu*. It would perhaps be taking things too seriously to suggest that Rall's comments have traces of *Deutsches Christtum* in them. It is more likely that after something of a eulogy of Hofmannsthal, Rall thought it wise to make a dutiful genuflection in the direction of the party throne. The book dates, after all, from 1936. The excerpts from *Manche freilich* ...and *Ballade des äußeren Lebens* are translated in order to give some idea of Rall's criticism. But it is impossible to convey the grammatical sense of his remarks as they are based wholly on orthodox German as opposed to Yiddish-German word-order.

PAGE 214

1   Schulausgabe, pp. 25–6.

PAGE 215

1   *Op. cit.* pp. 26–7.
2   The epitaph on Grimmelshausen's tomb comes to mind: 'Deutsch Volk belogen und betrogen / Im Streit um hohes Ideal / Durch Not und Elend durchgezogen / Aus Wunden blutend ohne Zahl / Einfältgen Herzens, tief verwildert, / Berührt doch von der Muse Kuß / Deutsch Volk Du warst, den er geschildert / Der arme Simplicissimus.' (German people, lied to and deceived in the struggle for a high ideal, dragged through want and misery, bleeding from countless wounds, simple of heart, thrown into deep confusion, yet touched by the muse's kiss, it was you whom he described—poor Simplicissimus.)
3   Hofmannsthal's personal attitude is difficult to assess, in so far as it is of importance in this study. The unreliable Rall observes: 'He did not really try to deny his Jewish ancestry, which incidentally amounted to only a quarter of his genetical constitution. But he did try to dismiss it as insignificant.' *Katholisches Schrifttum*, p. 64. One notes here the characteristic jargon of race-theory and suspends judgment. Rall may be right, however, if not altogether for the right reason. There is, as far as the present writer is aware, no autobiographical reference on Hofmannsthal's part to the Jews or to his own partly Jewish ancestry. The famous *Ganz vergessener Völker Müdigkeiten* scarcely signifies here. One can point to Hofmannsthal's lifelong friendship with Rudolf Borchardt, Richard

354

Beer-Hofmann and Artur Schnitzler—all of Jewish birth—and, of
course, to his collaboration over a quarter of a century with Max
Reinhardt. These facts do not seem to indicate any anti-Jewish
feeling on Hofmannsthal's part.

A further point of interest is the fact that Hofmannsthal must have
been familiar with the controlled (and largely theoretical) anti-
Semitism of Karl Lueger, *Oberbürgermeister* of Vienna from 1897
until his death in 1911. Apart, however, from two more or less
incidental references to Lueger (in *Gärten*, 1906, *Prosa*, II, 202–11,
and in *Aufbauen, nicht einreißen*, 1915, *Prosa*, III, 234–41), Hofmannsthal does not seem to have expressed any opinion of him.

All the above facts seem to indicate that the matter was not a
problem for Hofmannsthal, and that he had no particular feelings
on the subject.

PAGE 216

1 One is reminded in this passage of the apparently symbolical
visions of an apocalypse in some pre-war Expressionists, visions
subsequently realized many times over, for example Trakl's
Grodek. But the idea also recalls Shakespeare's use of supernatural
omen in, for example, *Julius Caesar*, *Macbeth*, and *Hamlet*.
2 Schulausgabe, p. 69.
3 *Op. cit.* p. 68.

PAGE 220

1 *Op. cit.* pp. 29–30.

PAGE 221

1 *Op. cit.* p. 31.
2 It is worth noting that this and other features of the Grand Almoner's
mode of speech have been noted as characteristic of Guevara.
James Fitzmaurice Kelly, for example, observes: 'He was...
deliberately eloquent and he drops with astonishing facility into
the declamatory style....He has many notes; is sarcastic, ironical,
dignified, confiding. He sometimes has a flight of stately phrasing.
He has, it is true, a tiresome trick of talking as if he were in the pulpit,
and his oleaginous eloquence is not always attractive...like
Seneca, he resorts to violent antithesis and three-piled metaphor.'
A New History of Spanish Literature (Oxford, 1926), p. 190.
There is no Grand Almoner in *La vida es sueño*. It is therefore

possible that in creating him, Hofmannsthal was influenced, consciously or unconsciously, in style as well as in content, by Bishop Guevara. Guevara, incidentally, was Commissioner of the Inquisition at Valencia and Granada prior to becoming a bishop. This may have been in part a reason for the Almoner's original title of Grand Inquisitor (see pp. 226–7), as the 'spirit' of Guevara certainly plays a considerable part in this scene.

3 Schulausgabe, p. 31.

PAGE 222

1 *Ibid.*

2 See p. 221, note 2 above.

3 *Op. cit.* p. 31. Translation is rather free here in order to try to suggest something of the Almoner's alliterative and aphoristic brevity (*ʒu reiten anstatt ʒu raten*).

PAGE 223

1 *Op. cit.* pp. 31–2.

PAGE 224

1 *Op. cit.* p. 34.

PAGE 225

1 Obviously the kind of thing which was in Hofmannsthal's mind when he wrote the letter to *Dial* (see also pp. 174–5, 167, note 2 (p. 340)): 'These figures, each one by itself in a niche surrounded by Gothic foliation, belong to that world which we encounter in Flemish and northern French tapestries of the fifteenth century . . . .' *Aufʒeichnungen*, p. 295. Hofmannsthal refers here to single figures —statuary in niches—as prototypes of his single figures in *Große Welttheater*. The principle, style and milieu are comparable, however.

PAGE 226

1 This might be compared with Hebbel's equally marked technique in the closing lines of a scene. With the action of a scene over, he often throws in a brief statement which forces it on again, as the mind leaps forward to the consequence: e.g. *Herodes und Mariamne*, Act II, scene 7: '*Alexandra*. The King! *Joseph*. In the city? *Alexandra*. Already in the castle.'

2 Here, as elsewhere in the drama, Anton's miming byplay is reminiscent of Leporello in Mozart's *Don Giovanni*. Not only have

the two characters an obviously common ancestry, but the traditional (Viennese) manner of portraying Leporello emphasizes the mime—as, for example, in his humorous behaviour after the Don's disappearance in flames.

3   13 October 1922. *Briefwechsel*, pp. 98–9.

1   The origin of this phrase is not biblical despite its obvious associations. In the *Buch der Freunde* there is the following entry which throws light on Hofmannsthal's idea in a surprising manner: 'On his deathbed Georg Büchner had in his delirium spasmodic revolutionary visions. In the pauses between them he was heard saying in a solemn voice: "We do not have too much pain but too little, for by pain we come to God. We are death, dust and ashes—how can we complain?"' *Aufzeichnungen*, p. 33.

1   Schulausgabe, p. 45.

1   *Op. cit.* p. 47. There is a striking resemblance between Hofmannsthal's setting and Philip II's suite in the Escorial. See Garrett Mattingly, *The Defeat of the Spanish Armada* (Pelican, 1962), pp. 89–90. This 'connection' is discussed in the following paragraphs.

1   *Op. cit.* p. 52.
2   See Trübner (Berlin, 1956), VII, 76–8. *Trabanten* were originally foot-soldiers. The life-guard of Maximilian I were known as *Trabanten* and Charles V appeared at the Augsburger Reichstag in 1530 with a noble retinue of 300 *Trabanten*. Normally the word can mean followers in good and bad ('hangers-on') senses.

1   *Op. cit.* p. 47.
2   Letter of 13 October 1922. *Briefwechsel*, p. 98.

1   It is easy to forget this point. Hofmannsthal's later plays are mainly depictions and discussions of ideas. This should not blind the reader to an important fact: that these dramas were written as plays for the theatre. As discussed above in various places, they were created out of a live and complex tradition. In this tradition

the visual-mimetic element was of almost equal importance with the spoken word. The non-German critic has few opportunities to see Hofmannsthal's dramas. Points which are obscure in the study are often clarified as soon as the action is *seen* in the theatre. Hofmannsthal was a skilled exponent of stagecraft. His preoccupation with this aspect (a *leitmotif* of his correspondence over a quarter of a century with Richard Strauss) proves that he was a man of the theatre at all times. Curt Hohoff discussed this aspect of Hofmannsthal in a very interesting, if somewhat apologistic manner. See 'Hofmannsthals Lustspiele', *op. cit.* 369–83.

2 *Briefwechsel*, pp. 98–9.

3 *Hamlet* is a very good instance. The function of *Wallensteins Lager*, and the early scenes of *Egmont* preceding Egmont's dramatic entrance during Act II, scene 1, are further comparable illustrations of this technique.

PAGE 234

1 Schulausgabe, p. 50. Translation hardly gives the sinister force of 'Verstellung'.

2 *Op. cit.* p. 49.

PAGE 235

1 Hofmannsthal did have a particular affection for *Egmont* during this period of his life. See chapter 8.

2 Schulausgabe, p. 50.

PAGE 236

1 *On Some Problems in the Study of Goethe's Imagery.* Bulletin of the M.H.R.A., no. 21, 1949 (England), pp. 16–17.

PAGE 237

1 Letter to Burckhardt, 9 October 1923. *Briefwechsel*, p. 140. See also p. 72.

PAGE 238

1 Schulausgabe, p. 50. See also p. 116, note 3, of this study.

2 Requadt's comparison of Sigismund with the Madman (*Das Kleine Welttheater*, 1897) indicates a significant line in Hofmannsthal's development.

3 'Sprachverleugnung und Mantelsymbolik im Werke Hofmannsthals', *DVjss*, II (1955), 276–7.

PAGE 239

1   The image itself seems to be characteristic of Hofmannsthal's baroque tradition. It is picturesque, even somewhat exaggeratedly colourful, and has a tone of cruel, physical hurt.

2   *Sprachverleugnung*, p. 277.

3   Schulausgabe, p. 52.

PAGE 240

1   'Bauer und Diener', in *Beiträge zu einem deutschen Calderón*, I, 104. Author's italics, in order to convey emphasis implicit in original.

2   *Sprachverleugnung*, pp. 277–8. For Requadt's quotation from the *Buch der Freunde*, see *Aufzeichnungen*, p. 78.

3   This again is in the tradition of Maria Theresia, so much admired by Hofmannsthal. No less a *Grand Seigneur* than Kaunitz asserted that 'the common man is the strength of the nation'.

4   *Prosa*, III, 348. See also p. 128 of this study.

PAGE 241

1   Hohoff follows Hofmannsthal in distinguishing sharply between *Volk* and *Masse*. See also p. 155, note 4 (p. 339).

2   'Hofmannsthal's Lustspiele', p. 383. An excellent detailed study of this theme is J. B. Bednall, 'The Slav Symbol in Hofmannsthal's Post-war Comedies'. See *German Life and Letters*, XIV, nos. 1–2 (1960–1), 34–44.

3   Possibly a reminiscence of the scene between Hamlet and Gertrude, with Polonius behind the arras (Act III, scene 4).

PAGE 242

1   The verse is translated here to demonstrate the comparison between the words of Carlos and those of Sigismund. The translation (with a few modifications) is that by R. D. Boylan in *The Works of Friedrich Schiller. Historical Dramas, etc.* (London, 1871), p. 38.

2   Schulausgabe, p. 59.

PAGE 243

1   *Op. cit.* p. 61. This speech of Basilius has the ring of a personal-political testament—in somewhat heightened form, admittedly. It might perhaps be interesting and relevant to investigate the influence on certain history-conscious literary artists of such Habsburg political testaments as those of Charles VI, Maria Theresia, or Archduke Francis Ferdinand.

PAGE 244

1 Schulausgabe, p. 62.
2 *Sprachverleugnung*, p. 279.
3 *Op. cit.* p. 278.
4 *Hofmannsthals Wandlung*, in *Über Hofmannsthal* (Göttingen, 1958), p. 160. The expression paraphrases Hofmannsthal's original in *Der Priesterzögling*, *Dramen*, III, 493.

PAGE 245

1 *Prosa*, III, 349. See also p. 129.
2 *Prosa*, III, 348. See also pp. 128, 240 of this study.
3 Schulausgabe, p. 18. See also p. 210.

PAGE 246

1 Schulausgabe, p. 67.

PAGE 248

1 Schulausgabe, p. 69.

PAGE 249

1 *Sprachverleugnung*, p. 279. The original is obscurely expressed and the translation is, one hopes, not unfair to it—especially in view of the critical remarks which follow.
2 Schulausgabe, p. 50. See also p. 238 of this study.
3 *Op. cit.* p. 38.
4 *Sprachverleugnung*, p. 278.
5 Schulausgabe, p. 70.

PAGE 250

1 *Sprachverleugnung*, p. 279.
2 Schulausgabe, p. 71.
3 *Sprachverleugnung*, p. 279.

PAGE 252

1 Schulausgabe, p. 73.
2 *Op. cit.* p. 74.
3 The *Passauersegen* (lit. blessing of Passau) provides a nice touch of local colour. Steiner (*Dramen*, IV, 511) says that 'it protects one from possible wounds'. Freytag (*Bilder aus der deutschen Vergangenheit*, 1859–67) describes this amulet in 'Aus dem Jahrhundert des großen Krieges : 2 : Der dreißigjährige Krieg : Soldatenleben und Sitten' (Insel-Verlag, vol. II, n.d., pp. 207–12). Freytag discusses

the origin of *Passauerkunst* (pp. 207–8) and its possible derivation as a corrupt form of *Pessulanten*. He also discusses (pp. 210–11) the *Passauer Zettel* and describes how these amulets were made, inscribed and bound under the left arm. Freytag, moreover, refers (p. 210) to Grimmelshausen's (not wholly accurate) account in *Satyrischer Pilgram*, pt. 2 (1666) and *Das wunderbarliche Vogelnest*, pt. 2 (1675). For details see, for example, *Vogelnest*, pt. 2, chap. 25, in *Simplicianische Schriften* (Munich, 1958), p. 528.

4 Schulausgabe, p. 72. My italics.

PAGE 253

1 This is a variation of the technique discussed on p. 247.

2 Schulausgabe, p. 76.

PAGE 254

1 *Op. cit.* p. 77.

2 *Hofmannsthal und Goethe* (Hameln, 1947), p. 81.

3 Schulausgabe, p. 77.

PAGE 255

1 *Op. cit.* p. 78.

PAGE 256

1 *Op. cit.* p. 77.

2 A comparison, for example, with Edgar Mowrer's chapter 'A Showman of Genius' in *Germany Puts the Clock Back* (Penguin, 1937), pp. 198–207, will confirm this.

3 Schulausgabe, p. 79.

4 See p. 200. Olivier uses the same oaths in the present scene.

PAGE 257

1 *Horrib.* p. 77.

2 Schulausgabe, p. 4.

3 This practice is perhaps comparable with a controversial habit of Thomas Mann, who 'used' features, characteristics, ideas, etc., of such men as Hauptmann (Peeperkorn), Stefan George (Daniel Zur Höhe), Nadler (Georg Vogler), Lukács (Naphta), etc., without (necessarily) implying any further association between the real and fictional characters. But Mann's practice, as with the ideas represented by George-Höhe and Nadler-Vogler, is much more complex and polemical than the one under discussion here.

PAGE 258

1 Schulausgabe, p. 80.

2 The first speech contains the kind of natural and unselfconscious poetic idiom frequently encountered in unspoilt peasant communities. George Thomson discussed this phenomenon, with notable reference to the Irish peasantry, in his pamphlet *Marxism and Poetry* (London, 1945), pp. 35, 54–6. The elemental metaphor in the last speech is pure Expressionism. It should be stressed, despite any great visible interest in the expressionist movement on Hofmannsthal's part, that the composition of the first version of *Der Turm* was contemporary with the climax of expressionist fervour. Sigismund himself is in some respects the kind of 'new man' who was almost a stock figure for some expressionist dramatists, e.g. Georg Kaiser, *Die Bürger von Calais*. See also pp. 167–8, 279.

PAGE 259

1 *Sprachverleugnung*, p. 280.

2 Schulausgabe, p. 80. A dalmatic is a wide-sleeved and rather loose-fitting ecclesiastical vestment. It was apparently a robe worn by persons of rank in the early Christian centuries, on the pattern of a dress worn in Dalmatia. The dalmatic and the golden crown represent therefore the union of spirit and power. It is probable that Hofmannsthal was familiar with the traditional regalia of the Holy Roman Emperors of the German Nation (publicly exhibited in the Vienna Hofburg since 28 December 1826). A dalmatic was an important feature of this and is symbolically appropriate for one who, like Hofmannsthal's Sigismund, was supposed to unite secular and spiritual power within himself. A very interesting description and history of both the regalia and of the coronation procedure is Fritz Traugott Schulz, *Die deutschen Reichskleinodien* (Leipzig, 1934). The dalmatic is described on p. 16 and illustrated on p. 23.

3 Anton prevents the mood from becoming exaggerated or sentimental. His semi-humorous sense of reality is in the best tradition of his type.

4 *Op. cit.* pp. 80–1. The technique here has an obvious similarity to the rhythmic choral speech of expressionist drama. See R. H. Samuel and R. H. Thomas, *Expressionism in German Life, Literature and the Theatre* (Cambridge, 1939), especially pp. 43–9. It is odd

that this otherwise admirable study seems to have ignored possible expressionist tendencies in the later work of Hofmannsthal, although *Elektra* (1903) is briefly considered, pp. 2, 44, 73. An obvious contact between Hofmannsthal and expressionist technique was Max Reinhardt. Reinhardt was as noted for his memorable productions of expressionist dramas (e.g. R. J. Sorge, *Der Bettler*; Georg Kaiser, *Die Bürger von Calais*) as for his lifelong collaboration with Hofmannsthal in the production of most of his dramas. This collaboration is amply documented in, for example, Hofmannsthal's correspondence with Bodenhausen (*Briefe der Freundschaft*), cited above in various places, and most markedly throughout his correspondence with Strauss (*Strauss–Hofmannsthal: Briefwechsel*), likewise cited at various points in this study. See also *Max Reinhardt* and *Reinhardt bei der Arbeit, Aufzeichnungen*, pp. 325–49. See also p. 40, note 2 (p. 318).

PAGE 261

1   *Hofmannsthal und Goethe*, pp. 81–2.

PAGE 262

1   *Erinnerungen an Hofmannsthal*, p. 27. One recalls here Hofmannsthal's depiction of the Germans in *Die Briefe des Zurückgekehrten* (1907), *Prosa*, II, 321–57: see, for example, pp. 332–3. See also pp. 120, 124–5, 151 of this study.

PAGE 263

1   Burckhardt, *Erinnerungen an Hofmannsthal*, p. 28. The full text of Hofmannsthal's letter (20 January 1929) is in *Briefwechsel*, pp. 302–3. It was not written from Germany but from Rodaun, and was in reaction to Burckhardt's letter of 12 January 1929, pp. 299–300.

2   Schulausgabe, p. 84.

3   *Ibid.*

4   This notion was foreshadowed in Sigismund's remark to Julian early in Act IV, p. 70: 'Future and present at the same time. I understand completely what you yourself put into me when you carried me up...beneath the stars which rise above the tower—for you have raised me up in this way in order to keep my soul pure from the sterility of despair.' In the present instance the image of 'stars' doubtless bears the traditional association of appointed fate and destiny, a driving destiny which is with Sigismund day and night.

PAGE 264

1 *Op. cit.* p. 98.

2 *Julius Caesar*, Act I, scene 2: '*Casca.* ...for he swounded, and fell down at it; and for my own part.... *Cassius.* But, soft, I pray you: what! did Caesar swound? *Casca.* He fell down in the market-place, and foam'd at the mouth, and was speechless. *Brutus.* 'Tis very like: he hath the falling sickness.'

It is of incidental interest to note that the historical Don Carlos was an epileptic, although Schiller (and Verdi) retain only the merest trace of this. One wonders if some chance association of ideas led Hofmannsthal from Carlos to Caesar—or indeed Caesar to Carlos. The result in either case is a noteworthy constituent of the drama. See also pp. 280–1.

3 Schulausgabe, p. 96. This episode is discussed in detail later in the present chapter.

4 *Dramen*, I, 419–20 and 421–31.

5 *Sprachverleugnung*, p. 272.

6 *Briefe der Freundschaft*, pp. 78–80.

PAGE 265

1 The original is 'Es wohnt bei Euch nicht zur Miete, sondern im eigenen Palast'.

2 Schulausgabe, p. 87.

3 *Op. cit.* p. 85.

4 'Palatine und Bannerherren': a typically colourful phrase. 'Palatine(s)' is of course encountered in several languages. It is perhaps worth noting that in Hungary under the Habsburgs 'there...existed such powerful institutions as that of the Palatine, who possessed vice-regal status...'; see Robert Kann, *A Study in Austrian Intellectual History from Late Baroque to Romanticism* (London, 1960), p. 20. *Bannerherren* were, historically speaking, great lords who were entitled to fly a full (square) banner, as opposed to the pennant of lesser lords. *Bannerherren* played a significant part in Hungarian history and this was possibly Hofmannsthal's immediate source. Translation cannot give much impression of the cosmopolitan and slightly exotic flavour of such passages as this, which are typical of Hofmannsthal in what might be called his *k.u.k.* (imperial and royal) or old Austrian mood.

5 'Bodyguard' is a poor substitute for *salva guardia*—see preceding note.

PAGE 266

1   Schulausgabe, p. 86.
2   *Op. cit.* p. 87.
3   I am very grateful to Dr Herbert Steiner for this verbal information.

PAGE 267

1   See, for example, *Ad me ipsum, Aufzeichnungen*, pp. 242–3.
2   *Prosa*, I, 99–112. The extracts quoted are on pp. 103–4 and 108.

PAGE 268

1   Schulausgabe, p. 101.
2   See pp. 197–8, 203.
3   *Op. cit.* p. 87.

PAGE 269

1   *Briefwechsel*, p. 99.
2   A curious point of incidental interest arises in connection with the
    simulacrum of Basilius. Already in the palace scene (p. 61)
    Sigismund abused Basilius as follows: 'It's not the first time that I
    have had to strangle a fox with my bare hands. And he stank like
    you' (Pushes him away).
       The apparition of Basilius is, as stated, alternately that of man
    and fox. Hofmannsthal could have found good, recent precedent
    for this kind of fantastic reality in Kafka's *Die Verwandlung*!

PAGE 270

1   *Erinnerungen an Hofmannsthal*, p. 70. It is a pity that Erika Brecht
    could not be more exact ('Round about 1925'). The first version
    of the play appeared in 1925 (see bibliographical note at end of
    chapter 8 for details), and it would be interesting to know just
    when Hofmannsthal introduced this theme. According to a letter
    to Strauss of 8 November 1924, *Briefwechsel*, pp. 517–18, the
    drama was completed 'last week'. Erika Brecht's book seems on
    internal evidence to have been written during World War II—thus
    many years after the events recalled, and to some extent only from
    memory. This could explain the vagueness and discrepancy of
    'round about 1925'. As a whole the passage tends to confirm the
    suggestion made on p. 251 that Hofmannsthal was interested in the
    Russian Civil War and was sufficiently familiar with it to adapt
    certain themes.
2   *Op. cit.* p. 70.

PAGE 271

1   One recalls Broch's comments: 'the flood of associations and memory-images whose symbol-chains and symbol-associations remained indomitable in Hofmannsthal's novels to the point of destructiveness'. Introduction to *Selected Prose* (of Hofmannsthal) (London, 1952), p. xii. There is of course a good deal more to Hofmannsthal's stories than that—as Broch himself demonstrates.

2   Schulausgabe, p. 108.

3   'Der Turm', in *Das Deutsche Drama vom Barock bis zur Gegenwart*, ed. Benno von Wiese (Düsseldorf, 1958), II, 265–83. The extract quoted is on pp. 275–6.

PAGE 272

1   *Faust* I: Dungeon, *Gretchen* to *Faust*: 'Day! Yes, day is breaking, the last day is breaking in.' Hofmannsthal, like Goethe, makes skilful use of the pathetic fallacy. Neville Cardus once summed up the force and point of this idea in a manner curiously appropriate here: 'A sunset in the Indian Ocean once bowled me over because it was like the closing scene of *Götterdämmerung*. I suppose I am a far-gone case of the Ruskinian pathetic fallacy; the external universe must appeal to me as a theatre or as a series of dissolving views, with the lantern turned inwards to my own soul.' *Autobiography* (London, 1947), pp. 250–1.

2   Schulausgabe, p. 91.

PAGE 273

1   One recalls particularly the camp of the Tartar chieftain Khan Kontchak, where Igor is held captive. The Diaghilev–Fokine production appeared in the main European capitals in the years immediately preceding the war. Hofmannsthal knew their work. See his vignette on Nijinsky, *Prosa*, III, 145–8.

2   Schulausgabe, p. 93.

3   *Op. cit.* p. 94.

PAGE 274

1   *Ibid.* It is probably no coincidence that two of the Oldest Lord's superlatives ('Großmächtigster! Unüberwindlichster!') are an exact echo of the form used by the burgomaster of Prague in addressing Ottokar at the height of his power (*König Ottokars Glück und Ende*, Act I, scene 2, line 409).

2 *Ibid.*

3 Letter to Burckhardt, 11 May 1919. *Briefwechsel*, p. 14. See also opening of chapter 5.

4 Letter to Burckhardt, 7 April 1926. *Briefwechsel*, pp. 200–1.

PAGE 275

1 Schulausgabe, p. 95. See also chapter 3, pp. 102–3 in which some connection is suggested between Prince Eugene and Sigismund in their 'mythical' proportions.

2 *Der Dichter in Zeiten der Wirren: Dem Andenken des Grafen Bernhard Uxkull,* first published as part of *Drei Gesänge* (1921), then as part of *Das Neue Reich* (1928), now in *Gesamtausgabe der Werke: Endgültige Fassung* (Berlin, 1937), IX, p. 39. The translation of this poem, by Olga Marx and Ernst Morwitz, seems to be particularly felicitous and the relevant part is therefore printed above. See *The Works of Stefan George* (Chapel Hill, 1949), pp. 296–7.

PAGE 277

1 Schulausgabe, p. 96.

2 *Ibid.*

PAGE 278

1 *Hofmannsthal und Goethe,* p. 82.

2 *Sprachverleugnung,* p. 280.

3 *Prosa,* III, 379. Hofmannsthal's views on *Ausgleich* with the Slavonic East were noted in chapter 4.

4 The original is rather ambiguous: 'und er zählt nicht die Völker, die ihm gehorchen.'

5 Schulausgabe, p. 96.

6 Of incidental interest is the fact that, consciously or unconsciously, Hofmannsthal endowed Sigismund with several of Alexander's personal qualities, as related by Plutarch. The personal charm, kindliness towards the soldiers, the violence on occasion—common to both figures—are obvious enough and could be chance similarities. It is perhaps not a coincidence, however, that Alexander's affection for and trust in his physician are virtually repeated in the relationship, sustained to the end, between Sigismund and the Doctor.

7 Regarding Frederick II, it is perhaps worth noting that on at least one occasion in this scene Sigismund expresses himself in a way

which directly recalls the idea of *Stupor Mundi*: 'I will not be your ruler in the way which is familiar and easy for you, but in a way which will astonish you' (p. 97). One might also note that in 1927 Hofmannsthal named Ernst Kantorowicz's biography of Frederick II as one of his five books of the year. See *Aufzeichnungen*, p. 373. It would be rash to assume any real connection other than possible 'atmospheric reminiscence', especially as Hofmannsthal's choice dates from 1927, the year in which Kantorowicz's book was first published. This was of course two years *after* the appearance of the first version of *Der Turm* (Bremer Presse edition). However, certain features of Frederick II as noted by Kantorowicz in his extremely detailed work (*Frederick the Second: 1194–1250*, trans. E. O. Lorimer, London, 1957) do indeed remind one of Sigismund—and of the Children's King! E.g. the progress of the 'Child of Apulia' through Swabia, Alsace and the Rhineland; the picture of Frederick as 'the Beggar Prince knocking at the gate of Constance,...the dream atmosphere of childhood enveloping him' (pp. 59–60); the imperial, loftily testamental tone of Frederick's *Book of Laws* (1231) outlined on pp. 224–36 (cf. Sigismund's definitions and pronouncements in the present scene); and the legends around Frederick's name: 'Frederick would come again,...to raise the Empire...to glory and to brilliance. He would bring justice and peace, he would hang the shield on the dry tree and lay down the sceptre of the world' (p. 688).

These reminiscences and similarities, it must be emphasized, cannot be proved. Hofmannsthal, however, had certainly heard of Frederick II before 1927! And if, indeed, the historical figure and the legends about him were in his mind when creating Sigismund and/or the Children's King one can only emphasize again that such a method is in accord with his known habit of drawing characters by some degree of 'historical analogy' (Julian the Apostate, Don Carlos, etc.). See, for example, pp. 235–7, 280–1 of this study.

8   Of the abundant evidence of this, Hofmannsthal's review of Karl Anton Rohan's *Europäische Revue* (1926), *Prosa*, IV, 326–33, is perhaps the most concise and explicit.

PAGE 279

1   Gerhard Meyer-Sichting, Schulausgabe, p. 109.

2   It is of incidental interest to note that Archduke Francis Ferdinand intended to refuse coronation in Hungary until the Magyar nobility

had come to heel. His dislike of the Magyars was notorious. It is quite possible that, without further identification of the two figures, Hofmannsthal used the Archduke's example as a symbol of Sigismund's will.

3 *Op. cit.* p. 97. It is difficult to know exactly what Hofmannsthal means by *Schindanger*. It is rare in modern German and bears the meaning of some sort of rubbish-tip. *Schinden*=to flay: *Anger*= meadow or common. Thus knacker's yard, the meaning given by Langenscheidt (1929), seems reasonably accurate. But the word (like *Schindhaufen*) also has a darker overtone, that of a place of execution outside the city walls.

4 See p. 275. That Attila was in Hofmannsthal's mind there is perhaps confirmed by Sigismund's reference to him here.

PAGE 280

1 See p. 264 for discussion of this particular point.

2 William Rey has shown the importance of the Oedipus symbol and of Hofmannsthal's own Oedipus dramas as a kind of substratum for *Der Turm*. See *Das Deutsche Drama*, II, 268–72, 275. See also Rey, 'Geist und Blut in Hofmannsthals *Ödipus und die Sphinx*', in *German Quarterly*, XXXI, 2 (1958), 84–93.

PAGE 281

1 It is worth recalling that Plutarch praised Caesar's fortitude and courage in the field in face of his affliction: 'For, concerning the constitution of his body, he was...often subject to headache, and otherwile to the falling sickness:...but yet therefore yielded not to the disease of his body,...but contrarilie, took the paines of warre, as a medicine to cure his sicke bodie, fighting always with his disease, travelling continually.' *North's Plutarch* (London, 1930), III, 411. Sigismund's fortitude in struggling bravely but vainly against the old, diseased order is a development of the symbol.

2 *Erinnerungen an Hofmannsthal*, p. 71.

PAGE 282

1 *Hofmannsthal und Goethe*, p. 83.

2 *Op. cit.* p. 71.

3 Schulausgabe, p. 100.

PAGE 283

1   *Op. cit.* p. 102.

PAGE 284

1   *Hofmannsthal und Goethe*, pp. 83–4.

PAGE 285

1   *Dramen*, IV, 450, 451.
2   Concerning this notion of 'innocence', Requadt commented with respect to the contrast between Olivier and Sigismund: 'And it is not so much following Calderón's fable as the logic of the symbol itself that Sigismund in *Der Turm* is naked, and that on going out into the world the ceremony of "clothing" him is performed with great pomp. Expressed thus in symbol we have the conflict of two worlds: that of the naked son of a king, and that of Olivier, who is all "world", and who therefore, in the final version...struts across the stage, clad "wholly in iron and leather".' *Sprachverleugnung*, p. 277.

PAGE 286

1   *Dramen*, IV, 455. *Herr* (*Achten auf den Herrn*) has a double meaning, that of gentleman and that of master or lord. Anton includes this latter meaning.
2   *Dramen*, IV, 456.
3   *Op. cit.* p. 457.
4   *Erinnerungen an Hofmannsthal*, pp. 42–3.

PAGE 287

1   *Dramen*, IV, 459.

PAGE 288

1   One recalls particularly *Richard II* and *Boris Godunov*.
2   *Der Turm* (1925), Schulausgabe, p. 101.

PAGE 289

1   William Rey, *Das Deutsche Drama*, II, 280.
2   *Hofmannsthal und Goethe*, pp. 81–2. See also p. 261 of the present study.
3   *Op. cit.* p. 83.

PAGE 290

1   *Erinnerungen an Hofmannsthal*, p. 58.

PAGE 291

1 *Op. cit.* pp. 19, 41, 43.
2 *Op. cit.* p. 70.
3 In *Dramen*, IV both versions are printed. See bibliographical note for details. There is no editorial comment as to preference or to Hofmannsthal's own views.
4 *Briefwechsel*, p. 168.

PAGE 292

1 *Op. cit.* p. 212.
2 'In memoriam Hofmannsthal', *Neue Rundschau*, II (1929), 584.

PAGE 293

1 See *Essex und sein Richter, Aufzeichnungen*, pp. 357–60.
2 2 August 1926. *Briefwechsel*, p. 219.
3 *Aufzeichnungen*, p. 240.

PAGE 294

1 *Sprachverleugnung*, pp. 281–2.
2 'In memoriam Hofmannsthal', p. 589.
3 In both essays of Requadt cited in this study he refers to the allegedly 'operatic' ending of the version of 1925. He uses the term in a rather derogatory sense, as opposed to the technical sense in which the term has been used from time to time in the present study. See 'Hofmannsthal', p. 61 and *Sprachverleugnung*, p. 280.
4 Schröder, 'In memoriam Hofmannsthal', p. 589.

PAGE 295

1 Theologically speaking the two ideas do not seem to be mutually exclusive. The second view—of 'hope and aspiration'—is, incidentally, powerfully propounded by Josef Nadler. See 'Hofmannsthal und das Sozialproblem', *Neue Rundschau*, II (1929), 653.
2 *Op. cit.* pp. 45–7.

PAGE 296

1 *Op. cit.* pp. 44–5. Hofmannsthal recalled this conversation when he was working on the second version of *Der Turm*. See p. 292. He seemed to be convinced that he was capturing the ideas which he had sensed on the earlier occasion, but one could hardly say that 'a spirit of reconciliation, the future, . . .' shines out of the conclusion to the later version.

2 *Erinnerungen an Hofmannsthal*, p. 40.

3 See p. 293.

PAGE 297

1 'Über das Drama', in *Ahnung und Aussage* (Gütersloh, 1952), pp. 298–300.

PAGE 303

1 Jakob Laubach gives an excellent account of various performances from the first performance (February 1928) onwards, together with quotations from various critical notices in the press. See *Hofmannsthals Turm-Dichtungen, Entstehung, Form und Bedeutungsschichten* (Diss., Fribourg, Switzerland, 1949). The published version of this work (Fribourg, 1954) includes an appendix (pp. 131–2) which records the most important performances up to the end of 1953. Erika Brecht gives a very thoughtful account of the first performance, in which she emphasizes the prophetic nature of the play. See *Erinnerungen an Hofmannsthal*, p. 69.

2 This statement is based on an eyewitness account given by Bernt von Heiseler in a letter to the writer.

PAGE 304

1 'remoteness...solemnity of': the original is 'pathetische Distanz'.

2 Letter of 22 September 1922. *Briefwechsel*, p. 95.

PAGE 306

1 Introduction to *Selected Prose* (of Hofmannsthal), *op. cit.* pp. xxiv–xxv.

2 Literally, 'saturated with culture'.

PAGE 307

1 'Erinnerungen an Hofmannsthal', in *Die Gestalt des Dichters im Spiegel der Freunde* (Vienna, 1949), p. 240. Concerning Kassner's following statement about the absence of dénouement in Hofmannsthal's dramas, see also p. 209, note 3 (p. 352). Hofmannsthal fulfils the first of Hebbel's requirements, and probably the second (in the third and fourth acts of both versions). One doubts whether, dramatically speaking, either solution to the fifth act 'must be so'. Relevant to Kassner's remarks is Hermann Stresau's critique of Heinz Hilpert's recent production of *Das Bergwerk zu Falun* (1899) in the *Deutsches Theater* (Göttingen). See *Frankfurter Allgemeine Zeitung*, 19 September 1960, p. 14.

PAGE 308

1 *Modern German Drama* (London, 1959), pp. 75–6.

2 It may be helpful in the present context to recall Alewyn's remarks on the baroque theatre. These are cited in connection with *Jedermann*. See pp. 79, 81–2.

PAGE 309

1 'Hofmannsthal: A Classic of German Poetry in the Twentieth Century', in *Universitas* (English lang. ed.), IV, 1 (1961), 76. Hill's quotation is from *Die Bühne als Traumbild, Prosa*, II, 75.

PAGE 310

1 Difficult to translate, it might be expressed as those abiding factors which join people and societies together and to their past—in terms of customs, traditions, social forms, etc.

PAGE 312

1 In *Die Gestalt des Dichters im Spiegel der Freunde*, pp. 257–9.

SELECT BIBLIOGRAPHY

I. WORKS OF HOFMANNSTHAL

Where possible the *Gesammelte Werke in Einzelausgaben* have been used. This series has been published by S. Fischer Verlag, Frankfurt/Main, under the editorship of Herbert Steiner. The fifteen volumes which constitute the edition proper appeared at intervals during the period 1945–60. It is understood that several additional volumes will also appear in due course. These will contain various fragments and letters additional to those published already in specific volumes of correspondence. Concerning the latter I have made extensive use of the following:

Hugo von Hofmannsthal — Eberhard von Bodenhausen: Briefe der Freundschaft. Ed. Dora Freifrau von Bodenhausen. Düsseldorf, 1953.

Hugo von Hofmannsthal — Rudolf Borchardt: Briefwechsel. Ed. Herbert Steiner. Frankfurt/Main, 1954.

Hugo von Hofmannsthal — Carl J. Burckhardt: Briefwechsel. Ed. Carl J. Burckhardt. Frankfurt/Main, 1956.

Briefwechsel zwischen George und Hofmannsthal. Ed. Robert Boehringer. 2nd ed. Munich, 1953.

Hugo von Hofmannsthal — Florens Christian Rang: Briefwechsel. With note by Berhard Rang. *Neue Rundschau*, III (1959), 402–48. The note is in 'Zu diesem Heft' at the end of the issue.

Richard Strauss — Hugo von Hofmannsthal: Briefwechsel. Ed. Franz and Alice Strauss, and Willi Schuh. Zürich, 1952.

N.B. There is no edition of Hofmannsthal's slender but important correspondence with Josef Redlich. However, I was able to use Hofmannsthal's letters to Redlich, ed. by Helmut Fiechtner and published in *Wort in der Zeit*, VII (1956), 16–30.

WORKS CONSULTED

Works either on Hofmannsthal or which at some stage refer directly to him. Hofmannsthal literature is extensive, especially in the smaller forms—essays, articles, memoirs, etc. It would be impracticable to list all works read which have had some bearing on the present study. The choice has thus been limited by two factors, usefulness and accessibility while the study was being written: by far the greater part was composed in Australia.

Adorno, Theodor W, 'George und Hofmannsthal: Zum Briefwechsel'. In *Prismen: Kulturkritik und Gesellschaft*. Suhrkamp, 1955, pp. 232–82.

Alewyn, Richard, *Über Hugo von Hofmannsthal*. Göttingen, 1958. This contains essays written and published over a period of twenty years: 'Hofmannsthal und diese Zeit' (1949), 'Jugendbriefe von Hofmannsthal' (1935), 'Unendliches Gespräch' (1954), 'Hofmannsthals Anfang: "Gestern"' (1949), 'Der Tod des Ästheten' (1944 and 1949), 'Hofmannsthals erste Komödie' (1936), 'Der Unbestechliche' (1956), 'Andreas und die "wunderbare Freundin"' (1956), 'Hofmannsthals Wandlung' (1949).

Auernheimer, Raoul, 'Hugo von Hofmannsthal als österreichische Erscheinung'. *Neue Rundschau*, II (1929), 660–6.

Baumann, Gerhart, *Österreich als Form der Dichtung*. Off-print from *Spectrum Austriae*, pp. 583–613. Vienna, n.d., probably 1956.

Bednall, J. B., 'The Slav Symbol in Hofmannsthal's Post-war Comedies'. *German Life and Letters* (n.s.), XIV, 1–2 (1960–1), 34–44.

Bergstraesser, Arnold, 'The Holy Beggar. Religion and Society in Hofmannsthal's Great World Theatre'. *Germanic Review*, XX (1945), 261–86.

Bergstraesser, Arnold, *Hofmannsthal und der europäische Gedanke*. *Kieler Universitätsreden*, Heft 2. Kiel, 1951.

Bithell, Jethro, *Modern German Literature*. London, 1939. Bithell devotes a comparatively lengthy and somewhat contentious section to Hofmannsthal.

Bollnow, O. F., 'Zum Lebensbegriff des jungen Hugo von Hofmannsthal'. *Unruhe und Geborgenheit*, Stuttgart, 1953.

Borchardt, Rudolf, The following essays in *Prosa*, 1 of Borchardt's *Gesammelte Werke in Einzelbänden* (see 2, Literary background and environment, under Borchardt): 'Brief über das Drama an Hofmannsthal', pp. 77–85; 'Hofmannsthals Prosäische Schriften', pp. 86–9; 'Eranos Brief', pp. 90–130; 'Über Hofmannsthals Erzählung', pp. 131–5; 'Hofmannsthals Lehrjahre', pp. 136–62; 'Hofmannsthals Wirkung', pp. 197–205; 'Hofmannsthals Unsterblichkeit', pp. 206–12; and in *Reden*, 'Rede über Hofmannsthal', pp. 45–103.

Braun, Felix, 'Encounters with Hofmannsthal'. *German Life and Letters* (new series), II (1948–9), 1–12.

Braun, Felix, 'Das Welterlebnis Hofmannsthals'. In *Das musische Land*. Innsbruck, 1952.

Brecht, Erika, *Erinnerungen an Hofmannsthal*. Innsbruck, 1946.

Brecht, Walther, 'Ad me ipsum und seine Bedeutung'. *Jahrbuch des Freien Deutschen Hochstifts* (1930), pp. 319–53.

Brecht, Walther, 'Die Vorläufer von Hofmannsthals Jedermann'. *Österreichische Rundschau*, IV (1924), 271–87.

Brecht, Walther, 'Fragmentarische Betrachtung über Hofmannsthals Weltbild'. *Eranos*. Munich, 1924 (volume commemorating Hofmannsthal's fiftieth birthday), pp. 18–24.

Brecht, Walther, *Grundlinien im Werke Hofmannsthals*. *Euphorion*, XVI. Ergänzungsheft (1923), pp. 164–79.

Broch, Hermann, 'Zu Hofmannsthals Prosaschriften'. *Neue Rundschau*, II (1951), 1–30.

Broch, Hermann, Introduction to *Selected Prose* (of Hugo von Hofmannsthal)—in translation by James and Tania Stern. London, 1952. Amongst Broch's posthumous papers there was found a much longer and more detailed essay on Hugo von Hofmannsthal: this work—'Hofmannsthal und seine Zeit: Eine Studie'—is now in *Gesammelte Werke: Dichten und Erkennen*. Essays, I, 43–181. Zürich, 1955.

Burckhardt, Carl J., *Erinnerungen an Hofmannsthal und Briefe des Dichters*. Munich, 1948.

Burckhardt, Carl J., 'Begegnungen mit Hofmannsthal'. *Neue Rundschau*, III–IV (1954), 341–54. This was a special issue to mark the eightieth anniversary of the birth of Hugo von Hofmannsthal. It includes contributions by Richard Alewyn, Ernst Robert Curtius, Rudolf Borchardt, Rudolf Kassner, Edgar Hederer, Reinhold Schneider, Herbert Steiner, Max Kommerell, Olga Schnitzler, letters of Hofmannsthal to Schröder, Schnitzler, S. Fischer, etc., in addition to various rare or hitherto unpublished works of Hofmannsthal himself.

Burckhardt, Carl J., 'Zu Hugo von Hofmannsthals Lustspiel Der Schwierige'. *Neue Rundschau*, I (1960), 133–7.

Curtius, Ernst Robert, 'Hofmannsthal und die Romanität'. *Kritische Essays zur europäischen Literatur*. Berne, 1950, pp. 164–71.

Curtius, Ernst Robert, 'Hofmannsthals deutsche Sendung'. *Kritische Essays zur europäischen Literatur*. Berne, 1950, pp. 158–64.

Curtius, Ernst Robert, 'George, Hofmannsthal und Calderón'. *Kritische Essays zur europäischen Literatur*. Berne, 1950, pp. 172–201.

Emrich, Wilhelm, 'Hofmannsthals Lustspiel: Der Schwierige'. *Wirkendes Wort*, I (1955–6), 17–25.

Fahrner, Rudolf, *Dichterische Visionen menschlicher Urbilder in Hofmannsthals Werk*. Publications of the Faculty of Arts, University of Ankara, no. 100. Ankara, 1956.

Fiechtner, Helmut A., ed., *H. v. H.: Die Gestalt des Dichters im Spiegel der Freunde*. Vienna, 1949. Contributions by (among others) Rudolf Borchardt, Hermann Bahr, Max Clauss, Thomas Mann, Max Mell, Josef Nadler, Rudolf Alexander Schröder, Richard Strauss, Helene Thimig, Franz Werfel, etc. Many of the essays in this volume have also been published elsewhere. Several of those which were especially useful in the present study (Burckhardt, Wassermann, etc.) are listed independently.

Franckenstein, George, Address at commemorative festival in Salzburg, 1948. With biographical note by H. F. Garten. *Contemporary Review*, February 1949.

Fuchs, Albert, 'Hugo von Hofmannsthal: thèmes et horizons spirituels'. *Etudes Germaniques*, III, 4 (1948), 355–81.

Fuchs, Albert, 'Ein großer Österreicher und Wir'. *Bulletin de la Faculté des Lettres de l'Université de Strasbourg*, XXXI (1952), 108–22.

Garten, Hugo F., *Modern German Drama*. London, 1959. Garten devotes a short but penetrating section to Hofmannsthal.

Gilbert, Mary E., 'Hugo von Hofmannsthal and England'. *German Life and Letters*, I (1936), 182–93.

Gilbert, Mary E., Introduction to *Hofmannsthal. Selected Essays*. Oxford, 1955.

Gilbert, Mary E., 'Recent Trends in the Criticism of Hofmannsthal'. *German Life and Letters*, V (1951–2), 255–68.

Gundolf, Friedrich, 'Loris'. *Europäische Revue*, IX (1930), 672–6.

Hamburger, Michael, 'Hofmannsthals Bibliothek: Ein Bericht'. *Euphorion*, LV (1961), 15–76.

Hederer, Edgar, 'Über die Aufzeichnungen Hofmannsthals zu einem Xenodoxus'. *Neue Rundschau*, III–IV (1954), 424–36.

Hederer, Edgar, 'Hofmannsthals Weg und Vermächtnis'. *Hochland*, XLVI (1953–4), 311–23.

Hederer, Edgar, *Hugo von Hofmannsthal*. Frankfurt/Main, 1960.

Heiseler, Bernt von, 'Hugo von Hofmannsthal'. *Die Sammlung*, XII (1957), 425–32.

Heuschele, Otto, *Hugo von Hofmannsthal: Dank und Gedächtnis* (1929). Tübingen, 1949.

Heuss, Theodor, *Hugo von Hofmannsthal: Rede des Bundespräsidenten Theodor Heuss gehalten bei der Eröffnung der Festspiele der Stadt Bad Hersfeld am 3. Juli 1954.* Tübingen, 1954.

Hill, Claude, 'Hofmannsthal: A Classic of German Poetry in the Twentieth Century'. *Universitas* (English lang. ed.), IV, 1 (1961), 63–77.

Hohoff, Curt, 'Hofmannsthals Lustspiele'. *Akzente*, IV (1955), 369–83.

Jászi, Andrew O., 'Die Idee des Lebens in Hofmannsthals Jugendwerk'. *Germanic Review*, XXIV (1949), 81–107.

Jens, Walter, *Hofmannsthal und die Griechen*. Tübingen, 1955.

Jens, Walter, 'Der Mensch und die Dinge. Die Revolution der deutschen Prosa'. *Statt einer Literaturgeschichte*. Pfullingen, 1957, pp. 59–85. Deals with Hofmannsthal, Rilke, Musil, Kafka, Heym.

Kluckhohn, Paul, 'Die Wende vom 19. zum 20. Jahrhundert in der deutschen Dichtung'. *Deutsche Vierteljahrsschrift (DVjss)*, I (1955), 1–19.

Koch, Franz, 'Hofmannsthals Lebens- und Weltgefühl'. *Jahrbuch des Freien Deutschen Hochstifts* (1930), pp. 257–318.

Kommerell, Max. *Hugo von Hofmannsthal*. Frankfurt/Main, 1930 (inaugural lecture).

Kraus, Karl, 'Hofmannsthal und die Bezüge'. *Die Fackel*, Vienna, nos. 717–23 (March 1926), pp. 62–7.

Laubach, Jakob, *Hugo von Hofmannsthals Turm-Dichtungen, Enstehung, Form und Bedeutungsschichten*. Diss. Fribourg (Switzerland), 1954.

Laubach, Jakob, 'Hofmannsthals Weg von der Magie zur Mystik. Zu seiner dramatischen Nachlese'. *Wirkendes Wort*, IV (1950–1), 238–45.

Martini, Fritz, *Deutsche Literaturgeschichte von den Anfängen bis zur Gegenwart*. Stuttgart, 1948. Martini's short section on Hofmannsthal is in quality much above the usual survey-type note (the entire work is only 614 pages in length). Hence its inclusion here.

Martini, Fritz, *Wagnis der Sprache: Interpretationen deutscher Prosa von Nietzsche bis Benn*. Stuttgart, 1954. Relevant to this section of the bibliography is Martini's interpretation of an extract from *Andreas*.

Metzeler, Werner, *Ursprung und Krise von Hofmannsthals Mystik*. Munich, 1956.

Meyer-Sichting, Gerhart, 'Hofmannsthals Turm. Eine Einführung und Deutung'. *Merkur* (Stuttgart), III (1954), 209–26.

Mühlberger, Josef, *Hugo von Hofmannsthal: Franz Kafka. Zwei Vorträge*. Esslingen, 1953.

Nadler, Josef, 'Hugo von Hofmannsthal: oder Welt im Traum. Aus Anlaß der Gesamtausgabe seiner Werke'. *Wort und Wahrheit*, VII (1952), 938–43.

Nadler, Josef, 'Hofmannsthal und das Sozialproblem'. *Neue Rundschau*, II (1929), 647–54.

Nadler, Josef, 'Hofmannsthals Ausklang'. *Hochland*, XXVI (1929), ii, 616–21.

Naef, K. J., *Hugo von Hofmannsthals Wesen und Werk*. Zürich, 1938.

Naumann, Walter, 'Hofmannsthals Auffassung von seiner Sendung als Dichter'. *Monatshefte* (Madison), III (1947), 184–7.

Naumann, Walter, 'Das Visuelle und das Plastische bei Hofmannsthal'. *Monatshefte* (Madison), III (1945), 159–69. This is an interpretation of *Ad me ipsum*, a fact not indicated by the title.

Naumann, Walter, 'Die Form des Dramas bei Grillparzer und Hofmannsthal'. *DVjss*, I (1959), 20–37.

Oswald, Victor A., 'The Old Age of Young Vienna'. *Germanic Review*, XXVII (1952), 188–99. The title is rather misleading. The essay is devoted to Bahr, Beer-Hofmann, Hofmannsthal and Schnitzler. It contains some very perspicacious remarks on *Große Welttheater*, *Der Schwierige*, and on both versions of *Der Turm*.

Pannwitz, Rudolf, 'Hofmannsthal in unserer Zeit'. *Neue Rundschau*, I (1924), 139–43.

Pestalozzi, K., *Sprachskepsis und Sprachmagie im Werk des jungen Hofmannsthal*. Zürich, 1958.

Pulver, Elsbeth, *Hofmannsthals Schriften zur Literatur*. Berne, 1956.

Rall, Theodor, *Deutsches Katholisches Schrifttum Gestern und Heute*. Einsiedeln/Cologne, 1936. Rall devotes a short but contentious section of his work to Hofmannsthal.

Requadt, Paul, 'Hugo von Hofmannsthal'. *Deutsche Literatur im XX. Jahrhundert*. Ed. Hermann Friedmann and Otto Mann. Heidelberg, 1954.

Requadt, Paul, 'Sprachverleugnung und Mantelsymbolik im Werke Hofmannsthals'. *DVjss*, II (1955), 255–83.

Rey, William H., 'Hofmannsthal: Der Turm'. *Das Deutsche Drama*, II, ed. Benno von Wiese (Düsseldorf, 1958), 264–83. This is an extended version of an essay which appeared in *Euphorion*, XLVII (1953), 161–72.

Rey, William H., 'Gebet Zeugnis: ich war da. Die Gestalt Hofmannsthals in Bericht und Forschung'. *Euphorion*, L (1956), 443–78. This is of particular value in that it is a splendid survey of recent Hofmannsthal scholarship into which Rey weaves his own valuable contribution. This is additional to his comments on the works discussed. Rey's approach to the later Hofmannsthal is especially stimulating and reasoned. His preference, incidentally—see pp. 475–8—is for the second version of *Der Turm*.

Rey, William H., 'Geist und Blut in Hofmannsthals *Ödipus und die Sphinx*'. *German Quarterly*, XXXI, 2 (1958), 84–93.

Rey, William H., 'Selbstopfer des Geistes: Fluch und Verheißung in Hofmannsthals *Der Turm* und Thomas Manns *Doktor Faustus*'. *Monatshefte* (Madison), IV (1960), 145–57.

Rey, William H., *Weltentzweiung und Weltversöhnung in Hofmannsthals Griechischen Dramen*. Philadelphia, 1962.

Roeffler, Albert, 'Hugo von Hofmannsthal'. *Bilder aus der Neueren Deutschen Literatur*. Frauenfeld/Leipzig, 1933.

Rychner, Max, 'Hofmannsthals *Turm*'. *Welt im Wort*, Zürich, 1949, pp. 211–45.

Rychner, Max, 'Der Briefwechsel: Hofmannsthal — Rudolf Borchardt'. *Arachne*. Zürich, 1957, pp. 154–65.

Rychner, Max, 'Der Briefwechsel: Hofmannsthal — Carl J. Burckhardt'. *Arachne*. Zürich, 1957, pp. 166–83.

Rychner, Max, 'Hofmannsthal: Prosa I und II'. *Sphären der Bücherwelt*. Zürich, 1952, pp. 88–109.

Rychner, Max, *Hofmannsthal*. Four essays: 'Hofmannsthal und diese Zeit', 'Das Schrifttum als geistiger Raum', 'Bildung', 'Die Berührung der Sphären'. *Zur europäischen Literatur*, Zürich, 1951, pp. 69–98.

Schaeder, Grete, *Hugo von Hofmannsthal und Goethe*. Hameln, 1947.

Schaeder, Grete, 'Hofmannsthals Weg zur Tragödie. Die drei Stufen der Turm-Dichtung'. *DVjss*, II–III (1949), 306–50.

Schaeder, H. H., 'Bemerkung zu Hofmannsthals Turm'. *Neue Rundschau*, VII (1928), 84–7.

Schröder, Rudolf Alexander, 'In memoriam Hugo von Hofmannsthal'. *Neue Rundschau*, II (1929), 577–93.

Schröder, Rudolf Alexander, 'Zeit und Gerechtigkeit. Gedanken zum Werk Hofmannsthals zur 25. Wiederkehr seines Todestags am 15. Juli.' *Merkur*, VIII (1954), 603–17. In view of the lifelong friendship between Schröder and Hofmannsthal, it is worth noting that most of Schröder's various essays on Hofmannsthal are now in vol. II of the *Gesammelte Werke*, Berlin, 1952, pp. 801–63.

Schumann, Detlev W., 'Gedanken zu Hofmannsthals Begriff der "Konservativen Revolution"'. *P.M.L.A.* LIV (1939), 853–99.

Sofer, J., *Die Welttheater Hugo von Hofmannsthals und ihre Voraussetzungen bei Heraklit und Calderón*. Vienna, 1934.

Staiger, Emil, *Meisterwerke deutscher Sprache*. Essay on *Der Schwierige*. Zürich, 1948, pp. 225–59.

Steiner, Herbert, 'Erinnerungen an Hofmannsthal'. *Deutsche Beiträge zur geistigen Überlieferung*. Ed. Arnold Bergstraesser. Chicago, 1947, pp. 203–7.

Steiner, Herbert, 'Über Hugo von Hofmannsthal'. *Monatshefte* (Madison), VII (1950), 321–4. This short article is concerned exclusively with Hofmannsthal's posthumous papers, a fact not indicated by the title.

Steiner, Herbert, *Zur Hofmannsthal-Ausgabe*, I. *Bericht und Berichtigung*. Berne, 1959. Steiner discusses here (among others) Werner Volke's essay on his edition of Hofmannsthal's works (*DVjss*, II (1958), 305–15).

Thomese, Ika Alida, *Romantik und Neuromantik mit besonderer Berücksichtigung Hugo von Hofmannsthals*. The Hague, 1923.

Vuillermoz, E., 'Les festivals de Salzburg: la résurrection moderne d'un mystère du moyen âge'. *Illustration*, 22 August 1931.

Wassermann, Jakob, *Hofmannsthal der Freund*. Berlin, 1930.

Weischedel, Hanna, 'Hofmannsthal-Forschung 1945 bis 1958'. *DVjss*, I (1959), 63–102. This is a valuable adjunct to Rey's survey above.

Wellesz, Eugen, *Das Salzburger Große Welttheater*—description of the (first) production. *Musical News*, 22 September 1922.

Wiemann, Heinz, 'Gedanken zu Goethes *Faust* und Hofmannsthals *Welttheater*'. *Studies in Language and Literature presented to August Lodewyckx*, Melbourne, 1948.

Wiese, Benno von, *Die deutsche Novelle von Goethe bis Kafka*. Düsseldorf, 1956. The interpretation of *Reitergeschichte* (pp. 284–303) is relevant to this bibliography.

Zweig, Stefan, *Die Welt von Gestern. Erinnerungen eines Europäers*. Stockholm, 1947.

2. LITERARY BACKGROUND AND ENVIRONMENT

Works listed here fall for the most part into one of two categories: (i) works which refer to epochs (e.g. Baroque) or figures (e.g. Grillparzer) of the past which/who influenced Hofmannsthal or to which/whom he felt in some way akin; (ii) contemporaries of Hofmannsthal whose work and activity throw light on his outlook and development, e.g. R. A. Schröder.

Atkins, Stuart, 'Goethe, Calderón and *Faust, der Tragödie zweiter Teil*'. *Germanic Review*, XXVIII (1953), 83–98.

Bach, Rudolf, 'Die Kronratsszene in *Faust* II'. *Neue Deutsche Hefte*, IV (1954), 263–73.

Bahr, Hermann, *Meister und Meisterbriefe um Hermann Bahr. Aus seinen Entwürfen, Tagebüchern, und seinem Briefwechsel.* Selected and with an introduction by Josef Gregor. Vienna, 1947.

Baumann, Gerhart, *Franz Grillparzer. Sein Werk und das österreichische Wesen.* Vienna, 1954.

Berger, Kurt, *Die Dichtung Rudolf Alexander Schröders.* Marburg/Lahn, 1954.

Borchardt, Rudolf, *Gesammelte Werke in Einzelbänden.* 8 vols. to date. Stuttgart, 1956 (?1955—no date is given in vol. I, *Reden*. The first review seen by the writer was in *Gegenwart*, Frankfurt/Main, 24 February 1956). The following essays in *Reden* were of special interest: 'Revolution und Tradition in der Literatur' and 'Schöpferische Restauration' (delivered, it is interesting to note, at the University of Munich, 9 March 1927, i.e. only five weeks after Hofmannsthal's 'Schrifttum als geistiger Raum der Nation', delivered there on 27 January 1927). Also relevant in *Reden* are 'Die geistesgeschichtliche Bedeutung des 19. Jahrhunderts' and 'Die neue Poesie und die alte Menschheit.'

Brecht, Walther, 'Österreichische Geistesform und österreichische Dichtung'. *DVjss*, IX (1931), 607–27.

Clara, Abraham a Sancta (Ulrich Megerle), *Werke.* Wiener Akademie der Wissenschaften. Ed. K. Bertsch. Vienna, 1943.

Forster, L. W., *The Temper of Seventeenth Century German Literature.* Inaugural lecture delivered at University College London, 7 February 1951.

Haas, Willy, *Die Literarische Welt.* Munich, 1957. This was very useful in a general way, but there are numerous references to Hofmannsthal, notably pp. 42–8, 68–70, 133–4.

Hankamer, Paul, *Deutsche Gegenreformation und deutsches Barock* (1934). Stuttgart, 1947.

Heiseler, Bernt von, *Ahnung und Aussage*. Gütersloh, 1952. Relevant here were essays on R. A. Schröder, E. G. Winkler and 'Über das Drama'.

Hennecke, Hans, *Rudolf Borchardt: Eine Einführung in sein Werk und eine Auswahl*. Wiesbaden, 1954.

Hohoff, Curt, *Geist und Ursprung: Zur Modernen Literatur*. Munich, 1954. Relevant were essays on R. A. Schröder and Josef Roth ('Österreich, mein Österreich').

Holthusen, H. E., *Ja und Nein: Kritische Versuche*. Munich, 1954. Particularly relevant was essay on R. A. Schröder.

Kann, Robert, *A Study in Austrian Intellectual History from Late Baroque to Romanticism*. London, 1960. This is an invaluable account of 'the typical elements and...cyclical pattern of Austrian intellectual development'. One should perhaps draw particular attention to parts 2, 4 and 5: 'Abraham a Sancta Clara' (pp. 50–115), 'Joseph von Sonnenfels' (pp. 146–244), and 'The Swing of the Pendulum (Era of Francis I, 1792–1835)' (pp. 259–302). There is also a highly detailed series of bibliographical notes (pp. 303–39) in addition to the very useful select bibliography (pp. 341–6).

Katann, Oskar, 'Die katholische Literaturbewegung von Muth bis Muckermann'. *Die Zeit im Buch*, II (1950).

Kelly, J. M., *A New History of Spanish Literature*. Oxford, 1926.

Kommerell, Max, *Beiträge zu einem deutschen Calderón*. 2 vols. Frankfurt/Main, 1946.

Kühnelt, H. H., 'E. A. Poe und die phantastische Erzählung im österreichischen Schrifttum von 1900 bis 1920'. *Festschrift für Moritz Enzinger*. Innsbruck, 1953.

Lange, Victor, *Modern German Literature, 1890–1940*. Ithaca, 1945. Hofmannsthal is treated in the essay 'Anti-Alexanders' (along with Nietzsche, Rilke, George, etc.). But the main significance of this book to the present study lies in its presentation of what Lange calls a 'critical outline' of the period. Hence its inclusion here.

Mann, Thomas, Radio talk on 'Germany and the Germans'. *Listener*, vol. XXXVII, no. 959, 12 June 1947.

Marcus, Aurelius (Emperor), *Meditations*. Trans. Jeremy Collier, rev. by Alice Zimmern. Scott Library no. 19. London, n.d.

Martini, Fritz, 'Expressionismus'. *Deutsche Lit. im XX. Jahrhundert*. Ed. H. Friedmann and O. Mann. Heidelberg, 1954.

Martini, Fritz, *Wagnis der Sprache: Interpretationen deutscher Prosa von Nietzsche bis Benn*. Stuttgart, 1954. See also section 1.

Milch, Werner, *Ströme, Formeln, Manifeste. Drei Vorträge zur Geschichte der deutschen Lit. im 20. Jhdt.* Marburg/Lahn, 1949.

Musil, Robert, *Der Mann ohne Eigenschaften*. Hamburg, 1949.

Nadler, Josef, *Franz Grillparzer*. Vienna, 1952.

Naumann, Walter, *Grillparzer. Das dichterische Werk. Urban-Bücher; die wissenschaftliche Taschenbuchreihe*, no. 17.

Naumann, Walter, 'Grillparzer und das spanische Drama'. *DVjss*, III (1954), 345–72.

Oberholzer, Otto, *Richard Beer-Hofmann. Werk und Weltbild des Dichters*. Berne, 1947. Beer-Hofmann was a close friend of Hofmannsthal and the book has a good deal that is of value to say about Hofmannsthal himself. Oberholzer's work is a kind of parallel volume to Naef's large-scale interpretation of Hofmannsthal (see section 1), to which Oberholzer refers frequently. Ideally the two books should be read in conjunction with each other. Both, by the way, are extended versions of doctoral theses, written in the first instance under the direction of Robert Faesi (Zürich).

Pannwitz, Rudolf, *Beiträge zu einer europäischen Kultur: Aufsätze und Vorträge*. Nürnberg, 1954. Despite later estrangement Hofmannsthal was well acquainted with Pannwitz and expressed himself very positively about his work. Hofmannsthal's correspondence with Bodenhausen (*Briefe der Freundschaft*) gives an indication of Hofmannsthal's views on Pannwitz's importance, together with an impression of his personal relations with and attitude to Pannwitz. But this latter is a very vexed subject indeed!

Pevsner, Nikolaus, *An Outline of European Architecture*. Pelican, 2nd rev. ed. 1951. Not, strictly speaking, a literary reference, but more appropriate here than elsewhere.

Plutarch, *North's Plutarch*. Vol. 3. London, 1930.

Richards, I. A., *Principles of Literary Criticism*. London, 1944.

Samuel, R. H. and Thomas, R. H., *Expressionism in German Life, Literature and the Theatre*. Cambridge, 1939.

Schröder, R. A., *Gesammelte Werke*. 5 vols. Berlin, 1952. Relevant here are vols. II and III. These include essays on Borchardt, Boden-hausen and E. R. Curtius, which are in vol. II. Relevant in vol. III are 'Kunst und Religion' and 'Dichtung und Dichter der Kirche'. See also section 1.

Schweitzer, Albert, *Selections*. London, 1953.

Thomson, George, *Marxism and Poetry*. London, 1945.

Wassermann, Jakob, *Caspar Hauser oder die Trägheit des Herzens* (1908). *Forum-Bücher*. Amsterdam/Stockholm, 1939.

Wassermann, Jakob, *Lebensdienst: Gesammelte Studien, Erfahrungen und Reden aus drei Jahrzehnten*. Leipzig/Zürich, 1928.

Yates, Douglas, *Franz Grillparzer. A Critical Biography*. Vol. I. Oxford, 1946.

3. THEATRICAL AND DRAMATURGICAL BACKGROUND

Alewyn, Richard, 'Der Geist des Barocktheaters'. *Festgabe für Fritz Strich*. Berne, 1952.

Bahr, Hermann, *Burgtheater*. Vienna, 1919.

Becher, Hubert, 'Die geistige Entwicklung des Jesuitendramas'. *DVjss*, XXI (1941), 269–310.

Dörrer, Anton, *Tiroler Fasnacht innerhalb der alpenländischen Winter- und Vorfrühlingsgebräuche. Österreichische Volkskultur, Forschungen zur Volkskunde*, vol. 5. Vienna, 1949.

Farga, Franz, *Die Wiener Oper von ihren Anfängen bis 1938*. Vienna, 1947.

Flemming, Willi, 'Die Erfassung des Epochalstils barocker Schau-spielkunst in Deutschland'. *Maske und Kothurn*, vol. I, 1–2 (1955), 109–40.

Flemming, Willi (ed.), *Barockdrama: Das Ordensdrama. Deutsche Lit.: Sammlung literarischer Kunst- und Denkmäler in Entwick-lungsreihen: Reihe Barock: Barockdrama* (5 vols.), vol. II. Leipzig, 1930. Contains *inter alia*, in addition to Flemming's introduction, a transl. (1635) by Joachim Meichel of Jakob Bidermann's *Cenodoxus* (Augsburg, 1602; Munich, 1609). It will be recalled that Hofmanns-thal based his (projected) drama *Xenodoxus* (see *Aufzeichnungen zu einem X.* and accompanying essay by Edgar Hederer in *Neue Rundschau*, III–IV (1954), noted in section 1 of this bibliography) on Bidermann's Latin drama. Meichel's German translation is certainly the most accessible version for the modern reader. N.B. Hofmanns-thal's *Aufz. zu einem X.* are now in *Dramen*, IV, 483–99.

Fontana, O. M., *Wiener Schauspieler von Mitterwurzer bis Maria Eis*. Vienna, 1948.

Goedeke, Karl, *Every-Man, Homulus und Hekastus*. Hanover, 1865.

Gregor, Hans, *Die Wiener Oper*. Vienna, 1931.

Hartl, Eduard, 'Die Entwicklung des Benediktbeurer Passionsspiels'. *Euphorion*, XLVI (1952), 113–37.

Hartl, Eduard (ed.), *Benediktbeurer Passionsspiel: Das St Galler Passionsspiel*. *Altdeutsche Textbibliothek*, no. 41. Halle/Saale, 1952.

Hebbel, C. F., *Mein Wort über das Drama*. 1843.

Kindermann, Heinz, *Hermann Bahr: ein Leben für das europäische Theater*. Graz/Cologne, 1954.

Kindermann, Heinz, *Theatergeschichte der Goethezeit*. Vienna, 1948.

Krause, Ernst, *Richard Strauss*. Leipzig, 1955.

Kronacher, Alwin, 'Goethes Faust, zweiter Teil, als Theaterstück'. *Germanic Review*, XXIII (1948), 42–54.

Laube, Heinrich, *Das Burgtheater*. Vienna, 1868.

Mell, Max, *Alfred Roller*. Vienna, 1922.

Michael, Wolfgang, 'The Staging of the Bozen Passion Play'. *Germanic Review*, XXV (1950), 178–95.

Müller, Johannes, *Das Jesuitendrama in den Ländern deutscher Zunge vom Anfang (1555) bis zum Hochbarock (1665)*. 2 vols. *Schriften zur deutschen Lit.*, vols. VII and VIII. Ed. for the Görres-Gesellschaft by Gunther Müller. Augsburg, 1930.

Nadler, Josef, *Literaturgeschichte Österreichs*. A general literary history. But Nadler's account of the developing theatrical genres of Austria is of high quality and is comparatively detailed.

Nicoll, Allardyce, *World Drama*. London, 1949.

Pfister, Kurt, *Richard Strauss*. Vienna, 1949.

Pichler, Adolph, *Über das Drama des Mittelalters in Tirol*. Innsbruck, 1850.

Reinhardstöttner, Karl von, *Die Darstellung des Todes und des Totentanzes auf den Jesuitenbühnen*. Leipzig, 1897.

Rommel, Otto, *Die großen Figuren der Alt-Wiener Volkskomödie. Hanswurst, Kasperl und Staberl, Raimund und Nestroy*. Vienna, 1946.

Rommel, Otto, *Ferdinand Raimund und die Vollendung des Alt-Wiener Zauberstückes*. Vienna, 1949.

Rommel, Otto, *Die Alt-Wiener Volkskomödie. Ihre Geschichte vom barocken Welt-Theater bis zum Tode Nestroys*. Vienna, 1952.

Rommel, Otto, 'Rokoko in den Wiener Kaiserspielen'. *Maske und Kothurn*, I, 1–2 (1955), 30–46.

Schreyvogel, Frederick, 'Der Weg des Burgtheaters'. *Maske und Kothurn*, vol. I, 1–2 (1955), 69–79.

Senn, Walter, *Musik und Theater am Hof zu Innsbruck*. Innsbruck, 1954.

Skalicki, Wolfram, 'Das Bühnenbild der Zauberflöte von der Uraufführung bis zu Oskar Strnad'. *Maske und Kothurn*, 1956. Begun in Heft 1 (pp. 2–34), concluded in Heft 2 (pp. 142–65).

Sonnenfels, J. von, *Briefe über die wienerische Schaubühne. Wiener Neudrucke*, no. 7. Vienna, 1884.

Stammler, Wolfgang, *Der Totentanz. Entstehung und Deutung*. Munich, 1948. Could with equal justice be listed in section 2.

Stumpfl, Robert, *Kultspiele der Germanen als Ursprung des mittelalterlichen Dramas*. Berlin, 1936. This book has to be used with great care. Stumpfl was a convinced National Socialist and this is often very apparent. This should not deter one, however, from acknowledging much that is genuine, original and stimulating. On the other hand it must in fairness be stated that such an authority on this subject as Wolfgang Michael writes of Stumpfl's book as 'unreliable and unscholarly'. See Michael's review of *A Swiss Resurrection Play of the Sixteenth Century* (N. S. Arnold, A Columbia University Dissertation. New York, 1949) in *Germanic Review*, XXVI (1951), 235–7.

Strich, Fritz, 'Das europäische Barock'. *Der Dichter und die Zeit* (especially pp. 97 ff.). Berne, 1947.

Wackernell, J. E., *Altdeutsche Passionsspiele aus Tirol*. Graz, 1897.

Weltner, J. *Alphabetisches Verzeichnis der Schauspielaufführungen im Hofburgtheater* (1776–1888). Vienna, 1889.

Zingerle, Otto von, *Die Sterzinger Spiele nach Aufzeichnungen des Vigil Raber. Wiener Neudrucke*, nos. 9 and 11. Vienna, 1886.

4. POLITICAL AND HISTORICAL BACKGROUND AND ENVIRONMENT

Barkeley, Richard, *The Road to Mayerling: Life and Death of Crown Prince Rudolph of Austria*. London, 1958.

Bergsträsser, L., *Politischer Katholizismus*, no. 3 of series *Der Deutsche Staatsgedanke: zweite Reihe — Die Parteien und der Staat*. Munich, 1922.

Bidez, J., *Kaiser Julian und der Untergang der heidnischen Welt*, transl. from French by Hermann Rinn. *Ro-ro-ro Bücher. Rowohlts Deutsche Enzyklopädie*, no. 26. Hamburg, 1956.

Bodenhausen, Dora, Freifrau von (ed.), *Eberhard von Bodenhausen: Ein Leben für die Kunst und Wirtschaft*. Cologne, 1955.

Burckhardt, Carl J., *Gedanken über Karl V*. Cologne, 1954.

Burckhardt, Carl J., *Gestalten und Mächte*. Zürich, 1954. Particularly relevant are essays on Maria Theresia and Gentz. Also in this volume is a splendid essay, 'Grillparzer und das Mass'. This should really be in section 2. Burckhardt's book is, considered as a whole, of essentially historical character. Hence its inclusion here.

Burckhardt, Carl J., *Reden und Aufzeichnungen*, Zürich, 1952. Especially relevant are Burkhardt's reminiscences of Vienna, 1918–19. This has no connection with Burckhardt's *Erinnerungen an Hofmannsthal* (see section 1 of this bibliography) which also describes this period.

Duch, Arno (ed.), *Josef Görres: Auswahl*. 2 vols. No. 12 of series *Der Deutsche Staatsgedanke: erste Reihe — Führer und Denker*. Munich, 1921.

Eckhardt, Hans von (ed.), *Friedrich von Gentz: Auswahl*. 2 vols. Munich, 1921.

Franz, Georg, *Erzherzog Franz Ferdinand und die Pläne zur Reform der Habsburger Monarchie*. Vienna, 1943.

Gooch, G. P., *Maria Theresia and Other Studies*. London, 1951.

Görlitz, Walter, *Marc Aurel: Kaiser und Philosoph*. Stuttgart, 1954.

Kallbrunner, Josef, *Kaiserin Maria Theresias Politisches Testament* (with epilogue by Clemens Biener). Vienna, 1952.

Kann, Robert, *The Multi-National Empire*. 2 vols. New York, 1950.

Kann, Robert, *The Habsburg Empire: A Study in Integration and Disintegration*. New York, 1957.

Kantorowicz, Ernst, *Frederick the Second: 1194–1250* (trans. E. O. Lorimer). London, 1957.

Kiszling, Rudolf, *Erzherzog Franz Ferdinand von Österreich-Este*. Graz/Cologne, 1953.

Kretschmayr, Heinrich, *Maria Theresia*. Vienna, 1925. See Hofmannsthal's review of this—*Geschichtliche Gestalt*—in *Prosa*, IV, 295–301.

Mann, Golo, *Friedrich von Gentz: Geschichte eines europäischen Staatsmannes*. Zürich, 1947.

Marboe, Ernst (ed. and chief contrib.), *Das Österreichbuch*. Vienna, 1948.

Meyer, Henry Corde, '*Mitteleuropa*' *in German Thought and Action: 1815–1945*. International Scholars' Forum: a series of books by American scholars, no. 4. The Hague, 1955. This is a very lucid and incisive account of an extremely complex and controversial subject. The final chapter (pp. 346–65) is a detailed bibliographical essay in appropriate sections according to particular aspects of the subject. This is an invaluable guide to the mass of literature on the theme which varies enormously in standard and 'Tendenz'.

Mitis, Oskar von, *Das Leben des Kronprinzen Rudolf*. Leipzig, 1928.

Mohler, Armin, *Die Konservative Revolution in Deutschland, 1918–1932: Grundriß ihrer Weltanschauung*. Stuttgart, 1950.

Mowrer, Edgar, *Germany Puts the Clock Back*. Penguin, 1937.

Müller, Adam, *Schriften*. 4 vols. Ed. Arthur Salz. Munich, 1920– .

Naumann, Friedrich, *Mitteleuropa*. Berlin, 1915.

Redlich, Josef, *Das Politische Tagebuch J.R.s., 1908–1919. Veröffentlichungen der Kommission für Neuere Geschichte Österreichs*, no. 40. 2 vols. Ed. Fritz Fellner. Graz/Cologne, 1954.

Redlich, Josef, *Austrian War Government*. Yale, 1929.

Redlich, Josef, *Emperor Francis Joseph of Austria*. London, 1929. Hofmannsthal named this as one of his three books of the year, 1928. See *Prosa*, IV, 515; also chapter 3, p. 84, note 1 of this study. There is no mention of a translator. Redlich taught for many years in the U.S.A. The translation is possibly his own.

Ridley, F. A., *Julian the Apostate and the Rise of Christianity*. London, 1937.

Ritter, Gerhart, *Die Neugestaltung Europas im 16. Jahrhundert*. Berlin, 1950.

Schulz, Fritz Traugott, *Die deutschen Reichskleinodien*. Leipzig, 1934.

Shepherd, Gordon, *The Austrian Odyssey*. London, 1957.

Steed, Henry Wickham, *The Habsburg Monarchy*. London, 1914.

Taylor, A. J. P., *The Habsburg Monarchy: 1809–1918*. London, 1948.

Wandruzka, Adam, *Das Haus Habsburg: Die Geschichte einer europäischen Dynastie*. Stuttgart, 1956.

INDEX

Abraham a Sancta Clara (Ulrich Megerle), 118, 224, 344
Addison, Joseph, 338
Aegidius Albertinus, 218
Aeschylus, 31
Alewyn, Richard, 8, 9, 11–12, 79, 81–2, 244, 324, 326, 373
Alexander the Great, 100, 188, 264, 278, 367
Almoner, Grand (at French court), 227
Alps, Austrian, 119, 173
Alsace, 124, 368
Andrian, Leopold von, 182, 345
Anschluß, 2, 7, 23
Atkins, Stuart, 339
Attila, 141, 275, 279, 369
Augsburger Reichstag (1530), 357
Ausgleich (with Hungary, 1867), 4, 86, 326, 332–3
Ausgleichpolitik, 108, 126, 128, 130, 132, 135, 262, 277–8, 339

Babylon, 217, 225
Bahr, Hermann, 9, 185, 345
Barkeley, Richard, 334–5
Baroque, 24, 29–34, 50–2, 55, 75, 77, 79, 81–2, 152–3, 165, 173, 179–80, 195, 197, 212–13, 216, 218–21, 224, 229, 257, 272, 294–5, 308–9, 316, 344–5, 350, 359, 373
Barrès, Maurice, 312
Bauer, Otto, 132
Becher, Johannes R., 341
Bednall, John B., 359
Beer-Hofmann, Richard, 354–5
Benedictine drama, 31
Bentley, Eric, 346
Bergstraesser, Arnold, 179, 182, 341–3, 345
Berlin, 13, 28, 128, 173, 318–19, 343
Berners, Lord (John Bourchier), 218
Bettler, der, 54, 363
Bidermann, Jakob, 316–17
Bismarck, Prince Otto von, 104, 120, 124, 127
Bithell, Jethro, 62–3, 172
Blume, Bernhard, 325
Bodenhausen, Eberhard von, 16, 28, 80, 86, 123, 129, 136, 138, 264, 314–15, 341, 352

Bohemia, 1, 33, 104, 107, 118–19, 201
Bonaparte, Emperor Napoleon, 4, 99, 104, 114, 142, 145, 148, 328
Borchardt, Rudolf, 10, 325, 332, 354
Boris Godunov, 203, 273, 370
Borodin, Alexander, 273
Borysthenes river (Dnieper), 198
Boylan, R. D., 359
Brant, Sebastian, 347
Braun, Felix, 330
Brecht, Bertolt, 170, 179
Brecht, Erika, 155, 269–70, 281–2, 291, 344, 365, 372
Brecht, Walther, 9, 206–9, 319, 349–50
Brenan, Gerald, 179, 345
Broch, Hermann, 9, 10, 119, 305–6, 366
Bruck, Karl Ludwig von, 134
Büchner, Georg, 357
Burckhardt, Carl Jakob, xiii, 72, 93, 105, 144, 150–1, 153–4, 156, 185, 193–4, 198, 204, 208–9, 226, 232, 262, 269, 286, 290–2, 295–6, 304–6, 335, 337–8, 343, 348, 358, 363, 367
Burckhardt, Jakob, 107
Burdach, Konrad, 350
Bürger von Calais, die, 167, 362–3
Byzantine emperors, empire, 190, 198, 266, 348

Calderón de la Barca, Pedro, 11, 153–4, 156, 166–7, 173, 179–81, 184, 186, 240, 338, 343, 345–6, 370; *El gran teatro del mundo*, xii, 156, 179–80, 186, 339; *La vida es sueño*, 184–6, 222, 298, 351, 355
Calmberg, Ernesta, 342
Campbell, Roy, 346
Cardus, Neville, 366
Carlsbad Decrees, 145
Carmina Burana, 55
Carnuntum, 116, 346
Catherine the Great, Empress of Russia, 105
Catholicism, 21, 25, 32, 38, 64–5, 68, 70–1, 77–8, 141–2, 152–4, 156–7, 169–70, 174–5, 181, 184, 206, 209, 227, 278, 289–90, 295, 322, 352–3